ANCIENT LEGENDS
OF
ROMAN HISTORY

THE ORIGIN OF ROME. A POMPEIAN FRESCO RECENTLY FOUND

Ancient Legends *of* Roman History

BY
ETTORE PAIS

Translated by
MARIO E. COSENZA

BOOKS FOR LIBRARIES PRESS
FREEPORT, NEW YORK

First Published 1905
Reprinted 1971

INTERNATIONAL STANDARD BOOK NUMBER:
0-8369-6661-9

LIBRARY OF CONGRESS CATALOG CARD NUMBER:
74-179532

PRINTED IN THE UNITED STATES OF AMERICA
BY
NEW WORLD BOOK MANUFACTURING CO., INC.
HALLANDALE, FLORIDA 33009

To my wife and affectionate companion
ANNETTA
On the twenty-fifth anniversary
of our wedding

PREFACE

WITH the exception of a few pages which have already appeared in Italy, this volume was written in America. The majority of the chapters were prepared as lectures for the Lowell Institute of Boston. The others were read before Columbia University, Harvard University, the University of Wisconsin, and the University of Chicago.

The present volume contains special and minute demonstrations of subjects already succinctly treated by me in my *Storia di Roma,* and represents new studies and new experiences. The judgments of intelligent and honest critics have been considered. Nevertheless I uphold and affirm the fundamental views set forth by me in my previous works. This is not the result of obstinacy. It is the logical conclusion of an objective and untiring examination of facts.

The conclusions attained in my *Storia di Roma* have been the source of many controversies in my native country. In compensation, however, they have gained for me the sympathy of the scientific public in the other countries of Europe, and also in America. It is natural, then, that I, who have been so cordially welcomed by the American universities, should present to the English-speaking public of this country these and future results of my researches.

The volume has been composed under the shadow of the universities already mentioned. I feel it incumbent upon me, therefore, to extend my sincere thanks to the professors who so kindly aided me. It is impossible to mention all. I trust, however, that it may be granted me to express my gratitude, in a particular manner, to Professors A. L. Lowell and W. T. Sedgwick, of the Lowell Institute; Professors J. C. Egbert and N. G. McCrea, of Columbia University; Professors C. H. Haskins, M. H. Morgan and J. H. Wright, of Harvard University; Mr. M. S. Prichard, of the Museum of Fine Arts, Boston; Professors D. C.

PREFACE

Munro, M. S. Slaughter and F. I. Turner, of the University of Wisconsin; President W. R. Harper and Professors F. F. Abbott and J. F. Jameson, of the University of Chicago.

My special thanks are due to Professor Harry Thurston Peck, of Columbia University, who has kindly undertaken to read the English version of my young compatriot, Mario E. Cosenza.

ETTORE PAIS

NEW YORK, *February* 15, 1905.

CONTENTS

CHAPTER I

THE CRITICAL METHOD TO BE PURSUED IN THE STUDY OF THE MOST ANCIENT ROMAN HISTORY 1

CHAPTER II

THE EXCAVATIONS IN THE FORUM ROMANUM, AND THEIR IMPORTANCE FOR THE MOST ANCIENT ROMAN HISTORY . . 15

CHAPTER III

THE ORIGINS OF ROME, AND A NEW POMPEIAN FRESCO . . . 43

CHAPTER IV

ACCA LARENTIA, THE MOTHER OF THE LARES AND NURSE OF ROMULUS; AND THE MOST ANCIENT DIVINITIES OF THE PALATINE 60

CHAPTER V

THE STORY OF THE MAID TARPEIA 96

CHAPTER VI

THE SAXUM TARPEIUM 109

CHAPTER VII

THE LEGEND OF SERVIUS TULLIUS; AND THE SUPREMACY OF THE ETRUSCANS AT ROME 128

CHAPTER VIII

THE LEGENDS OF THE HORATII, AND THE CULT OF VULCAN . 152

CONTENTS

CHAPTER IX

The Fabii at the River Cremera and the Spartans at Thermopylæ 168

CHAPTER X

The Legends of Lucretia and of Virginia, and the Cults of the Prisci Latini 185

CHAPTER XI

The Legends of Spurius Mælius, Servilius Ahala and Lucius Minucius 204

CHAPTER XII

On the Topography of the Earliest Rome 224

EXCURSUS I

The Stips Votiva of the Niger Lapis, and the Faliscan Museum of Villa Giulia 242

EXCURSUS II

The Authenticity of the Etruscan Tile from Capua, and the Supremacy of the Etruscans in Campania . . . 250

EXCURSUS III

The Relations between the Square Palatine, the Square Palisades in Emilia, and the Pretended Terramara of Tarentum 257

EXCURSUS IV

Cælius Vibenna, the Friend of Romulus, Servius Tullius, and Celer the Slayer of Remus 264

EXCURSUS V

Servius Tullius and the Lex Ælia-Sentia 268

EXCURSUS VI

The Topography of the Via Nova, the Vicus Orbius or Sceleratus, and the Vicus Cyprius, or Good 272

ILLUSTRATIONS

THE ORIGIN OF ROME. A POMPEIAN FRESCO RECENTLY FOUND	*Frontispiece*	
THE CAPITOLIUM	*Facing Page*	6
TEMPLE OF VESTA. ANCIENT RELIEF	" "	12
THE CAPITOL	" "	12
THE ARCHAIC STELE OF THE FORUM	" "	16
ANCIENT BASE, CIPPUS AND PILLAR BENEATH THE NIGER LAPIS	" "	18
ALTAR OF THE YEAR 9 B.C., WITH ARCHAIC OUTLINES (Magazino Comunale, Roma) . . .	" "	18
CAMPANIAN INSCRIPTIONS OF THE END OF THE REPUBLIC (Naples Museum)	" "	20
MONUMENTS BENEATH THE NIGER LAPIS		21
GREEK INSCRIPTION FROM S. MAURO FORTE NEAR MATERA (Naples Museum)	*Facing Page*	22
CAMPANIAN INSCRIPTION NOT EARLIER THAN THE FIFTH CENTURY (Naples Museum)	" "	24
ITALIC INSCRIPTION NOT EARLIER THAN THE FOURTH CENTURY	" "	24
VENETO-LATIN INSCRIPTION (Museum of Este)		24
THE NIGER LAPIS	*Facing Page*	28
THE ORIGIN OF ROME, AFTER AN ALTAR FROM OSTIA	" "	46
THE TEMPLE OF MAGNA MATER IDÆA ON THE PALATINE	" "	46
COIN, WOLF NURSING TWINS		50
COIN, WOLF NURSING TWINS		50
COIN OF THE GENS CÆSIA, SHOWING THE LARES		52
THE MOST ANCIENT WALLS OF THE PALATINE, ATTRIBUTED TO ROMULUS	*Facing Page*	52
COIN SHOWING THE LAURELLED HEAD OF JANUS		64
THE NORTHWESTERN CORNER OF THE PALATINE	*Facing Page*	68
THE NORTHEASTERN CORNER OF THE PALATINE (CURIÆ VETERES)	" "	68
WESTERN END OF THE FORUM, WITH A GENERAL VIEW OF THE PALATINE	" "	78

ILLUSTRATIONS

Coin of the Gens Cæsia, Showing the Lares		93
Coin of Turpilianus		97
Coin of L. Titurius		97
Church of S. Maria in Araceli, Seen from the North. (The Site of the Temple of Juno Moneta)	Facing Page	104
The So-Called Tarpeian Rock	" "	104
The Tabularium, between the Capitolium (Templum Iovis) and the Arx (Templum Iunonis)	" "	110
The Mamertine Prison	" "	120
Remains of Walls Attributed to Servius Tullius	" "	140
Nemi and the Lacus Nemorensis	" "	142
Aricia and the Lacus Turni	" "	146
The Mons Velia	" "	150
Palazzo Caffarelli, on the Site of the Temple of Jupiter Capitolinus	" "	154
Coin of the Gens Horatia		158
Coin of the Gens Valeria		165
A Roman Divinity (Magazino Comunale, Roma)	Facing Page	166
The Island of the Tiber	" "	166
Coin of the Gens Valeria		167
Map of Rome, Fidenæ and Veii	Facing Page	174
View of Veii (From Dennis, Etruria)	" "	178
View of Veii	" "	178
The Country of the Prisci Latini	" "	188
Monte Cavo (Mons Albanus) and the Lake of Albano	" "	194
Remains of the Basilica Æmilia, on the Site of the Tabernæ Novae	" "	198
Coin of L. Mussidius Longus		199
Valley of the Lacus Turni	Facing Page	200
Plan of the Forum		210
Site of the Tabernæ Novae	Facing Page	212
The Aventine and the Porta Trigemina	" "	218
Plans of the Most Ancient Rome	" "	234
The Etruscan Tegula from Capua (Berlin Museum)	" "	250
The Temple of Castor and a Corner of the Palatine	" "	260
Ancient Walls of the Palatine	" "	264
Ancient Gate of Republican Times Assigned to the Age of the Kings	" "	270

ANCIENT LEGENDS OF ROMAN HISTORY

CHAPTER I

THE CRITICAL METHOD TO BE PURSUED IN THE STUDY OF THE MOST ANCIENT ROMAN HISTORY

THE greatness of the deeds of the Roman people and the charm of the beautiful land of Italy explain why, from the Renaissance on, the early history of Rome has many times been the subject of thought and investigation. Philosophers and statesmen such as Machiavelli, Montesquieu and G. B. Vico based upon those early tales theories of constitutional law, or laid the foundations of a future philosophy of history. Historians and scholars such as Beaufort and Niebuhr availed themselves of the same material to establish the canons of the new historical criticism.

The period of Roman history extending from the origins of the city to the Punic Wars is a very attractive one to the thinker. There are many causes for this powerful attraction. An inexhaustible quantity of legendary material is fused with the story of internal events and with philosophical maxims. The noblest sentiments of humanity and a respect for law are represented as having guided the actions of the persons and the people to whom was entrusted the task of founding the Roman State. This organism appears so well developed, even from the beginning, that several critics of past generations ventured to assert that Rome had known no infancy.

Enthusiasm for ancient Rome draws ever new and living power from the eloquent and glowing pages of Cicero and Livy. The political wisdom of the Romans has been transmitted in a body of laws which is not destined to perish even in modern times. Upon Roman foresight, too, was modelled in part that complete organization represented by the Roman Catholic Church, which, with the arts of the ancient pagan statesmen, has succeeded and still succeeds in swaying so great a part of human conscience.

Side by side, however, and yet entirely separate from this admiration for Rome, a new influence was gradually appearing. This was the critical method, which endeavored to distinguish the true from the false, and to eliminate, or at least to simplify, contradictory versions. Its object was to determine what should be chosen, and what discarded. It has ended with denying the occurrence of a large proportion of the events examined. In a similar manner, the study of the contradictions in the old Biblical texts and the Gospels has caused the rise of free criticism in the study of the problems of religious history.

The movement in the critical study of Roman history had already attained large proportions at the time of the Renaissance with the Italian Lorenzo Valla. It received a great impetus from Gronovius and Perizonius. Beaufort, the French scholar of the eighteenth century, established the principles of the new criticism with rigorous logic and keen perception. Thus it may be said regarding the study of the earliest Roman history (in its substance if not in its details), that the principles of Beaufort have never been surpassed,—not even by the most advanced and conscientious German criticism. It is true that it was left for Niebuhr and the German school to establish the standards of ulterior investigations with greater precision of method and with the aid of investigations in related sciences. The complexity of the subject, however, the various ways in which this portion of Roman history could be investigated, and the variations of critical tendencies in related organisms or in the study of other historical periods, have given a life and a direction to such researches quite different from those intended by Niebuhr.

The opinion of this illustrious German scholar was that legendary and poetical material formed the substratum of all the early tales of Roman deeds. This belief was given a poetic exposition by a great historian,—Lord Macaulay. Others, like Schwegler, endeavored instead to discover an historic nucleus, buried beneath a great number of secondary traditions and later interpolations. Theodore Mommsen, finally, with keener eye and greater knowledge of the Roman world, saw that not only the period referring to the origins of Rome, but also subsequent eras, had been subjected to an extensive process of official falsifications.

Upon undertaking to narrate the deeds of the Roman people, Theodore Mommsen did not consider it fitting to expound the primitive period. This was enveloped in a long series of falsifications. He limited himself, therefore, to tracing out that which, in his opinion, formed the permanent and unfailing elements of historical narrative, namely, those elements of a constitutional character which he redintegrated and reconstructed from the more or less questionable data of later ages. In a series of special papers, Mommsen, nevertheless, undertook a minute examination of some of the most ancient legends. He thus demonstrated that elements of a constitutional character, though attributed to the earliest centuries of Rome, were in fact derived from late annalistic compilations of the times of Sulla and of Cæsar. These later traditions he clearly distinguished from the comparatively trustworthy annals of the second and third centuries B.C.

Mommsen's fundamental conception was that the earliest annalists (such as Fabius Pictor) wrote succinct narratives, which were later utilized by the Greek Diodorus of Sicily. He maintained that the most ancient data were expanded by an infinite number of falsifications by such writers as Licinius Macer and Valerius Antias. Mommsen, finally, was guided by the concept that the fundamental and ancient characteristics of the traditions regarding the constitution were worthy of belief, and that the narratives of Roman history had a firm foothold in the Fasti preserved in the Regia of the Roman Forum.

However worthy of our highest respect these theories of Mommsen may be, they nevertheless meet with insurmountable obstacles. A minute and careful examination of the political constitution of Rome reveals the same impurity of sources that is generally acknowledged with reference to the narration of her external events. I shall render this fact still more evident in future researches. The statements concerning the various Valerian and Horatian laws have no greater value than those regarding the laws of the Decemvirate or the social laws of the fourth century B.C.[1] The official story of the Roman constitution was derived, in great part, from those same annalistic sources of the first century B.C. (such as Licinius Macer), which evolved the pseudo-history of the agrarian agitations beginning with the fifth century. This history merely reflects the tendencies and political ideals of the progressive parties of the last centuries of the Republic.

On the other hand, there is no reason for suspecting that the annalistic sources of the Gracchan and Hannibalic periods are much purer than those of the ages of Sulla and of Cicero. We grant that both the increase in rhetorical culture and the development of Latin prose writing gave occasion to the creation of new frills and to the invention of quantities of false details. It is nevertheless true that a minute examination of the statements traceable to the annalists of the second and third centuries B.C. reveals the same tendencies and the same falsifications.

Fabius Pictor, the earliest Roman annalist, has, in this respect, no greater value than Licinius Macer, the contemporary of Cicero. Licinius glorified, and even invented, the history of the plebeian Licinii. He narrated a series of political struggles in which the ancestors of his family were supposed to have played a prominent part. Fabius, too, glorified the deeds of his patrician family. He related the story of a battle at the River Cremera, in which struggle three hundred and six of his family perished in the same manner and at the same time as Leonidas and his three hundred Spartans at Thermopylæ. Licinius and Valerius Antias, in recounting the deeds of the fifth century, depict a struggle and a political constitution which are a faithful reproduction of conditions in their own age. Fabius Pictor similarly attributed to the pseudo-King Servius Tullius the political constitution and the number of tribes which, indeed, existed only in his own times.

Mommsen expounds in a marvellous manner the fundamental and precise ideas and development of the Roman constitution. He has not been able, however, to free himself from a tendency towards the method characteristic of jurists,—a method which urges them to form abstractions without due consideration of historical flexibility, the powerful influences of surroundings, and the development of analogous situations in other countries. In opposition to his method and his endeavor to reconstruct the earliest constitution of the Roman people, there stands the entire history of this people,—a history very recent in all its manifestations and very doubtful in all that precedes

THE CRITICAL METHOD

the fifth century. In opposition to Mommsen, also, is the explicit declaration of Polybius, who affirmed that he was quite ignorant of the private and political institutions of the ancient Romans.[2]

Moreover, the conception to which Mommsen adhered is not exact. The great historian and scholar held that the Roman deeds earlier than the fourth century are to be considered as a skeleton (so to speak) representing the summary indications of the Annales Maximi and of the Fasti which were used by the early annalists. This conception, in fact, encounters two difficulties: the existence of such Fasti as sources for authentic history, and the strictly non-Roman character of the narrative of the earliest national deeds.

An examination of the fragments of the earliest annalists (such as Fabius Pictor, Cato and Calpurnius Piso) clearly proves a direct use of Greek sources. Our opinion of the excessive brevity employed by the early Roman annalists is greatly exaggerated. Let us remember the copious particulars of the origins of Rome given by Fabius, who drew from the Greek Diocles. Let us recall, too, the many details given by both Calpurnius Piso and Cassius Hemina in speaking of Romulus.[3] Moreover, this dependence of the early Roman annalists upon Greek sources corresponds with the state of their political relations and of their literary and material civilization. It is, too, in full harmony with the explicit declaration of Dionysius of Halicarnassus. This historian compiled a list of the Sicilian authors who had written the story of Roman deeds, beginning with the fifth century and Antiochus of Syracuse, and ending with Callias, Hieronymus of Cardia and Silenus of Calacte.[4]

The Greeks, and particularly those of Sicily, were the first to narrate the history of Rome. This is paralleled with the fact that the earliest Roman annalists wrote in Greek. It is, then, impossible to conceive of the origins of Roman historiography without due consideration of the Greek sources by which, according to the plain statements of the ancients themselves, the earliest Roman annalists were inspired.[5]

Surely the preservation of the ancient Fasti in the Regia and the compilation of the Annales Maximi did not give a true and great incentive to Roman historiography. Even granting that the Fasti which have come down to us are a faithful reproduction of the most ancient ones, we could only deduce that the earliest Romans preserved a list of their magistrates and triumphs. If, moreover, we are to accept the affirmations of the ancients, we shall conclude that also the annals of the pontiffs, which were called Maximi, contained merely a list of magistrates and their deeds, and of the meteorological phenomena (such as eclipses) that had been observed during the year. To this was added the information as to whether or not the year had rendered large crops. These annals, in short, were a species of official civil, military, financial and meteorological bulletin.[6]

The fragments of the Annales Maximi that have been preserved are far more numerous than is generally supposed. I have been preparing an edition of these for some time. They disclose the fact that they are by no means of very ancient date, and that they contain scattered anecdotes and religious tales. The earliest compilation of these annals (if indeed there was one) should have resembled, in certain respects, the Fasti which at the end of the Republic and the dawn of the Monarchy were exhibited on the Regia. But if such documents had furnished positive chronological data and undoubted indications of magistrates, we would not be able to understand the long series of confusions in the chronology of the ancient Republic. These confusions hold sway not only in the fifth century, but also in the fourth, and even for a great part of the third.

Evident and flagrant contradictions in giving or omitting the names of the dictator or consuls frequently occur. Magistrates unknown to other authors were by some freely inserted among the lists of magistrates. Livy either accepts the various traditions or declares his ignorance of what principle to adhere to in discarding certain lists, generally accepting the testimony of the earliest annalists. On other occasions he confesses complete inability to distinguish the true from the false. Moreover, he never refers to the existence of ancient monuments which might be of value in deciding the point in question. All these facts prove indisputably (to those who are not slaves to prejudice) that the annalists of the first century, as well as those of the third, did not possess monumental Fasti to which they could safely adhere.[7]

THE CAPITOLIUM

THE CRITICAL METHOD

Dionysius is very much inclined to place belief in all the native documents referring to the earliest Roman history. In endeavoring, however, to establish one of the fundamental dates of Roman chronology, he refers to the different opinions of annalists on the subject. On another occasion he dwells upon the rather doubtful value of documents belonging to the archives of a Roman family.[8] And when, in endeavoring to solve a doubt concerning the Fasti, he declares his faith in the Annales Maximi, he actually depends upon the forgeries of Licinius Macer. Even by Cicero and Livy we are taught how little faith is to be placed in such documents.[9]

There remain, it is true, the Fasti of the Regia, called Capitolini from their being preserved to-day in one of the palaces crowning the Capitoline. Mommsen believed them to be the key and foundation for the study of Roman history. He deemed it necessary to determine with precision whether they were cut in one rather than in another decade of the Augustan age.[10] Let us freely consider the disastrous results to which we are led by the study of the chronology and of the Fasti, not only of the early Republic, but also of the fourth and third century B.C. We shall then recognize that such a question as the age in which the Fasti were cut is of altogether secondary importance as compared with the value of their contents.

From indications in the Fasti themselves, and from a comparison of annalistic data, it clearly results that they do not represent the most ancient sources, but indeed are themselves dependent on recent works. The Capitoline Fasti are to be classed with the *elogia* of the Augustan age which adorned the Roman Forum. Like these they are the result of the researches of scholars,—men who begin with the generation of Varro, Cicero and Cornelius Nepos. I have already set forth elsewhere various observations regarding the questionable value of the chronology of the Roman Fasti.

I shall defer the question to a special study of a character exclusively chronological,—a minute and careful examination of the Fasti of the Roman Republic. Here it will be sufficient to affirm that, in indicating the *prænomina* and *nomina* of the magistrates, the Fasti reveal the use of sources which the texts themselves declare not to have been the most ancient. The entirely recent character of their compilation fully agrees with the constant use therein of *cognomina*.

There is no positive reason for attributing greater value to the Fasti than to the records of triumphs cut and preserved upon the same edifice. For these latter are derived from the same sources as the consular Fasti. Moreover, regarding the names of the conquerors and the dates of their triumphs, these records do not depend on primary sources, but indeed (like the *elogia* of the Forum) upon authors of very recent ages. Thus they often present data that are utterly devoid of historical value.

The fundamental conception of Mommsen, then,—that one might attain to the knowledge of the earliest Roman history through the study of the institutions and the Fasti, —does not accord with reality. An examination of the facts leads, instead, to the sad conclusion that Roman history appears as an adult organism from the very origins of the city, thanks to the development, or rather to the incipient decline, of Hellenistic civilization. The virgin and comparatively uncultured energies of the Roman people were enveloped in the atmosphere of the fully mature Greek civilization. The result was that the young organism was granted neither the occasion nor the time to develop gradually and along individual lines.

Greeks were the first narrators of Rome's fortunes. Ennius and Nævius, who first moulded the elements of the epic and of the national history, were but Hellenized Oscans. Fabius Pictor, Cincius Alimentus, Postumius Albinus and Acilius could not escape this influence. They, too, wrote in Greek. And though contrary to his will, nevertheless on account of the irresistible demands of culture and of the times, even the elder Cato is caught in this current,—Cato, who, protesting vehemently against Greek culture (though thoroughly imbued with it), writes in Latin the deeds of his country.

Born under such influences, and as the result of such conditions, Latin historiography gathered and from the very beginning reproduced the ancient patrimony, the very conventional material of the rhetorical historiography and the historical *epos* of the Greeks. The history of the development of historical poetry and historiography,—as also the entire life of the Roman people,—may be compared to that of a vigorous youth from a mountainous district who is received within the lordly halls of an ancient family. Such a youth, though retaining all the energy and crudeness of his native soil, will, nevertheless, assimilate more or less completely the elements of the more refined and elegant life which he is called upon to live.

Greeks participated in the compilation of the Roman national history. The more or less familiar knowledge of the literary, moral and political products of the Hellenic world gave to the story of Roman deeds the semblance of precocious maturity. It gave to it the aspect of a civic wisdom which is merely the reflection of the completed cycle of Greek culture which was instilled into the youthful Roman blood. At times this culture regained its youth, but more frequently it underwent a process of deterioration.

It was a characteristic of the Roman people that it did not always allow itself to be transformed or overcome by the Greek atmosphere. The external form of the Roman annals reflects, at times, certain archaic qualities fitting to the Latin stock. This form is enveloped in the legends and in the moral and political reflections of a maturer age, which are due, at one time, to the pen of a thoroughly Hellenized Roman poet, at another, to a statesman imbued with Greek doctrines. On the whole, the products of a national character prove a familiar acquaintance with the religious, artistic and political problems already propounded and discussed by the declining Hellenic world.

The drama of Plautus and the song of Lucilius are both adaptations from the Greek. The national epics of Nævius and of Ennius, as well as the logos or annals of Fabius, represent the grafting of Greek arguments upon Latin themes. The Gracchi, the reformers of the social constitution, were dependent upon Hellenic sources; Pænetius and Poseidonius were teachers of the Romans. Similarly, Greek are the models for the temples and statues, whether Semo Sanctus be reproduced as an archaic Apollo, or whether the temple of Ceres be decorated by artists from Sicily and Magna Græcia.

That which in the beautiful and marvellous Roman legends appears to be the fruit of spontaneous national sentiment, is almost in every case the result of mature artistic reflection. It is the work of Roman writers and poets thoroughly trained and fully acquainted with all the situations in Greek poetry. Such Roman authors had been trained, above all, in the schools of Alexandria and Pergamum,—schools which, rather than offering the fresh flowers, provided them only with an artificial product,—no longer vivified by the marvellous and virgin activity of the Hellenes. Thus the treatment of social and political problems, and the story of the agrarian agitations (which at times seem to be a characteristic of Roman historiography) are the result of later political elaboration. Above all, they represent the practical tendency of historiography, which had already taken such a course in the works of Xenophon and Theopompus, and which continued to serve as the medium for expressing personal views on the principles of the Hellenic States.

The legendary elements of Hellas were borrowed. Exotic events were reproduced. But this was not sufficient to complete the picture of national history. This history arose only when in Greece there had flourished for a long time the study of topography and of monuments; when, from Herodotus to Polemon, an infinite series of scholars had turned their attention to such documents—documents which in all times and in all regions constitute the humblest sources of national history.

Houses, public edifices, simple statues, religious tales and the temples offered material that was by no means neglected in Greece. Such monuments, then, naturally attracted the attention of one who, whether Greek or Latin, undertook to narrate the deeds of Rome. This material was all the more zealously investigated because of the intense desire to complete the *lacunæ* that so frequently occurred in the knowledge of the national history. The longing increased disproportionately; it was stimulated by the increasing power and dominion of Rome. It grew in the same proportion as the eagerness of illustrious families to ennoble still more their genealogy, and to enrich the deeds of their more or less authentic ancestors. We shall discuss several times in this volume how and when topographical data and religious tales contributed to the formation of the earliest Roman history.

It is not my purpose, moreover, to present here a minute exposition of the development of Roman historiography, inasmuch as this has already been done elsewhere. To others can be entrusted the more careful solution of problems connected with the religion, the Annales Maximi, the chronology and the Fasti of the Roman people. In this volume it will be sufficient to have established how some of the more famous legends came into existence, and how they were expounded. Those legends have been discussed that struck the fancies of our fathers and inspired their sentiments; legends which had great efficacy in moulding the thought, the political life, and the literary development and history of Europe.

He who casts only a superficial glance at the method pursued by me, and at the conclusions reached in this volume, may find that the results of my labors are negative ones—that the critical method is of advantage only in stripping the laurels of the Roman people, and that, if the conclusions drawn are true, the only result must be to destroy the charm of the ancient history of Italy and its culture.

If the results were really thus to operate, we could not do better than to accept them as the results of pure truth. There are statesmen, or rather politicians, who have had a rhetorical training in moral maxims, and who are imbued with a patriotism more or less sincerely felt. This they use for personal ends, to conceal their true conduct, or else to intoxicate the masses. Such men have, naturally, good reason for deploring a loss in their stock of weapons. In a similar manner, an impresario would be in the greatest despair if, as the result of fire, he would find himself and his actors suddenly deprived of the scenery and wardrobes by which inferior persons appear in the fantastic atmosphere of princes and illustrious men.

Scholars who devote themselves to study and to the search for truth do actually search only for the truth and for the sake of truth. They heed not the immediate results of their researches. Their endeavor is that the researches may be exact, and that their results may be the mirror of truth. They are fully aware that the real object is light and truth, that error will be dispelled by light, and that truth will ultimately reign.

In our case, however, the conclusions reached are by no means negative. Still less are they of such a nature as to cause discomfort to the patriot, or to the scholar who lovingly studies the Fasti of the ancient Italian nation. A purely negative work is one that destroys without constructing something new in its place, without searching for the reasons which justify the destruction. In case of the elimination of an error, a work even purely negative would in itself still be of great advantage. But surely that criticism is not purely negative which traces the various discordant passages of the ancient authors, investigates the causes of the formation of the different versions, and ascertains which version is the more ancient and which the more recent. Such criticism, on the contrary, is quite constructive. It discovers the persons and the facts which gave vigor to the ancient traditions. It reproduces the general atmosphere that gave rise to such inventions, and reconstructs the history of the era which gave them birth. Finally it explains the conception of the ancients regarding their own primitive history,—the history which they had built up and narrated.

From such researches, the conclusion might be drawn that the history of a given people is less ancient than later tradition would have us suppose; and that, through national vanity common to all peoples, the writers of that nation increased, embellished and rendered more august the period of their formation. With all this, however, we would not be destroying, but rather constructing. For, we would thereby obtain a true and sincere conception of the primitive conditions of such a people.

The study of the texts, and the comparison of the political and constitutional history of the Romans with that of other peoples, prove that at Rome, as elsewhere, there occurred a long process of falsifications. These forgeries were (so to speak) genealogical in character. Latium and the summits of the seven hills of Rome may have been occupied by human races many centuries before the age of the vases and bronzes found by the architect Giacomo Boni. In these vases and bronzes certain learned persons see I know not what confirmation of the legends and falsifications of the late annals. The political history, the true and proper political history which is embodied in actual persons and events, begins at Rome only towards the fifth century. If any events worthy of history occurred at Rome before this time, no one was in condition to gather and preserve them. Polybius and Livy both recognized as the chief principle of historical criticism that there can be no trustworthy and sincere history where there have not been contemporary historians.

This is not the case for resorting to the argument of the ancient convivial songs, which were supposed to constitute

TEMPLE OF VESTA. ANCIENT RELIEF

THE CAPITOL

THE CRITICAL METHOD

the most ancient source of Roman history. Such songs were already lost in the times of Cato and Cicero.[11] Those still extant in the time of Dionysius were not strictly historical. They were, at times, sacred and religious tales. If the ancients did truly sing the deeds of Coriolanus, it must not be forgotten that they similarly recounted the deeds of Romulus and Remus.[12] If, moreover, the convivial songs known to Cato had been preserved, the gain for the true history of Rome would have been meagre indeed. History exists only when there are limitations of time and space. All the valuable and abundant data regarding the Homeric epic have not in themselves been capable of establishing more than vague and uncertain theories regarding the historic contents of the poem.

A comprehensive study of Roman history proves that the true and great development of the Roman people began only towards the middle of the fifth century. It suddenly asserted itself as the result of rapid and vigorous action. Similarly rapid was the rise of the Arabian tribes which bore from the heart of the desert the voice of the Prophet. A like phenomenon was manifested in the conquest or colonization of the Indies and the New World by the English.

The rapidity with which the Romans became masters of preceding civilizations and spread their authority over the world may lessen the admiration for them in the bourgeoisie greedy for noble ancestry, or in some petty nobles who live exclusively in the squalid remains of the past. A thoughtful Italian, however, assists with great satisfaction at the rapidity and impetus with which his ancestors conquered so honorable a place in the history of the world. In a similar manner, a well-thinking American is justly proud of the recent origin of the history of his country. He observes with contentment the rapid and gigantic progress made from the not-distant day when the declaration of the independence of his country was proclaimed to the world.

The majority of Roman annalists were patriots. They were, too, genealogists and demagogues rather than true historians. They rendered less clear the true picture of the early national history, with their countless and more or less deliberate forgeries. There were not lacking, however, other Roman writers who brought into relief the uncertain sources of the history as commonly accepted. Cicero himself, who in many ways was a representative of the nation's vanities, recognized the falsity of these origins. Livy is not destitute of critical science, as (on the contrary) are those scholars who base themselves on his work (without a clear conception of his intentions) and accept the ancient tales. Livy himself often strongly emphasizes the uncertain character of the earliest history. This portion of history he presented in synopsized form, placing it as an introduction to his careful and truthful exposition of times less remote and historically more certain.[13] Politicians and genealogists like Valerius Antias and Licinius Macer devoted their labors to augmenting the number of ancient fancies and misrepresentations. Ovid, however, genuinely echoed the general feeling, exclaiming:

O quam de tenui Romanus origine crevit.[14]

Hail, then, to Rome, which from such modest beginnings rapidly rose to be mistress of the Mediterranean and of the uncultured West. Glory to the race which descended from the valley of Rieti and the mountains of northern Abruzzi, and which gave to the Peninsula a political unity defined by the chain of the Alps and the shores of the sea. Foreign dominations, the tyranny of a theocratic government, and the degeneration due to union with inferior races from beyond the sea have for a more or less long period weakened this splendid political and moral unity. But it is under the banner of Rome, and with the name of Rome, that that race will one day exercise in a greater degree its influence upon the civilized peoples of the world.

CHAPTER II

THE EXCAVATIONS IN THE FORUM ROMANUM, AND THEIR IMPORTANCE FOR THE MOST ANCIENT ROMAN HISTORY

WHOSOEVER undertakes to trace the most ancient history of the Italian peninsula is immediately impressed by the disparity of the material at his disposal. He finds a relative abundance offered by Etruscan civilization (beginning with the eighth century B.C.), but a great scarcity of such material in Latium. The solution of the problem is not difficult. It must be remembered that at Rome, and in the neighboring regions, the civilization of the Empire modified the earlier strata, and that the spade of the excavator uncovers remains similar in character to those already offered by the necropolis of Tarquinii or that of Præneste. The Esquiline has already disclosed to us its archaic necropolis. The Forum, thanks to the zeal of Giacomo Boni, is now disclosing the sepulchres of the most ancient inhabitants of Latium. It is restoring to light monuments which were once seen by the annalists of the second century and the contemporaries of Varro and Cicero, but which had already disappeared in the generation of Livy and Augustus.

The important excavations of Boni have naturally attracted the attention of the civilized world; and the contents of the archaic inscription upon the four sides of the stele have exercised the ingenuity of the most eminent scholars. It is natural that every one should have hastened to offer the contribution of his own observations; and it is likewise natural that such haste should have caused premature judgments and should have diffused some error. It is not surprising that to-day, after five years, the ancient inscription still refuses to reveal its meaning. We must consider that it is written in a Latin far different from that employed after the third century B.C., and that we have in our possession but little more, perhaps, than a third of the entire monument.

Of all the words inscribed upon the stele, very few have reached us entire: *sacros, regei, kalatorem, iouxmenta, iuvestod, liquoiod.* It is vain to endeavor to complete the broken words without formulating (as has been the case even with the best scholars) the strangest conjectures. By the words *iouxmenta capia* many scholars have thought themselves authorized to suppose that the inscription refers to animals, such as horses or oxen, and to ceremonies connected with the *rex*. But there have not been lacking eminent scholars,—for instance Mommsen,—to deny the possibility of such signification. At any rate, the sacred character of the inscription is evident, and no one has doubted that the word *regei* is the dative of the noun *rex* and not the passive infinitive of the verb *regere*.[1]

Vain, however, would be every attempt to determine through what circumstance the *rex* came to be mentioned in our inscription. The calendar published for the first time about 304 B.C. by Gnæus Flavius is, by some ancient and also by some modern scholars, ascribed to the time of the Decemvirate rather than to the kingly period. According to this calendar the *rex sacrorum* appeared in the Forum on the 24th of February, or the feast of the Regifugium,—that is, a ceremony closely connected with the end of the year. He appeared also on the 24th of March and on the 24th of May,—the latter being a day on which (according to a very probable conjecture of Mommsen) it was lawful to make one's testament in the *Comitia Calata*,— in the presence, that is, of the Quirites gathered in *curiae*. It is to be noted, however, that the *rex sacrorum* did not present himself to the public only three times during the year. On the Nones of each month, and from the Capitol, he indicated to the people the various holidays. He offered sacrifices on the days called *agonales;* and on the day sacred to the worship of Consus he was seen upon his horse-drawn chariot in the Circus Maximus.[2] When in our inscription, therefore, mention is made of beasts of burden, it does not follow that these must necessarily be connected with the *rex sacrorum* rather than, for example, with the Quirites who had to assist at the sacred rites performed by the *rex*. We know that at Rome, as in Greece, it was the custom to sacrifice to the gods animals still untamed by the yoke. The exceptions that can be noted in Thebes, Rhodes and Rome itself do not authorize us to believe (as has been done) that in those cases reference was made to sacrifices.[3] But even if this were so, we would find in the *tabulae* from

THE ARCHAIC STELE OF THE
FORUM ROMANUM

Iguvium a rite which would explain the words *iouxmenta capia*. One might, indeed, believe that the Forum inscription alludes to some ceremony similar to that of the Umbrian city,—in which oxen and cows were pursued as enemies which the citizens endeavored to *capere*. With this ceremony of the Iguvini we might compare the Roman festivals of the Poplifugium and of the Vitulatio (July 5th).[4]

Iumenta are mentioned also in a text so badly mutilated that it is impossible to complete it. In this there is mention also of the *Vinalia rustica* of August, sacred to Jupiter. Furthermore, *iumenta* are referred to on the occasion of the feast of the Septimontium (the 11th of December), one of the natal days of Rome.[5] It would be easy to understand why they should have been spoken of in our inscription, if to it could be referred certain passages stating that in this vicinity chariot-races and sacrifices of horses took place. I refer to the feast of the 15th of October, in which the inhabitants of the Subura and those of the Sacra Via fought for the possession of the head of the right-hand horse on the winning chariot.[6] If it were my intention to give other analogous cases and hypotheses, I would recall that it was the duty of the augurs to prevent yoked animals from giving rise to the so-called *iuge auspicium* in the presence of the magistrates; and that, in the fully historic age, the inferior magistrates and Roman knights were obliged to dismount on the arrival of the consul. Likewise, in the most ancient period the patricians appeared in chariots drawn by horses. And, finally, it may be recalled that the road which led from the temple of Carmentis to the Forum, in the direction of the Vulcanal and the *niger lapis*, was called the *Vicus Iugarius*.[7]

I refrain from accepting any of the suppositions just made. My aim has been merely to show how many conjectures can be ventured about a single word; to show how necessary it is to proceed with the utmost caution and to discard all fantastic explanations.

A certain light, however, seems to come from the fragmentary word *sora*. Milani has thought of connecting this word with the cult of Soranus (worshipped by the Hirpini), who, by the explicit testimony of ancient texts and monuments, was at one time identified with the Solar god Apollo, and at another time with the god of the dead,— Dis Pater.[8] Wissowa does not admit this identification.

Similarly he has not understood that Acca Larentia, a sepulchral deity, could be associated with the worship of Jupiter. But his doubts are not valid as against the proofs offered by the monuments themselves. The god Soranus represented, at the same time, both the light and the darkness.[9] We know from explicit statements that Vulcanus and Summanus were worshipped in one cult and in one temple, Vulcanus representing the diurnal activity of the Sun, Summanus the nocturnal. Nor is it any marvel (as Hülsen thinks) that the name of Vulcanus, the Sungod of the Faliscans, should be met with in the Forum. For it should be remembered in this connection, that the Romans of the Palatine performed ceremonies on the Lupercalia entirely analogous to those of the ancient Hirpini of Mount Soracte.[10] Furthermore, we know too little concerning the names of the most ancient Roman divinities to marvel at that of Soranus. It will be sufficient to recall that, even in the beginning of the Empire, few persons knew that the most ancient Romans had worshipped Strenia, Vica Potæ, Mutunus and Summanus. And this, too, in spite of the fact that the worship of the last had been, originally, as important as was later that of Jupiter Capitolinus himself, or Tarpeius.[11]

The finding of Apollo Soranus in the Forum and in the area of the Comitium should not surprise us. The Etruscan soothsayers caused to be erected in the same place (and in memory of Vulcan) the statue of Horatius Cocles. The statue of the god was then removed to the neighboring Vulcanal that it might be better illuminated by the Sun.[12] If it be considered that the foot of the Capitoline Hill formed, in most ancient times, a *sepulcretum* like that of the Velia and of the Palatine, we shall deem it quite natural to find here the mention of a cult sepulchral in character. This will agree with the name of the neighboring region, *doliola,* which some explained by the presence of ancient sepulchres on that site, and which by others was connected with the ancient *sepulcretum* discovered by Boni at the foot of the temple of Faustina.[13] This, finally, will be in accord with the fact that in the Comitium, where later the tomb of Romulus and the Rostra were situated, it was the custom to deliver funeral orations.[14]

The archaic stele of the Forum, then, seems to record the memory of sacred ceremonies performed in honor of the

ALTAR OF THE YEAR 9 B. C., WITH ARCHAIC
OUTLINES. (MAGAZINO COMUNALE, ROME)

ANCIENT BASE, CIPPUS AND PILLAR BENEATH THE NIGER LAPIS

god of the dead,—Soranus,—and under the direction of the *rex*, the supreme head of the State religion.

We shall arrive to the same conclusion by examining the statements of ancient authors concerning the monument which they supposed to be hidden beneath the *niger lapis*.

II

According to information which can be traced to Varro, there was beneath the *niger lapis* a monument adorned by two lions, and believed to be the tomb of Romulus.[15] One of the sources known to Dionysius of Halicarnassus, however, attributed the same monument to Faustulus, the shepherd who reared Romulus, but instead of speaking of two lions made mention of only one. It was probably the same source who asserted that in that place there was a stele commemorating the valor of Hostus Hostilius,—facts, these latter, which correspond very well with those known to Verrius Flaccus.[16] The value of these statements is purely mythological and legendary. Nevertheless, the sepulchral character of the foundations forming the substratum of the monument covered by the lions has been now clearly demonstrated by Professor Studniczka, of the University of Leipsic.

With a perspicacity equal to his learning, Studniczka has compared an entire series of Greek and Etruscan monuments. With these he has proved that the monument considered by the ancients as the tomb of Romulus can belong, as regards its architectural features, to a period extending from the fifth to the second century B. C. It is also the merit of Studniczka to have successfully braved the question of the stratigraphy of the soil in which the monuments rest. From the presence of certain objects found near the tomb, and attributed to the sixth and even seventh century B.C., the official publishers of the excavation had deduced that the sepulchre did truly belong to so remote an age. Only a few months after the discovery I questioned the value of what was being published as complete and certain information. Nearly a year had first to pass, however, and the loud outcry of all scholars became necessary, before the facts were published, at least less imperfectly. From these it became evident that the so-called *stips votiva* of the monument was composed of a conglomeration of objects extending from the seventh or sixth century to as late as the seventh century B.C.[17]

The careful study of Studniczka has now demonstrated that the monuments in question are embedded in strata later than that following the Gallic fire, and as recent as those of the age of Cæsar and Augustus. Traces of the Gallic fire are seen in a stratum containing the remains of those bricks that were distributed by the State to the citizens on the rebuilding of the city.[18] The tomb of Romulus and the stele, however, do not rest upon this stratum, but on another which is one meter higher; and between these two strata there is clearly visible still a third stratum,—the level of the Curia Hostilia as rebuilt after the departure of the Gauls. Both tomb and cippus were surrounded and covered by stones and various other materials, to which the name *stips votiva* has been given.

Bearing in mind the dedication of a statue representing the wolf with the Twins, made by the Ogulnii in 266 B.C. at the *ficus Ruminalis,* and considering the age indicated by the architectural character of the tomb of Romulus, Studniczka is inclined to date the latter at about 300 B.C. On the other hand, by regarding the palæography of the inscription, which is generally attributed to the sixth, and by some even to the fifth, century B.C., he concludes that the cippus is of the sixth century, and that it was replaced *in situ* on a more recent stratum. Similar was the procedure of the Athenians (he observes) after the departure of the Persians.

These conclusions of Studniczka are surely worthy of consideration, and I think that certain topographical facts can be urged in his support. A mere glance at the arrangement of the monuments shows that the tomb of Romulus, the archaic stele and the neighboring pavement have three different orientations and represent three different periods. In addition, if the cippus with its four inscribed surfaces had originally been placed in such a position as to be easily read, this end was frustrated by the building of the tomb of Romulus so close to it. This fact obliges us to assume a more remote age for the cippus than for the tomb of Romulus. In this regard I might recall that Cicero affirmed having once seen the Rostra adorned by the statues of the Roman orators killed by the Veientes in about 426 B.C., and also the column bearing the treaty of peace

CAMPANIAN INSCRIPTIONS OF THE END OF THE REPUBLIC. (NAPLES MUSEUM)

between the Latins and Spurius Cassius.[19] This document, according to the official annals known to Livy and to Dionysius, was drawn up in the year 480 B.C. Livy would, therefore, seem to have good reason for declaring that, on the departure of the Gauls, diligent search was made for all the written monuments which the barbarians had overturned.[20]

I do not intend to repeat here my observations as to the perfect credibility of this statement; nor do I desire to discuss whether or not Cicero saw the original monuments themselves, and whether they are to be assigned to the

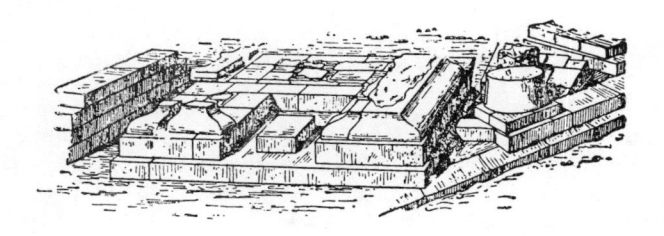

fifth century B.C. I deem it essential, however, to bring into relief the fact that, before resorting to the hypothesis of Studniczka, it is fitting to verify whether the inscription of the cippus must necessarily be assigned to the sixth century, and whether there be not arguments for maintaining that the stele rests upon its original stratum. To answer such questions, it is necessary for us to discuss the problem of the palæography of the inscription.

III

When we consider the external form and the direction of the writing, the cippus does not present any chronological data helpful to us in our task. For, indeed, we find this form of monument and this direction of writing throughout Latium and Magna Græcia in an age far more recent. The same is true among the Veneti at least as late as the third century B.C. An even later limit is offered by the two Capuan cippi here presented, which are either of the latter part of the second century or, more probably, of the first century B.C.

The three diacritic points and the boustrophedon direction of the writing have been regarded as undeniable proofs of the antiquity of the stele. The laws of Solon are cited in this respect to prove that our monument is of the sixth century B.C. But such a comparison was not necessary, nor even to the point. I do not delay over the three diacritic marks that separate the words of the stele, because they are frequent in Greek inscriptions of the fifth century B.C., and appear, though rarely, in Attic inscriptions later than 403 B.C.[21] To this must be added the fact that the three points are found in Italic monuments of a much later age.

I do not, moreover, attach excessive importance to the archaic form of the letters, because epigraphists know well that such forms are to be found here and there in the various States of Greece later than the middle of the fifth century B.C. Even the closed ⊟, which is, perhaps the most archaic form in our inscription, and which was seized upon as a special proof of its antiquity, is found in the inscription of Hiero recording the victory of Cuma in 474 B.C.,[22] and in Arcadian inscriptions of the fourth century. This letter appears in the Etruscan tegula of Capua of the fourth or even the third century; and in Etruria letters of such form continue (according to the testimony of a bilingual inscription) until the subjugation of the country by the Romans.[23]

Mommsen has noted that the letter r in our inscription is represented by the form P rather than by the form R, which appears in the most ancient Roman monuments,—that is, on coins.[24] But the earliest Roman coins are not anterior to the beginning of the fourth century B.C., and this, consequently, does not necessarily lead us to the fifth century, and still less to the sixth. It would seem, then, that greater importance must be given to the boustrophedon order of writing. But who is not aware that at Crete this order still continues in the fifth century, if not later? Not to cite other instances, who does not know that we have traces of boustrophedon in the inscription of Pantare of Gela, which is not much earlier that 505 B.C.?[25] Finally, the stele of S. Mauro Forte near Matera (which is of the fifth century), both in its boustrophedon order, in the char-

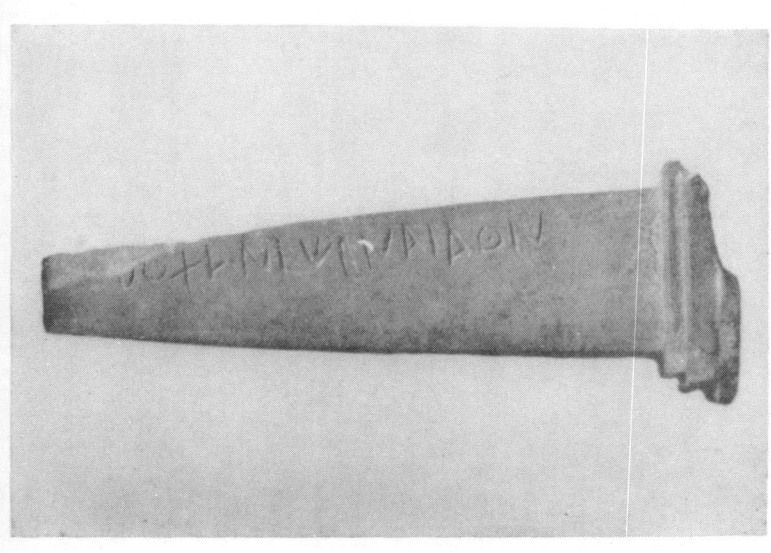

GREEK INSCRIPTION FROM S. MAURO FORTE, NEAR MATERA. (NAPLES MUSEUM)

acter of many of its letters, and even in its external form, recalls the one lately discovered at Rome.

But there is still more. An examination of the Italian dialectic inscriptions teaches us that archaic letters, the three diacritic points and the boustrophedon order are precisely the characteristics of the great majority of the inscriptions of Picenum, of the Marrucini, of the Pæligni and of the Marsi. Such inscriptions are not, as a whole, earlier than the fourth century. And, surely, at least as late as the third century we find Venetian inscriptions with very archaic letters similar to those of our inscription, and with the boustrophedon direction of the writing.[26]

The historic, and not epigraphic, character of this study does not permit me to proceed to a minute palæographical examination of the inscription. I confine myself, therefore, to inviting the readers to make for themselves, as I have done, a careful comparison of the stele with Oscan, Etruscan and Italic inscriptions. Whosoever will undertake such examination will find that those graphic elements, on account of which some have thought that the stele of the Forum was inscribed in the sixth century or perhaps in the seventh century B.C., are of such a nature as to be assigned even to the end of the fifth century B.C. A sufficient proof of this is offered by the Etruscan *tegula* from S. Maria di Capua Vetere. This, also, has the boustrophedon order; it has diacritic marks of one, two and three points, and, probably, is not earlier than the fourth century. Perhaps it is even more recent.[27] A further proof is furnished by the boustrophedon inscription of Caso Cantovios, which is attributed, by those who specialize in such studies, to the year 300 B.C., but which (to state my opinion frankly) gives me the impression of being still more recent.

The persistency of such archaic characters among the peoples of the Peninsula cannot be explained by the isolation in which they lived. For, even laying aside many other considerations, it is well known that the coast of Venetia was visited by the Corcyraei and Tarentini as early as the fifth century, and was finally settled by the Syracusans. Likewise, the civilization of the Sabine races during the fourth century is explicitly testified to by the ancients. The persistency of forms which in Greece tend to disappear in the latter half of the fifth century is especially due to the fact that the Italic races retained for a long time the original forms,—forms which they employed at the time when they directly or indirectly learned the art of writing from the Greeks. The Veneti, as we learn from a bilingual inscription, continued to write with archaic letters and from

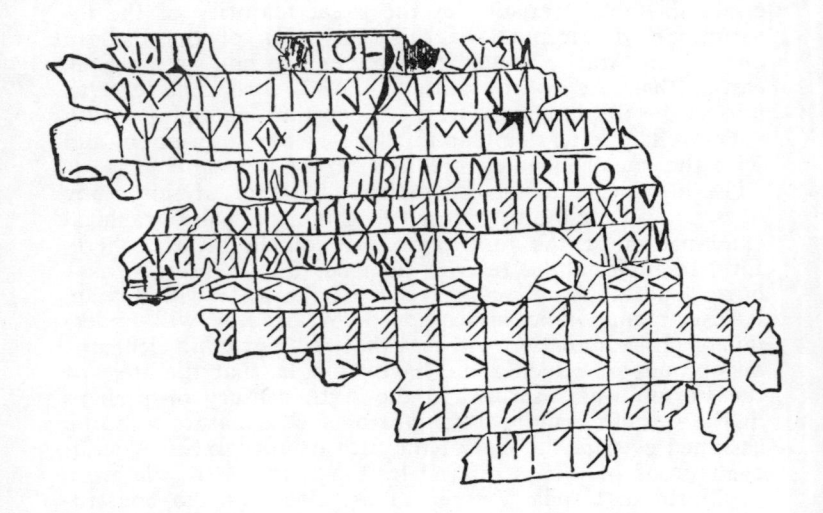

right to left after they had learned to write Latin inscriptions, with letters of more recent form, and in the direction from left to right. For this same reason, the Oscans and Etruscans continued the use of archaic characters and the direction from right to left as late as the third century. If, then, among these and other races of Italy there came, later, a time when they perfected and elaborated their graphic characters, such elaboration is not to be attributed to the successive modifications of the Hellenic alphabets, but rather to a local evolution of characters learned *ab antico* from the Greeks.

In short, the comparison with the Greek inscriptions on the one hand, and with the Italic dialectic inscriptions on the other, does not present a single fact which compels us to believe that the Roman stele belongs to the sixth century B.C., or to an even more remote age. It obliges us, rather, to consider whether, perchance, it be not later than the

ITALIC INSCRIPTION NOT EARLIER THAN THE FOURTH CENTURY

CAMPANIAN INSCRIPTION NOT EARLIER THAN THE FIFTH CENTURY B.C. (NAPLES MUSEUM)

end of the fifth, and, we may add, than the beginning of the fourth century B.C.

An examination of the few Roman inscriptions of the earliest times would not lead us to different conclusions. The *fibula Prænestina* demonstrates that, as late as the sixth century, characters similar to those of our stele were employed at Rome. The Duenos bowl of the Quirinal, published by Dressel in 1880 (attributed by some scholars to the fifth century, and by many others equally authoritative to the fourth and even the third century B.C.), proves for how long a period certain archaic forms were retained in Rome. Nor is this the case to refer to the earliest Roman coins, on which the word *Roma* is written in somewhat less archaic forms, and in the direction from left to right. We shall omit, therefore, considerations upon the age in which were written inscriptions that can, in some cases, be attributed to a period later than the fourth century. We shall, however, emphasize the fact that there are no Roman coins earlier than the second half of the fourth century, and that the retrograde order of writing is found on Roman coins that are not earlier than 268 B.C.[28]

In regard to questions of this nature, it does not seem to us that we should blindly follow the rigid rules of certain archæologists and palæographists. From a few graphic strokes of different ages and of different monuments they are drawn to chronological conclusions which they deem certain. For instance, the letters upon the stones of the Servian walls,—walls which are to-day assigned by the most authoritative critics to the fourth century,—may have a form more or less recent than the characters on some other monuments, without bringing as an absolute consequence the necessarily anterior or posterior age of these latter monuments. Again, whoever has given but a glance at the forms of letters inscribed on the monuments of Italy during the close of the Middle Ages and throughout the Renaissance, has immediately noticed that forms of writing altogether different (such as the half-uncial and the Latin) interchange on monuments of the same period. And that this state of affairs obtained also in ancient times is proved by coins of the Greek city of Croton, dating about 400 B.C. In those years, in fact, Croton coined money on which, side by side with the new alphabet employing the sign *K* in the direction from left to right, there were still used archaic letters, including the form ρ, and written in the direction from right to left.

Also at Rome there may have been employed in the same century, and even in the same years, forms of writing entirely different from each other, determined by the habits of the writer as well as by the character of the monument and the material used. I do not desire to plunge into minute and useless comparisons. I limit myself to observing that, in the archaic stele of the Forum, the different sides have been inscribed with more or less dissimilar characters. This fact, from the purely epigraphic standpoint, might authorize the hypothesis (which I, however, would consider erroneous) that the stele was inscribed in different ages. Above all, it is worthy of note that in the same inscription there have been employed different forms for indicating both the "m" and the "u", the latter being at times given as a *V,* and at others as an *I*.

Thus, any one who, in applying himself to the solution of this problem, has not armed himself with preconceptions and prejudices, must necessarily come to the conclusion that we lack sufficient precise data for maintaining one hypothesis rather than another. We do not think that exact limits can be fixed, having at our disposal merely the *fibula Prænestina* on one hand and the letters on the Servian wall and the Dressel bowl on the other. Considering the different character of these monuments and the different language employed, it is not easy to establish comparisons between them. I confess that I cannot understand the ease with which linguists of merit derive chronological data from such meagre and mutilated documents. I hardly deem this the occasion for establishing comparisons with other literary texts (such as the Twelve Tables) which have not, perhaps, reached us entirely in their original form. The same prudence is undoubtedly necessary in palæographical criticism.

We are entirely lacking Roman inscriptions that can be referred with certainty to the fourth, fifth and sixth centuries. More numerous and less insecure dates are, on the one hand, furnished by the Greek inscriptions (particularly by those from Magna Græcia), and on the other by the inscriptions of the Oscans, the Etruscans and other Italic peoples. Epigraphists are well aware that if an inscription with characters similar to those on the archaic stele of the Forum had been found on Attic soil, it would necessarily be assigned to the seventh century; whereas had it been found in various regions of the Peloponnese, it might be attributed even to the fifth century. The same elasticity of bounds is of avail, and with still greater justice, upon Italic soil.

There is no doubt that the sixth century would be the proper age of an inscription inscribed with such characters, if only it had been found in Sicily and in Italic soil. Nothing, however, would prevent such monument, even if found in the regions mentioned, from being attributed to the late fifth century. Among the Etruscans, the Oscans and the Veneti an inscription with similar characters might very reasonably be assigned not only to the fifth, but also to the fourth and even to the following centuries. The same holds true, in even greater degree, for the races of central Italy, such as the Marsi, the Pæligni and the Sabini. In regard to Rome, all the elements for comparison have disappeared, with the exception of the Dressel bowl and the letters of the Servian wall of the fourth century. Consequently, we can reach no better conclusion than that the inscription on the stele can be referred with equal probability to the sixth, the fifth, or to the beginning of the fourth century.

It is natural to think that Rome, which was situated on the banks of the Tiber and had been hailed as a Greek city as early as the fourth century,[29] should have received the seeds of Greek culture not later, nor in lesser degree, than had the Etruscan coast towns. Everything, indeed, favors the hypothesis that at Rome, as at Tarquinii and Cære, inscriptions were written in the fourth century in Greek characters. Latin epigraphy rapidly changed its characters from the middle of the fourth century, as is partly deduced from coins. Though showing itself bound in many ways to the Greek letters, it gradually assumed a character of its own, fundamentally distinct from the writing of the Etruscans, the Umbrians and other Italic peoples. This change must be connected with that rapid political transformation through which Rome, already head of the Latin league and ally of Capua and Naples (between 338 and 327 B.C.,), became the first State in Italy, joined in fresh relations with the Greek element, and renewed every detail of its customs and its culture. This renewed and refreshened culture may, in its turn, be closely related to the publication of the laws and the Fasti from 312 to 304 B.C., under the care of Appius Claudius and his collaborator, Gnæus Flavius.[30]

It is probable that, on account of this great transformation, Rome abandoned at one stroke its ancient system of writing, in the same manner as at Athens the archonship of Eucleides marked the transition from the old to the new alphabet. The epigraphy of the stele is anterior to this important reform. This fact, however, does not enable us to decide whether the stele is of the sixth, fifth or beginning of the fourth century, when the boustrophedon order, the three points and the archaic letters still continued among other races of the Peninsula. Surely we are not encouraged to assign a great antiquity to the art of writing among the Romans, by the statement of an ancient author that the Romans began to employ the stilus only in the time of Porsena.[31] The one certain fact is that the stele rests upon a stratum later than that representing the era of the Gallic fire, 387 B.C. There is no proof that the monument is of a period anterior to that historic event. At the same time, nothing excludes the possibility of its having been inscribed in the years immediately following that catastrophe.

IV

There remains but one defence to those who assign the stele to the sixth century,—namely, that in the inscription there is mention of a *rex*. It is clear (they argue) that if the *rex* is an actual king, we are led back to the sixth century B.C. But this supposition is not based upon valid arguments. There is no reference in the inscription to any fact which can be ascribed to the political authority of the *rex*. The mention of Soranus recalls, rather, the religious activity of the *rex*. Finally, even if mention had been made of a political *rex,* such statement would not have brought us back to 509 B.C., firstly because it is by no means certain that the kings were expelled from Rome in that year, and secondly, because we do not know the precise time when the *rex sacrorum* was once for all substitued for the political *rex*.

I shall not delay to demonstrate the falsity of the story of

THE NIGER LAPIS

EXCAVATIONS IN THE FORUM

the expulsion of the Tarquins from Rome. This I have proved elsewhere, and the same conclusions had partly been obtained by Mommsen. It is sufficient to consider, for instance, the story of the first consul, Tarquinius Collatinus, who, together with Brutus, was invited to resign from office. This tradition was a parallel to that which made the Tarquins leave Rome as the result of a tranquil revolution. In addition, the date, 509 B.C., assigned to the expulsion of the kings is a synchronism utterly lacking in value. The founding of Rome was fixed at 814 as well as at 753, when the institution of the Ephors was established at Sparta. In like manner, it was asserted that Rome had been founded in the same year in which Carthage arose.

I omit mentioning many synchronisms somewhat less certain, but shall note that the Roman revolution for which the plebs seceded to the Sacred Mount was placed in more or less the same days in which the Syracusan Kyllirioi expelled the *gamoroi*. Likewise, the slaughter of the Fabii at the Cremera was made to coincide with that of the Spartans at Thermopylæ. To the laws of Solon there chronologically corresponded (more or less) those of Servius; and the reign of Numa was erroneously made to fall in the times of Pythagoras. It is equally worthy of note that the adoption of the laws of the Twelve Tables was fixed in the same year in which, at ancient Thurii, the Protagorean code was proclaimed. Furthermore, the terrible plague which broke out at Athens was paralleled, by the Roman annalists, with a similar pestilence which spread over Rome in the year 433 B.C. The mention of the temple of Apollo in the latter case proves that the synchronism is a false one; for, that temple was erected only in the year 353 B.C. Finally it is not an isolated and accidental fact that the Tarquins, the authors of the principal Roman temple, should have been expelled from Rome in the very year in which the Pisistratidæ, the authors of the principal temple of the Acropolis, were expelled from Athens.

It is more important for our purpose to examine the relations between the political *rex* and the *rex sacrorum*. Livy plainly states that, on the abolition of the former, the *rex sacrorum* was created for the purpose of performing those sacrifices which had previously been the exclusive care of the political *rex*.[32] But, inasmuch as there are grave reasons for doubting, indeed for resolutely denying, the expulsion of the Tarquins, we should obviously ask whether the political *rex* and the *r x sacrorum* did not represent but one charge,—a charge which slowly and gradually transformed itself from a political office to one purely religious. The history of the relations between the political and the religious authority in Rome urges us to accept the second hypothesis. During the last centuries of the Republic, we see how the political and the civil authorities of the *pontifices* were continually encroached upon by the prætors and consuls. An examination of the religious hierarchy of the *rex sacrorum* as compared with that of the *pontifices* makes it clear that these latter, in preceding ages, must have gradually stripped the *reges* of their religious and civil authority. For, though the *reges* occupied the first place in the hierarchical scale,[33] and the *pontifices* the fourth, nevertheless we see that in the second century the office of *rex* was shunned by those who desired to pursue a political career.

That the conditions of the *rex* were different in the early centuries of the Republic is evident from various circumstances (such as the occurrence of *interreges* and *interregnum*), and from certain rights of the political magistrate retained by the *rex sacrorum*. The names *interrex* and *interregnum*, which answered to real and uninterrupted activities only till the beginning of the Punic Wars, prove false the conception that the Romans, with the pretended expulsion of the Tarquins, entirely abolished the civil functions of the *regnum*. The character of the *rex* clearly appears from certain indications of Pliny referring to the period of the last Samnite Wars,—indications which fix a date by naming the *rex* then in office. It is well known, moreover, that, till the end of the Republic, the *rex* played a conspicuous part in the official proclamation to the people of the feasts of the calendar.[34]

Consequently, we do not believe that in the year 509 B.C. the political *rex* was expelled, and that he was succeeded by a purely religious *rex*. It is more rational to believe that, from the beginning of the fifth century, the authority of the *rex sacrorum* gradually diminished, and that it was absorbed by the *prætores* and *tribuni militum* on the one hand, and by the *pontifices* on the other. In like manner the *interrex* was finally, after the times of Pyrrhus, supplanted by the *dictator* for the election of magistrates. We find that the *rex* existed in the fifth century at Tarentum and at Veii; and we find him in even later ages in the cities of Etruria (e. g., at Clusium), and among the Italic people of southern Italy.[35]

There is no ground for supposing that there was, at Rome, a more rapid political evolution than elsewhere. Even if such were the case, rather than believing in the fantastic date of 509 B.C., it would be more fitting to assign such change to the middle of the fifth century, when a band of Sabines, by establishing themselves on the Quirinal, gave origin to the people of the Romani and Quirites. In this period occurred those important political changes which tradition connected with the legends of the Decemvirate (450-445), with the re-establishment of the tribunate of the plebs, with the Valerio-Horatian law (449), with the creation of the censorship (444), and, finally, with that of the *tribuni militum consulari potestate* (443 B.C.). In other words, in the years from 509 to 443 B.C., for which there is a more or less falsified list of consuls and dictators, I would not hesitate to recognize that period in which the regal authority was gradually stripped of its military and civil attributes. During this period it was confined within that circle of civil and religious powers which we must regard as continuing throughout the whole of the fourth and beginning of the third century, under the form of the *interreges* so frequently mentioned for that period.[36]

Granted this condition of affairs, the mention of *rex* in our stele leads to no chronological conclusion. Even if it were anterior to the Gallic fire, such consideration would by no means lead us to date the cippus earlier than 509 B.C. The mention in our inscription of only sacred functions connected with the *rex* agrees very well with a *rex sacrorum* of an age later than the departure of the Gauls. Nothing, therefore, obliges us to believe that the stele was replaced *in situ* after the Gallic catastrophe; and such conclusion is confirmed also by a new examination of the problem of topography.

V

The Ogulnii, in 296 B.C., dedicated near the *ficus Ruminalis* a statue representing the wolf nursing the Twins. On this account Studniczka was, as we have already seen, led to assign the tomb of Romulus to c. 300 B.C. Such conclusion is without great value. There is no proof that the dedication of the above-mentioned statue took place in the Comitium and near the *ficus Ruminalis* situated by the statue of Attus Navius, rather than near the more ancient *ficus Ruminalis* of the Lupercal. For here, as we learn from the ancient authors and the Pompeian fresco herewith presented, there was a bronze statue representing the wolf in the act of nursing the founders of the city.

A more important element seems to be contained in the fact that Varro declares the tomb of Romulus as being behind the *rostra*. We know that the Rostra were built in 338 B.C., after the great naval victory of the Romans over the Antiates. In a similar manner, as a consequence of the victories of L. Camillus and Gaius Mæcius over the Volscians and Latins, and of the conquest of Naples between 338 and 327, Rome became not only the recognized and undisputed head and centre of the Latin confederacy, but also the foremost nation of the Peninsula. By the same Camillus (according to a version worthy of consideration) there was erected in that year the temple of Saturn, which other writers attributed to King Tarquin.[37] During those years the Forum was becoming filled with worships imported from other Latin cities; and therefore, on account of the ever-increasing importance of the worship of the Capitoline Jupiter (who had protected Rome against the Gauls), and because the city was now spreading over the Quirinal and the neighboring hills, the slope of the area sacred to Vulcan and the place originally destined for military exercises became the political centre of the community.

The Palatine naturally lost a great part of its religious and political importance, and the chief cults connected with it were consequently transported to the Comitium. Just as men then talked of the house of Romulus as no longer on the Palatine, but on the Capitoline, so in the Comitium (attributed by some to Romulus himself) the founder of the city was supposed to have created the *mundus*. In this region,—that is, in the Vulcanal adjacent to the Comitium, —Romulus was also supposed to have gathered his people. From this place he had disappeared, and here, according to others, he had been buried. Legend, indeed, asserted that the *ficus Ruminalis* of the Palatine passed to the Comitium in virtue of a miracle of Attus Navius. From this it is evident that all the cults of the Palatine were transferred to the Comitium.[38]

The legend which affirmed that Romulus was transformed into the god Quirinus and snatched to heaven does not quite agree with the monument that was supposed to guard his bones. It was natural, therefore, that there should arise the tradition (reported by the Dionysius), that Romulus, during the struggle with the Sabines, was struck by a rock while standing on the spot where his tomb was later pointed out. The missile, however, was supposed to have wounded him only; and on that spot Faustulus, instead, was supposed to have been killed, while endeavoring to separate the Twins engaged in their fratricidal combat.[39]

This story, therefore, transferred to the Comitium still another legendary element originally closely connected with the Palatine, over whose *pomerium* Remus was supposed to have leaped. But the Comitium already had its myths before the year 338, in which the Rostra were built. Legend affirmed that it was built by Tullus Hostilius, or Tarquinius Priscus, or in the time of the augur Attus Navius, who marked out the *templum* which, by other legends, was connected with King Hostilius. A third tradition, instead, ascribed the reclaiming of this region from the marshes to the second Tarquinius.[40]

With these contradictory traditions there is in close relation still another, to the effect that the Curia Hostilia was founded, not by Tullus Hostilius, but by his grandfather, Hostus Hostilius,—the first husband of Hersilia, wife of Romulus. There were legends, it is true, which spoke of Hostus Hostilius as of a person living even after the wars against the Sabines. According to some, he perished instead during that period, and his tomb was supposed to have been marked by a stele recording his virtues, and situated in a conspicuous part of the Comitium. Everything, then, would seem to warrant the assumption that our stele is precisely the monument to which the ancients referred. But since the text of the stele says nothing of Hostilius, and still less of his military virtues, it is clear that the reference was to some monument earlier than the tomb of Romulus, and oriented with the more ancient plan of the Curia Hostilia,—that is, the curia of the *hospites*. It may well be that before the invasion of the Gauls there was, on the site of the Curia Hostilia and Comitium, a sacred enclosure in which the *hospites* (strangers) were received, and in which military exercises took place.

From the diagram of the strata presented by Studniczka, it is clear that the stele and the tomb of Romulus, rather than reposing on the stratum above the one representing the Gallic fire, rest on the stratum above this second one even. This fact naturally gives rise to the belief that between 386 B.C. (the year in which the Gauls departed) and 338 B.C. (when the Rostra were built), there must have taken place an elevation of the ground of the Comitium. We do not know what were the causes of this elevation. Nevertheless, we are warranted in assuming that it was due to the sudden sinking of the Forum connected with the legend of Curtius, and to the subsequent filling in of the abyss. The less remote and more probable date for this event is 362 B.C. That the abyss of the *lacus Curtius* extended towards the Vulcanal and the *niger lapis* is deducible, I think, from the fact that Curtius was supposed to have precipitated himself into the abyss by starting from the temple of Concord, which indeed overlooked the Vulcanal and the Comitium.[41]

We shall, then, establish the fact that, both on account of its different orientation and its position as regards the tomb of Romulus (which was afterwards built against it), the archaic stele represents a monument anterior to the former. But, inasmuch as the stratum on which it rests is not that of 386 B.C., but a later one, there results the obvious conclusion that, as far as the stratigraphy of the monument is concerned, it belongs to the years extending from 386 to 338 B.C. Perhaps (as I suspected a few months after its discovery) the stele is to be assigned to the year 362 B.C.[42] This chronological conclusion, indeed, is contradicted neither by the occurrence of the word *rex* in the stele nor by the palæographical examination already made.

VI

We have thus determined, as far as was possible, the date of the tomb of Romulus and of the archaic cippus. Before establishing what advantage for the most ancient history of Rome is to be derived from these discoveries, let us glance at the ancient *sepulcretum* which Boni has laid bare not far from the slopes of the Velia and the foundations of the temple of Faustina.

From the poverty of the tombs, the archaic household utensils, and the scarcity of traces of contact with Greek vases, some ill-advised critics have arrived at the conclusion that this *sepulcretum* belongs to the seventh, eighth, or even ninth century B.C. From the presence of proto-Corinthian vases, the more recent tombs have been assigned to the sixth century B.C. The more ancient tombs have been referred by some to the year 753, on the supposition that Rome was really founded in that year; whereas the tombs of the sixth century have been considered ample and sure proof of the reclaiming of the Forum in that century—the time assigned by tradition to the works of the Tarquins. To me all these conclusions seem purely arbitrary. We lack the chronological limits within which such pottery as the above was made. It may belong to the seventh or eighth century, or even to an earlier age; and, on the other hand, nothing excludes their continuing throughout the fifth century. The presence of proto-Corinthian vases of the sixth century is not an absolute terminus, because there is every probability that such vases continued to be imported and preserved at Rome even in a much later age. To pretend to establish the chronology of the Roman *sepulcretum* according to the exact ages which specialists ascribe to the various species of Greek vases is equivalent to deriving the date of a Catholic Church from the exotic material adorning it, and belonging to various periods.

It is needless to insist on the well-known fact that vases belonging to an earlier age in Greece may continue for a long time in Rome. Similarly, in the latter city (as we learn from the declarations of Boni himself) forms of sixth and seventh century vases were continued, for ritual reasons, till the late Empire. Surely the texts imply that for a long time,—that is, till the age of Pyrrhus and the Punic Wars,— the Romans remained faithful to the traditional custom and used poor and rough vases of earth and wood.[43] The assertion that the *sepulcretum* at the foot of the Velia ends with the period of the Tarquins is proved false by tradition itself, which states that on that spot, even after the expulsion of those kings, there were the sepulchres of the Valerii.[44] The theory, too, that it was the Tarquins who recovered the Forum from the waters is proved false by the fact that tradition attributed this work to Tullus Hostilius (the beginning of the seventh century) as well as to 362 B.C.—the occasion of the vortex calmed by the self-sacrifice of Curtius.[45]

The poverty of this necropolis, and the lack of gold, rather than pointing to a remote antiquity, demonstrate the sober and earnest character of the Roman people till the Punic Wars. It will be sufficient to recall that Cornelius Rufinus was expelled from the Senate by the famous Fabricius for having abused the use of silver cups, and for possessing some quantity of silver plate. All will recollect the surprise of the Carthaginian ambassadors at finding the same dinner-set in all the houses of the senators by whom they had been invited. For, the senators had gathered all their presentable ware, and had borrowed it from one another in turn. The great scarcity of gold explains, also, that passage in Pliny in regard to the worship by the Quintii of a golden coin—a poverty which confirms the declarations of the ancients that the most ancient community of the Palatine was composed of poor shepherds, that the magistrates themselves were clothed in humble skins, and that the houses were wretched huts covered with thatch and cork:

> *Frondibus ornabant quæ nunc Capitolia gemmis*
> *Pascebatque suos ipse senator oves.*

I know not whether the contemporary presence of inhumation and of cremation tombs (such as in this *sepulcretum*) be in favor of the theory which assigns it to the seventh and eighth, and even ninth century. Even admitting that these tombs are of the eighth century (in which tradition placed the origin of Rome), or else date back to a period by centuries and centuries earlier than the eighth (as some have thought), there would not result from this fact any confirmation whatsoever of the traditions and legends of the regal period. The zoölogy of man is one thing; political history, another. We know the history of Florence only from about the year 1000 A.D.; we have, also, the most ancient notices regarding the Roman *Florentia* in the time of Sulla. To no one, however, would it occur to make the public history of that city begin in the eighth century B.C., merely because there were found, in the very

centre of the Roman *Florentia,* vases of the Villanova type.
The critic who would aim to narrate the mediæval history
of Florence for the period preceding the year 1000 A.D.
would find himself in the same position as those contemporaries of Dante's ancestors who, in repeating old legends,
talked of Fiesole and Rome.

If future excavations will bring to light similar or even
more ancient *sepulcreta,* they will but prove that primitive
tribes established themselves upon the hills of the Septimontium about the year 1000 B.C., and, let us say, in even
earlier times. From all this, however, there will never come
the slightest corroboration of the legends of the ancients,
whether of Romulus, or of Numa and his loves with the
nymph Egeria, or of Servius Tullius, the creator of the
institutions of public and private law, the son of the god
of the hearth, and the lover of the goddess Fortuna.

VII

We shall not tarry amidst the confutations of coarse and
puerile errors; let us rather dwell upon the real and positive
gain derived from the latest excavations.

Let us immediately affirm that the *sepulcretum* discovered
by Boni has made evident that which the ancient authors
already clearly stated—namely, that the Roman Forum was
a region outside the *pomerium* and devoted to burial purposes. The ancients, in fact, make mention of tombs of
the Valerii at the foot of the Velia in the early years of the
Republic, and declare that in 275 B.C. it was permitted to
bury Fabricius in the Forum.[46] The references to the tomb
of Acca Larentia on the slopes of the Lupercal, and of the
Servilii and Cincii not very far from that place, are to be
thought of in connection with the sepulchres of the Claudii
upon the slopes of the Capitoline.[47] The archaic *sepulcretum* discovered near the temple of Faustina, the tombs
which were said to exist near the Comitium in the place
called *doliola,* and, finally, the stele sacred to Soranus, cause
the belief that, in the most ancient times, there were tombs
also in the region later occupied by the Comitium. Such
sepulcreta on the slopes of the hills facing the Forum must
have had the same relations to the cities above as those
which we now see between the *sepulcretum* of Volsinii

(Orvieto) and the ancient walls on the crest of the plateau on which that city was founded.

We know from the ancients that the region of the Forum was once a marsh; and from authentic reports we learn how, still in the time of Horace, the floods of the Tiber extended to the temple of Vesta and the neighboring Regia. The quantities of stones and pebbles near the tomb of Romulus prove that this ground was continually elevated; and the legend of Curtius, who, in 362 B.C., hurled himself into the abyss, indicates that the task of reclaiming the Forum had not yet been completed by that year. The statement that the Forum was reclaimed in the regal period is as little worthy of belief as that which attributes to the Tarquins the building of the famous Cloaca Maxima. For the excavations of Boni have demonstrated what I had already suspected—namely, that the Cloaca Maxima is a work of the Republican period.

The marshy area of the Roman Forum had at times been employed for military exercises. Here, in the marsh of the Caprificus (which extended from the foot of the Palatine to the Vulcanal and the adjacent Comitium), Mettius Curtius, the mythical ancestor of the Curtius of 362 B.C., had been on the point of being drowned; here Romulus harangued his army, and from this place, finally, had he disappeared. The sepulchral, and at the same time military, character of this region appears from the cults honored therein. At the foot of the Palatine we see the temple of Castor and Pollux. This cult (Greek in origin) was connected with the Roman cavalry which, from 304 B.C., on the Ides of Quintilis passed before it in the review called *equitum transvectio*. Here, too, was the temple of Mars,—the Regia,—a cult which, as we learn from Vitruvius, had to be outside the city;[48] and here was the temple of Janus, situated beside the Cloaca Maxima, which marked the limits of the most ancient *pomerium* of the Septimontium.

We do not possess sufficient material to warrant a discussion as to whether there was any chronological relation of contemporaneousness or succession between the sepulchral and the military purposes of the Forum in earliest times. In our case, the very facts that, after instituting the Comitium and the Rostra for civic functions, the pretended tomb of Romulus was placed there and that the custom arose of praising the dead in that locality, cause us to think that its sepulchral purpose was not immediately obliterated from the minds of the Romans. This supposition is in accord with the statement that, in 275 B.C., permission was granted to bury the remains of Fabricius in the Forum. Nothing, therefore, excludes the possibility that the sepulchral character of the area afterwards occupied by the Comitium should have been felt later than 386 B.C. Indeed, no historical fact denies that there was maintained in this locality the memory of the worship of the god Soranus, inasmuch as that of Mutunus on the Velia continued till the time of Augustus. At any rate, the fact remains that the ground occupied by the Forum was originally outside the boundaries of the ancient city, and that it was reclaimed, not in the time of Romulus or of the Tarquins (as various contradictory traditions suppose), but as a consequence of the predominating of the cults of the Capitoline over the divinities of the ancient Palatine, and of the ever-continuing extension of the city over the Quirinal and the Esquiline.

The defence presented by the Capitol during the invasion of the Gauls (who instead became masters of the Palatine) established the religious centre of the nation on the extremity of that hill. On the other hand, the growing power of Rome and the sudden accession of foreigners caused the Rome of the fourth century B.C. (as in our own days in 1870) to spread over the plateau of the Quirinal and of the Esquiline. The final proof of this is offered by the extension of the Servian city and of those walls attributed to the kings, which to-day all competent critics assign to a period following the Gallic fire.

With the rebuilding of the city after the departure of the Gauls, the Forum began to be the true religious and political centre of the nation. Therefore, in the same year in which the barbarians left Rome the temple of the god Mars, who had to be worshipped outside the *pomerium,* was transported beyond the Porta Capena. For the same reason there were transported thither the rites of the *hastæ* and of the Horatii, —a worship originally connected with one of the most ancient parts of the Septimontium,—the Velia.[49] The Curia Hostilia, from being the military headquarters where *hospites* might be fittingly received, became the seat for civil transactions; and the *hospites* were, after the year 296 B.C., welcomed in the temple of Bellona in the Campus Martius. The valley of the Forum, from which the Tiber was easily reached, was protected, as by high fortifications, by the converging slopes of the Capitoline, the Esquiline, the Velia, and the Palatine. With full justice, therefore, did L. Furius, in about 338 B.C., erect on the slopes of the Capitoline the temple of Saturn,—the state-treasury; and for like cause were the temple of Vesta and the Regia considered the homes of the most sacred cults of the nation and the palladium of its *arcana*. As a result of these changes, the marsh Caprea or of the Caprificus was now located in the Campus Martius, so that the Tarentum was transferred to the same place from that region of the Velabrum opposite to the Insula Tiberina.[50]

To sum up, the founding of the temple of Mars at the Porta Capena in 386 B.C. (388 B.C. according to Varro), the building of the Rostra in 338 B.C., the erection of the temple of Bellona in 296 B.C., and the burial of Fabricius in the Forum in 275 B.C., mark the extreme limits of this transformation. Moreover, we meet with clear evidence of the fact that the Forum, until the time of Fabricius, and even of Duilius, did not form part of the city of the Seven Hills.[51]

VIII

The results derived from the topographic discoveries in the Roman Forum are, consequently, in favor of critical studies rather than the confirmation of old follies. We are drawn to the same conclusion by the examination of the historical value of the archaic stele and of the tomb of Romulus. It has been said,—and it has often been repeated,—that the discovery of these monuments serves to prove the erroneousness of critical studies and to confirm old traditions. The results of modern criticism would have been severely shaken had a monument been found contemporary with Romulus and Numa, and capable of proving the existence of those mythical characters. The so-called tomb of Romulus, however, is revealed to be, with all certainty, a work of the fourth century. Nothing proves that the stele belongs to a different period. Even admitting the latter to be of a period anterior to the Gallic invasion (let us say of the sixth century), I do not see that from this any arguments can be drawn in favor of the traditional legends. Such confirmation would have been possible had the tomb truly been of the eighth rather than of the fourth century, and if the stele, instead of recording sacred ceremonies, bore the eulogies of Hostus Hostilius. But, inasmuch as its age and its contents are so widely different, we must recognize that we have here a new example of the arbitrary manner in which the ancient annalists described and determined the age of the earliest monuments of their national history.[52] We shall arrive to the same conclusion when, in speaking of Servius Tullius, we shall see that the law of the *servus rex* of the temple of Diana Aventinensis was attributed to the sixth king of Rome.

In the meantime, we shall place the stories of the tomb of Romulus in the same category with the statues referred by the annalists to the time of Romulus and Tatius, and also with that statue of Junius Brutus, first consul of the Republic, which (as the ancients themselves observed) was so very similar in features to the Junii—well-known plebeians of the late Republic. The stele of Hostus, too, will be classed with the eulogy of Romulus, written (it seems) in Greek characters and placed in the Vulcanal after the capture of Cameria. It may be classed also with the legal code attributed to Servius Tullius, and exposed in the Forum long before Gnæus Flavius had thought of publishing the Fasti and the calendar. The facility with which annalists attributed to the time of the first king of Rome monuments that were but by few decades earlier or later than the Gallic fire, is clearly evidenced by the legend of the *lacus Curtius*, which the annalist Piso placed in relation with Romulus, which Lutatius and Cornelius assigned to 445 B.C., and which Procilius and Livy attributed to the year 362 B.C.

The indications of the ancients regarding the date of the monuments hidden by the *niger lapis* will, with good reason, be placed in comparison with those regarding the temple of Flora, which Varro affirmed as having been founded by the mythical King Tatius, but which, instead, was not built earlier than 238 B.C. Finally, we shall contrast such indications with the statue of Jupiter, which Titus Quinctius is supposed to have taken from the Prænestini in 380 B.C. and to have dedicated on the Capitol, though (as is well known) it was dedicated later than 197 B.C. by T. Quiritius Flamininus, the conqueror of Philip, King of Macedonia.[53]

We shall not stop to confute the errors of a group of critics who, to establish a given idea or hypothesis, have not disdained to resort to the unworthy artifice of deliberately concealing the facts relative to the excavations, and who revealed only those data which were likely to give to the monuments a more ancient date than that which they truly possess. These so-called critics are those same persons who, with a method and tendency anything but scientific, deceived the good faith of scholars in the formation of the Faliscan Museum of Villa Giulia; and who, not long since, endeavored to brand as false the Etruscan tegula from Capua.[54] Their methods have taught us what value to place upon their declarations. Let us hope, however, that in the progress of time the study of our national antiquities may not be clouded by sentiments which are not inspired by the purest love of truth.

Having thus ascertained that the theories set forth by us have successfully withstood the test of the latest excavations, let us turn with confidence to the examination of the ancient legends of the Roman people.

CHAPTER III

THE ORIGINS OF ROME, AND A NEW POMPEIAN FRESCO

THE influence which Rome has exerted upon the entire world is inestimably great; the number of those who have learned her history and her legends is countless. Few legends, consequently, have been so generally diffused as that of the birth of Romulus and Remus. It is, perhaps, quite unnecessary to recall the various particulars to scholars, or even to cultured men and women.

The maid Rhea Silvia, or Ilia, was the daughter of an Alban prince whose throne had been usurped by his brother, Amulius. Rhea Silvia is forced to become a vestal virgin, and her brother is killed. By this means Amulius rids himself of the fear that his usurpation may give origin to revengeful attacks on the part of his brother's children.[1] Rhea Silvia, however, while going to the grove of Mars to procure water for her sacred duties, meets the god and becomes his bride.

Amulius, greatly enraged at this fact, condemns Rhea Silvia to death for having thus broken her vows; but Anthos, his daughter, who was bound to her cousin by ties of the most intimate friendship, saves the life of the guilty vestal. Silvia, accompanied by Anthos, is subsequently led to prison; her sons, instead, are destined to perish. The shepherds of the Alban king carry them whither the Tiber washes the slopes of the Palatine, and there abandon them in their cradle. On the subsiding of the waters, however, the cradle is thrown upon a rock, and the little ones are cast upon the wet sands.

A she-wolf saves them from imminent death. She stands tenderly over the twins, and licks the slime from their small bodies. It chanced that Faustulus, the chief swineherd of King Amulius, passed in that vicinity, and was astounded at the sight which met his eyes; the more so that the she-wolf was not alarmed at his approach in the slightest degree. He lifts the god-born infants in his arms, and carries them to his wife, Acca Larentia. The latter retains them as her sons, until, having become brave and robust leaders of shepherds, they engage in encounters with the king's men. There follow, in quick succession, their acknowledgment, the restoration of the ancient Alban king, and the founding of the square city of the Palatine.[2]

It is not my purpose to examine the individual elements of this legend, nor to determine how it came to be formed, nor how it developed. I have treated these questions in my *Storia di Roma*. I have there brought into relief the Greek character of this legend; I have there cited parallel tales which the Greeks related of the founding of numberless other cities, both of Greece proper and of Magna Græcia. It was my endeavor, in my History, to determine also the reasons and the manner in which the Hellenic legend was transplanted to Latin soil.[3] In these pages I propose, rather, to examine a new Pompeian fresco, which contains the particulars of the legend as recounted by the ancient authors, and which, in addition, presents elements hitherto misunderstood.

In regard to the legend itself, it will be sufficient to recall that other myths and traditions connected the origin of Rome with the arrival of the Arcadians and Evander, and also with the coming of the Argives and Hercules. The feast of the Lupercal (which was sacred to Faunus) was similar to that celebrated by the Peloponnesians of Arcadia and of Messenia in honor of Pan or Evander. In other words, Faunus, or Faustulus, the god known under the name of Innus and the form of a goat, was made the first dweller of the Palatine.[4] As in the Hellenic myths, moreover, he was placed in relation with the Greek Herakles. The latter, it will be remembered, was represented, according to the various versions, as having been either kindly or unkindly received by Cacus, the primordial Vulcan of the Palatine.[5] In this form of the ancient Greek myth there figures also Pales, the goddess presiding over the flocks of the Palatine. Moreover, in certain authors Pales was represented as the wife or the daughter of Faunus; while in others she was transformed into the youth Pallas, son of Evander.[6]

These ancient myths underwent a great transformation as the result of the changed political conditions of Rome and of Italy, particularly after the first Punic War and during the Hannibalic period. Rome, from a State aspiring to preponderance in the Peninsula only, was obliged by circumstances to transform itself into a State aspiring to the hegemony of all the third Mediterranean basin,—consequently, into a nation of the first rank even in the affairs of the Greek Orient. The peculiar relations of Pergamum with Syria and with the other States of Asia Minor and of Greece more than ever strengthened the bonds of friendship between the former State and the most powerful city of the Italian peninsula.

It was to the interest of Rome to create a strong, compact party in the East. In ancient times cults and religious legends had the same importance which to-day is assigned to national or ethnographical origins,—above all, in such matters as the joining of interests based on politics and on commerce. It therefore happened that the Phrygian goddess of the hills and woods,—the Mater Idæa or Silvia, —who was so widely honored in Asia Minor and who was worshipped under the form of a rock at Pessinus,—became identified with Silvia, the goddess of the Alban hills and woods. The latter, in turn, was already connected, in Latium, with the legend of the Phrygian Æneas.[7] This new element served to confirm more than ever the story of the Phrygian and Trojan origin of Lavinium,—a story accepted by Sicilian writers as early as the end of the fifth century,—that is, by the sources known to Aristotle.[8]

The victory of Rome over the Latin confederation (in the middle of the fourth century) caused to be transported to Rome the cults and legends of Lavinium, of Ardea and of Aricia,—all of them cities of the Alban Hills. Similarly, the Hannibalic War fused these religious elements of the Prisci Latini with others that were purely Asiatic. In 204 B.C. there was transported to Rome the stone of Pessinus,—the symbol of the Mater Magna Deum, the mother of the founders of Rome. Contrary to the custom of Roman religious laws, this foreign deity was received within the limits of the Palatine,—to speak more exactly, it was harbored within the temple of Victoria herself, which tradition affirmed to have been consecrated by Evander. In the immediate vicinity there was later erected a special temple to the Mater Magna. It was situated by the side of the temple of Victory, which had been erected upon that crest of the hill overlooking the Lupercal,—that is, overlooking the grotto in which the she-wolf was supposed to have found and nurtured the Twins.[9]

In examining, then, the fundamental elements of the legend regarding the origin of the city, it results most clearly that it gathered and fused together two different and entirely separate myths. The more ancient legend (and, at the same time, the simpler and more natural one) was based on the conception that the goat and the wolf of Mars were the sacred totems of the nation. The early Romans, as well as the Piceni and the Hirpini, worshipped the *picus* (woodpecker) and the wolf. In addition, they (as also the Gauls) paid divine honors to geese; and the Sabelli worshipped the bull, which they pursued on occasion of the *ver sacrum*.[10]

The earliest tradition, and, therefore, the one which we should consider indigenous, placed Rome under the protection of Pales, the goddess of the flocks. It assumed, too, that the slopes of the Palatine were inhabited by wolves. The divine founders of the city had for this reason been represented as nursed by a she-wolf inhabiting the caverns at the foot of the hill. As the result of conceptions which to-day are not readily understood, the she-wolf became considered the mother of the Twins and also of the Lares. Hence, Acca Larentia, the personification of the she-wolf, was placed in relation with the goat-god Innus, or Faustulus, who reared Romulus and Remus.

The feast of the Lupercalia (which fell on the 15th of February) must be connected with this cult and belief. During that feast the priests, who had been instrumental in prolonging its existence, ran naked at the foot of the Palatine, and struck with straps of goat-skin those women who desired to become mothers. The priests symbolized the god Innus or Lupercus himself.[11] These rites and ceremonies represent to us the earliest beliefs of the ancient Romans. They were partly changed in the official tradition on account of new and foreign elements which were introduced into the Palatine,—an influx due to a change in both the tastes of the people and in their beliefs. Faustulus and Acca Larentia had been divinities of the Palatine and the parents of the Lares,—the founders of the city. They had been, respectively, a goat and a she-wolf. Faustulus then became the chief swineherd of the Alban king; and the she-wolf was transformed into Acca Larentia, his wife, styled *lupa* on account of her loose morals. Furthermore, the legends and the cults of the

THE ORIGIN OF ROME, AFTER AN ALTAR FROM OSTIA

THE TEMPLE OF MAGNA MATER IDÆA ON THE PALATINE

Lupercal, which had been closely connected with the Palatine, were arbitrarily placed in relation with the myths of Alba.[12] The artificial character of this relation was due to the necessity which the Romans felt of considering themselves the direct heirs of the Alban cults when, in the fourth century, they established their power over Latium. I have shown that the Twins whom Amulius had destined to death were stranded at the foot of the Palatine, and that they were found by Faustulus. Faustulus was, in origin, the god of that region; but on this occasion according to some writers he was a swineherd of the Alban king, and merely chanced to pass in that vicinity.[13]

This mixture of elements originally so widely diverse was accepted in the Greek version set forth in the beginning of the third century by Diocles of Peparethos. It was repeated by Fabius Pictor, the contemporary of Hannibal, who had been sent as ambassador to Delphi after the disaster at Cannæ; it was accepted by Cincius Alimentus, an early native annalist of Rome. This version, which thereafter became official, is found in the works of Livy, of Dionysius of Halicarnassus, and of Plutarch; and we see it reproduced on monuments. It is this same legend, finally, which we recognize in the Pompeian fresco, of which we present a copy.

This remarkable fresco was discovered nearly two years ago at Pompeii, while I was director of the excavations. For reasons which do not concern me, the commission entrusted with the preparation of the *Notizie degli Scavi* did not see fit to publish it. Through my efforts, however, it has formed part of the collection of ancient frescoes in the National Museum of Naples for the period of about one year.

In the background of our fresco we see the peak of Monte Cavo, the highest of the Alban Hills, on whose summit stood the temple of Jupiter Latiaris. The scene of Silvia, who abandons the temple and altar of Vesta and proceeds into the grove of Mars, is not, however, represented as we would have expected. In other words, the scene of action is not the Alban Mount, but the Palatine. The temple of Vesta is readily identified from the smoking altar, and from the poker abandoned by the guilty vestal. It is natural to think, then, that the temple situated on the opposite elevation and near which Silvia lies sleeping is the temple of Mars and the *curia* of the Salii, to which she was supposed to have gone to draw water. It is that very locality in which the sacred *lituus* of Romulus was found, in spite of the burning of the city by the Gauls.[14]

The cults and the temple of Mars at Rome were always outside the *pomerium*.[15] It is natural, then, to ask if, before the city included the entire Palatine hill, there was not a more restricted Rome in the neighborhood of the *ficus Ruminalis*, of the Lupercal and of the temple of Victory. In no other way can we understand that passage of Antistius Labeo, who, in speaking of the seven hills, distinguished the Cermalus (where Romulus was born) from the Palatine.[16] With this same explanation there agrees, also, the fact that the feast of the god and hero Pallas, on the 21st of April, was quite different from that of the Lupercalia, on the 15th of February. The latter, indeed, was connected with the Ruminalis fig-tree.[17] It must be remarked, finally, that the distinction between the Palatium and the Cermalus is clearly shown in the official records of the sacrifices of the Argei.

The ancient authors affirm that the hut of Romulus (still shown under the Empire) was made of wood and of straw.[18] We cannot say whether it is due to the artist's fancy or to some other cause that, in our fresco, this hut is represented as a temple of Greek structure. Many other details of the painting will surely give origin to debates among scholars. The branch which is seen near this temple appears to be a *caprificus,* similar in character to the *ficus Ruminalis* represented on a lower plane of the painting. It is a detail which cannot be accounted for, but it must not have had great importance in the mind of the artist. I do not dwell on the opinion that we have represented here the spear which Romulus threw to the Aventine and which, having taken root there, became a tree. We know, in fact, that the tree was a *cornus* and that it grew by the house of Romulus.[19] It is doubtful, too, whether one may regard it as the crook (*lituus*) of Romulus or that of Attus Navius; or the vine which figures in the legend of this priest and which, even later, was the symbol of the authority of the centurions. The shape of the tree recalls rather the *caprificus* which is represented on a lower plane of the painting, and which we find mentioned in connection with the Comitium, the temple of Saturn, and the statue of Marsyas

THE ORIGINS OF ROME

in the Forum Romanum. It is to be observed, moreover, that the *caprificus* is represented on two other ledges of the hill.

The Sun, which appears in the sky drawn by white coursers, is an element lacking in the version of Livy. It is, however, recorded in the more extended version of Dionysius, who says that when Silvia met Mars the Sun was darkened. The author of our fresco has represented the Sun in this manner, at a time preceding the violation by the god.[20] The darkening of the Sun is a characteristic touch which other versions placed in relation with the death of Romulus.[21] Likewise, in the more diffused epitome of the story of Diocles, a conspicuous part is played by the intercession of Anthos, who saves the life of Silvia.[22] And so, in the second plane of the painting, and beneath the figures of the three priests who are pointing to the guilty vestal, Anthos and Silvia are represented as being thrust towards the prison.[23]

The third scene is still more remarkable, for it represents elements partly known to the official tradition, and partly irreconcilable with it. In the extant epitome of Diocles there is reference to a spring whose sources were in the Lupercal. A glance at the Pompeian fresco shows at once that the scene takes place in a cave whence water flows towards the marsh of the Velabrum. The figure in the left hand corner is in full accord with this conception, representing, indeed, a nymph of the Tiber. It is a character which appears in the family traditions of the Fabii, who considered themselves the descendants of a *nympha Tiberina* and of Hercules, and who played so conspicuous a rôle in the cult of the Lupercalia on the Palatine.[24]

It is likewise worthy of note that our painting calls special attention to the rock near the *ficus Ruminalis*. It is, surely, that *saxum* upon which, according to the versions of Diocles and of Dionysius, the cradle of the Twins was stranded. Since the stone is square, it is possible that it is the symbol of the *Roma Quadrata*. Of this, however, we shall speak separately. The group of the she-wolf nursing Romulus and Remus immediately reminds us that at the foot of the Lupercal, and near the *ficus Ruminalis,* there was a similar archaic bronze statue.[25] A comparison of our group with the one represented on the coins of the Pompeii Fostuli and of Satrienus shows that the painter of the Pompeian

E

fresco did not express a creation of his fancy, but, on the contrary, faithfully reproduced an actual original,—in all probability that same bronze group dedicated by the ædiles

Ogulnii in 296 B.C.[26] The she-wolf, following closely upon the official tradition as expressed by Diocles of Peparethos and by Fabius, is represented as turning to lick the infants who are lying in the slime. This characteristic touch is met with, not only in the texts of historians such as Livy and Dionysius, not only in extant monuments, but also in the divine poems of Ennius and of Vergil:

> *Fecerat et viridi fetam Mavortis in antro*
> *Procubuisse lupam: geminos huic ubera circum*
> *Ludere pendentis pueros, et lambere matrem*
> *Impavidos; illam tereti cervice reflexam*
> *Mulcere alternos, et corpore fingere lingua.*[27]

We must, also, observe the special care of the artist in representing the *ficus Ruminalis,* traces of which were still believed to be visible under the Empire.[28]

With those elements of our painting that are common in the official tradition there are contrasted others that are of the greatest importance. We are not surprised, indeed we think it quite natural, to see on the left a *nympha Tiberina;* for, it is expressly stated that the nymphs of the Tiber, who animated the waters at the foot of the Palatine, were sacred to Rhea Silvia.[29] As we have already said, it was from one of these nymphs that the Fabii traced their descent. Furthermore, we do not consider it strange that on the altar from Ostia (of which we present a copy) there is represented, not a nymph of the Tiber, but the Tiber itself. Indeed, the Tiber was, according to the well-known legend, the husband of Rhea Silvia; he was the god of the stream which washed the foot of the Palatine, or rather, which partly surrounded the Palatine through the marsh of the Velabrum.

We cannot, however, understand why in place of Faustulus, who was supposed to have found the Twins, we see, instead, a female figure accompanied by Hermes. There is no hint of this in the official tradition; yet also in the *ara Casali* do we see the shepherds thus arranged. The Pompeian fresco belongs to the last period of Greek painting. Like similar Pompeian paintings, in which is represented on various planes the story of Dædalus and of Icarus, it shows the full influence of Alexandrine art. This fact might, at first sight, lead us to imagine that we have here a creation of the artist's fancy, and that in this painting (as in the *ara Casali*) we have the prototype of those scenes representing the *Presepio* and the birth of Christ.[30] Perhaps the Christian *Presepio* is but the continued representation of the birth of Romulus.

The fidelity with which the other elements of the fresco are reproduced leads, however, to quite different conclusions. What is thus obscure at first sight becomes quite clear by consulting the Fasti of Ovid. In speaking of the Feralia, one of the many inter-related feasts of the month of February and one dedicated to the worship of the dead, Ovid relates that Jupiter became enamored of the fountain Juturna. This fountain was situated at the northern angle of the Palatine, near the temple of Vesta and beneath the ridge on which was situated the shrine of the Lares. The designs of the god were divulged by the sister of Juturna, namely, by Lara or Lala, who revealed the god's love also to the jealous Juno. Jupiter, highly incensed, punished her by tearing out her tongue, thus rendering her dumb,—Muta. In addition, he entrusted her to Mercurius, or Hermes, to be led to the lower regions. In the meantime, Lala was beloved by Hermes:

> *Fitque gravis, geminosque parit, qui compita servant*
> *Et vigilant nostra semper in urbe, Lares.*[31]

We shall not delay in explaining in detail the legend given by Ovid. Lara, or Larunda, was originally the mother of the Lares,—divinities which constantly preserved their chthonic character, and which were ever considered the gods of the soil, of the ways and of the subterraneous world.

Lara was later transformed into Lala, by derivation from λαλεῖν. This explains why the Lares or Larvæ (the shades of the dead) were called *silentes,* and why *Muta* or *Tacita* was said to be their mother. Lara or Lala, in fact, is merely the mother of the Lares and the nurse of Romulus and Remus.[32] The cult of the public Lares, whose altar was situated not far from the Porta Mugonia (a site even later considered one of the corners of the city of Romulus[33]), was soon associated with that of Romulus and Remus. Indeed, the Twins were themselves considered Lares, and consequently Cassius Hemina, the early annalist, affirms that on the miraculous parturition of the sow Romulus himself erected the temple of the *Lares Grunduli.*[34]

We can, therefore, readily comprehend the scene in our painting by considering that it represents the above-named fusion of cults. We are to recognize in the group in question Mercury accompanying Lala, or better, Acca Larentia. The cult of the latter (as we are explicitly told by the authors) was located at the end of the Nova Via, and at the foot of the Velabrum. In other words, it was situated by the side of the Porta Romanula and of the Lupercal,— in the region within which were worshipped the divinities Volusia and Angerona.[35] This mingling of cults is not surprising; for both Angerona and Acca Larentia were chthonic deities connected with the death of the Sun. The former, indeed, was represented with closed lips as the goddess of Death and of Silence. Her image, *ore obligato atque signato,* stood in the *sacellum* of the goddess Volusia, which was near the Porta Romanula, the Lupercal and the sepulchre of Acca Larentia. This fact naturally explains why some should have thought that Angerona kept secret the unknown name of the city of Rome,—a name which it was not permitted to pronounce nor even divulge.[36]

The Pompeian fresco, then, rather than representing a creation of the artist, offers us topographical data of the

THE MOST ANCIENT WALLS OF THE PALATINE, ATTRIBUTED TO ROMULUS

highest importance. It is incumbent upon us, consequently, to endeavor to determine more exactly the identity of the two divinities in the lower corners of the painting.

We have already seen that one of these figures represents a *nympha Tiberina;* and that the female figure accompanied by Mercury is the goddess Lala or Acca Larentia. The hypothesis consequently suggests itself that the *nympha Tiberina* is the sister of Acca Larentia,—namely, the nymph Juturna.

It is, however, more difficult to establish the identity of the divinity which is represented upon a pedestal within a niche, and which is by the side of the group of the wolf with the Twins. We must immediately declare that it would be the height of folly to insist on any precise determinations. For, near the Lupercal, too, there was a statue representing the ancestress of the Cincii and of the Servilii, who was by some considered the mother of Romulus.[37] On the other hand, we must recognize that the statue represented in the fresco seems to be a part of the Lupercal itself. Acca Larentia has already been represented in the figure escorted by Mercury. We can, then, believe the figure in question to be the goddess Rumina herself (the personification of the *ficus Ruminalis*), who, together with Jupiter Ruminus, was worshipped by the shepherds of the primitive Palatine.[38] We should remember that the Lupercal, as well as the sepulchre of Acca Larentia, was situated near the Porta Romanula and near the fountain,— in other words, at the end of the Nova Via. Furthermore, we are told that here, too, were the *sacellum* of the goddess Volusia, the curia Acculeia (of Acca Larentia), and the statue of Angerona.

Whatever may be the opinion to be accepted in regard to this last figure, it is necessary for us to emphasize the fact that the new fresco unites and fuses elements belonging to three different versions. The official tradition of the vestal Rhea Silvia and of Anthos is represented in the first and in the second plane, together with the still more ancient element of the wolf nursing the Twins. This latter element was never destroyed by the legend of Rhea Silvia as mother of Romulus. Furthermore, we see these two stories conected with the myth of Acca Larentia, who was transformed into Lala, or Muta, or Tacita, the mistress of Mercury and the mother of the Lares.

This fusion depends, in part, from the fact that the temple of Mercury was in the Circus Maximus, not very far from the bank of the Tiber, and close to the altar of Hercules and to the sepulchre of Acca Larentia. In the chapter devoted to this goddess we shall see that the proximity of these temples gave rise to the tale of the love of Hercules and Acca. It is quite natural, then, that circumstances of the same kind should have suggested the story of the love of Mercurius (who guided the souls of the dead) for the sepulchral goddess, Acca Larentia. It should also be considered that the cult of the Lares near the Porta Mugonia was, in origin, more closely connected with that of Romulus and Remus, who were nursed by Acca, the mother of the Lares.

Nothing, however, obliges us to accept the views of some modern critics, who believe the story of Acca to be the creation of the scholars of the Augustan age and of even later times. The connection of the cult of Romulus and Remus with that of the Lares Grunduli is expressly testified to in the passage already cited from Cassius Hemina, an annalist of the second century B.C. This passage proves, therefore, that we need not accept the view which to-day holds sway, and that the opinion which I have set forth is worthy of greater consideration. At any rate, we reach the conclusion that we have, in the monuments, the same fusion of different Greek and Latin elements which is characteristic in the old Roman poets and annalists.

The Pompeian fresco is not the fancy of some obscure provincial artist. It is a copy of a famous painting, which represented one of the many combinations of the myths referring to the origins of Rome. It faithfully reproduces both the group of the she-wolf nursing the Twins, and the peaks of the distant Alban Hills. We are inclined to believe, therefore, that it gives with sufficient exactness also the grotto of the Lupercal, as it was before the times of Dionysius. This writer states that the outline of the grotto was, in his time, no longer recognizable, on account of the various edifices which had gradually been erected on the site. Dionysius declares that he had not been successful in discovering traces of the cults of the primordial Palatine divinities (such as Pallas), of which (he informs us) Polybius had spoken nearly a century and a half earlier, and of which also Vergil has preserved the memory.[39]

THE ORIGINS OF ROME

It is possible, therefore, to suppose that also the highest point of the Palatine, on which we see the temple of Mars and the slumbering figure of Rhea Silvia, represents to us the ancient form of this hill. To speak more exactly, it may be a reconstruction as conceived by the Romans of the first century B.C. The frequent allusions of Varro and of Ovid to the ancient form of the Palatine and of the Forum cause the belief that they made accurate and personal observations. This in turn obliges us to consider the Pompeian fresco worthy of the closest attention also in this respect.

The official tradition persistently affirms that Rhea Silvia went to the grove of Mars. The ritual laws preserved by Vitruvius (which agree with topographical data) prove (as we have seen) that the cult of Mars was never received within the *pomerium* of the city, but that it was established outside the gates. It would result, then, that the curia of the Salii and the hut of Romulus were outside the walls of the most ancient city of the Palatine Hill.[40] This shows on what insufficient grounds some ill-equipped archæologists concluded that Rome was, originally, a square city like the square wooden palisades of the Æmilian region. We shall return to this question hereafter. The fresco proves that the most ancient Rome was on that part of the Palatine Hill where were situated the temple of Victory, the grotto of the Lupercal, and the Porta Romanula. It should be especially noticed that the *ficus Ruminalis* and the square stone are in the centre of the painting, between the she-wolf and Acca Larentia.

We are thus reminded that with this tree both the name and the origin of Rome are connected. Modern authors have thought that the name of *Roma* is to be explained by *Rumon,* the ancient name of the Tiber, and by the root which in Latin means *to flow.* Consequently they have thought that *Roma* means *the river.*[41] This same etymology is employed by I. Guidi in connection with the name of the *Porta Romanula,* the ancient gate of the Palatine, which was situated near the Lupercal and the temple of Volusia. This opinion is to-day generally accepted. It appears to me that modern scholars have beaten a false track, and that the ancients have offered us, instead, genuine elements of interpretation. The latter affirm that the *ficus Ruminalis* was also called *Romularis* and *Romula.*[42] They declare, too, that the cult of the *ficus Ruminalis* was identical with that of *Iupiter Ruminus* and of the goddess *Rumina* (the protecting goddess of nursing infants), to whom libations of milk, and not of wine, were poured.[43]

Nothing forbids our believing, indeed all the evidence favors our believing, that the ancients judged well when they affirmed that the Latin name for the nursing breast, *rumis* (from which milk flows), was the same name by which the *ficus Ruminalis* was called,—a tree from whose fruit flows a milky juice.[44] Ennius sang of the

Fici dulciferæ, lactantes ubere toto.[45]

The source of Pliny is quite right when, in closely connecting the name of Romulus with the *ficus Ruminalis,* it affirms that Romulus had been protected by this tree.[46] Romulus, *rumis* (the breast), and the *ficus Ruminalis* are related thoughts. It is, therefore, quite natural that not wine but milk only was to be used in the sacrifices which Romulus was said to have established.[47] We are not surprised that the Tiber should have been named *the stream* (Rumon) from a radical identical with that of *Rhenus*. The fundamental importance of the *ficus Ruminalis* in the cult of the Lupercal is proved by the fact that when, towards the middle of the fourth century, the Forum Romanum became the centre of the city, there was transported to the Comitium a sapling of the *ficus Ruminalis* which continued to be called by the parent name.[48] This demonstrates how altogether wrong the modern and the ancient scholars are who combat the explicit declarations of the ancient authors, and who affirm that the *ficus Ruminalis* has absolutely nothing in common with the legend of Romulus.[49] The truth lies in the opposite view. As Festus and, apparently, also Varro affirms, the name *Porta Romanula* did not mean the gate that led to Rome,[50] nor, as some modern scholars maintain, the gate which led to the river or to the current. It signified the gate where the *ficus Ruminalis* or *Romularis* grew,—the place in which was situated the shrine of the goddess *Rumina* and of *Iupiter Ruminus*. In fact, *Ruminus* and *Ruminalis* bear the same relation to *Romanus* as *Romanus* to *Romulus*. The Porta Romanula, indeed, was called also Romana.

The earliest Romans named their city from the fig-tree,—

among all peoples regarded as the symbol of fruitfulness. It was from the fig-tree that their inhabitants derived the names of the Latin cities of Ficana and of Ficulea. Some Greek cities similarly derived their name from σῦκον, that is, the fig-tree.[51] The sacred character of the *caprificus*, and the importance attached to it, were closely related with the origin of the city. Therefore we can readily understand why a branch of the old fig-tree was transported to the Comitium in the Forum Romanum, and why it was planted near the puteal of Attus Navius and the tomb of Romulus. This significance of the *caprificus* caused it to be planted, also, near the statue of Marsyas in the Forum, near the temple of Saturn, and, finally, near the lacus Curtius where the *sidentia fundamenta imperii* were situated.[52]

By duly considering the importance of the fig-tree in the cults of the ancient Romans, we may understand many of their beliefs and ceremonies. Not only does it become clear why the tree sacred to Jupiter Ruminus had the virtue of warding off the lightning-bolt,[53] but we can also understand why Romulus was supposed to have died in the marsh *Caprea*, that is, of the *caprificus*. This marsh was, originally, not in the Campus Martius, but in the Velabrum,—the place where Romulus was born, or where he had been exposed.[54] Finally, with this cult of the *ficus Ruminalis*, or with the very name of the city of Rome, is to be connected the feast of the *Nonæ Caprotinæ*,—that is, the day in which, according to some, Romulus disappeared from mortal eyes.[55] The meaning of this feast is *the feast of the Caprificus;* by others it was connected with the cult of Juno Caprotina; by still others with that branch of the fig-tree with which the maid-servant Tutela saved the Romans, either from Etruscans, or Volscians, or Fidenates, or Ficulneates.[56]

The Romans, moreover, could not have been alone in attributing such great importance to the fig-tree, or in naming themselves from that tree. We have seen that the Ficulneates and the Ficani in Latium did the same. It would be a long task to make a complete list of those cities which in Italy, as elsewhere, drew their names from other trees, such as the pear-tree, the cypress, the oak, and others. One may think of the Italian towns Cerreto and Frassineto, and of the American Oakland, Red Oak and

Cypress City. I deem it more convenient to place in relief the fact that the fig-tree and the vine play a fundamental rôle in the legends of the founding of Chalcidian Rhegium and of Spartan Tarentum. The Greek colonists who founded Rhegium had been ordered by Apollo to found their city only when they should come upon a woman in the embraces of a man. They established themselves on the banks of the river Apsias, where they saw a vine twining round a *caprificus*.[57] Likewise, the Spartan founders of Tarentum, in obedience to divine will, stop where the plant, τράγος,—the *caprificus*,—kisses the salt waves and wets the end of its hoary chin.[58] This last legend (as I have already noted in my *Storia della Magna Grecia*[59]) is to be explained by the climatic conditions of the peninsula Sallentina, where the sea winds prevent all trees on the shores from bearing fruit, with the exception of the very prolific fig-tree. In Attica the fig-tree was considered to be the most ancient of trees, and on that account sacred.[60] It was similarly regarded at Rome.[61] Like reasons, then, guided the Romans and other peoples of antiquity in naming their cities, and consequently themselves, from the fig-tree. The wonderful fruitfulness of this tree has made it a very common one throughout the Italian peninsula,—so much so that it has become a byword for things abandoned and worthless. Ancient Italy, as well as ancient Greece, was very rich in oaks and fir-trees, but sadly poor in fruit-bearing trees. Therefore, we can readily understand how the fig-tree came to be held in the highest estimation. We can understand, too, the anecdote of the Persian monarch who waged war aginst the Athenians, to become the master of the land which produced such sweet fruit. We can, finally, comprehend why the denouncers of the frauds perpetrated at the Athenian custom houses should have been called sycophants.

At Rome, both in the Lupercal (the cradle of the city), and in the Comitium (the later political centre), divine worship was offered to the fig-tree, the symbol of Fecundity. The cenception of Fecundity, together with that of Victory, is, in fact, the basis of all the cults of the most ancient Roman community. By this conception of Fecundity were inspired the ancient feasts of the Consualia, so called from the god Consus, of the Fordilicia, from the *fordæ* or pregnant cows, and also the feasts of the Palilia and Lupercalia.

In all these feasts the fundamental idea is the thriving and increasing of the herds and flocks. During the Empire a temple was raised to the goddess Fecunditas, the successor of the most ancient divinities of the same kind.[62] Cicero, in enumerating the public sacrifices which were to be made by the Roman State, undoubtedly represented the national and the religious feeling when he reminded the Romans that some days were to be devoted *ubertatem lactis feturæque*,—that is, for the abundance and richness of the milk and the increase of the herds.[63]

CHAPTER IV

ACCA LARENTIA, THE MOTHER OF THE LARES AND NURSE OF ROMULUS; AND THE MOST ANCIENT DIVINITIES OF THE PALATINE

THE legend of Acca Larentia, the dweller of the Velabrum and the nurse of Romulus, does not, at first sight, appear rich in poetic elements. The mythical stories referring to this winter deity seem to be important only in illustrating Roman topography and the Roman calendar. And yet it is not so. Few myths, on the contrary, present such abundant material for the study of the most ancient Roman religion and of the development of the most ancient legends. It is a myth in which Greek and other foreign elements superimpose themselves upon indigenous ones. This divinity has often been the subject of research in modern times, having been studied, among others, by Mommsen himself. It seems to me, however, that the true character and importance of this legend has not yet been properly understood, and that it is necessary to present a new interpretation, deduced from new points of view.

I deem it necessary to state briefly the salient elements of the two stories of Acca Larentia as given by the ancient authors.

The 23rd of December was the day of the Brumalia, that is to say, the feast of the *Bruma,* the shortest (*brevissima*) day of the year. Festal celebrations were held on that day at the foot of the Palatine, in that region of the Velabrum bounded by the Tiber on one side, and on the other by the Circus Maximus. The feast was sacred to the goddess Acca Larentia, and sacrifices were offered to her by the Roman pontiffs. Inasmuch as the feast was among the most solemn and the most important of the ancient calendar, it was mentioned by the Fasti. Why, then, were such sacrifices made? Two reasons were given, one entirely different from the other. According to some, the establishment of the cult was due to the fact that Acca Larentia (called *lupa* on account of her loose morals) had been the wife of the shepherd Faustulus and the nurse of Romulus; and that, upon her death, she had left Romulus as heir, having already adopted him in place of one of her twelve children, who had died. Romulus had for this reason established the cult of Acca on the spot where she had disappeared from mortal eyes, and had created the college of the twelve Arval Brothers,—the twelve sons of Acca,—the twelve months of the year.

Others related the story differently. From the same place at the foot of the Palatine another woman of loose morals had disappeared, whose beauty had won the affections of a god. It was related that, in the reign of Ancus Marcius, the priest of Hercules challenged the god himself at play. Hercules won, and the priest not only prepared for him a good supper, but also led to him Acca the hetaira. The god loved her; and, on her leaving his temple, imposed the condition upon her that she should kiss the first person whom she might chance to meet. It so happened that a wealthy Etruscan named Tarutius met her, was charmed by her, and left her his large patrimony at his death. Acca in her turn left this as a heritage to the Roman people, who thus came into possession of the territories of Semurium, Lintirium, Turax and Solinium, and who, as a sign of their gratitude, later established an annual festival in her honor.[1]

Which of these two legends is the more ancient? And what relation does one bear to the other? I leave out of consideration the unsuccessful attempt of Bæhrens (followed by others in basing his arguments on the corruption of texts), who came to the conclusion that instead of Larentia one ought to read Laurentia, and who transforms Acca into a deity of the Latin city of Laurentum. Against such conclusion I shall oppose the official reading of the Fasti themselves, which always give Larentia and never Laurentia. Indeed, all that we shall have to remark hereafter will tend to prove that Acca Larentia is simply the mother of the Lares.[2] Moreover, I do not deem this the proper occasion for undertaking a minute examination of the opinions of Zielinski (followed by Wissowa), who denies any sacred and legendary character to a form of the legend which he considers to have been merely the subject-matter of a comedy. Also this theory will be confuted by what I shall remark. Finally, I do not consider even

Mommsen's opinion a happy one, who believes the legend of Acca Larentia to be a late product of the age of Sulla.[3]

Without denying that annalists of the stamp of Licinius Macer and Valerius Antias previously elaborated this legend, it seems to me that there are certain elements which prove that this legend had been told even earlier than the third century B.C. I do not think that the more ancient form of the myth is represented by the story of Hercules and his passion for the hetaira. An examination of the various data of the tradition shows that the cult of Acca Larentia was, at an early period, connected with that of Angerona, of Dia, of Dea Bona, and of Flora. This connection must very soon have given occasion for varied stories, which (as far as I know) have not yet been well examined.

I shall begin by affirming that the fundamental character of the goddess has not been properly explained. Mommsen wrongly considered it an inexplicable enigma that, in the Roman calendar, the day sacred to Acca Larentia,—a sepulchral deity,—should have been sacred also to Jupiter,—the solar deity. The supposed enigma is, on the contrary, a most natural fact. Jupiter, the god of light, was considered subject to all the vicissitudes to which the other solar divinities were subject—namely, to perish and come to life again each year. The 23rd of December, the festal day of Acca and of Jupiter, was the day of the Brumalia, the shortest day of the year. It was the day of death for the god of light, just as the 25th of December, when the days begin to grow longer (a day later changed into Christmas both by chance and by our religion), was the birthday of Sol Invictus.

Everyone is aware that in Greece Zeus was considered a chthonic deity.[4] At Crete the very tomb of Jupiter was pointed out; at Sparta and at Tarentum there was indicated that of the solar god, Apollo Hyacinthus. In Asiatic Hatra the temple of the Sun was (as is known) an absolutely dark place;[5] and, likewise, there was worshipped at Sparta a Jupiter, ruler of the Darkness — Zeus σκοτεινός. At Rome it seems to have been different. Jupiter Vulcan, the god of light, was in absolute opposition to the corresponding Jupiter Summanus or Nocturnus.[6] Again, the day of the Brumalia was, at Rome, dedicated to Jupiter; at Argos the same day was sacred to Jupiter Nemeus.[7]

ACCA LARENTIA

Wissowa, therefore, has beaten an absolutely false track when, in endeavoring to solve the pretended enigma as seen by Mommsen, he concludes it to be entirely accidental and fortuitous that the 23rd of December was sacred to both Jupiter and Acca Larentia.[8] To attain this result, he too easily discards the data furnished by the ancient authors, who expressly say that the cult of Jupiter was connected with that of Acca.[9] Inasmuch as the ancients placed the worship of Tellus (the Earth) in close relation with that of Jupiter, it should not be surprising that the latter is found in connection with that of Acca Larentia, also a chthonic deity.[10] Acca Larentia was actually said to be the mother of the Lares—that is to say a deity particularly chthonic. Surely such declarations of the ancients cannot be impaired by the doubts of modern scholars caused merely by questions of quantity. For these lose much of their power when it is considered that *Lares* is to *Lārentia* in the same manner as to *Lārvæ,* and as *Lārentia* is to *Larunda.*

II

In order to understand completely the meaning of the cult and of the legend of Acca, it is necessary to make some preliminary remarks upon the calendar and Roman feasts.

It is a characteristic common to the Roman and to many other religions (both ancient and modern), that one and the same divinity was worshipped under different names. Persephone was called by various names at Syracuse; and, at Cyzicum, Cybele was honored under the titles of Dindymene and Plakiane. The Catholic worshipper does not act differently in attributing to the Mother of our Saviour the various appellations of Holy Virgin, Santa Maria, Madonna, Addolorata, Assunta and others. In like manner Janus was, according to his various manifestations, called Junonius, Quirinius, Consivius, Clusius, or Patulcius. Furthermore, Carmentis was invoked under the name of Prorsa and, again, of Postvorta;[11] and no one is ignorant of the fact that the knowledge of these various appellations formed, in the beginning, the secret science of the Roman priesthood and was a matter of scruple among the faithful.

Still another common characteristic must be kept in mind

if we wish to grasp the meaning of the cult of Acca. The custom of honoring one and the same deity through several successive days *per triduum* or *per novem* has been noted in Rome, in Syracuse, and in Macedonia; and at Rome, as in other Hellenistic States, there existed, also, the custom of dedicating to the worship of the same divinity the successive odd days of the month.[12] For instance, the 11th and 15th of January were sacred to Carmentis; the 21st, 23rd, and 25th of March to Mars; the 7th, 9th, 13th, and 15th of June to Vesta; and the 5th and 7th of July were dedicated to the worship of Juno Caprotina. The same fact holds true for the worship of the dead. To the Lemures or Larvæ were sacred the 9th, 11th, and 13th of

May; and the 15th, 17th, and 21st of February to the sepulchral worship of the Lupercalia, Quirinalia, and Feralia.

A mere glance at the Roman calendar will show that certain portions of the year, or of months, were sacred to the worship of related divinities. April was sacred to the goddess of the standing corn and of wine, and to the divinities which presided over the parturition of animals. March was sacred to the god of arms. To the worship of the earth and of the dead were especially dedicated the months of December, February, and May. According to the religious ideas of the Romans, there existed a close relation between the worship of the earth and the awakening and dying of the year on the one hand, and the souls of the dead on the other. This fact serves to explain how it was that the 1st of May was sacred to the Lares Præstites (the protectors of the city), the 9th, 11th, and 13th to the Lemures; and how, in the second half of the same month, there fell the feast of the Ambarvalio, or lustrations sacred to the goddess Dia and the fields. Thus the reason immediately presents itself why also the Earth and the Lares were worshipped in the month of December, in which occurred the Feriæ Sementivæ—feasts intended to conclude the day sacred to Acca Larentia.[13] Indeed, according to various Roman systems the year ended with December rather than with February.

This is not the occasion for expounding at length why the beginning of the sacred and the civil year should have been fixed at about the time of either the autumnal or vernal equinox, or of the winter or summer solstice; nor why the tribunician year should have begun on the 10th of December, while the consular year should have been made to coincide with the first part of March and with the end of January; nor why, finally, September and the period of the summer solstice should have been the beginning of the sacred year, which, in the earliest times, had been closely related to the civil year. It behooves us here rather to note that the expiations made to the dead and their protecting deities towards the end of the year explain why the entire month of February was sacred to the dead. In the most ancient calendar we find that in this month fell the feast of the Lupercalia,—sacred to Faunus,—and the Quirinalia, which was connected with the death of Quirinus or Romulus. In February, also, fell the feast of the Feralia, sacred to Lara, the mother of the Lares. On the 24th of the month was the feast of the Regifugium, connected with the end of the Monarchy,—a day which, together with the preceding (the Terminalia), marked the close of the most ancient year. If not in the most ancient year, surely in the less ancient calendar of the Republic, the 11th of February, which was sacred to the Genii, and the 22nd, on which was celebrated the feast of the Charistia, were considered days of mourning.

If, after such examination, we turn to the month of December, we shall discover similar cults. We find the worship of Faunus or Lupercus; and, corresponding to the political festival of the Regifugium, we see the civic feast of the Septimontium,—the 10th of December. Beginning from the Ides, moreover, all the celebrations of this month are dedicated to sepulchral deities. The 13th was dedicated to the goddess Tellus; the 15th, to Consus, and was celebrated in the Circus Maximus; the 17th, to Saturn; the 19th, to Ops. The 21st of the month was sacred to Dia, the goddess venerated by the Arval Brothers; the 23rd, to Acca Larentia; and when, in 179 B.C., the worship of the Lares Permarini was established, the 22nd of December was chosen as the day for that feast. Finally, it is to be noted that it is not through mere chance that, in the reformed calendar, the Compilalicia were celebrated during successive days in the end of December,—a worship of the Lares Viales which the ancients connected with that of Saturn, the very tvpe of a chthonic god.

In natural harmony with such close relations between the days and the months are, also, the relations between the various divinities worshipped on those days. We have already seen that the Lares and the mother of the Lares were celebrated in December, in February and in March.[14] Let us now observe how the same divinities reappear, at times, under different names.

Lara or Larunda, expressly called the mother of the Lares (a goddess, therefore, of chthonic and sepulchral character), was, according to infallible data, called Mania also. She was consequently thought of in connection with the Manes.[15] She was worshipped, too, under the name Muta or Tacita.[16] But the goddess Muta or Tacita was the same divinity as that one which was worshipped under the name of Angerona, whose festival fell on the 21st of December,— a day sacred to Dia, the chthonic deity of the Arval Brothers. Angerona, furthermore, was worshipped in the precinct sacred to Acca, in the sanctuary and at the altar of the goddess Volusia.[17]

The associations of worships, and the identifications to which the ancient texts lead us, do not stop at this point. From these, in fact, we learn that the 1st of May was sacred to Maia, who, in turn, was at times called Bona Dea, at others Fauna, Fatua and Ops.[18] We therefore believe that Fauna or Fatua (by the ancients identified with Bona Dea) was none other than that divinity which is at various times called the wife, the daughter, or the sister of Faunus or Lupercus,—that is to say, of Faustulus, the inhabitant of the Lupercal. Inasmuch, then, as the wife of Faustulus was also Acca Larentia, there is nothing more natural than to conclude that Bona Dea was identical with Acca Larentia.

III

If the examination just made has led us to recognize the chthonic character of Acca Larentia, we must not disguise the fact that the method which has been followed by us is exposed to certain dangers. We might, for example, identify more or less allied worships, which precisely for this reason were confused, first by the priests, and subsequently by the Roman scholars. Though such fusion may have been determined, in certain cases, by plausible reasons, it is only too evident that in others it was due to an excessive tendency to fuse worships altogether different in origin. This tendency modern criticism has rightly endeavored to avoid. To determine with precision, therefore, those cases in which the ancients were right, constitutes one of the most difficult problems in the study of Roman religion.

Nothing, for instance, prevents our considering Consus and Saturn as divinities identical in substance. Moreover, it is evident why Ops, the wife of the former, was at times considered the wife of the latter. Nevertheless it is absolutely certain that, originally, the worship of Consus in the Circus Maximus was distinct from that of Saturn at the foot of the Capitoline. In like manner, Diana and Lucina were epithets referring to the same deity; and yet the temple of the latter was on a site far different from that of the former. Everything points to the conclusion that divinities closely related to one another were also worshipped in a common region. Thus the temple of Mater Deum Idæa of Pessinus was close to the Lupercal, and not far from the grove sacred to Bona Dea, precisely because of her chthonic character and that of the divinities to which the adjacent land was sacred.

On the other hand, we have sufficient data for establishing that in other cases the same divinity was worshipped under different names. I see no reason for doubting that Vica and Strenia, who were worshipped on the Velia, belonged to one and the same worship; or that Semo Sancus (or Sanctus), and Deus Fidius, whose temples were on the Quirinal, were one and the same divinity. This I have already demonstrated on another occasion. The cause of some of these identifications is to be sought for in a very early fusion of worships different in their ethical character.

However, to return to our case, the problem which confronts us is to determine whether or not Acca Larentia and the divinities with which she was connected belonged to but one worship or to different ones, cognate and related even though only through reasons of topography.[19]

In the present case, both the first and the second statements seem to be verified. Acca Larentia was absolutely confused with Flora, because both were considered hetairæ who had made donations of territory to the Roman people, and because both were connected with ceremonies relating to the sowing of the fields.[20] On the other hand, there are abundant arguments with which to prove that the relation and the connection between the worships of Angerona, Tacita, Dia, Acca Larentia, and the Lares were not accidental. The problem, which is very complicated in its religious aspects, may be simplified (at least in part) by working towards the solution offered by the ancients. This I do not think has yet been done with sufficient care, not even from the point of view of topography.

Let us, then, begin by asking where was the sepulchre of Acca Larentia? To this question we can, fortunately, give a sufficiently exact answer. We know that it was in a very conspicuous place of the Velabrum and near the foot of the Palatine, where the valley of the Circus Maximus began, and precisely at the point where the Nova Via terminated. The same exact indication is given for the place where, on the day sacred to Dia (the 21st of December), Angerona was worshipped.[21] It is not, therefore, accidental that the altar of Volusia (upon which sacrifices were offered to Angerona) should have been in the Curia Acculeia,—that is to say, of Acca Larentia.[22] Since the goddess Angerona, as was befitting a sepulchral deity, was represented with a closed mouth, it is also clear why Lara and the mother of the Lares should have been called Tacita or Muta. Tacita or Muta had her sacrarium not very far from the fountain of Juturna (on the slope of the Palatine), and near the sepulchre of Acca.[23] The name Muta or Tacita was very appropriate to the mother of the Lares,—that is to say, to the goddess of the Manes who have lost their speech and were hence called *taciti* and *silentes*.[24] Finally, assuming that there was some contact between the worships of Angerona and Acca Larentia, the nurse of Romulus, it is readily explained how the popular belief arose that the

THE NORTHWESTERN CORNER OF THE PALATINE

THE NORTHEASTERN CORNER OF THE PALATINE.
(CURIÆ VETERES)

ACCA LARENTIA

secret of the true name of Rome was connected with the goddess Angerona.

The worship of the goddess Dia took place at the boundaries of the ancient *ager Romanus*,—that is to say, at the fifth milestone from Rome on the Via Campana, where the *Acta* of the Arval Brothers were found. This fact by no means excludes the possibility that, originally, such worship may have taken place also in the vicinity of the temple of Angerona. Indeed, even under the Empire the first and the last days of the celebrations of the Arval Brothers were held in the Roman Forum.[25] The principal divinities invoked in the *Carmina* of the Arval Brothers were Mars, the Lares and the Semones. This fact seems to contradict the hypothesis that their worship was actually connected with that of Acca Larentia. Nevertheless, the opinions of Masurius Sabinus and of other authors, who placed Acca Larentia in direct connection with the Arval Brothers, do not seem to be entirely the results of wild imagination.

But were Angerona or Tacita, Dia, Acca Larentia and Volusia divinities very closely related to one another and honored in one locality or *sacellum?* or were these simply the different epithets of one and the same divinity?

In the present state of our knowledge we have, fortunately, sufficient data for answering this question,—at least in its religious aspect,—with all the certainty that could be desired. The 11th and 15th of January were sacred to Carmentis; the 9th, 11th and 13th of May, to the Lemuria; the 13th and 15th of February, to the Lupercalia; the 13th, 15th, 17th and 19th of December, to the divinities of the earth,—Saturn, Consus, Tellus and Ops. Likewise, it is but proper to infer that also the 21st and 23rd of December were sacred to but one deity, at times called Dia, at others Larentia. Thus we are necessarily drawn to the absolute identification and fusion of all these various worships. The most natural conclusion is, therefore, that the different worships mentioned above were very closely related, and that they took place either in the same area or in neighboring localities.

The relations just noted between Acca Larentia, the mother of the Lares, and Dia, the goddess of the fields, receive still greater confirmation from the fact that the worship of Angerona, or of Dia, was performed within the area of the goddess Volusia. Volusia, according to some texts, was an epithet of the goddesses Dia and Acca Larentia.

In fact, as we have already seen, sacrifices to the goddess Angerona were offered in the sanctuary and upon the very altar of Volusia. They were performed in the Curia Acculeia, situated at the extremity of the Via Nova, where the sepulchre of Acca Larentia was located. Whether Volusia was simply another name for the two divinities just mentioned, or whether it represented a divinity closely connected with them, we come, nevertheless, to the conclusion that there existed a worship dedicated to the goddess of love at the foot of the Palatine. For, Volusia, under the appellation of Libertina, was considered a goddess in her very nature analogous to Venus.[26] We find that the cult of Volusia was associated with that of the Mother of the Earth and of the Lares,—that is to say, of the *genii* of the dead. It does not seem unreasonable, therefore, to suppose that it may have had a character similar to that which the ancients attributed to the goddess Libertina, who was, at one and the same time, the goddess of Love and of Death.[27]

Some modern critics (among whom Wissowa) have called into doubt the declarations in this regard made by the ancients. They have thought it possible to prove that the scholars of the Varronian age were better able to understand the true essence of a deity whose worship had already become partly obsolete, and had been identified with different ones. They seem to me, however, to have but little justice in so doing. They may be right in maintaining that the primitive meaning of these worships underwent a gradual transformation, and that it was later rediscovered, so to speak, only through scientific integrations.[28] There is no proof, however, that the integrations of the ancient scholars themselves in respect to Libertina were not near the truth. Furthermore, from the moment that we find in the *lucar* of Libertina a temple sacred to Venus, it seems permissible to deduce from these concomitant facts the substantial identity of the two divinities.

I see no reason for asserting that the ancients wrongly believed the goddess Libertina to correspond to Aphrodite Epitymbia of Delphi.[29] Similarly, I do not find sufficient cause for excluding the statement that at Rome, as elsewhere, the worship of the reviving seasons, of the gardens, of vegetation and of love, should have been conceived of

under the aspect of the dying season and vegetation and
of life that perishes. Certain similarities between the worships of different peoples are not, after all, the results of
importation. Even the most ancient Rome had cults
similar to those of the Babylonian Istar and to the Asiatic
Aphrodite, who descended into Hell in search of their
lovers. Ceres, the Italic goddess of creation, was identified
with the Greek Demeter, who, once a year, descended
into Hades in search of Kore.

In conclusion, I do not find valid the arguments which
deny that Volusia was a divinity of love similar to Libertina.
Since the goddess Volusia was worshipped in the Curia
Acculeia,—that is to say, of Acca Larentia, the mother of
the Lares,—I would find therein the explanation of the fact
that Acca Larentia, who was a chthonic deity, came at the
same time to be considered an hetaira,—in other words, a
goddess of purely physical love. It was precisely for this
reason that, as we have already stated, she was later confused with Flora, the protecting goddess of courtesans.

Topographical relations similar in character to those which
we have just traced between the cults of Acca Larentia,
Dia, Angerona and Volusia existed between those of
Faunus, Hercules and Bona Dea. The Lupercal, as is well
known, was situated in the immediate vicinity of the
sepulchre of Acca Larentia referred to above. This fact
would suffice to explain why Acca Larentia was identified
with the wife of Faustulus and the nurse of Romulus.
To Romulus the establishment of the feast of the Brumalia
(i.e., the worship of Larentia) was attributed, and he was
supposed to have created the college of the twelve Arval
Brothers. These, in turn, instituted the worship of the
Lares Grunduli.[30] The great vicinity of the Lupercal to
the Curia Acculeia and to the sepulchre of Acca Larentia
may suggest in what way the mother of the Lares became
the nurse of Romulus and Remus. Finally, nothing excludes the hypothesis that originally the conception of
Romulus and Remus was closely connected with that of
the Lares,—that is, of the enchoric divinities which presided over the hearths and homes.

Similar considerations can, I think, explain why mention
of Acca Larentia was made in connection with Hercules
and his sacristan. The temple and altar of this god were
between the Velabrum and the Circus, and distant from

the sepulchre of Acca by some 150 yards. The vicinity of the two *sacraria*, and the coincidence of ceremonies common to both deities, may have given origin to the story of the relations of one divinity with the other. Likewise, the vicinity of the temple of Saturn to that of Janus gave occasion to many different stories as to the relations of those two gods. It is not necessary to demonstrate how the story of the good reception of Saturn by Janus had its origin precisely in this topographical circumstance.[31] Reasons of vicinity between the temples of Hercules and Saturn caused many and varied tales, some of which obtained the honor of being considered authentic history and of forming part of the public annals of the Roman people.[32] A like cause established the tales of relations between Evander, the dweller on the Palatine, and his mother, Carmenta, whose tomb was to be seen at the Porta Carmentalis.

I omit examining the thousand other analogous cases,—as, for instance, the myth of Janus and Camese, of Hercules and the *sacella* of the Argives. Without wandering very far from our subject, it will be sufficient to recall the cult of Hercules, whose statue was erected in the Forum Boarium, and its relation with that of the god Cacus, who had his domains on the adjacent crest of the Palatine,— that is, where also Romulus is supposed to have had his house. Such topographical elements, in fact, gave origin to the well-known legend of the death of Cacus, who originally was the earliest god of the Palatine,—its Vulcan. Later ceremonies may have contributed to establishing even greater relations of a topographical character. It is certain that on the 21st of December (before the day of the Brumalia, which was sacred to Acca Larentia) sacrifices were made to Ceres and to Hercules.[33] Such sacrifices may have been due to earlier Hellenic worships based on the relations between Demeter and Herakles,[34] as well as to the immediate vicinity of the temples of Ceres and of Hercules. The precinct sacred to this god could not, in fact, have been more distant from the temple of Ceres than from the sepulchre of Acca Larentia. The same reasons of vicinity (as we have remarked in the preceding chapter) seem to account for the version of Ovid,—a version relating the love of Hermes (Mercury) for Acca.

To have placed the Roman Larentia in special connection

with the Greek god would seem to have added an important element to the legend. It must be remembered that near the sepulchre of Acca Larentia there was the altar of Volusia, who, if not to be identified with Acca Larentia, was at least connected with her worship. It was told that Hercules had relations with all the nymphs he met on his travels; and the hero, consequently, was supposed to have had relations also with the various female divinities of the Palatine.[35] It was, therefore, quite natural that he should have been connected with Volusia, the goddess of Love. Since Volusia was the goddess of Love and of the sepulchral deity Angerona, and since Acca Larentia was a goddess similar in character to the latter, it naturally resulted that mention should have been made of the relations of Hercules with Acca as with a *nobile scortum* rather than with a chaste maiden.

There is a further proof of the fact that reasons of topographical vicinity gave origin to legends relative to the ancient divinities of the Palatine. This I shall draw from another worship,—that of the Bona Dea. It was narrated that Hercules, after having killed Cacus, in vain searched the Velabrum for a place where he might quench his thirst. The laughter of some nymphs guided him to a spring; but the nymphs, who were performing the mysterious rites of Bona Dea, asked him to depart. Hercules then retaliated upon them by excluding women from his worship. By this legend the ancients explained how it was that men were excluded from the worship of the Bona Dea.[36] This worship has generally been localized on the Aventine, at the base of the Remuria, where the famous temple of the Bona Dea Subsaxonea was situated. The explicit account of Propertius, however, contradicts this interpretation. According to this author, it appears, instead, that the action took place in the Velabrum, not far from the Lupercal and from the sepulchre of Acca Larentia.[37] Here, therefore, must have been the most ancient temple of that goddess.

We arrive to the same conclusion by considering that Bona Dea (as the ancients had already recognized) was identical with the goddess generally called Magna Mater, Ops, Fatua or Fauna.[38] In the Pompeian wall-painting here reproduced the question arises whether the goddess by the side of a spring or fountain of Juturna is a nymph of the river Tiber or Bona Dea. Bona Dea was a chthonic deity, considered at various times as the daughter, sister, or even wife of Faunus. Her sacred grove was at the foot of the Palatine, beside the Lupercal,—the home of Faunus. The legend of the arrival of Hercules to this grove, of his retaliation and the exclusion of women from the rites of the Ara Maxima are all, therefore, easily explained as the effects of religious ceremonies performed in two sanctuaries situated so near to each other.

Even in the case of Tarutius, the rich Etruscan who afterwards wedded Acca Larentia, reasons of topography are of avail. It is difficult to separate his nationality as an Etruscan from the existence of the Vicus Tuscus which led from the Forum to the Velabrum, and near which was the sepulchre of Acca Larentia. Furthermore, this Tarutius immediately recalls that Teratios, who, according to a secondary form of the legend of Romulus, exposed the latter on the banks of the Tiber,—in other words, in the Velabrum which adjoined the Vicus Tuscus.[39] Perhaps Tarutius was a local divinity, to be compared with the vestal Taracia, who (as well as Acca Larentia) left to the Roman people the land bordering on the Tiber. Perhaps, too, he is to be compared with the territory of Turax, one of those which Acca donated to Romulus and to the Roman people.

Arguments based on topography have been of value in understanding for what reasons the two legends of Acca Larentia arose: the hetaira beloved by Hercules and afterwards by Tarutius, and the spouse of Faustulus and nurse of Romulus. We have not, however, been able to establish which of these versions is the more ancient; and, much less, which bears a purely national stamp, and which a foreign. The story which would seem the more genuinely Roman is that which makes Romulus nursed by a she-wolf rather than by an hetaira. But such version not only presents traces of later reasoning,—such as the substituting of Faustulus for the god Faunus or Lupercus,—but, indeed, was related by the earliest Roman annalist in imitation of a Greek model. This should not surprise us, inasmuch as also all the other legends relative to the Palatine were modified by contact with Greek literature. For instance, Pales, the goddess who presided over the fecundity and parturition of animals, yielded (even though for a short time) to the youthful Pallas and to the homonymous nymph beloved by Herakles. Likewise, Faunus was transformed into Evander; and Cacus, the god of fire and the earliest deity of the Palatine, became the robber who was slain by Herakles.

IV

That version of the legend which relates the wager made by the idle sacristan with the god Hercules is not inconsistent with these topographical relations. Nothing proves that the version which connected Acca with Romulus was invented by a late annalist. As we have seen, both Cincius Alimentus (one of the earliest Roman annalists) and Cassius Hemina spoke of the worship of the Lares Grunduli, who were placed in relation with Romulus.[40] This, certainly, does not favor the hypothesis of Mommsen that Licinius Macer and Valerius Antias were the first to invent or to introduce the relations between the Twins and the mother of the Lares. To solve the question of the literary genesis of the various traditions regarding Acca Larentia, it is, perhaps, necessary to keep present still a third tradition. This, as far as I have been able to discover, has not yet been noticed. It has been preserved for us by Ovid. In speaking of the Lupercalia and of the ceremonies performed on that occasion, Ovid states:

> *Sed cur præcipue fugiat velamina Faunus,*
> *Traditur antiqui fabula plena ioci.*[41]

He then relates how Faunus, having seen Hercules in company with Omphale, became enamored of the latter, and endeavored to introduce himself into the cave of the two lovers. Faunus, however, was but little successful. For, being deceived by the female garments in which (according to the well-known legend) Hercules was robed, he, instead of approaching Omphale, who was in the embraces of Hercules, in the darkness fell upon the body of the hero himself. He was consequently violently hurled from the high couch by the god thus suddenly awakened. To this story, which explained the lines,

> *Veste deus lusus fallentes lumina vestes*
> *Non amat et nudos ad sua sacra vocat,*

Ovid soon adds another explanation; and after having said.

Adde peregrinis causas, mea Musa, Latinas,[42]

presents the story of the Roman ceremony of the Lupercalia, connected with the family rites of the Fabii and the Quintilii, which latter were made to date as far back as the rivalry between Romulus and Remus.

The story told by Ovid offers us an example of the many Roman ceremonies and worships which counterbalanced those of the Greeks. Thus, the Lupercalia were identified with the Lycæa of Arcadia, and the Arcadian Evander (in other words Faunus) was made an ancient king of the Palatine.

We have not sufficient data at our disposal for determining how and when the Hellenic worship of Pan (the rival of Herakles for the love of Omphale) arose on Latin soil. Still less can we establish what author was particularly responsible for localizing upon the Palatine the Greek legend in connection with the Lupercalia. It is, perhaps, sufficient for our purpose to recall that the above version of Faunus and of Herakles has its counterpart in the better-known story of Pan, who flees in horror at the sight of Hermaphrodite, whom he had accosted in the belief of finding a charming maiden. This latter form of the myth finally gained the superiority also in the Roman world,—a fact proved beyond question by the Pompeian wall-paintings in which it is so frequently represented. Likewise, it is to be observed that the version of Ovid brings to mind another myth, given by the same poet and referring to the relations of Priapus with Vesta. This latter story reveals the same origin, and is a proof of that contact between the Greek and the Roman cults which became so frequent, particularly after the third century B.C.[43]

The myth of Faunus as rival of Hercules is not an isolated fact. It is an element closely connected with the story which makes Faunus the enemy of Hercules and his victim, and also with that fable which makes Herakles the lover of the wife, or daughter, of Faunus. Consequently, Herakles, and not Faunus, would be the true father of Latinus.[44] There needs not great discernment to see that the cults just mentioned, as well as the one described by Ovid, have as their subject-matter the loves of Hercules and the adulterous wife of Faunus, on one hand, and the desires and passions of Faunus himself for the mistress of Hercules on the other. They have, moreover, a common foundation with the more diffused legend of Acca Larentia,—that is to say, with the immoral wife of Faustulus or Faunus, the mistress of Herakles and the bride of the rich Tarutius. All these versions place in close relation Hercules, the god worshipped in the Velabrum below, and the goddess who dwelt in the Lupercal or at its base, and who was by some considered the wife of Faunus.

An apparently different and yet characteristic touch is presented to us by the idle sacristan who challenges Hercules at play, and who, being beaten, prepares a supper for the god and conducts to him the beautiful Acca Larentia. Considering the analogies already noted, we might suppose that the sacred ceremonies of the worship of Hercules were related to the sacellum of Tarutius and to the sepulchre of Acca Larentia.[45] It will be easier to comprehend this element of the legend if we shall recognize in the idle *ædituus* of the temple the god Faunus himself. In fact, the most ancient annalists (Cincius Alimentus and Cassius Hemina) affirm that the ancient Romans, in using the word *fana,* employed also the form *faunæ*. This equation became extended also to the goddess Fauna, wife of Lupercus or Faunus, who was also called Fata, or Fatua.[46] This is not the place for delving into the real philological value of such an equation. It is sufficient for us to establish the fact that the ancient writers did admit it, and to affirm the probability that the rather recent elaboration of the myth was preceded by a more ancient form of the legend. In place, then, of the sacristan, or *fanaticus,* who made the wager with Hercules, Faunus himself must be thought of as the speaker,—that is to say, Faustulus, the husband of Acca and the rival of Hercules. By substituting, therefore, the name of Faunus for *fanaticus,* it will be easily understood how the story of the *ædituus* as enemy of Hercules arose.

Having reached this point, it would be desirable to trace the development of the entire legend, from its beginnings at the time of the earliest annalists of the third century B.C. to the age of Sulla. The loss of the more ancient historical literature, however, prevents our proceeding more at length and more minutely in our analysis. We are fully satisfied in having established the fundamental meaning of the legend. We shall proceed, therefore, to the examination of the society in which this legend was born, the more so that such investigations will indirectly lead us to the solution of the preceding problem also.

We shall not tarry in the examination of the legal points in the legend of Acca, such as the adoption of Romulus and the will of Larentia. These questions, notwithstanding what has been said to the contrary by some jurists, are of no importance in the history of early Roman law. They merely reflect legal conditions of the third and the second century,—a time when such institutions had already been long established, and had already undergone many transformations.

We shall here emphasize the fact that the cult of Acca Larentia,—as well as those of Consus, Saturnus, Ops and Ceres,—belongs to a group of indigenous divinities,—divinities which, though in time more or less transformed by frequent contact with Hellenic culture and religion, nevertheless retained a thoroughly Roman name and character.

The sanctuary of Acca Larentia (like that of Venus Murcia) was situated outside the most ancient *pomerium* of the Palatine, and near the altar of the goddess Volusia. This would indicate, firstly, the original sepulchral character of the worship of the Lares; secondly, that the area adjoining to and beneath the Palatine, on the side towards the Velabrum, was devoted to the same purposes as the slopes of the Velia and the Capitoline. In other words, they were occupied by those sepulchres which were wont to adorn the gates and the roads of ancient cities,—sepulchres of which at Rome, and elsewhere, we are to-day finding such extensive remains.[47]

The mother of the Lares, and, at the same time, the goddess of the earth, was the protectress of all the Roman territory. Thus it is readily understood how the legend arose of the donation of land to the Romans by Acca. These lands, according to our texts (which, perhaps, are corrupt), were the territories of Semurium, Turax, Lintirium and Solinium. Precisely where they were is not told us. The territory of Turax recalls that Tarutius who gave his lands to Acca. In even greater degree it reminds us of that Gaia Taracia who, according to a similar version, left to the Romans the Campus Tiberinus,—that is to say, the

THE WESTERN END OF THE FORUM, WITH A GENERAL VIEW OF THE PALATINE

Campus Martius. From a vague, yet sufficiently secure, statement of Cicero we gather that the *ager* Semurium must not have been distant from the Campus Martius. Inasmuch as Acca Larentia was placed in connection with the Arval Brothers by the ancients themselves, the suspicion may, perhaps, be entertained that the Semones were the divinities invoked by the Arval Brothers together with the Lares. Semurium, therefore, may have been the name of the territory sacred to the Semones. We cannot define more closely the limits of this region, and still less indicate, even in a vague manner, where the territories of Lintirium and Solinium may have been.[48]

Bearing in mind the region occupied by the sepulchre of Acca, however, it would seem obvious to believe that she donated to the Roman people all the originally marshy territory of the Velabrum. Similarly, the nymph or vestal Tarpeia (or Taracia, or even Fufetia) was supposed to have donated the equally marshy territory known, at first, as the Campus Tiberinus or Tarquinius, and later as the Campus Martius.[49] In the most ancient period, the Palatine was surrounded by two currents of water, which rendered the Forum marshy. One of them crossed the Vicus Tuscus, the other descended through the valley of the Circus Maximus. In this respect the ancient texts are very explicit.[50] There is no doubt that this isolated position of the Palatine was the reason for its choice as a place of defence.

The legend, therefore, which spoke of gifts of land in the Velabrum and in the Campus Martius would seem to refer to a time when those localities, having been useless marshes in the past, were reclaimed for the benefit of the Roman people. They recall, too, those public works which the accepted tradition attributed to the Tarquins. That the legend of Acca should be referred to the times of Romulus, or of Ancus, rather than to those of the Tarquins, causes no surprise. For it has often been questioned whether certain facts attributed to the age of kings belonged to the reign of one king rather than to that of another. Cœlius, for instance, is supposed to have been the companion either of Romulus or of Servius Tullius, according as to whether the enlarging of the city was attributed to the former or to the latter ruler. The version which dated the donations of Acca Larentia in the times of

Romulus naturally go hand in hand with those other traditions which made the city of Romulus extend over all of the later Septimontium.

The tradition which makes Acca Larentia and Tarutius contemporaneous with King Ancus is in close relation with a story which later became official. According to this, King Ancus settled the conquered Latins in the marshy valley of the Aventine (where the temple of Venus Murcia was), extended the Roman territory as far as Ostia, and was the first to construct a bridge connecting the Velabrum with the right bank of the Tiber.[51] There is, therefore, a natural correspondence between the reclaiming from the marshes of both the Aventine and the Velabrum, and between the land donations of Acca Larentia and King Ancus. Likewise, there is, probably, a close relation between the rich Etruscan Tarutius of the Vicus Tuscus and the Etruscan Tarquinius who is supposed to have reached Rome during the reign of Ancus.

V

In its topographical and religious aspects the myth of Acca Larentia presents but minor difficulties. To our modern way of thinking, difficulties arise as soon as we learn that the divinity to whom the Roman pontiffs, once a year, offered public worship in the Velabrum, and who was considered to have been the nurse of Romulus, the very founder of the city, should have been represented as an hetaira. This difficulty is not to be explained by the hypothesis that a stern divinity was, later, transformed in character by the mere idle talk and the etymologies of Greek scholars. Furthermore, the declarations of Cato the Elder, who already called her an hetaira,[52] cannot be considered a consequence of his reading of those Greek authors who, from Timæus on, narrated anecdotes of Roman history.[53] Let us grant, for the moment, that the conception of Acca was gradually transformed, just as Faustulus gradually supplanted Innus, or Faunus, and just as the nymph Pallas replaced Pales. Nevertheles, it makes a strange impression upon us to see that Cato,—the austere glorifier of Roman deeds,—should have told the version making of the goddess Acca Larentia,—the mother of the Lares of his country,—a mere courtesan.

In the solution of this problem there is but one thing that will aid us,—to put aside entirely those ideas, both ancient and modern, which constantly strive to cast the light of idealism upon every particular referring to the origin of the Roman people. We should, rather, recognize the absolutely rough and primitive character of the pastoral community which, in earliest times, inhabited the Palatine Hill.[54]

The rough and nature-symbolizing character of Faunus or Innus, the goat-god who renders fecund Pales, the she-goat and goddess honored on the Parilia, was never entirely obliterated by the later additions and modifications of the legend of Romulus and of the foundation of the city. The feast of the Lupercalia, in which the most distinguished citizens,— for instance, the patrician family of the Fabii,—ran naked round the *pomerium,* striking with straps of goat-skin those women who desired to become mothers, recalled only too vividly the origin of a ceremony which to us seem obscene.[55] The feast of the Lupercalia, which apparently constituted one of the most sacred and most important ceremonies of the earliest Rome, had, consequently, a meaning and a form altogether rough and brutal. It is easily understood, therefore, that, inasmuch as the priesthood of the Lupercalia continued for century after century, the feast itself should gradually have clashed with customs that were becoming more and more refined, and, at the same time, more and more refinedly corrupt. Writers of the stamp of Ovid adapted the legend to the new customs.[56] On the other hand, those persons who were less attached to the primitive customs of the Palatine community ended by regarding as disgusting those ceremonies which were repugnant to the culture and the good taste of the later age.[57]

The Lupercalia were not the only ceremonies in which the crudeness of the primitive community of the Palatine was manifested. Those ceremonies were analogous, in certain respects, to those rites of the Hirpinian Sorani which revealed the barbarity of the Faliscan custom.[58] The crude character of the ancient cults of the Palatine is revealed, also, in the festivals relative to matrimony. I leave aside certain data which would prove beyond question the primitive common ownership of women, and the custom (still to be met with among some savage races) of conceding the new bride to one's friends. I limit myself to certain facts of an

G

undeniable nature,—to the ceremony in which lewd words were pronounced at the wedding ceremony by those present.[59] Again the new bride performed a shameful ceremony in the presence of the god Mutunus on the Velia, to whom, as late as the last years of the Republic, sacred honors were paid. Even he who does not allow himself to be too much influenced by the polemics and the invectives with which the earliest Christian writers systematically assailed the pagan religion, must admit that, at least in this respect, they had the most perfect right to raise the cry of scandal.[60]

The fearful brutality of customs is not at variance with what we know of the most ancient Roman life, in so far as regards the relations between parents and children. Roman legend, to be sure, speaks of the chastity and the modesty of women; but, at the same time, it confirms the fact that cases were frequent in which women drank wine in secret, and became guilty of witchcraft. Even the chaste Bona Dea is related to have disregarded the prohibition to drink wine, and, in consequence, to have been struck dead.[61] But let us abandon legend and come to facts. We shall then notice that such faults, rather than testifying to the perfidy of the women of the Palatine community, demonstrate the roughness and the barbarity of their men. The Roman women lived beneath the yoke of an iron discipline. They finally, it is true, emancipated themselves, lived with all license and even dominated their lovers and their husbands. But this does not exclude that, in the most ancient period, they were subjected to laws that were absolutely brutal. The matron surprised in the act of drinking wine in secret was actually punished with death.[62]

The severity of the primitive custom, and the acceptance, in time, of others less severe, is indirectly proved by legendary tales. It is handed down that, on the recurrence of the Consualia (the rape of the Sabines), and of the Carmentalia (the siege of Veii and of the Capitol), the concession was made to women of abstaining from all servile tasks and of riding in vehicles.[63] Beautiful and later literary tradition, in Rome as elsewhere, strives, as we shall see in subsequent studies, to nobilitate all the legends in which woman takes part. The gravity of the *mater. familias* is then contrasted with the laxity of the women of the conquered races. Roman legend, for instance, glorifies the Sabine women, Lucretia, Cloelia, and the companions of Veturia and Vo-

ACCA LARENTIA

lumnia. Like the official Spartan legend, it strives to prove that its women were the mirrors of virtue. Those ancient writers, however, like Aristole, who had no interest in thus glorifying the Spartan women, inform us that they were very corrupt, and that the laws framed for the purpose of restraining them were of no avail whatsoever.[64]

In regard to the sons, custom was equally severe and cruel. By the side of the *ius necis*, the father exercised in a most brutal way the right of sale. The son, as is well known, had to be emancipated three times before being entirely free from this danger. Furthermore, even the attaining of curule offices did not remove the son from the *potestas* of his father.

When conditions were such, valor, frankness and many other manly virtues had frequent occasions for manifesting themselves. But, when women were considered more or less as objects of merely material pleasure, or as a domestic tool, when the begetting of children, who could be sold, might have been judged simply as an increase in one's movable property and stock, the nobler sentiments of the soul must have had but little play.[65] The sentiment of love could not have had but a purely physical expression, just as purely physical and brutal was the form of the cult of Faunus and of Pales, worshipped on the feast of the Parilia. The divinity which presided over love, therefore, could not have been conceived of but under the personification of the energies of purely animal reproduction.

Consequently, the identification of Acca Larentia with a courtesan and with Flora, and, finally, her association with Volusia, do not represent a later development of the literary tradition, nor the more or less worthless imaginations of foreign and of Latin scholars. They represent, rather, one of the fundamental conceptions of the primitive Roman society.

Even after 238 B.C., when the cult of Flora was introduced at the advice of the Sibylline books, this goddess, who symbolized the blossoming and unfolding of vegetation, was identified with an hetaira. This identification was all the more natural because the life of the fields, fecundity, voluptuousness, love and prostitution were fused into but one conception by the inhabitants of the crude and primitive Palatine community. Its grade of culture, however, was equal to that of other Latin communities. Prostitution was closely connected with the worship of Juno Caprotina, a divinity which under the form of a she-goat was originally honored throughout Latium by *scorta* of servile condition. It is natural that in this primitive state (which for so long retained traces of its original constitution) the bull and the cow, sacred totems also for other Italic races, should have become the symbols of the *iustæ nuptiæ*, and of the establishment of State and family according to certain laws of *ius* and *fas*.[66]

Physical reproduction outside the family, therefore, and love in the wider connotation of stimulus to reproduction, could not have had any other meaning than prostitution. The totem which was to symbolize such a conception was necessarily the she-wolf or she-goat, or some other sacred animal which could not possibly represent wedded life. The ancients tell us that in Latin *lupa* signified *scortum;* and from this explanation it is clear how the transition took place from *lupa,* the nurse of Romulus, to the conception as *lupa* of Acca Larenti the wife of Faustulus. That the equation of *lupa* to *scortum* is a true one, is proved by the word *lupanar*.[67] This same story leads us to affirm that, rather than with the sacred animal identical with Faunus (the goat) Acca Larentia was originally connected with the she-wolf,—the animal to which the cave of the Lupercal was sacred, and which symbolized nomad life.[68]

In fact, we are to suppose that Acca Larentia, whose tomb was near the Lupercal, was originally honored as a real wolf,—that is, as the strongest and the most vigorous animal that roamed through the Latin land. It was precisely for this reason that she was considered the worthy nurse of Romulus, the son of Mars, who, as is well known, was represented by the *lupus Martius*. If Acca was, in reality, the *lupa Martia* who nursed the founder of the city,[69] the legend of the vestal who became the mother of Romulus when going to draw water in the grove of Mars, and in company with Mars, would then present itself as a later embellishment.[70] On the other hand, the identification of Acca Larentia with the *lupa Martia* would reëstablish the primitive elements of our legend, which considered the Roman people the sons of the sacred wolf. In a similar manner the Hirpini, the Piceni and the Sabelli considered themselves the descendants and the allies of the sacred bull, of the woodpecker and of other sacred animals.

ACCA LARENTIA

In case this solution be accepted, we shall have explained why Acca was considered the mother of the Lares, the dead progenitors of the Roman people, and why Mars was invoked not to bring harm upon the Romans. We shall, too, come to the conclusion that the ancients spoke of relations between the Lares, Acca Larentia and Faustulus because the cults of these divinities were closely connected with one another, and were, consequently, localized in adjacent places. Thus the sepulchre of Larentia was rightly situated near the Lupercal, if indeed it did not form part of it.

We do not deem it wise, however, to proceed further and by more subtle researches to the signification of the primitive elements; neither do we expect to find complete clearness in the conceptions of primitive societies. Clearness and simplicity are the results of learning, and not of uncultured minds. We do not agree with those who, pursuing a path which we had hoped forever abandoned, see ancient learning, recondite wisdom and profound mysteries where, originally, there was nothing but darkness and ignorance. The intelligence and the state of development of the most ancient priests of the Palatine could not have been much superior to that of the minds of primitive peoples even to-day living in a state of nature. Clearness of conception cannot be expected in a people who confused themselves with the animals with which they lived, and from which they believed themselves to be descended; who, not being able reasonably to explain natural phenomena, thought it both true and natural that a man should be converted into a wolf, and that one animal should be changed into another; who, finally, considered animals, stones and trees divinities to which expiations should be offered and sacrifices made.

VI

For 160 years after the foundation of their city, the Romans, according to ancient testimony, had no images of their various divinities.[71] This is equivalent to saying that only in the time of the first Tarquinius was plastic art introduced. There needs not a long examination to realize the chronological value of such information. We are, in fact, led by it to the times of Tarquinius Priscus, who dedicated a temple to the Capitoline triad, and who was the son of that Demaratus Corinthius who brought with him the artists Eucheir, Eugrammos and Diopos,—the first to teach plastic art to the Italic peoples.[72] This information corresponds, also, with data given by the texts, according to which the most ancient plastic works to decorate the Capitol came from Veii.[73] If this fact proved nothing else, it would be useful in demonstrating the erroneous opinion of the ancients who spoke of statues of the kings of Rome, and also of modern archæologists who, though utterly lacking chronological data, are disposed to give great weight to such vain fancies.[74] This knowledge is useful in still another respect. It teaches us an important truth regarding the most ancient religion, the establishment of which was attributed by the Romans either to Romulus or to Numa,—namely, that the earliest Romans did not worship divine beings under human form. Their successive worships were, in fact, those of the sacred animals, of the waters, of the trees and of the rocks.

The dwellers of the Palatine worshipped and feared the ferocious wolf who ensnared their flocks, and whom they supposed, whether rightly or wrongly, to inhabit the cave of the Lupercal. At the same time, they rendered sacred homage to Faunus and to Pales, protective divinities of their herds, who, naturally enough, were not supposed to have a form different from that of the animals guarded by them. That even the Lares had, in the conception of the early Romans, the form of domestic animals, is not improbable. Indeed, a painter of the age of Nævius represented the Lares with the tail of a bull.[75] It may well be that the story of the ancient annalist, Cassius Hemina, regarding the *sacrarium* of the Lares Grunduli (dedicated by Romulus when the sow so miraculously gave birth to her litter of thirty), indicates that upon the Palatine there was a sanctuary of the Lares worshipped under the form of pigs. Similarly, Faustulus was said to be a swineherd.[76] This becomes all the more probable when it is considered that at Lavinium, whence this myth found its way to Rome, there were to be seen statues of the sow and her litter to which divine honors were paid.[77] In a like manner, at Lavinium were honored the statues of the eagle, of the wolf and of the fox,—the symbols of the Latin nation.[78] In regard to the transformation of a god from one form to another, it is sufficient to recall the worship of Bona Dea, who was supposed to have changed into a snake,— the reason for which serpents were maintained in her temple.[79]

In addition to the worship of animals, we have, also, that of stones, of fire, of water and of trees. On the Quirinal there existed a worship of Jupiter under the form and name of a stone, as is proved by the existence of various cippi of the Palatine *pomerium,* which, until a late period, were considered divinities.[80] This belief corresponds with that of the *lapis manalis,* which was preserved in the temple of Mars outside the Porta Capena, and which was carried in sacred procession whenever rain was desired.[81] As regards fire, it is sufficient to recall the worship of Cacus, and of Caca his sister,[82] and the ceremonies which were performed on the Parilia. It is not necessary to mention many proofs for the worship of water. We need merely recall the feasts sacred to the Tiber and to the fountains which, in the feasts of the Volturnalia and the Fontinalia, appeared even in the most ancient calendar. As to trees, it would be natural to believe that Jupiter, who was worshipped on the remaining hills of the Septimontium under the form of an oak-tree, beech-tree or osier, should have assumed analogous forms on the Palatine also.[83] A conspicuous proof of this fact is furnished by the spear of Romulus, which, hurled from the Aventine, was supposed to have become a leafy tree.[84] It is further evidenced by the cult of the *ficus Ruminalis,* which was identified with that of Jupiter Ruminus.[85]

I omit presenting complete statistics of the divinities which were worshipped by the Palatine community. I shall end this portion of our study by recalling that special and divine honors were paid also to Sterculus or Stercutus, the son of Faunus, who gained immortality for having discovered the art of fertilizing the fields.[86] Stercutus was worshipped under the name of Pilumnus also; and, surely, he, as well as Pitumnus, was considered one of the *dei coniugales.*[87] All this may be easily conceived of in a community where man and wife were, as we have already seen, placed on a level with the bull and the cow, which, together with the pigs and other domestic animals, lived in the same huts with their masters. This was perfectly natural, too, among a people who often placed themselves on a level inferior, rather than superior, to the animals with which they lived. With this conception of themselves and òf their divinities, the members of the Palatine communities adopted such names as the Porcii, Asinii, Suilli and others. Furthermore, they named their cities Bovillæ. or Gabium,—that is to say, the place for their oxen,—and dubbed with the name of *ovilia* (the sheepfolds) the place in which the sovereign Roman people gathered to perform their supreme functions as electors. Finally, this conception serves to explain why the community which dwelt on the Palatine was called a *grex* or flock,[88] and eminent men were styled *egregii*.

The picture of the Palatine community which we have been gradually drawing is not a conclusion to which we have been led by the painstaking examination of forgotten fragments only. It results, in equal measure, from the explicit declarations of the texts of the ancient writers. Cicero, in the passage already quoted referring to the nature of the ceremonies of the Lupercalia, concluded that this festival belonged to an ancient, rural community.[89] And Vergil, in a celebrated passage idealizing the ancient pastoral life of the Romans, and glorifying the primitive myths of Latium, pictured for us the materialism of the conceptions of the early Palatine dwellers by making Evander exclaim,

Hæc nemora indigenæ Fauni Nymphæque tenebant,
Gensque virum truncis et duro robore nata,
Quis neque mos neque cultus erat . . .[90]

The material and the moral conditions of the Palatine. as revealed by the cults that were there cherished, entirely correspond with those of all the other ancient Italic peoples. Only in regard to the Etruscans is the observation true (at least in part) that they were of a higher grade of civilization,—a progress due, of course, to rapid and frequent commercial contact with the Greeks.

It is readily seen that divinities that were not anthropomorphic, but that were worshipped under the forms of animals, or water, or plants, or stones, could not offer material for a large and abundant poetry, and still less for historical legend. Poetry and legend would have developed gradually but surely, even though the Roman people, slow and backward as it was in its historical and its literary evolution, had not come into contact with other peoples. These races crystallized, so to speak, the incipient stage of Roman literary development, and, by their old heritage of conventional cults and legends, despoiled of its fruits the fresh poetic energies of the Latin race. The continuous and insistent relations between the Greek and the Latin races, and, above all, the literary contact beginning with the first Punic War, did not permit Roman theology to develop itself into a purely national poetry. By the grafting of Latin themes upon old historic Greek ones, the national element very rarely gave occasion to the formation of such legends as those of Picus or of Vertunnus, the lover of Pomona, and of Lara or Larunda, who was beloved by Mercurius, or of Flora pursued by Zephyr. The chroniclers, strictly Greek in training, succeeded, at times, in rendering poetic a material rough and theological in character; but more often they presented an infinite series of old Hellenic stories made new by the mere introduction of Latin characters.

This phenomenon manifested itself in the worships of the Palatine divinities, as well as throughout the entire field of Latin religion and mythology. It developed from the predominating worship of Hercules. Whether Lupercus be the subject of investigation, or Faunus, or Pales, or Bona Dea, or Acca Larentia, or Cacus or Caca, it will be found in every case that Hellenic myths are repeated, with those modifications due to their adaptation to new soil.[91] As the result of causes that I have elsewhere explained, the fundamental cult of the Palatine became that of Romulus, associated with that of the Magna Mater Idæa of Pessinus who, in 191 B.C., was given a place of worship in the vicinity of the Lupercal. The worship, however, which first transformed the primitive stories of the Palatine, was that of Hercules, who was honored in the Velabrum not far from the Porta Capena which leads to Campania. Indeed, according to both myth and history, the cult of this god probably came from Campania.[92] The antiquity and the importance of this cult made even the most ancient Roman historians believe Rome to have been founded by Hercules, and to have been, consequently, a Greek city from its very origin.[93] Certainly, the importance of the cult and the immediate vicinity of the other sanctuaries gave origin to the legends examined above,—legends which, though retaining here and there traces of national touches, nevertheless softened the character of the national cults.

The meagre knowledge of the development of the ancient world which was had in the past, and morbid, ill-considered national honor, had proposed the idea (still vainly defended by some inexperienced persons) that Rome had a poetic history and a mythology equal in importance to the Hellenic. Disinterested and unprejudiced study leads us to discard as false those ideas which the Romans themselves but partly sustained,—sustained, too, only when, after Greece had already become decadent and abased, it seemed inconvenient to acknowledge the merits of the conquered, —of those to whom they were really indebted for their cults. In the most ancient period, the Roman historians themselves (with the possible exception of Cato) hastened to recognize the efficacy of Greek culture and the importance of the cult of Hercules. They asserted, indeed, that Rome was a city Greek in origin.

Considering the Hellenic character of their civilization they were not altogether wrong. The temple of Ceres was transformed and decorated by Greek artisans, and Italiot types were adopted in the national coinage.[94] The Romans, in civilizing themselves, civilized also their gods, so to speak, and refined them. Faunus, from a rough goat, became a pious and beneficent shepherd; and his wife Pales became a charming maiden. Bona Dea became the subject of a pretty legend. The worship of the uncultured Cacus yielded to that of Hercules, who destroyed him; and the feast of the Palatine,—that is, of the tutelary divinities of the Palatine,—gave occasion to the beautiful and charming legend of the youth Pallas, son of Evander,—a legend which, already accepted by Lucilius,[95] suggested to Vergil one of the most tender and most delicate episodes of his poem.

The cult of Hercules, which, as we have seen, modified all the adjacent cults and those more or less distant from the Palatine, seems to have had still more important results as regards the development of Roman civilization. For, among the Romans (a military people) the cult of Hercules came to be of such great importance that a tenth of the war booty was dedicated to that god. In still more ancient times, the custom prevailed of carrying in the triumphs and with great solemnity the archaic statue of

Hercules, which was worshipped in the Forum Boarium, and which was considered so old as to be thought the work of Evander himself.[96] Hence, what the ancients tell us is fully credible,—namely, that the cult of this god had the power of modifying other Roman rites. As is well known, human sacrifices continued at Rome to a very late age. Certain ceremonies performed on the Lupercalia demonstrate the truth of this statement. The Roman theologians, with a pretty legend (which is the mere repetition of an analogous one already widely diffused among the Greeks) narrated how pious King Numa had obliged Faunus and Picus to discover a means of substituting bloodless expiations of garlics or onions for human heads.[97] We know, too, that human sacrifices were made also to the Mother of the Lares. This barbarous rite (which confirms what we have already remarked concerning the uncultured and ferocious inhabitants of the Palatine community) was supposed to have been abolished by Junius Brutus, the first consul of the Republic,—that is to say, by that same person who later fearlessly assisted at the execution of his sons.[98]

Another version, however, appears to have been very widely diffused,—a version which attributes to Hercules the merit of having abolished the bloody rites rendered to Saturn, and of having substituted for men those stuffed figures that were thrown into the Tiber on the day of the Argei.[99] We might be led to think this statement purely fantastic; but it is certain that the cult of Saturn, originally a purely Italic one, was performed entirely according to Greek rite in the historic period.[100] Likewise, it is known that in the temple of the Italic Ceres, adjacent to the sacred precinct of Hercules, worship in the Greek rite was performed by priestesses imported either from Sicily, or from Naples, or from Velia.[101] The influence of Hercules upon the neighboring indigenous cults being once admitted, it is readily understood why on the 21st of December, the day sacred to the goddess Dia and to Angerona, sacrifices should have been made in the Curia Acculeia to Hercules and to Ceres. To conclude, the cult of Hercules had the power of transforming Acca Larentia, the she-wolf and bride of Faunus the goat-god, into the faithless wife of Faunus or the shepherd Faustulus, and, finally, into the courtesan of the Greek Herakles.

VII

The preponderating of the myth of Herakles over all the cults of the Palatine and of the neighboring regions seems to coincide with the fourth century and with the beginning of the earliest historical period. As far as can be judged, it is in relation, also, with that more ancient phase of Roman civilization which drew its origin from Sicily and from Magna Græcia. To this phase there succeeded, as the result of the first Punic War and of the direct relations with Greece and with the Hellenic States of Asia Minor, a period in which new cults and new myths exercised their influence upon Roman society. Positive reasons (as I have elsewhere shown) brought about the reception of the cult of the Mater Idæa of Pessinus within the *pomerium* of the Palatine; and this, too, though contrary to all laws. That which had not been conceded to Ceres, to Hercules, to the Dioscuri and to Æsculapius, and which later was to be denied to Venus Erycina herself, was granted, however, to Rhea. This goddess, for public reasons and by the influence of Greek authors, came to be considered the mother of Romulus,—Romulus, no longer the son of a she-wolf, but, indeed, of a vestal virgin.

The myth of Herakles had forced into a secondary position Faunus, the goat, and Acca, the she-wolf. The official acceptance of Rhea Silvia (the Mater Idæa), to whom a temple was conceded near the Lupercal in 191 B.C., transformed Acca, the mother of Romulus, into his nurse, whether she had previously been considered merely a she-wolf (as in the more ancient form of the myth), or whether, according to more recent versions, she had been talked of as the faithless spouse of the shepherd Faustulus. The story of Romulus and Remus was told for the first time by Diocles of Peparethos, on the lines of an ancient and very widely diffused Greek legend. But even this leaves out of consideration those Lares Grunduli or Præstites whose worship on the Velia continued till the age of Augustus. In other words, just as Acca Larentia, the she-wolf, was substituted by Rhea Silvia, the mother of the Twins later nurtured by the she-wolf, so the Lares Grunduli, the sons of Acca Larentia (the mother of the Lares), were supplanted by Romulus and Remus. These, in turn, were supposed to have erected a sanctuary to the Lares Grunduli. In brief, just as the second form of the legend did not entirely destroy the first, so the third version did not destroy, but only rendered subordinate the

details of the second. In the official tradition of the age of Augustus (preserved for us in Livy and in Dionysius), as well as in the Pompeian fresco referred to above, we see as three distinct characters Rhea Silvia, the she-wolf, and Acca Larentia, the spouse of Faustulus.

VIII

If we have succeeded in illustrating and understanding this, the most ancient of early Roman legends, and if we have been successful in comprehending entirely the religious and the moral conscience of the early strata of Roman civilization, we are indebted, not so much to the texts of the ancient classical writers, but, in a far greater degree, to the earliest Christian writers. These, full of holy zeal, and aided by an ideal of virtue and of sacrifice which was so very dissimilar from actual conditions in the setting civilization of the Romans, allowed themselves to be spurred forward at times altogether beyond the just measure. They considered as an integral and fundamental characteristic of pagan civilization that which, at bottom, merely represented its earliest strata, or those superstitions that were afterwards stamped out by the maturer and gentler forms of civilization. The church writers had a polemic aim in view. They assailed their enemies at the exact spot where their armor had its strongest links. Consequently, they had neither eyes nor mind for distinguishing the gems of the Gospel from the rough and crude conceptions of the early Hebrew race, interpreting them all as idealities and as deep allegory hidden from profane eyes.

We modern scholars, in dedicating ourselves to the study of those ancient legends which reveal to us the most ancient treasures of the culture and the morality of antiquity, have, naturally, no polemic aim, no material end to attain. We are guided only by the love of scientific truth. While grateful to the Christian writers for having preserved for us the most ancient data of Roman religion, we nevertheless direct our energies to the task of tracing its gradual and continuous development. Finally, we establish the fact that the Romans, too, traversed all those stages of brutality and of rough materialism that we constantly find at the cradle of all civilizations.

A mere glance at the long course of Roman civilization will make evident how true it is that he who attains success, not by evil arts, but by his own virtues, does not disdain lovingly to admit his humble beginnings. Still less does he endeavor to conceal them by false and pompous origins. A group of what are, after all, insignificant modern writers and ill-advised patriots raises the cry of scandal whensoever the historian places in their true light the origins of a people that later was to rule the lands washed by the Mediterranean. Ovid surely echoed the ancient national spirit when he said,

Non ego te, tante nutrix Larentia gentis,
Nec taceam vestras, Faustule pauper, opes.
Vester honos veniet, cum Larentalia dicam.[102]

In the midst of her splendid military triumphs, Rome never concealed, but instead reverently recalled, her humble origin. The cult of the omnipotent Jupiter Optimus Maximus Capitolinus never cast into oblivion that of the ancient Pales, the goddess of the flocks, whose feast on the 21st of April was ever considered the birthday of the city. And we of to-day, to whom Rome has, together with Greece, transmitted the sacred heritage of its culture, do not scorn the earliest, the primitive civilization of the Palatine. We do not scoff at the race which chose as its progenitor the wolf, the strongest animal of Latium, the one which endangered their houses and their sheepfolds. Rather shall we meditate on that which time produced in the people who emerged from such narrow, modest bounds, and shall repeat with Propertius, the gentle Umbrian poet:[103] "Oh, she-wolf of Mars, thou best of nurses, what a city grew from thee!"

Optima nutricum nostris lupa Martia rebus,
Qualia creverunt mœnia lacte tuo!

CHAPTER V

THE STORY OF THE MAID TARPEIA [1]

THE youth who is learning Roman history, as well as the mature man who likes to refreshen his memory of the stories of the past, thinks with pleasure of the tale of Tarpeia. He reads that the daughter of Spurius Tarpeius (the guardian of the Capitoline citadel), while going outside the walls for the purpose of drawing water, was bribed by the gold of Titus Tatius, the leader of the Sabines; and that, urged by the desire of possessing the golden bracelets and jewelled rings of the enemy, she promised to throw open one of the gates. Titus Tatius and his men, however (so the story continues), did not give her the reward which she expected. They pretended to keep their faith; but, instead of giving her the golden and precious ornaments which they carried on their left arm, they threw upon the Roman maiden the shields supported by that same arm. Such was the reward of treachery.[2] Tarpeia, however, is not an historical person, and it is not true that, in the beginning, she was considered an infamous maiden.

Fabius Pictor and Cincius Alimentus, the most ancient Roman writers of their national history,[3] represented the character of Tarpeia as that of a guilty person, and the version that was accepted by them prevailed.[4] Other annalists, however, did not present the story in the same way. L. Calpurnius Piso, who flourished somewhat less than a century later (namely, in the era of the Gracchi), endeavored, in narrating the earliest Roman history, to clear it of that which seemed either little credible or absurd.[5] This author put forth a version which seemed more probable also to Dionysius of Halicarnassus.[6] How was it possible that Tarpeia should have aimed at betraying her countrymen, when these honored her, later, by erecting a sepulchre on the very spot where she had fallen? Why did they not rather dig up her bones and scatter them abroad? Why did they yearly (as later became the custom) perform sacred rites in honor of one who had betrayed her country?

THE MAID TARPEIA

Calpurnius Piso, therefore, thought himself authorized to present this story somewhat differently. According to him, Tarpeia conceived the noble idea of merely pretending to turn traitor in order to save her country. Consequently, she demanded as reward for her pretended treachery, not the ornaments of gold, but the shields, so that the Sabines might, when unarmed, be the more easily overcome by the Romans. Tatius and his followers were to be received within the citadel; and a secret messenger, who afterwards betrayed her, was to notify Romulus that the Sabines could be easily overcome. These therefore, in the belief that the maiden had allowed herself to be bribed by the rich armbands, prepared to remove the ornaments from their arms.

It was with astonishment that they heard the request for their shields. Titus Tatius thereupon understood that Tarpeia had tried to deceive him, and, consequently, gave orders to throw the shields upon her and to kill her.

The version given by Piso must have appeared more natural to several ancient writers. It was therefore accepted by Dionysius of Halicarnassus.[7] Livy himself does not disdain to refer to Tarpeia, even though it be in only a few words.[8] For this same reason, in the last century of the Republic, certain families that boasted of their Sabine origin did not disdain to remember Tarpeia on their coins. The Tituri, indeed, represented her (as far as can be judged) in the act of separating a Sabine and a Roman,—

perhaps Titus Tatius and Romulus. In other words, there was ascribed to Tarpeia that which legend commonly ascribes to the Sabine women who had been ravished, and who had become the mothers of the Romans.[9]

These two are not the only versions of the story of Tarpeia. Propertius (the famous elegiac Roman poet) was acquainted with a third. According to him, the Roman maiden became enamored of Titus Tatius, and for him betrayed her country. Tarpeia, having come out of the citadel to draw the water sacred to Vesta,

> *Vidit arenosis Tatium proludere campis*
> *Pictaque per flavas arma levare iubas:*
> *Obstupuit regis facie et regalibus armis,*
> *Interque oblitas excidit urna manus.*
>   .   .   .   .
> *Sæpe tulit blandis argentea lilia Nymphis,*
> *Romula ne faciem læderet hasta Tati.*

And, having seen the blond-haired king, she exclaimed:

> *Ignes castrorum et Tatiæ prætoria turmæ*
> *Et formosa oculis arma Sabina meis,*
> *O utinam ad vestros sedeam captiva Penates,*
> *Dum captiva mei conspicer ora Tati.* [10]

It has been wrongly stated by some[11] that Propertius was the only writer to adopt such a version. On the contrary, it is to be found registered in more ancient authors, though in great part different in form.

Plutarch was aware that, according to some writers, Tarpeia was the daughter of Titus Tatius; that she had, indeed, been guilty of treachery, but against the Sabines, and because urged to it by Romulus; and that, on this account, she had been punished by her father. Among those who thus told the story of the Roman maiden was also Antigonus,—a Greek historian not later (not to say earlier) than the first Roman annalists.[12] From Plutarch we learn, moreover, that, according to the poet Simylos, Tarpeia had become enamored of Brennus, the Gaul; that she had betrayed her country's Lares in the hope of becoming his wife; and that the Gauls had thrown their splendid armbands upon her corpse.[13] Plutarch falls but little short of pronouncing Simylos insane, and considers this version absurd.[14] Surely, no one will say that these stories are deserving of faith. Nevertheless, no one can fully agree with Plutarch (who approached so very near to the official version) who does not at the same time consider the character of Tarpeia as historic; and authentic the story of the betrayal.

The deed attributed to Tarpeia is pure legend, and, as such, was capable of being narrated in a thousand different ways, not one of which, in our opinion, has reason to be considered more truthful than another.

It is evident that, even before Fabius Pictor and Cincius Alimentus had undertaken to narrate the deeds of their country, a rather numerous group of Greek authors must have occupied themselves with writing the earliest Roman history. These authors range from Callias of Syracuse and Timæus to Silenus of Calacte, from Agathocles of Cyzicus to Diocles of Peparethos. Very often, however, such works were historical novels, not history. We know that the story of Romulus and Remus as recounted by Fabius and then repeated by all historians, both Greek and Roman, was but a fantastic invention set forth for the first time among the Greeks by Diocles of Peparethos. Those versions that had the good fortune of being accepted by the more influential Roman annalists ended by becoming official; the others were rejected and forgotten, known only to such scholars as Varro, Juba and Plutarch. This fact, however, does not imply that they are unworthy of consideration.

Of the two versions given by Plutarch, apparently the stranger is that which makes Tarpeia contemporary with Brennus and with the siege of the Capitol by the Gauls. Between this version and the official one there is a difference in time of more than three centuries and a half. But is it at all certain that the legend of Tarpeia contains, within itself, anything historic that may be attributed to the age of Romulus? This is far from being the case. Tarpeia is as much a mythical person as were the first kings. Moreover, even by the official traditions (as we shall prove later) she was placed chronologically in the age of Numa and in still later times.

In close relation with this fact we find that the ignominious signification attached to the Tarpeian Rock was connected, by some, not with Tarpeia, but with a certain L. Tarpeius of the times of Romulus.[15] From the comparison of certain legends with that of Tarpeia, Petronius Sabinus shows that she was connected with another betrayal, which occurred in the age of King Tarquinius or Tarpeius.[16] Likewise, the story of Curtius, which the annalist Piso attributed to the age of Romulus, is to be assigned to 445 B.C., according to Cornelius and Lutatius. By Procilius it was placed still later, namely, in 362 B.C.[17] The poet Simylos, therefore, at the very most, did not commit any graver error than did the authoritative annalist Piso. At any rate, it is to be remarked that what the former asserted is, in a certain measure, confirmed by a passage in an author sufficiently authoritative. Polyænus (who drew from good sources) affirms that the Gauls made a compact that one of the gates of the Capitol should always remain open; and that the Romans, after having conquered the enemy by means of snares, and in order to appear faithful to a sworn compact, built an open door upon an inaccessible rock. Polyænus thus undoubtedly refers to the Mons Capitolinus or Tarpeius.[18]

This condition, according to other authoritative Roman sources, was also in close relation with the story of Tarpeia, and with the compact established between Romulus and Tatius that one gate of the Capitol should always be open to the Sabines.[19] Even the pseudo-Plutarch, who attributes to the time of the capture of Ephesus by the Gauls a story absolutely identical with that of Tarpeia, assumes a Roman original for the legend. In this, the Roman Tarpeia is connected with the siege of the Capitol by the Gauls.[20] The precious armbands are pronounced the motive for the betrayal, both in the case of the Gauls and in that of the Sabines. The jewelled rings of which Fabius spoke, however, do not befit the Gauls. This proves that the ancient Roman annalist, in speaking of Tatius and of his fellow-soldiers, had present the rich Sabines of his own days.[21]

The full and complete prevalence of that version which made Tarpeia contemporary with Titus Tatius rather than with Brennus did not depend upon the existence of very ancient and authentic Roman annals anterior to the third century B.C. We know that such annals never existed. It depended rather upon those later observations, topographical in character, by means of which it was thought possible to fix, chronologically, so great a part of the legendary history of Rome. It was, in fact, the belief of the majority that the temple of Vesta and the Regia in the Forum had been established by Numa.[22] It is obvious that Numa could not have established in that place the centres of the cults which represented the very existence of the city, unless the Capitoline and the Quirinal already formed part of the *pomerium*. It seemed, therefore, conclusive that the Capitoline had been occupied at a time later than the founding by Romulus of the square city on the Palatine, and earlier than the reign of Numa. Consequently, the occupation of that hill was attributed to the Sabines, who were already masters of the Quirinal.[23] All this is redintegration—the fruit of later antiquarian research. It is not serious historical tradition. Indeed, there were not lacking those who asserted that the temple and the cult of Vesta were to be attributed, not to Numa, but to the very founder of the city—Romulus.[24]

It is somewhat probable that, originally, the myth of Tarpeia was assigned to the times of the Gauls (who gave origin to other fantastic tales), and that the version of the poet Simylos did not stand altogether isolated. Indeed, it is worthy of note that the legend of M. Manlius Capitolinus, the so-called defender of the Capitol, states that he lived on the spot where afterwards rose the temple of Juno Moneta—in other words, on the identical spot where, according to tradition, the Sabine Titus Tatius had had his palace.[25]

The version of Antigonus,—that makes Tarpeia a Sabine rather than a Roman,—contains nothing that should surprise us. Does not Livy himself, for instance, show his uncertainty as to whether the Horatii and Curiatii were respectively Romans and Albans, or vice versa?[26] Furthermore, this version seems to agree with the claims of the Sabine and Roman families of the Petronii and Titurii, who claimed Tarpeia as their own. It may well be that the coin of the Titurii, which shows Tarpeia between the shields of a Sabine and a Roman,—of Tatius and of Romulus,[27]—represents the myth as it was related by Antigonus and by those other writers whom Plutarch has not deemed necessary to name.

We cannot declare in what age the poet Simylos lived, nor fix with precision upon the time in which Antigonus wrote his Histories of Italy. Since, however, there are good reasons for believing that the Greek Antigonus was not later than the earliest Roman annalists, and since his version was accepted by families that boasted of their Sabine origin, I see no reason for dismissing him so summarily. Still less do I think unworthy of examination the motive for which (according to such version) Tarpeia failed to perform her duty.

The study of the most ancient Roman legends proves that they are, more or less, imitations of similar Hellenic stories, well known to the Greeks who first narrated the history of the Latin city.[28] It is, then, very possible that in speaking of Tarpeia,—the personification of the hill whence the guilty were hurled,—they localized upon the Capitol one of the many myths of women who failed in their loyalty towards their country.

Two are the motives which, according to the Greek legends as well as the laws of human character, urge the maiden to commit crime: love—if the soul is noble; if base, gain. The first,—love,—was that for which Medea, Ariadne, and the Megarian Scylla were supposed to have betrayed their kin. For a necklace, instead, Eriphyle sent Amphiaraus to certain death; for gold Arne betrayed her native Liphnum.[29] Such motives have actually been the cause of the loss of more than one fortress; and, limiting ourselves to only a few ancient examples, it will be sufficient to recall by what means Antigonus became master of the citadel of Corinth, and how Fabius Maximus retook Tarentum.[30] It was for one or the other of these two motives that, according to the ancient versions, Tarpeia, too, opened one of the gates of the citadel.

According to Fabius Pictor and Cincius Alimentus, Tarpeia was a shameless maiden—to be compared with Arne. Propertius, on the contrary, likened her to Scylla, who, upon seeing that Minos was besieging Megara, snatched the golden crest from the head of Nisus, her father, and killed him. Propertius compares Tarpeia also with Ariadne, who, on account of her love for Theseus, helped him in overcoming the Minotaur. Furthermore, just as Jason and Theseus afterwards abandoned Medea and Ariadne, just as Minos does not marry the faithless maid, but throws her into the sea, so Titus Tatius causes the Roman maiden to be killed. Giving due weight to the fact that Propertius had the episode of Scylla in mind when he wrote the story of Tarpeia, some have been led to suppose that the versions which made Tarpeia sin through love merely gave a Roman coloring to the Megarian legend.[31]

It is to be noted, however, that Tarpeia was not punished

THE MAID TARPEIA

(as we might have expected) by being the first to be hurled from the rock to which her name was afterwards attached.[32] She perishes, instead, buried beneath the shields which were substituted for the desired ornaments; or, according to the version of Simylos (so very much different, but, to a certain extent, confirmed by Appian [33] in this particular), upon her were thrown the glittering *armillæ*. Finally, according to the version accepted by Plutarch, the Sabines threw upon her both the *armillæ* and the shields.[34]

What fact gave origin to the legend of the *armillæ* and the shields, and, later, to the ambiguous request for the ornaments on the left arms? The various elements of such legends spring from the force of circumstances which differ much among themselves. They may spring from some topographical data, or from data offered by monuments, such as, in our case, those of the Tarpeian Rock and of the Porta Pandana. They may arise from etymological reasons; or, finally, from the mere reproduction of an element borrowed from some other legend.

It is not easy to decide to which one of these causes we must direct our thoughts. Perhaps we will not go far astray if we bear in mind the fact that the Tarpeian Rock was situated on that part of the Capitoline Hill facing the Quirinal, and not on the southern ridge of the hill. On the edge of the Arx was the temple of Juno Moneta—the mint of the Romans. Every monument of the Capitol and of the adjacent Forum gave origin to legendary tales and to explanations of various kinds. The presence of the mint may, therefore, have led to similar consequences. On the other hand, it is clear that, in the story of Tarpeia, there is an imitation of one of the many analogous legendary tales of Greece. It will be sufficient, in this respect, to recall the charming story of Polycrita the Naxian.

Because of the rape of Neaira, the new Helen (wife of Hypsikreon), the Milesians once waged war upon the Naxians. The neighboring Erythreans formed an alliance with them, and Diognetus, their leader, became enamored of the beautiful maid Polycrita, whom he had seen in a temple near the beleaguered city. Polycrita conceived the idea of taking advantage of his love for her to aid her own countrymen. She feigned to surrender herself to his wishes, on condition that he should bind himself by oath to maintain a certain promise. Diognetus, beside himself with love, consented, and soon found himself obliged to break faith with his allies, the Milesians. By another stratagem of Polycrita the Naxians succeeded in overcoming their surprised enemy and in regaining their freedom. The citizens did not fail to show their gratitude towards the maid. Indeed, in endeavoring to surpass one another in the honors bestowed upon her, they showered wreaths and precious ornaments for her head and bosom, and actually suffocated her beneath their great number. Later, a monument was erected to the patriotic maid on the spot where she had breathed her last.[35]

Polycrita, who saves her country, and Tarpeia, who betrays it, are two different and opposed characters. Not so great, however, is the difference between the former and that virtuous Tarpeia pictured by Calpurnius Piso, who is represented as merely feigning to yield to the desires of Titus Tatius, while in reality considering the safety of her countrymen. At any rate, there is a great similarity between the two legends. The Milesians march against Naxos to rescue a ravished bride; Titus Tatius and the Sabines besiege the Capitol in a war of vengeance for their ravished women. Polycrita and Tarpeia die of suffocation—in the one case caused by the wreaths and the crowns that were thrown upon her, in the other, by the *armillæ* and the shields. In the story of the capture of Rome by the Gauls there is, also, a curious legend of a certain maid called Philotis or Tutela, who, by stratagem, succeeds in freeing the Romans from the harassing attacks of the Fidenates and of other neighboring peoples. Such a legend is the reproduction of an identical story of Smyrna. Are we, then, to believe that the story of the Naxian Polycrita, so broadly diffused among the Greeks, exercised some influence upon the legend of Tarpeia? Or was this Roman story fashioned upon the model of a nearer and more similar myth?

In the history of the Greek colonization of Lesbos, an unknow Alexandrian poet recounts the story that Peisidike, daughter of the King of Methymna, having become enamored of Achilles (who was besieging the city) agreed to open the gate of the citadel on condition that she should become his bride. Achilles consented; but, on becoming master of the city, he gave orders to his soldiers that, on account of her treachery, they should kill the maid by heaping stones upon her.[36] Also this legend of the Lesbian

THE SO-CALLED TARPEIAN ROCK

CHURCH OF S. MARIA IN ARACELI, SEEN FROM THE NORTH. (THE SITE OF THE TEMPLE OF JUNO MONETA)

Peisidike has many points in common with that of Tarpeia as given by Propertius. It is very probable that he who first related the love of the Roman maid had in mind the above legend as well as many other similar tales.[37]

However this may be, we must consider what feeling, more than any other, induces the heart of woman to attempt either good or bad enterprises. We shall thus, perhaps, come to the conclusion that, according to the ancient historians (or rather Greek chroniclers), it was not desire of gain or ornaments, but love, guilty love for the enemy of her country, that urged Tarpeia to throw open one of the gates of the Capitol.

Tarpeia, however, whether guilty through love or through the desire for gain, is not a Roman conception. We cannot establish whether or not the story that Tarpeia was killed by Tatius because she would not divulge the secrets entrusted to her by Romulus dates from very ancient sources.[38] Before the end of the Republic the legend had already been formed that the evil signification of the Tarpeian Rock as a place for punishment was caused, not by Tarpeia, but by a Lucius Tarpeius, who had opposed Romulus. Doubtlessly Calpurnius Piso had good reason for protesting against the generally accepted tradition that Tarpeia had betrayed her country. To us, who know so little concerning the most ancient rites that were purely Roman in character, as well as to the Roman annalist it seems strange that the memory of one reputed a traitor should have been honored with annual sacrifices.

It does not result from this that the explanation offered by Piso is a valid one. His version, however, together with others, enables us to establish that Tarpeia was, originally, a beneficent deity. Indeed, it is related that her image was to be seen in the temple of Jupiter.[39] Tarpeia is the personification of the *Mons Tarpeius,* which was called *Capitolinus* only after the erection, by the Tarquins, of the temple of Jupiter Capitolinus.[40] In truth, the words *Tarpeius* and *Tarquinius* are but two forms of the same word.[41] *Tarpeia* stands in the same relation to *Tarquinia* as the *Saxum Tarpeium* to the *scalæ Tarquitiæ* in the same locality. Granting, then, that the temple of Jupiter was built by the Tarquins, it must needs follow that only in the time of those kings was the hill called Tarpeius. Even leaving this argument aside, it is evident that the vestal Tarpeia, who was seduced by Titus Tatius while drawing water for her sacred duties,[42] is simply the tutelary deity of the Tarpeian Hill. She is precisely that Vestal Tarquinia who, having donated to the Romans the plain of the Tiber below the Capitol, was honored with a statue, and was granted a privilege of which she never availed herself,—the permission to marry.[43] This vestal Tarquinia is, in turn, evidently identical with the vestal Tarpeia who was one of the four virgins first chosen by Numa to that honorable office.[44]

The conception of the vestal Tarquinia or Tarpeia as a person benevolent to the Roman race stands in perfect opposition to that of the betrayer of the Capitol. That they are but one and the same person is clear from the fact that, in the original legend, this guilty and treacherous vestal was not made the daughter of Spurius Tarpeius.[45] She herself was the guardian of the Capitol which she delivered to Tatius. In short, one person was separated and distinguished into two. There are not lacking other examples of this process in the pseudo-Roman history. In this same manner the deity Acca Larentia was conceived of at one moment as the nurse of Romulus, at another as the mistress of Tarutius—in other words, as she who donated to the Roman people the fields of Solinium, Turax, and Lintirium.[46]

The fact that guilty persons were actually hurled from the Tarpeian Rock serves to explain the transformation of the good vestal into a traitor.[47] From this custom the conclusion was drawn that the first guilty person must have been the one who gave her name to the rock. Since she chanced to be the protecting goddess of the Capitol, it is natural that it should have been decided that Tarpeia failed in her duties when the Capitoline Hill was attacked, either by the Sabines or by the Gauls. The primitive conception, however, of the good and tutelary deity of the place was not entirely destroyed. Fabius Pictor and Cincius Alimentus, indeed, though asserting that Tarpeia has been guilty for the sake of the *armillæ*, related that, as soon as the Capitol was invaded, she awakened the Roman sentinels in order that they might warn the citizens of the danger to which they were exposed. The Sabines, therefore, found the fortress deserted.[48]

To the maid considered so guilty there was surely thus conceded one great extenuating circumstance, which reveals that the later versions did not succeed in effacing altogether the memory of Tarpeia, the good vestal. For this reason, there was substituted for Tarpeia (the goddess who gave her name to the Tarpeian Rock) that hypothetical L. Tarpeius of whom we have spoken, also contemporary with Romulus. For this reason, Lucius Calpurnius Piso defended her memory; for this reason, finally, were favorable traditions of Tarpeia cherished in the Sabine families of the Petronii and Titurii, and was it related that she had died a victim to her duty, and at the hand of Tatius.

Even when talk of her faults began, men hardly thought of her desire for Sabine gold. The worst crimes which could be committed by a vestal were those of allowing the sacred fire of Vesta to become extinguished, and of harboring in their souls an unchaste affection. The authentic history of Rome teaches us that it was not so extremely rare for vestal virgins accused of the latter crime to be buried alive.[49]

It is far more natural to believe that the most ancient legends affirmed that Tarpeia, as the Megarian Scylla or as Peisidike of Methymna, became enamored of the leader of the enemy, and that the Greek novelists of the late Alexandrian and Pergamean age, in adapting to the Roman goddess one of the many elements with which their mythological storehouse abounded, numbered Tarpeia among those

Ch' Amor di nostra vita dipartille.

The genius of the Roman people recognized and sanctified nothing but the wholesome and sacred love of country and of family. It might have been congenial to it to accept the noble and sublime legend of the rape of the Sabine women who, having become mothers, intervened between their brothers and their husbands, as the Titurii supposed Tarpeia to have done. It could not have acknowledged pleasantly the story of Tarpeia, who, conquered by her love for the hostile leader, betrays her country's Lares. It is, therefore, entirely natural that a keen and passionate poet like Propertius, imbued with the stories related by Phitetos and Parthenius, should have brought back to honor that form of the legend which we consider the more ancient.[50] Such version must have been incomprehensible and absurd to a Roman of the time of Fabius and Cincius. Even Calpurnius Piso, though defending the memory of Tarpeia, does not make mention of her love for Tatius, in spite of the fact that such version must have been known to him. By means of it he could have explained the colloquy between Tarpeia and Tatius, and the feigned concession of receiving the enemy within the citadel.[51]

The austere Roman, in defending her memory, did not picture her to himself as at all different from a well-mannered maiden of his own period, or from Lucretia, or Clœlia, or Virginia—all of whom were glorified by legendary history. He aimed with this story to present a model of sublime patriotism. Nor did Fabius Pictor and Cincius Alimentus have a different aim in view, though accepting the version that Tarpeia became guilty through the debasing desire for the golden armlets and the jewelled rings. The annals of the Roman people aimed to kindle the souls of its youth to the performing of noble and glorious enterprises, and to emulating the deeds of their ancestors. The sad story of the vestal, instead, simply taught (to repeat the words of the Roman historian) that "there must be no faith towards the betrayer of one's country,"—*ne quid usquam fidum proditori esset.*[52]

CHAPTER VI

THE SAXUM TARPEIUM

ON what point of the Capitoline was situated the *Saxum Tarpeium,* or that *Rupes Tarpeia* from which were hurled those condemned to death? This question forms one of the many problems of topography which, from the Renaissance on, have presented themselves to scholars, and have received answers widely different, and not always convincing. The earliest Italian topographers came to the conclusion that the *saxum* was situated on that portion of the southern ridge of the Capitoline which faces Piazza Montanara; or else, on that portion which faces the Via Tor de' Specchi. This view was strengthened by the fact that there was, in that vicinity, a small street named *Vicolo di Rupe Tarpeia,* and also by the existence of a church *sub Tarpeio*.[1] This view, however, was combated in 1819 by the French scholar, Dureau de la Malle. He called the attention of critics to two passages in Dionysius of Halicarnassus (VII. 35; VIII. 78), from which it clearly results that the Tarpeian Rock was situated on that part of the Capitoline facing the Forum Romanum.[2] From that time on the Tarpeian Rock has been sought for on that portion of the Capitoline above the Æquimælium and the Velabrum,—where ran the *Vicus Jugarius,* represented to-day by the Via della Consolazione. This is the location accepted by Jordan, Gilbert, Richter and Huelsen.[3]

In my opinion, neither the site facing the Circus Flaminius (the choice of the early Italian scholars), nor that on the southern ridge (according to the foreign critics just mentioned), is the true location of the *saxum.* Unless I be greatly mistaken there are grave reasons for believing that the *Saxum Tarpeium* was situated, not on one of the ridges of the southern portion of the Capitoline, but rather on the northern portion, where the *arx* and the temple of Juno Moneta were. In other words, it was situated on that part which, by means of a sloping ground which was later levelled down and enlarged, was joined with the Quirinal.

Before expounding in detail the reasons for which I believe that this latter view should be accepted, I deem it fitting to examine those arguments which were judged the solid foundation of the other views. I shall not stop to discuss the more ancient sites assigned to the *saxum*,— namely, those facing Piazza Montanara and the Via Tor de' Specchi. Dureau de la Malle has already noted the words of Dionysius, "the hill overlooking the agora," and again (in speaking of Spurius Cassius), his being conducted "upon the ridge overlooking the agora" and "hurled from the rock in view of the entire people." They prove conclusively that the *Saxum Tarpeium* faced the Forum over which it hung.[4]

I judge it proper, however, to emphasize the fact that, from those words, it does not at all follow that the rock was situated on that portion of the Capitoline Hill occupied by the temple of Jupiter. I would argue, rather, in favor of that portion where rose the temple of Juno Moneta. The word *agora*, which occurs in both the passages quoted from Dionysius, directs our thoughts to the region above the area of Concordia, and near the citadel and the temple of Juno Moneta. These places are somewhat distant from those overhanging the Vicus Jugarius and near the Capitolium, which indeed overlooked the Velabrum, and not the Forum.

Likewise, I do not find in the passages quoted any argument in favor of the statement that *Mons Tarpeius* originally indicated only the southern portion of the hill, where the temple of Jupiter Capitolinus was afterwards erected. In fact, the passages of the ancient writers which refer to the change of name from *Mons Tarpeius* to *Mons Capitolinus* do not compel us to agree, with modern critics, that the northern portion of the Capitoline was not called *Mons Tarpeius* also.[5]

Against such entirely arbitrary conclusions I shall oppose the inscription of Flavia Epicarides, priestess of the goddess *Virgo Cælestis*. It was found in 1892, in excavating for the monument to Victor Emmanuel II.,—that is, while excavating in that region of the Capitoline where the *arx* and the temple of Juno Moneta had been. In this inscription Flavia Epicarides is called a priestess "of the goddess Virgo Cælestis, the most propitious deity of this region of the *Mons Tarpeius*."[6] The expression *Mons*

THE TABULARIUM, BETWEEN THE CAPITOLIUM (TEMPLUM IOVIS) AND THE ARX
(TEMPLUM IUNONIS)

Tarpeius, consequently, equally with *Mons Capitolinus,* indicated the northern as well as the southern portion of the Capitoline. There are necessary, then, quite different arguments from those hitherto employed to establish the site which the ancients described with the name *Saxum Tarpeium.*

I do not stop to discuss minutely various other passages from which it has been wrongly deduced that the *Saxum Tarpeium* was not far from the Capitolium. These passages are, in my opinion, very ambiguous, and lend themselves to different interpretations. For instance, we read in Tacitus that, in the siege of the Capitol in 69 A.D., since the entrance had been barricaded, the various approaches to the Capitol were attacked near the grove of the *asylum,* and where the Tarpeian Rock is reached by the one hundred steps.[7] I fail to see how, from this passage, it can be unhesitatingly deduced that this stairway was on the southern portion of the hill, upon which the Capitolium was situated. The story in Tacitus, taken as a whole, gives the impression that, inasmuch as the direct approaches to the Capitol were well defended, entrance to it was sought by more distant paths. Such a path was the one near the grove of the *asylum* mentioned by Tacitus, situated beyond the limits of the southern elevation of the Capitoline.

The same author relates that " having quickly crossed the Forum and passed by the temples overlooking the Forum, they pushed forth their line of battle up the opposing hill as far as the first gate of the Capitoline citadel." By these words, then, he informs us that the field of action embraced also the northern region of the Capitoline, where the *arx* was situated. Precisely on that portion of the hill, which was crowned by the citadel, were the *Tarquitiæ Scalæ,* which are to be identified with the stairway of one hundred steps mentioned by Tacitus.[8]

It is not worth while to prove that no certain conclusion can be derived from the fragment of Festus. Lucius Terentius of the Vicus Tuscus. is there spoken of, who, as it seems, recovered from the fall from the Tarpeian Rock. It does not result from this passage (so full of lacunæ) that the Vicus Tuscus was beneath the *saxum*. In fact, we know from other sources that there were some Terentii called *Tuscivicani,* because they lived in that street.[9] Again, I do not give any weight to the circumstance that, by the poets, that part of the hill which was occupied by the Capitolium was sometimes called the *Rupes Tarpeia*. This ancient name indicated the entire Capitoline Hill, which, indeed, terminated in precipices at several points.[10] If the *Saxum Tarpeium*, therefore, is at times called *Rupes Tarpeia*, it does not mean that the latter name indicated exclusively that spot whence the guilty were hurled. It indicated, rather, the various portions and the generally rocky aspect of the entire hill.[11] In view of the inscription of Flavia Epicarides mentioned above,—from which we learn that also the northern portion of the Capitoline was called *Mons Tarpeius,*—it seems to me useless to discuss specious arguments, and to delay in finer distinctions as to the meaning of certain texts.

The name *Tarpeius* referred, originally, to the whole of the Capitoline Hill, just as the cult of Tarpeius and of Tarpeia (the most ancient divinities to yield to Jupiter Capitolinus, Juno Moneta and, finally, to the Virgo Cælestis), belonged both to the northern and to the southern portions of the hill.[12] Indeed, from the mutilated text of Festus regarding the *Saxum Tarpeium*, it could be deduced that this site was entirely separate from the Capitolium, and that it was on the opposite part of the *Mons Capitolinus*.[13] But, rather than give excessive importance to a text susceptible of various interpretations, I prefer to examine a passage from Livy, which, at first sight, would seem to favor the view opposed to that which I consider true.

In relating the death of Marcus Manlius Capitolinus, who was supposed to have been hurled from the Tarpeian Rock, Livy says that the same place was thus, in the case of one and the same man, a witness of his great glory and of his final punishment.[14] The Gauls (according to Livy's version) attempted to scale the Capitoline by climbing the precipice *ad Carmentis Saxum*. The natural conclusion, then, would be that Manlius was hurled from the precipice overhanging the Porta Carmentalis, not far from the region of the temple of Jupiter Capitolinus. This conclusion might seem all the more natural, because (according to an ancient tradition preserved by Cicero) Manlius had saved the *Capitolium*.[15] All favors the belief that the words of Livy, *locusque idem*, mean that Marcus Manlius met his death at the precise spot from which he had repelled the

THE SAXUM TARPEIUM

Gauls, and that they do not mean that the entire Capitoline Hill was a witness of his glory and his misfortune.[16] Nevertheless, against this seemingly simple conclusion there are many valid objections.

According to Livy, not only the *Capitolium* was in danger of being captured by the Gauls, but also the *arx*.[17] In addition, the tradition preserved by Livy constantly affirms that the house of Manlius was situated, not in the Capitolium, but in the citadel or *arx*, where later rose the temple of Juno Moneta.[18] The information which has reached us does not enable us to ascertain whether or not there was, originally, a legend which made Manlius the rescuer of the *arx* rather than of the Capitolium. Tradition itself informs us that in the moment when the Gauls were scaling the heights, Manlius was not the guardian of the *ad Carmentis saxum*, but of the *arx*, and that from there he hastened to the place of danger.[19] There are sufficient reasons for believing that, originally, the version of the house of Manlius upon the citadel (afterwards razed to the ground) was placed in relation with the version that Manlius had been hurled from the very spot where he lived and from which he had repelled the Gauls. We are inclined to believe that the rock known under the name of *Carmentis Saxum* was not the same that was generally distinguished by the epithet of *Saxum Tarpeium*.

There is a close connection between the legend of Marcus Manlius and that of Tarpeia,—a relation which I have endeavored to establish elsewhere. According to two different versions, it was determined, after the crime of Manlius, that no one should live in the *arx* or in the Capitolium.[20] Similarly, two different versions affirmed that the sepulchre of Tarpeius was situated near either the Capitolium or the *arx*. Only if the existence of these two versions be admitted can that passage of Plutarch be clearly understood, where it is said that, in the time of Tarquinius, the bones of Tarpeius were removed from the spot where they had rested (that is, from the spot where the temple of Jupiter was erected), and were placed in another portion of the Capitoline Hill.[21] This latter belief had its origin in the fact that at first delinquents were hurled from every precipice of the Capitoline Hill. Only with time,—when the different portions of the hill became occupied by edifices of various kinds,—did the necessity arise of confining the execution of the penalty to that place which seemed most fit for it. At any rate, because not even the passage from Livy furnishes us with the desired solution, we must seek for it elsewhere. We shall obtain it, perhaps, only by an investigation of what place, according to tradition, was the scene of action of the story of the maid Tarpeia.

Ancient tradition is quite consistent in placing in close relation the *Saxum Tarpeium* and the place of capital punishment with the betrayal of Tarpeia. The latter is described as the daughter of the guardian of the *arx*, and as having thrown open one of its doors to the Sabines. The variant versions, too, which speak of the treachery of Tarpeius rather than of Tarpeia, agree in stating that he was the guardian of the betrayed citadel.[22] From the moment, then, that the *Saxum Tarpeium* is placed in such close relation with the betrayal of the *arx*, it seems as though it were most natural to conclude that the *saxum* should be sought for, not so much on the southern elevation of the Capitoline Hill (where the Capitolium was), but rather on the northern, where the *arx* was situated. Here it is said that the Sabine Titus Tatius established his palace,[23] and here the house of Marcus Manlius Capitolinus afterwards arose,—that is, on that part of the hill which, under the Empire (as we learn from the inscription of Flavia Epicarides), still preserved the name of *Mons Tarpeius*.

This conclusion is confirmed by the version of the maid Tarpeia offered by Propertius. Regarding the motive which induced Tarpeia to betray the Romans, Propertius gives an entirely different explanation,—the love, namely, of the unfortunate maid for the Sabine chieftain. I have already endeavored to demonstrate that this romantic story is a reproduction of one of the most ancient versions of the legend.[24] It will suffice, here, to note that Propertius, as well as the writers followed by Livy, admitted that Tarpeia had occasion to see Titus Tatius, and had allowed herself to be induced to betray her countrymen by going outside the walls to draw water.[25]

But where was the spring? Livy does not deign to relate such purely legendary particulars. From his point of view, he was right. Propertius is, instead, naturally drawn to tell us where the "Tarpeian grove and the shameful sepulchre of Tarpeia" were, and where, finally, the spring was at which Tarpeia drew water. The Sabine king Titus Tatius (he says) pitched his camp in the Forum:

> *Atque ubi nunc terris dicuntur iura subactis,*
> *stabant Romano pila Sabina Foro.*

And, speaking of the spring, he adds,

> *. . . ubi nunc est Curia Sæpta*
> *bellicus ex illo fonte bibebat equus.* [26]

According to Propertius, Titus Tatius encamped at the foot of the *arx*. This entirely agrees with the story of Dionysius, which states that the Sabine king, on arriving from Cures and the North, occupied the plain between the Quirinal and the Capitoline.[27] The spring at which Tarpeia drew water was, therefore, in the region where later rose the Curia Hostilia. This, in turn, recalls both the *Tullianum*, which was so called from the *tullius* or spring which emptied within it, and the Porta Fontinalis.[28]

We have thus seen that the place in which Tarpeia was induced to betray her fatherland was localized at the foot of the *arx*. It seems, therefore, natural to believe that the *Saxum Tarpeium* (from which traitors were hurled) and the *sepulchrum* of Tarpeia (at which sacred rites were performed yearly) should be found on one of the rocks of the citadel above.

This hypothesis, in itself simple and natural, finds support in the statements concerning the use made of the southwest slopes of the *arx*,—that is, of the slopes facing the Forum. From a mass of authentic information we learn that these slopes served, at the same time, as both mines and prisons. Or better, it is manifest that the following ends were held in view: firstly, to isolate still more the Capitoline Hill, by widening and deepening the pass separating it from the Quirinal, and thus to render the citadel more inaccessible; secondly, to procure material for building the walls of the Capitoline, and, perhaps, also for draining and paving the marshy area of the Forum; thirdly, to guard the prisoners, part of whom (as we shall see later) consisted of prisoners of war, who were condemned to work in mines or *Lautumiæ*, as had already been done in the *Lautumiæ* of Syracuse. From these, indeed (according to the ancients), the Roman mines derived their name.[29]

Finally, we know that, in the vicinity of the *Lautumiæ* there were the *Tullianum* and the *scalæ Gemoniæ* or *Gemitoriæ*, upon which were thrown the bodies of the condemned. The circumstance that the spring of Tarpeia was near the *Lautumiæ,* the prison, and the *scalæ Gemoniæ,* renders it very probable that it is on this side of the Capitoline that the *Saxum Tarpeium* and the one hundred steps leading from the Forum to the *Rupes Tarpeia* must be sought.[30] This conclusion will appear still more probable if, going beyond the topographical limits of our problem, we shall examine its relation to the earliest penal code of the Romans.

II

What crimes were punished with death from the Tarpeian Rock?
The tradition gathered by Fabius Pictor and Cincius Alimentus is quite explicit. It placed the *Saxum Tarpeium* in relation with the crime of high treason.[31] It is true that the version defended nearly a century later by Calpurnius Piso spoke only of a pretended betrayal on the part of Tarpeia, who, on the contrary, was supposed to have notified Romulus of the compact she had made with the Sabines. It is also worthy of note that, according to this annalist, Tarpeia was a virtuous maiden, whose sepulchre was justly honored with public *inferiæ*.[32] Such version doubtlessly has preserved for us a very ancient characteristic, inasmuch as it recalls the early and beneficent deity of the Capitoline Hill.[33] But in so far as this version speaks of only a pretended betrayal, it bears the stamp of a correction of the earlier tradition regarding an actual crime of treason. The rectification itself confirms our belief that, even before the third century, the *Saxum Tarpeium* was connected with the crime of conspiracy against the security of the State.

Let us examine still further the cases in which (according to the annals) this rock was the scene of capital punishment. We find that it is mentioned in connection with those who, like Coriolanus,[34] attacked the privileges of the populace, or who, like Spurius Cassius[35] and Manlius Capitolinus,[36] aimed at becoming the tyrants of their country. The authenticity of these reports is not in the slightest degree guaranteed. Even the details concerning the deaths

THE SAXUM TARPEIUM

of these men are variously narrated by the different authors.[37] From the whole, however, it results that in the first centuries of Rome (according to the annals) the Tarpeian Rock represented one of the penalties for those convicted of *perduellio,* or crime against the State. For this reason, the execution of such sentences was entrusted to the tribunes of the people,—that is to say, to the representatives of the popular liberties.[38]

There are not lacking examples of traitors thus sent to death in the fully historic age. It is sufficient to recall the 360 deserters who were hurled from the rock in 214 B.C.,[39] the faithless hostages of Tarentum and of Thurii who escaped in 212 B.C.,[40] and the treacherous slave of P. Sulpicius.[41] Indeed, the numerous stories of Roman citizens who, in revolutionary times, met their death from the Tarpeian Rock, refer to so many cases of treachery. For, considering the different points of view, the enemies of any given party were judged guilty of overturning the constitution, and of impeding the natural development, or rather, the direct application of rights more or less acquired and recognized.[42]

Seneca, indeed, said that he saw different vices in many persons, and that he was called upon to heal the State; that for everyone's ill a cure was asked. He adds that, although the perverse dress must clothe the magistrate and the assembly be convoked at the sound of the trumpet, he would ascend to the tribunal neither raving nor hostilely inclined, but would recite the laws and its solemn phrases in a gentle and serious tone rather than in a raging voice; and that when he would condemn the criminal to be beheaded, and the parricide to be sewn up in a sack, when he would sentence the guilty to military torture and the traitor or public enemy to the Tarpeian Rock, he would do so without any show of anger, but with that appearance and feeling with which he would strike the serpents and other venomous animals. With these words, therefore, Seneca explicitly declares that the penalty of the Tarpeian Rock was one of several particularly decreed to those guilty of *perduellio,*—that is, to public enemies and traitors.[43]

Some difficulty may nevertheless present itself. As early as the laws of the Twelve Tables the *Saxum Tarpeium* was not spoken of in cases of *perduellio* or high treason, but indeed in cases of private crimes,—especially those of false testimony and theft on the part of slaves.[44] In addition, it must be remarked that, in some cases during the Empire, the *saxum* was mentioned in connection with witchcraft and incest.[45] These facts, however, bear no proof against our view. In the most ancient Roman law the State did not intervene in the judgment and the punishment of slaves.[46] It later entrusted to the father similar powers over his own sons. Therefore, it is easily understood how, by the side of a tradition which spoke of Spurius Cassius as being hurled from the *Saxum Tarpeium* (after a trial conducted by the *quæstores*), there should have been a second one which, if not more authentic, certainly bore the stamp of the more ancient Roman law,—one, namely, which represented him as being judged and slain by his own father.

From the fact that the Twelve Tables established the punishment of the Tarpeian Rock for the crime of evident theft, there can be derived, I think, still another argument in favor of a theory that I have elsewhere expounded. The legislation of the Twelve Tables, indeed, seems to be the fruit of a legal experience extending to a period much nearer to us than tradition partly affirms. It seems to represent a codification made, not in 451 B.C., but rather about 304 B.C., when Appius Claudius Cæcus and Gnæus Flavius (according to reliable notices) published the civil code and the *legis actiones*.[47] It should not surprise us that, with the development of legal procedure, with the increase and the multiplication of the functions of the State, and with the differentiating in the application of the laws, the *Saxum Tarpeium* should have become considered a fitting place of execution for various crimes other than that of high treason.

The punishing of private crimes did not necessarily require the direct intervention of the State in the earliest Rome. In that period the principle of the vendetta flourished in all its vigor, and the only crime for which the State resorted to capital punishment was that of plotting against the State itself.[48] Nevertheless, it is not inappropriate to observe that the punishment of a free citizen guilty of breaking his faith, and of the slave faithless to his master (whether in robbing him, as is foreseen by the laws of the Twelve Tables, or by surrendering him to his enemies, as in the case of the slave of P. Sulpicius), are both the direct and normal development of legal views and principles. The

Saxum Tarpeium, which originally represented one of the methods reserved for the punishment of traitors, became gradually used also in punishing those who broke their plighted faith towards private persons.[49]

The fundamental and original character of the *Saxum Tarpeium* was that of a place of punishment for crimes against the State. This results from a long series of incontrovertible facts. Furthermore, there is no doubt that the same character was attached to the prison beneath the citadel, and to the neighboring *scalæ Gemoniæ.* The latter, in fact, are mentioned by tradition only in cases of death for *perduellio,* of political revolutions, and, finally, of the crime of lese majesté towards the people, and (under the Empire) towards the Emperor.[50] In the present state of our knowledge, it is not easy to determine whether the *scalæ Gemoniæ* (which were in front of the prison), were, in substance, identical with the one hundred steps leading from the Forum to the Tarpeian rock,—in other words, identical with those ill-famed *scalæ Tarquitiæ,* the building of which was ascribed by tradition to King Tarquin.[51] At any rate, it seems to me that the two places must have been very close to each other, and that the bodies of those hurled from the Tarpeian Rock must have fallen into the *Lautumiæ.* These, in turn, were not only near the *carcer Tullianum,* but (in my opinion) were on the boundary of the *nemus Tarpeiæ.* Here were the sources of the spring emptying near the Curia—the spring whither, according to the myth, the maid Tarpeia had gone to draw water.[52]

III

The presence of the *Lautumiæ* and of the *scalæ Tarquitiæ* in the immediate vicinity of the Tarpeian Rock induces us to examine our problem from the historico-legal point of view. According to the theory set forth by Mommsen in his monumental work on penal law, forced labor in the mines was unknown at the time of the Republic. It was introduced (he says) only in the reign of Tiberius, in imitation of what was done elsewhere, perhaps in Egypt. Mommsen himself, however, states that the mines of the Italic and Siceliot cities had already been operated by condemned criminals.[53] Therefore, I do not see why a similar procedure should not be admitted also for Rome during a period relatively ancient—the more so that forced labor for crimes against the State is but the evolution and the later application of the conception of the labors to which the slave guilty towards his master had been condemned.

The ancient texts enable us to solve this problem in a sufficiently exact manner. According to the source of Johannes Lydus, Tarquinius Superbus invented instruments of torture, and established the penalty of *ad metalla*.[54] The same facts (but still more explicit) are to be read in Suidas, according to whom Tarquinius invented chains of wood and iron, scourges, the block, and the penalties of *ad metalla* and exile.[55] The same words are found in Johannes Antiochenus. The latter quotes Suetonius Tranquillus, in a passage saying of Numa the same that is said by the Chronographus of 354 A.D. This has induced Reifferscheid to assign to Suetonius, as to a common source, those words of the Chronographus referring to Tarquinius Superbus: *Hic prior hominibus invenit lautumias, tormenta, fustes, metalla, carceres, exilia.*[56] The view that such statements, instead of being traced back to Suetonius, find their source only in a late compilation of the second century of the Empire would not be a very just one. Even Lydus, as can be deduced from other passages, drew upon Suetonius.

The notices regarding Tarquinius Superbus come, in the ultimate analysis, from still more ancient sources. This can be deduced from a fragment of Cassius Hemina, an annalist of the second century B.C. This author, in speaking of Tarquinius Superbus, says that he had forced the people to build the sewers; and that when, on this account, many committed suicide by hanging, he ordered their bodies to be nailed to crosses.[57] Whether directly or indirectly, an ancient annalist is again the source for a similar statement in Pliny, where (as in other cases) Tarquinius Superbus is confused with Tarquinius Priscus. Pliny, indeed, after relating that the sewers were built by Tarquinius, says: " Since Tarquinius Priscus built that work with the hands of the people, and since it was difficult to decide whether such labor was more intolerable on account of its severity than its long duration, many Quirites escaped by committing suicide; and the king then hit upon a new and hitherto unthought of remedy, namely, to nail to the cross the corpses of all who died in this manner, to be looked

THE MAMERTINE PRISON

THE SAXUM TARPEIUM

upon by the citizens and, at the same time, to be torn by the wild birds."[58] In these two passages only the sewers are mentioned. It is to be observed, however, that such fragments can be fully understood only when those parts of Livy and of Dionysius are held in mind, in which it is narrated that Tarquinius Priscus (and especially Tarquinius Superbus) oppressed the people, compelling them to surround the city with a wall, to erect the temple of Jupiter Capitolinus, to build the Circus Maximus, and to dig the cloaca,—in a word, to fulfil the duties of *opifices* and *lapicidæ,*—of workmen and of stone-cutters.[59] Above all, it must be remembered that Tarquinius Superbus, in order to oppress the people, alone and without any counsellors exercised jurisdiction over capital offences, and by this means he was able to slay, drive into exile, and confiscate property.[60]

All the elements, then, in the passages cited (which seem to have Suetonius as a common source), actually date back to the annalistic compilations. I do not think that much importance should be given to the fact that, while the annalists speak of *operæ* and of *munia,* the passages traceable to Suetonius mention forced labor. For, undoubtedly, just as it was said in the original version that the rebellious were nailed to the cross, so there must have been also a suggestion of forced labor in the mines.[61]

Even the most ancient tales represented Tarquinius Superbus as the inventor of the severest laws in the early penal code. This we learn with complete certainty from the oration of Cicero *pro Rabirio,* accused of *perduellio* in 63 B.C.[62] On that occasion, in order to benefit the ultrademocratic party, it was thought fit to recall to vigor those very ancient penal sanctions which were preserved by the legend of Horatius, the slayer of his sister. To speak more definitely, the prosecutor evoked the *carmina cruciatus* of Tarquinius *crudelissimi ac superbissimi regis,* in which, among other things, it was ordered *caput obnubito, arbori infelici suspendito.* In other words, the laws of Tarquinius Superbus, which were supposed to have been obtained *ex annalium monumentis atque ex regum commentariis,* punished those convicted of *perduellio* with that crucifixion which, by annalists like Cassius Hemina and the other ancient writers cited above, was said to have threatened those disobeying the laws of Tarquin.

122   ANCIENT LEGENDS OF ROMAN HISTORY

The statements, therefore, of the Chronographus of 354, and of Johannes Lydus,—that Tarquinius invented the *lautumiæ* and other punishments,—have their origin in the ancient annals. With these facts there is in close relation the notice preserved in Festus, that Tarquinius had caused the *scalæ Tarquitiæ* to be cut—that is, the stairway leading to the Tarpeian Rock. King Tarquin, then, was considered the creator of the ancient and severe penal laws of Rome. His activities in this, as in many other respects, were moreover localized particularly upon that hill whose southern portion had been called *Mons Tarpeius* as late as his own reign. To sum up, with his name were connected the establishment of crucifixion as a punishment, of forced labor in the mines, and of many other kinds of torture.

Have these statements, however, any real historic nucleus, or have we before us a complex of legends?

I unhesitatingly accept the latter view. The same law which was attributed to Tarquinius was, by others, referred to the mythical King Tullus Hostilius, who had desired to apply it in the trial of Horatius.[63] Undoubtedly there is, in this latter story, a sacred legend which is to be connected with the cult of Jupiter Tigillus and his sister Juno Tigilla. This worship took the form of cross-shaped beams of wood inserted into the ground close together, and was held near a gate of early Rome.[64] In our case, however, it is urgent to bring into relief the very evident equation of *Tarpeius* to *Tarquinius,* and of *Tarpeia* to *Tarquinia.* The luckless maid Tarpeia who, for love of gold, betrays the citadel, is not essentially different from the legendary and benevolent vestal Tarpeia or Tarquinia, who donated the Campus Martius to the Roman people. Likewise the bad King Lucius Tarquinius, who held possession of the Campus Martius, is in no wise distinct from that Lucius Tarquinius (Tarpeius) whom Romulus caused to be hurled from the *Saxum Tarpeium.*[65] In conclusion, I think that Tarquinius Superbus, the author of the Roman criminal code, of the prison and of the *Lautumiæ,* is that same person who was by others called the guardian of the citadel and the father of the vestal Tarpeia.

The stories of his legal activities, consequently, must be considered as originating in the use afterwards made of those slopes of the citadel facing the Forum. In the same manner, with Tarpeius or Tarquinius was connected the founding of the chief temple of the nation on the most southern portion of the hill. On this spot there had been the temple of Tarpeius, or Vulcanus, or Summanus—a temple which, perhaps in the time of Marcus or of Lucius Furius Camillus (but surely after the Gallic invasion), became the temple of Jupiter Optimus Maximus and of the Capitoline triad.[66]

The entirely fantastic character of these stories does not prevent our recognizing the fact that, in the most remote period, the slopes of the Capitoline toward the Comitium and the Forum were used as *lapicidinæ* (quarries) and as prisons. According to tradition, this custom obtained in the time of the Tarquins—namely, during the sixth century. The Greek word *lautumiæ*, which is derived from the word in use among the Siceliots, would by itself, without any further proofs, lead us to a more recent time limit. Since, however, we cannot fix the precise date, let us pass over the question of chronology in this place. Let us remark, rather, that it may be held with sufficient certainty that at Rome the punishment of forced labor in the mines existed, not only during the Empire, but also in a far remoter age.

There was a great similarity, too, between the *lautumiæ* of Syracuse and the Capitoline *lautumiæ*—namely, that prisoners of war were guarded in both of them. This circumstance seems to result in a most evident manner from what Livy narrates for the year 198 B.C. He there speaks of the revolt of the Carthaginian hostages and of their slaves—a revolt which, starting at Setia, spread to the neighboring cities of Norba, Cercei, Præneste, and Rome. Only if it be admitted that such persons were actually guarded in the *lautumiæ*, can the words of Livy be understood, when he says of this revolt that the *triumviri* of the prison of the *lautumiæ* were commanded to keep a closer guard than customary.[67]

IV

We have thus established that death from the Tarpeian Rock and crucifixion were the two penalties for those guilty of *perduellio*. Tradition, however, records various other punishments for such crime during the earliest stage of the legal life of the Roman people. I omit examining the great majority of them, because they have no direct bearing upon our problem. I shall limit myself merely to recalling the death of Mettius Fufetius, torn to pieces by wild horses; of Turnus Herdonius, drowned in a spring; and of Spurius Cassius, no longer a consul, but a tribune of the people, and burned by flames. All these are legendary stories utterly lacking in historical consistency. Nevertheless, they have the merit of informing us what, according to the Romans of the third century, were the most ancient punishments—punishments then grown obsolete.[68]

I shall dwell a moment in the consideration of the death of Spurius Mælius, who, about 439 B.C. (as Spurius Cassius before him), aspired to royal authority. Legend says that he was killed by the dagger of Servilius Ahala. The annalists, on the contrary, while affirming this story as a whole, merely discussed the legal point at stake. They questioned whether or not Servilius Ahala had been invested with the powers of the *magister equitum,* and whether the slaying of Mælius had, consequently, been committed by the order and the will of a magistrate, or at the initiative of a private citizen. This second theory was, in fact, accepted by the earliest annalists; the opposite version (as it seems) was maintained by the defenders of strict legality. Among these were the authors who strove to find in their national history the forms of the existing constitutional law in all its rigid application, or who employed such tales in justifying given legal doctrines which were affirmed to descend from the earliest times of the Republic.

I do not intend, here, to examine in detail the value of these and of similar versions. Such examination would lead me beyond the just limits of this discussion—a discussion made from points of view so entirely different from those held by Mommsen, Pernice and Ferrini.[69] To trace how much truth there is in the stories of Spurius Mælius and of Spurius Cassius, it is not very useful to establish which of the ancient versions comes nearer the primitive law of the Romans. For, I believe that even the most ancient tradition presents a very greatly altered aspect of the historical facts—granting, even, that these actually occurred. The question whether or not he who aspired to absolute power over his country was *sacer* and could, therefore, be killed without regular trial, or whether the slayer could, without further ado, be absolved, and indeed rewarded, was the one question which must have agitated the minds of the most ancient annalists. These men were at the same time, indeed, the earliest Roman jurists.

Such questions must have been answered in various ways, according to the views already expressed in Greece during the fourth and the third centuries. In Greece there was no constant and absolute application of the principle that it was lawful to kill a tyrant immediately—as is affirmed on the authority of Solon [70] and as is repeated by Xenophon.[71] This is proved by the fact that at Eresus, in the second half of the fourth century, a formal sentence ratified by the people was deemed necessary, whereas, at the same time, the opposite theory was accepted at Chios and at Ilium. At Ilium, in fact, immunity and even rewards were decreed, in the third century, for the tyrannicide and for whomsoever slew the head of the oligarchy—just as, according to the more widely diffused Roman legend, was done in the case of Servilius Ahala.[72] The fact that Phanias of Eresus wrote a work on tyrannicide at the same time in which the law cited above was passed, proves that upon this point philosophers and jurists were not agreed.[73] The Greek discussions upon the question must have been examined by the Roman annalists. It is proved, firstly by the laws of the Gracchi, and secondly by the words of Dionysius concerning the lot of the sons of Cassius. In this passage the author contrasts the Roman laws with the Greek, which latter did or did not impose death upon the sons of the tyrants.

From the words of Dionysius, indeed,[74] it results that also at Rome (as in the Greek States) there was a time in which the sons of those who aspired to become tyrants were killed as well as their father. If, then, in the legislation which flourished in the last centuries of the Republic there is no trace of the transmission of the penalty even for crimes against the State, or if it was limited merely to the confiscation of property, it cannot be deduced from this that the Roman laws were superior to the Greek, as is affirmed by Dionysius and as is accepted by Mommsen.[75] Such a fact simply proves that, in this respect, there took place that same progress of ideas and that same softening of customs which, beginning with the third century B.C., gradually led to the substitution of exile and of other penalties, even in the case of State offences.[76] In the story of Spurius Cassius, however, there is an argument in favor of the view that the laws of the Republic (gathered together in the Twelve Tables) represent a very late stage of legislation. Such a legend teaches us that the legal development immediately following the publication of the Twelve Tables drew as from a storehouse upon the doctrines of Greek jurists and philosophers.[77]

I do not intend to express a different opinion concerning the historical substance of the legend of Spurius Mælius than that which I have already set forth.[78] I shall only recall that the *porticus Minucia,* the *Æquimælium* and the sanctuary of the god *Minucius* or *Minutius* near the Porta Trigemina had great influence in the formation of the legends referring to those characters. Likewise, the existence of the *lacus Servilius* at the beginning of the *Vicus Iugarius* and in front of the *Æquimælium* (where the house of Spurius Mælius was supposed to have been) may have had great part in fashioning the legend of that demagogue and of his death at the hand of Servilius Ahala.[79]

What is of paramount importance to us is to emphasize the circumstance that the *æquimælium* was situated at the foot of the Capitolium and near the *Saxum Carmentæ*. In other words, it was in the vicinity where, according to the generally accepted idea (in this study, however, opposed by me), the *Saxum Tarpeium* was situated. It is evident that if the *Saxum Tarpeium* had truly been there situated, the legend of Spurius Mælius would not have failed to take advantage of such a circumstance. As in the case of Marcus Manlius, the correspondence between the house of the demagogue and the place whence those guilty of *perduellio* were hurled would have been emphasized in this legend also. Since, then, this element is entirely lacking, and, on the contrary, there appears in its stead the dagger of Servilius Ahala, it is permissible to affirm that we have here a negative proof that the Tarpeian Rock was situated on the citadel. When, consequently, Dionysius says that those in the Forum saw the body of Spurius Cassius hurled from the rock, these words must be understood as referring to that part of the hill which overhung the Forum—namely, to that portion beneath which were situated the *lautumiæ* and the *Tullianum*.

If it were permitted to me to draw any conclusion from these observations, it would be: that the history of the most ancient penal laws of the Romans is but ill studied and investigated, unless a due regard be had for those topographical circumstances which gave life, not only to pure legends, but also to so many semi-historical tales of the early Republic.[80] Such method is of avail both for the penal and the civil laws. Hence, only if the circumstances of the topography in which the first phases of *ius civile* developed be held in mind can the stories referring to it be fully understood, as well as the impulses which fashioned and trained the body of the civil law in one way rather than in another.

CHAPTER VII

THE LEGEND OF SERVIUS TULLIUS, AND THE SUPREMACY OF THE ETRUSCANS AT ROME

THE general tendency of scholars is to admit that the first four kings of Rome were mythical beings. On the other hand, the view prevails that the last three kings belong to authentic history—in particular, to that period during which Rome and Latium were subject to the domination of the Etruscans. Several years ago I opposed such theory. I endeavored to demonstrate that the last three kings of Rome,—namely, Tarquinius Priscus, Servius Tullius and Tarquinius Superbus,—are quite as legendary as Romulus, Numa, Tullus Hostilius and Ancus Marcius. To-day, after having duly examined and weighed the objections presented, I reaffirm what I then set forth.

The principal argument of those who believe in the stories of the last three kings is the existence of the famous Etruscan tomb at Volci, which was discovered in 1857 by François.[1] On its walls there are represented various persons (among whom the Tarquins) who appear also in the Roman traditions. It is, therefore, fitting to begin with examining carefully the contents of such paintings.

The paintings of this famous tomb are arranged to correspond, so that opposite to the scene representing the combat between the two brothers Eteocles and Polynices there is a representation of a Cneve Tarchu Rumach in the act of being attacked by a certain Marce Camitlnas. Again, opposite to a scene of the Trojans who were slain to honor the funeral of Patroclus there is indicated (by means of names written on the painting) the Etruscan Caile Vipinas, freed from his chains by a warrior called Macstrna. There follow three more groups. A certain Larth Ulthes transfixes a Laris Papathnas Velznach; a Rasce wounds a certain Pesna Arcmsnas Svetimach; and, finally, a Venthi Cau(le)s? . . . plsachs is killed by the better-known Aule Vipinas.

Various critics have, during these latter years, dedicated themselves to the study of the relations and the meanings of these paintings. In addition to the well-known figures of Mastarna, of the two brothers Cælius and Aulus Vibenna, and of a Tarquin, there are figures entirely unknown to the versions in the Roman annals. Some have concluded that there is a unity of conception in the paintings, which correspond to each other in position. Others, however, basing their arguments on the diversity of treatment in the figures, and on the different Greek subjects expressed by them, have reached the conclusion that in this, as in other Etruscan tombs, there are elements referring to events and to scenes not closely related to one another.

With due regard to the writers who have treated this subject, I do not believe that there are any decisive arguments for accepting one view rather than the other. However, I incline to those who admit a certain unity of composition in the Etruscan paintings. Even accepting this view, there results no certain conclusion regarding the complete and precise interpretation of those scenes. For, if it be true that Mastarna and the two brothers Cælius and Aulus Vibenna had some connection with Gnæus Tarquinius of Rome (who, according to other views, belonged to an event quite different), there does not result any interpretation closely related to the facts known in Roman tradition. According to this, in fact, Lucius Tarquinius is slain by two shepherds, and at the instigation of the sons of Ancus Marcius. In the tomb painting, on the contrary, Gnæus Tarquinius is assailed by a certain Marce Camitlnas. I do not give any weight to the circumstance that, while in the Roman tradition Tarquinius is called Lucumo and later Lucius, in our painting he is styled Gnæus. Such changes of *prænomina* are very frequent even during the age posterior to the legendary era of Roman annals. Even granting that the person in question is one of the Tarquins who reigned at Rome, it is evident that we have absolutely no way of identifying the unknown Camitlnas.

It has been very cleverly thought that this Gnæus Tarquinius, instead of being one of the kings of Rome, was one of those princes who, after the revolution of 509 B.C., sought refuge among the Etruscans. It may be argued against this hypothesis, however, that the figures of Gnæus Tarquinius and of Marce Camitlnas constitute the principal part of the painting. They are, consequently, to be contrasted with the combat between the two Theban brothers,

Eteocles and Polynices. From the parallelism between the Greek and the Etruscan scenes depicted on the opposite walls of the tomb, it might be deduced that also in this case there was represented a combat between relatives, or, at any rate, between persons connected by some close bond. Furthermore, there are those who, neither admitting nor denying the idea of unity in all these paintings of Etruscan warriors, think it evident that the artist presented events which happened, not at Rome, but in Etruria—events which with our present knowledge, we are unable to determine.

We shall not delay in making vain and useless conjectures. We shall emphasize the fact that, in the painting referred to, characters are represented that are partly known also to Roman versions—namely, the two brothers Vibenna and Mastarna. The latter was identified, by some, with King Servius Tullius. In fact, the Roman annalists known to Varro spoke of Cælius Vibenna, a noble Etruscan leader who, on arriving at Rome, aided Romulus in his wars against the Sabine Titus Tatius.[2] It is not improbable that this Cæles Vibenna, the contemporary of Romulus, is identical with the Cæles whom Valerius Antias considered the leader of the Celeres—that is, of the knights elected for the first time by Romulus.[3] Verrius Flaccus, however, knew of writers who related that, on their arrival at Rome, the two brothers Cælius and Aulus Vibenna aided King Tarquinius Superbus.[4]

More precise details are furnished by Emperor Claudius. In his speech delivered in the senate, in favor of extending to the Gauls the rights of the curia, he says that Servius Tullius (according to the Roman annalists) was the son of the captive Ocrisia, but that, according to Etruscan writers, he was the faithful friend and companion of Cælius Vibenna. After a series of misfortunes he was supposed to have arrived at Rome with the remnants of the army of Cælius; and, having settled on the hill later known as the Cælian, to have named it in honor of his friend. He himself (the story continues) discarded his Etruscan name of Mastarna, and adopted that of Servius Tullius.[5] A mass of contradictory traditions was known to Tacitus, who affirms that the hill originally called Querquetulanus (from the trees covering it) was later named Cælius after a certain Cælius Vibenna, an Etruscan leader who settled upon the

SERVIUS TULLIUS

hill with the consent of Tarquinius Priscus, *or of some other king.* With these words, Tacitus states explicitly that the ancient authors disagreed on this question.[6]

To sum up, the perfect agreement in the names of the brothers Vibenna, the fact that Mastarna (in the painting from Volci) frees his friend Vibenna, and that Mastarna (or Servius Tullius) is called by Claudius the faithful friend of Cælius Vibenna,—furthermore, the circumstance that all the Roman versions agree in stating that there arrived upon the Cælian either Cælius or the remnants of his army under the leadership of Mastarna,—all these facts are, at first sight, in favor of the belief that there must be an historical nucleus to such narratives, and that this nucleus seems to be worthy of deep consideration. But whosoever would thus argue would give a proof of his superficiality. A careful analysis of all these elements proves, on the contrary, an entire lack of historical worth in these stories.

The first requisite for establishing an historical foundation is that there should be some chronological data. No time limits can be determined upon from the Roman versions, or from the painting. Verrius Flaccus and Emperor Claudius, it is true, affirmed that the brothers Vibenna arrived at Rome during the reign of the fourth king, Tarquinius Priscus. But Varro, an authority worthy of great consideration, affirmed that this event occurred in the times of Romulus.

This is not the place for insisting that, in the painting from Volci, there is represented a Tarquin of Rome; for, while some traditions stated that Lucumo of Tarquinii arrived at Rome in the reign of Ancus Marcius (whom he succeeded), others equally well accepted by the official Roman tradition made Lucumo (like Cæles) reach Rome in the times of Romulus.[7]

Does the painting from Volci, then, represent a Tarquinius of the era of the last three kings, or a Tarquinius of the time of Romulus? And, in case the former version should be accepted, what element is there, what fact, which authorizes us to prefer such version to the one accepted by Varro and by Dionysius of Halicarnassus? A very careful examination of the sources of Varro and of Verrius Flaccus leads, practically, to no results regarding the dating, and, consequently, the preference which should be given to one or to the other. A thorough study, on the contrary, of Roman annals leads to negative results as regards all that is affirmed in such discordant ways concerning the most ancient regal period and the first century of the Republic.

Nothing obliges us to give the preference to the Etruscan annals, which (as is well known) were not of more remote origin than the Roman annals. Even admitting the hypothesis that the painting from Volci is of the fourth century rather than of the third (to which, perhaps, it should be referred), conceding, too, that it is a faithful representation of a story accepted by an Etruscan annalist, we shall not have any ground for asserting that it represents an absolutely historical fact. Nothing excludes the possibility that it may be the repetition of a legendary tale more or less arbitrarily represented. And that the Etruscans had various traditions during the era in which lived the characters represented in the tomb painting is shown by a mirror from Etruscan Volsinii. Upon this are figured the two brothers Aulus and Cælius Vibenna, in the act of assailing the Latin Cacus.[8] This recalls the passage in the annalist Gellius, in which Cacus is placed in relation with the Tyrrhenian Tarchon.[9] Hence, the same persons are referred to the mythical age of Cacus, of Romulus and of Tarquinius. Similarly, the Etruscan who came to Rome, and who was known, at various times, as Tarchon, Lucumo, Lucumo of Tarquinii and Lucius Tarquinius, was made the contemporary of Æneas, of Romulus and of Ancus Marcius, and is respectively assigned to an age preceding the year 1000 B.C., to the eighth and to the sixth century.

This chronological identity is paralleled in other noteworthy particulars. The historian Tacitus says that, according to the different authors, Cælius Vibenna arrived at Rome in the reign either of Tarquinius Priscus *or of some other king*. He declares it a certain and undoubted fact that the Etruscan Cælius occupied the homonymous hill, and that the Etruscans guided by him settled in the regions adjacent to the Forum—the Vicus Tuscus deriving its name from the settlers.[10] A strong contradiction to the too positive affimations of Tacitus is to be found in the declarations of other authors. Verrius Flaccus knew of a version similar to that declaring that the Vicus Tuscus was named from the companions of Cælius Vibenna.[11] He seems, however, to relate an entirely different legend. According to this one, the famous Vicus derived its name from the Etruscans who passed through it in the time of Porsenna. Indeed, the sources known to Livy and to Dionysius of Halicarnassus stated that such event occurred after Aruns, son of Porsenna, had been killed in the siege of Aricia, when the Romans received the remnants of his army.[12]

We find this uncertainty and contradiction in all the notices relating to the Cælian Hill. Though some authors asserted that it had been occupied by the Etruscan Cælius, others said that only after his death had Mastarna (that is, Servius Tullius) established himself upon it.[13] The traditions known to Livy and to Dionysius agreed in affirming that the first occupant of the Cælian was Tullus Hostilius, who had there built his palace.[14] But whereas, according to Livy, the king had settled the Albans upon it, according to Dionysius it had long before been given over as a dwelling place to those Romans without a home. Finally, if we are to put faith in the sources of Cicero and of Strabo, the Cælian was first added to the city by the king who succeeded Ancus Marcius.[15]

Among the elements of this legend, one of the most characteristic is that of Mastarna. We see him, in the painting from Volci, in the act of liberating Cælius Vibenna; and Emperor Claudius, who related his constancy and true friendship for Cælius, added that, on arriving at Rome, he discarded his Etruscan name for the Roman one of Servius Tullius.[16] I do not think well of what has lately been conjectured in this regard—namely, that we have here a personal supposition of Claudius, who invented and established such an equation. I believe that Claudius here drew upon those authors who similarly stated that Lucumo of Tarquinii, upon coming to Rome, caused himself to be called Lucius Tarquinius. In like manner, it was said that Tanaquil (the latter's wife and an Etruscan) was identified with the person worshipped under the name of Gaia Cæcilia in the temple of Semo Sanctus or Dius Fidius. It is self-evident that the Latin divinity Cæcilia was the goddess of the hearth analogous to Cacus and to Caca (the ancient divinities of the Palatine), and that originally she had nothing in common with the Etruscan Tanaquil. It is also evident that the myth of the Etruscan Mastarna was arbitrarily fused with the strictly Latin one of Servius Tullius. It should cause no surprise that Mastarna is not mentioned in the secondary version to which Livy and Dionysius refer, since they omit recording several versions which, instead, are preserved by Vergil.[17]

From a linguistic point of view, it surely appears rather hazardous to contrast Macstarna with that Mezentius, King of the Cærites, whose name, perhaps, reappears in the Etruscan Mesapius. From the historical standpoint, however, Mezentius, the enemy of Tarchon and of Æneas, seems to be the prototype of Macstarna, the enemy of Tarquinius. Since the sources at our disposal do not permit us to trace further this important element of the legend, we must resume our examination of the remaining elements. We shall demonstrate that the ancient authors, in regard to the Etruscan supremacy in Latium, followed the same course that we shall find pursued in the formation of the Latin league and in the invasion of the Sabines.

Roman tradition speaks of an alliance with the Latins during the war of Romulus and Tatius, and of a war with the Albans and the subsequent removal of the population to Rome in the reign of Tullus Hostilius. This hegemony of Rome over the Latins is recorded both in the story of the foundation of the temple of Diana Aventinensis by Servius Tullius, and in that of the alliances established by the Tarquins. The alliance with the Latins reappears in the first years of the Republic—at the time of the victory over the Latins at Lake Regillus, as well as in the treaty of Spurius Cassius. It is mentioned, finally, on occasion of the renewal of the *fœdus* with Ardea in 443 B.C., and again after the historic victories of 340 B.C.

In all these stories there is merely a repetition of a series of events. Aside from what is referred to the regal period, the story of the battle of Lake Regillus is entirely mythical; and what is related concerning the *fœdus Cassianum* is more than doubtful. It may, indeed, be admitted that, towards the middle of the fifth century, there was a renewal of the ancient alliance with the Latins. But surely the statement is not worthy of faith that the Roman element preponderated over the Latin. In fact, only in 338 B.C., after the victories of Furius and of Mænius, and after the alliance with the Samnites of Capua, did Rome attain that eminent position which tradition would assign either to the time of Spurius Cassius, 493 B.C., or, still worse, to the age of the kings.[18]

Similar observations are of avail regarding the relations

SERVIUS TULLIUS

with the Sabines. Roman tradition, it is true, contains some stories meriting belief. From these it appears that the Sabine population which descended from the central plateau of the Peninsula (the modern Abruzzi) invaded and conquered Latium. Instead of admitting, however, that this invasion occurred in the beginning of the fifth century, it spoke of the aborigines who were supposed to have migrated in the time of the mythical Pelasgians. The Sabine element is spoken of in the era of Titus Tatius and of Numa, again about two centuries later (in regard to the admission of Appius Claudius and his five thousand clients, 505 B.C.), in the occupation of the Capitolium in 460 by the Sabine Appius Herdonius, and, finally, in the last Sabine wars, which were won in 449 B.C.

When all these stories are submitted to a searching examination it will be found that the Sabine invasions of the period of the Pelasgians and of Numa are to be relegated into the creations of a later historiography, but that a great invasion of the Sabines towards the middle of the fifth century must be conceded as historic.[19] With this historic invasion must be connected the arrival of Appius Claudius and the pretended victories over the Sabines.

Roman tradition, though regretfully and indirectly, nevertheless does admit the victory of Porsenna and the supremacy of the Etruscans. But, rather than admitting that the Etruscans were, for a longer or shorter time, masters of Latium, and that their dominion ended only at the intervention of the Sabines, it speaks of a war by Æneas and the Prisci Latini against the Etruscan Mezentius, King of Cære. In this war Æneas is aided by the Etruscan Tarchon and, afterwards, by the latter's son, Ascanius. The arrival of the Etruscans is again mentioned in the time of Lucumo, who hurried from Etruria to the aid of Romulus, or in the time of that other Lucumo who came to Rome from Tarquinii in the reign of Ancus Marcius. The presence of the Etruscans and the Sabines, finally, is to be recognized in the story of the war against Porsenna, followed by the arrival of Appius Claudius and his five thousand clients.

In fact, the same events are repeated several times, and are referred to different ages. The Etruscan Tarchon, the enemy of Mezentius and ally of Æneas, is but the reproduction of that Lucumo who came from Tarquinii. Likewise, Mezentius is, in certain respects, an anticipation of Porsenna. Mezentius takes part in the war in which figure the towns of Ardea and of Lavinium, retiring only after the death of his son, who was killed in battle against Ascanius, King of Alba. He recognizes the Tiber as the boundary between Latium and the Tyrrhenians. In the same manner, Porsenna makes peace and recognizes the confines only a short time before the death of his son, who dies battling against the Aricini.[20]

The chief aim of Roman tradition is to demonstrate that Rome, from its very beginnings, was mistress of Latium, and that, as early as the regal period, it became the centre of the Latin confederation. Roman tradition insists that the Sabines did not conquer Rome, but were admitted by a benevolent concession. It does not recognize an actual domination of the Etruscans, but affirms that these were hospitably received at Rome in the times of Tarquinius Priscus, or that, on occasion of the followers of Ancus, they were settled in the Vicus Tuscus. The victory of Porsenna (explicitly accepted by the sources of Tacitus and of Pliny)[21] is veiled over and rendered well-nigh irrecognizable by the stories of Roman heroism woven round it, and by the invention of a treaty in which the rôle of the conqueror is assigned to the conquered. The official tradition does not reconcile itself to admitting that the true beginning of the political history of the nation dates in the beginning of the fifth century, and that there were various breaks in the national existence, which were determined by conquests. It assumes, therefore, that the development of the State was merely modified by the influx of foreign elements that were spontaneously welcomed. In order, finally, to attain to a great antiquity, the same events were repeated again and again, thus reaching back into the mythical period, giving free scope to the formation of legends, and proceeding beyond the control of history and of chronology.

Etruscan supremacy in Latium and Campania is one of the most certain facts in the early history of Italy. There are lacking archæological data which would place such supremacy earlier than the sixth or the fifth century. We cannot derive from Roman tradition any chronological elements to serve this purpose. Roman annals were utterly unfit to fix with chronological precision relations with foreign peoples. Consequently, though slightly touching upon the relations with Sicily, they confused Dionysius, the

SERVIUS TULLIUS

tyrant, with Hiero of Syracuse.[22] Furthermore, it dated in 431 B.C. military operations of the Carthaginians in Sicily that are to be referred to the year 480 B.C. or to 409 B.C.[23] In order to determine the year in which the Etruscans attained the supremacy over Latium, and the year in which they lost, not only that, but even their power over Rome, it is far more profitable to examine the information furnished by the history of the more civilized peoples of those times.

The Etruscan expedition against Cumæ (dated by the Greek annalists towards the years 524, 504 and 474) is certainly worthy of consideration. In addition, there is no reason to doubt that towards 438 B.C. (according to Livy, c. 424 B.C.) the Sabines became masters of Capua, wresting it from the Etruscans, who had held it for about half a century. All the evidence is in favor of the belief that, as the result of a practically synchronous movement, the Sabelli became masters of Latium in those same decades. We are warranted in assuming that the years 449 B.C. (in which tradition dated the last Sabine War) and 443 B.C. (in which was renewed the *fœdus* with Ardea, the early capital of the ancient Latin confederation) represent the time limits within which the Etruscans were expelled. Tradition supposed that the Etruscans penetrated into Rome peacefully, and with the consent of the nation, as was assumed in the case of the Sabines also. Tarquinius Priscus, therefore, instead of being a conqueror, was welcomed as one who had migrated spontaneously, even as Attus Clausus. Roman tradition attributed the period from 616 to about 509 B.C. to the supremacy of the Etruscans. That this chronology has no claims to exactness appears from the fact that the two reigns of the Tarquins are a repetition of but one event. It results, too, from the chronological contradictions in these two reigns into which the earliest annalists fell (among whom Fabius Pictor), thus authorizing the rectification of Calpurnius Piso.[24] It clearly results, finally, from the fact that Servius Tullius is a character of Latin stamp, artificially inserted into the series of Etruscan rulers.

I have had occasion to set forth elsewhere what reasons compel us to admit that Lucius Tarquinius Priscus, or better, Lucumo of Tarquinii, is one and the same person with him who reappears under the name of Lucius Tarquinius Superbus. In mythology this same person is known under the title of Tarchon, the ally of Æneas, or of Tarchetios, King of Alba, or, finally, of Tarutius, the lover of the fair Acca Larentia. Here it will suffice to recall that the temple of Jupiter Optimus Maximus, or better, of Jupiter Tarpeius (supposed to have been founded by the Tarquins), was not in existence till the middle of the fourth century—that is, till after the Gallic fire. The cult of Jupiter Tarpeius was ascribed to the Tarquins as a consequence of the fusion of two such closely related names as Tarquinius and Tarpeius. These names, in their turn, correspond to those of the Vestal Tarquinia (of the time of the Tarquins), and of the maid Tarpeia, the divinity of the hill.[25]

The more ancient versions do not connect the works of the Tarquins on the Velia with those on the hills of the Septimontium. Indeed, if it were the case to speak of a Capitolium in this respect, we should think of the one on the Quirinal, and not of that on the Capitoline.[26] Of the remaining improvements ascribed to the Tarquins, the Circus Maximus and the *tabernæ* of the Forum are, by more reliable versions, assigned to the year 194 B.C.[27] The draining of the Forum and the building of the Cloaca Maxima belong to the last centuries of the Republic and not to the time of the Tarquins.[28] Similarly, only in the years following 339 B.C. did there arise that powerful political bond which brought Latium to the worship of Jupiter Capitolinus—by tradition (it will be remembered) assigned to the Tarquins.[29] Furthermore, the extent of the external wars waged by these princes is in accordance, not with the sixth and fifth centuries B.C., but rather with the fourth century. In short, there is neither an internal nor an external event which can be referred to the reigns of the two Tarquins and which, at the same time, is worthy of being reputed historic. I am strongly inclined to believe that the Tarquins, who are so closely connected with the conquest of Ardea, are one and the same thing with the mythical Tarchon, who aided Æneas in the war against the Ardeates.

If a future discovery should some day reveal the presence, at Rome, of an authentic prince named Tarquinius, there would result merely a confirmation of the chronological errors of Roman tradition in regard to the reign of the two Tarquins. Not the slightest corroboration could be obtained of the fantastic legends referring to these princes and to the prophetic Tanaquil. The strictly legendary character of these traditions results, too, from what the ancients have told us regarding Servius Tullius, whom Tanaquil reared in the palace, who was raised to the throne by her, and who later became the son-in-law of the first Tarquinius.

In the history of Servius Tullius there are elements of a fantastic character,—such as his birth due to the domestic Lar or to Vulcan, and his being constantly favored by the goddess Fortuna. There are, too, many legal and constitutional questions, which have been discussed and accepted in a greater or lesser degree by the most authoritative students of the history of Roman law. Let us, therefore, turn to the study of what we must designate as the most tangible part of the tale.

It was said that Servius published fifty laws upon contracts, that he had relieved the people of its debts and rescued it from usury.[30] Other versions, however, affirmed that the Decemvirs were the first to publish the laws, and the legislation attributed to them contained provisions that were, at times, ascribed to the kings. Those best acquainted with Roman traditions maintained that the laws were never written before the time of the Decemvirate,—an affirmation which entirely agrees with the conditions of a people not far advanced in civilization, and which entrusted the care of its laws to the memory of its priests and its magistrates.[31] The strongest proof of the falsity of the story regarding the laws of Servius (which are supposed to have abolished the *nexum*) is offered by the Roman authors themselves. They asserted that the *nexum* was abolished for the first time only in the times of the dictator Pœtelius. This brings us to the end of the fourth century B.C.[32] The liberal laws of Servius, and his pretended defence of the law, are in complete harmony with the character of a prince who was said to have been born of a handmaid, and whom it was proposed to contrast with Solon and with Cleisthenes.

There existed, in this story, a tendency to establish a chronological parallel to the history of Athens. This is evident from the annalists themselves, who affirm that Servius, in founding the temple of Diana Aventinensis as the centre of the Latin confederation, had drawn his inspiration from similar political institutions of the Ionian Greeks and of the Doric Pentapolis.[33] The ancient authors, moreover, declared that Servius had created the census. But recognized tradition denied both this story and those referring to every taking of the Roman census in times later than those of Servius. It persistently affirmed that the institution of the census arose for the first time in 444 B.C., or even in 433 B.C.[34] As regards the political constitution of Servius, known as the *comitia centuriata*, I deem it hardly necessary to recall the masterly observations of Bœckh, of Schwegler and of Mommsen. The last has pointed out that Fabius Pictor assigned to the times of Servius the political constitution of his own days.[35] It is no wonder, then, that Fabius Pictor and other annalists should have made Servius the author of the division of the Romans into the twenty-six, thirty-one and even thirty-five tribes. The number of twenty-six tribes was not attained till after the year 358,—that is, after the conquest of the Volscian territory and of southern Etruria, which tradition assumes as already won by the Etruscan kings, Tarquinius and Servius.

Servius Tullius, also, was supposed to have divided the city into the four urban tribes. From indications for the year 304 B.C. it can be deduced that only in that year (when Gnæus Fiavius published the laws,—the censorship of Q. Fabius and P. Decius) were the four urban tribes formed, to which were ascribed the descendants of freedmen.[36] Again, legend says that Servius laid the foundations of the temple of Diana Aventinensis, with the purpose of compelling the Latins to acknowledge the supremacy of Rome. But such supremacy was not attained till a far later period, and until 340-338 B.C. the Romans continued to participate in the league which gathered round the spring of the goddess Ferentina.[37] Moreover, the cult of Diana Aventinensis (as we shall see shortly) was closely connected with that of Diana Aricina. The Aricini, according to the official Roman tradition, ceded their cults to the Romans only towards 338 B.C.[38] If we should wish to go to a still greater antiquity in Roman tradition, in search of an event worthy of historical belief, we should find no other date than 443 B.C. In that year the Romans intervened in the affairs of Aricia and of Ardea, and seized territory which later, perhaps, formed part of the tribe *Scaptia*. This tribe, however, was formed only in the year 332 B.C.[39]

It is likewise stated that Servius Tullius, after having conquered the Etruscans, erected a temple to Fortuna on the right bank of the Tiber, and a second one to Mater Matuta

REMAINS OF WALLS ATTRIBUTED TO SERVIUS TULLIUS

in the Forum Boarium. From other accounts, however, we gather that the latter was erected only in the time of Furius Camillus, and the former by the consul Carvilius in even later times.[40] Servius, then, was placed in close relation with the temple of Fortuna and with the Forum adjacent to the temple of Mater Matuta, because certain traditions (which we shall examine more minutely) considered him the special lover of Fortuna. We shall not proceed further in these comparisons. We shall merely add that the version originally set forth by Greek annalists (according to which Servius Tullius was the first to coin money) is in opposition to all that we know of numismatics. For, not only actual and real copper money, but even the *as signatum* is assigned by numismatists to the fourth century, thus proving beyond doubt the artistic elaboration of this legend.[41]

The same is true of the Servian wall, or better, of the *agger* with which he was supposed to have strengthened Rome. A series of arguments (due especially to the acute discernment of Richter) have now established that such construction belongs, not to the mythical age of the kings, but to the fourth century B.C. I myself have already made clear that these walls, as well as the foundations of the Capitolium, are in harmony with the growth of Rome subsequent to the Gallic fire.[42] In short, there is not a single institution or event attributed to Servius which is not rather to be assigned to a much later age, or which is anterior to the fourth century B.C.

In this century the Greeks began to write the first narratives of Roman history,—narratives which preceded by nearly a century the efforts of the earliest Roman annalists. The deeds of Servius Tullius, therefore, were narrated at a time when the Roman plebeians had already won full independence and complete equality in the political field. At the same time, they began to encroach upon that patriciate which had, for so long a period, denied them any legal and political recognition whatsoever. Hence Servius, the son of a handmaid and born in slavery, became considered the natural author of the constitution and the census which supplanted the ancient patrician *curiæ*. He was, furthermore, placed in relation with all the cults plebeian in character, and so was considered the author of the Compitalia. As a plebeian king, he was believed to have had his palace on the Cælian, where those plebeians were settled who were destitute of fixed habitations. According to others, he lived on the Esquiline, the plebeian and suburban quarter which had been added to complete the circuit of the Palatine and the Velia. The authors of this artificial and false constitutional history not only attributed to Servius Tullius the enlarging of the city by these plebeian hills, but also explicitly declared that he had thought of making the Roman people free. The first consuls of the Republic were, consequently, supposed to have been elected according to memoranda left by Servius Tullius.[43]

As is now evident, all that is narrated in regard to the civil, the military and the constitutional activities of Servius Tullius forms a web of falsifications which must be discarded. To understand the real meaning of this king, and the elements which constituted his real personality, we must turn to the examination, not so much of· the imaginary history of the Roman constitution (which we customarily consider the object of accurate academic study), but rather of the ancient religious patrimony of the Romans and of the Prisci Latini.

In the territory of ancient Aricia, near the shore of the beautiful lake of Nemi, there was a famous sanctuary of Diana. This, according to archæological data and to the excavations there instituted, was erected in the fourth century B.C. The cult itself of this goddess, however, was a very ancient one, as well as that of the nymph Egeria,— that is, of a fountain flowing close by. The more ancient temple was supposed to have been erected by a certain Egerius, whom different authors described as a native of Tusculum or of Aricia. On account of the great similarity of his name with that of the goddess Egeria, the thought arises that he may have represented the masculine aspect of that same divinity. Indeed, it is well known that the ancient Latin priests, as well as those of other peoples, conceived of both the masculine and the feminine natures of the enchoric divinities, whom they invoked with the formula *sive mas sive femina.*

Another divinity was still more intimately connected with Diana Nemorensis,—namely the *Nemus*, that is, the grove of Aricia. Just as the Peloponnesian Artemis was enamored of Endymion, King of Elis, so Diana Aricina loved Virbius, from whom a street was named which led to the temple of the goddess. Virbius was a native Latin god. Owing to

NEMI AND THE LACUS NEMORENSIS

the extreme efficacy of Hellenism, Diana was soon identified with the Greek Artemis, and so the river and solar god Virbius was identified with Hippolytus, the son of Theseus and the beloved of Phædra. The cult of Aricia was, by some, considered as an offshoot of that of Epidaurus. For, it was affirmed that Virbius, after having been brought back to life, betook himself whither Æsculapius had assured him a tranquil existence. Others considered this cult to have sprung from that at Tauris, transported thence by Orestes also to Tauranium, near the Greek Rhegium. The fact that horses were not permitted to approach the grove of Aricia was placed in relation with the very name Hippolytus, and, too, with the *hippoi* or horses who had dragged and killed the Greek hero. The barbarous custom, according to which the priest of Diana Nemorensis always went about fully armed, for fear of being slain by his successor, suggested the connection with the cult of the Scythian Artemis.

The Aricini had very ancient relations with Magna Græcia and with the inhabitants of the Chalcidian Rhegium. Therefore they quickly accepted this faith, the more so because they believed that they had in their possession the bones of Orestes, brother of Iphigenia, who in turn, was the well-known priestess of Diana. Indeed, it was said that Orestes himself had introduced this cult in Aricia. This circumstance, added to the torch which adorned the statue of Diana Aricina, favors a belief in the direct derivation of the cult from Diana Phacelitis (the torch-bearer), worshipped by the Greeks of Rhegium and of Messana. Moreover, it was related that Virbius, on returning to life, assumed the appearance of an old man, and, though remaining unknown to others, was accorded an ignoble, yet immortal, existence near his beloved Diana.[44]

Virbius (according to the declarations of the ancients) was the name of a river.[45] Other texts inform us that Virbius was the Sun.[46] The two statements, rather than being mutually exclusive, are supplementary to each other,—for, the water which descends from the skies is transformed into fountains and rivers. Janus is, at one and the same time, the god of the Sun and of the waters; he is the lover of the fountains Camese and Juturna, and of the spring Venilia,— that is, of the nymph which represented the currents of the springs. Likewise, just as Hephaistos, among the Greeks was placed in relation with the ocean, so Vulcan, at Rome, was placed in close connection with the Tiber. Again, the mention of Egerius as founder of the temple of Diana, and, in even greater degree, certain remains found in the area of the temple, prove that the cult of the waters was closely connected with that of Diana Aricina also.[47] On the whole, it seems a probable supposition that the cult of Virbius and of Diana was related with the cult of the nocturnal light, and that it represents one of the many forms of popular and sacerdotal fancies regarding the relations between the Sun, and the Moon which illuminates the woods with its nocturnal light.

The most characteristic touch of the cult was, however, that one relating to its priest. As also in other places, he was considered an emanation and a perpetuation of the god himself. The god was considered a divinity which had to lead an ignoble life, and his priest had to be an escaped slave who, with weapons in hand for fear of being slain, continually wandered through the woods. Whosoever killed him became his successor, and inherited the name of *rex nemorensis*—that is, the king of the woods.[48] The general metamorphosis of the cult, and the softening of sentiments, brought it about that, to the writers of the end of the Republic, this cult already seemed strange. There was, however, nothing strange in such cult. It recalls the conditions obtaining in the earliest Latin civilization, reminding us of the roughness and the brutality of the Roman Lupercalia, and of the ferocity of the Luperci, or, better still, of the Hirpini on Mount Soracte. These latter, it will be remembered, in imitation of their totem, the wolf, lived entirely by rapine.[49]

Thus the priest of the *Nemus Aricinum*, as well as the god, is himself called *rex*. This brings to mind the asylum which Romulus established on the Capitoline Hill, and that other asylum on the Cælian where Tullus Hostilius or Servius Tullius received bandits and fugitives. The fact that the legend of the very humble origins of Rome was at no time rejected by the national tradition, and was only partly modified and softened in later ages, is in perfect harmony with this primitive phase of Latin civilization. Moreover, even to-day in certain regions of southern Italy (where forms of primitive social life still survive) the brigand inspires no averse feelings in the farmer, who does not avoid his society. The bandit is more often the subject of admira-

SERVIUS TULLIUS

tion than of fear in the mountain fastnesses of Calabria, Corsica and of Sardinia. Perhaps, too, one may note that, notwithstanding so many centuries of civilization and the softening of customs, the country round about Nemi and Genzano even to-day recall at times the ferocity of the ancient inhabitants of the Alban hills. Another series of facts illustrates, in still greater degree, the analogies, indeed the identity, of the cult of the lake at Aricia with that of Diana on the Aventine. The Aventine, being the region sacred to slaves and to fugitives of all the Latin nations, was always excluded from the *pomerium*. On this hill, not only did the slaves and fugitives find refuge (as for instance in the time of the Gracchi), but here, as well as on the Mons Sacer, was the tribunate of the plebs supposed to have been established. And the plebs, in fact, were originally composed of fugitive slaves and of those without masters.

These analogies extend, also, to the representatives of the cult in the two temples,—the one at Rome, the other at Aricia. The priest at Aricia was a *servus rex,* and Servius Tullius, sixth king of Rome, was likewise the son of a slave woman. The *servus rex* of Aricia had to be a fugitive slave and was obliged to flee continually for fear of assassination by the aspirant to his office. He was, indeed, the representative and the emanation of that Virbius represented as an aged man, who, under the name Hippolytus, had been trampled upon by the chariot-horses. Similarly, the old Servius Tullius in vain endeavored to flee in a chariot, and was trampled upon in the Clivus Orbius (or Urbius), where the temple of Diana was situated.[50] Indeed, the Clivus Virbius of Aricia was the street inhabited by beggars, and leading to the temple of Diana. Even to-day, in the popular speech of Italy, the Sun is called the father of the poor.

There are other points of contact still more remarkable. It is expressly said that Virbius was the Sun and the lover of Diana Aricina. This goddess was worshipped on the Ides of August,—in other words, in that month which the ancients gratefully placed under the guardianship (*tutela*) of Vulcan.[51] The ancients also said that Servius Tullius was the son of Vulcan, or of the Sun. To him were sacred the Nones of each month, and his birth was said to have occurred towards the Ides of August. This day, a festal day of the *servi* (slaves), was, too, considered the day on which King Servius Tullius dedicated the temple of Diana

L

on the Aventine. Though Virbius was the lover of Diana, Servius Tullius was beloved by Fortuna. In the sacred narratives officially accepted by the Roman priesthood, it was stated that Fortuna secretly visited Servius by night, entering by the door called Fenesta.[53] It is, therefore, easily understood how the various temples of Fortuna, and particularly that one in the Forum Boarium, were said to have been consecrated by Servius. The divinity worshipped in this temple seems to have been identified with Pudicitia Plebeia, a fact recalling the cult of Diana, which also at Aricia assumed special forms. So true is it, that she was there called Vesta, which reminds us of the Lares discovered in the temple of the goddess, and also of the fact that Servius was considered the son of the domestic Lar, or else of Vulcan.[54]

At any rate, it is certain that chaste Fortuna, who was accustomed to pay her visits by night and veiled, is strongly reminiscent of Diana approaching the sleeping Endymion. To this must be added the fact that the Dianium, which was situated near the vicus Urbius (the later called *sceleratus*) and which was inhabited by Servius Tullius, does not seem to differ from the temple and the sanctuary of Fortuna, or of Pudicitia Plebeia, who assisted Servius in his dying moments.[55] The bones of Orestes (which were transported from Aricia) were not buried in the Dianium on the Aventine, but beneath the temple of Saturn in the Forum.[56] The thought naturally arises that there may have been more or less similar cults in the different Latin cities, and that the two temples of Diana (at Rome and at Aricia) were not closely related to each other. Nevertheless, it must be remarked that Roman tradition is consistent in stating that the Aventine was inhabited by the Prisci Latini, and that the temple of Diana Aventinensis was erected by the entire Latin confederation.[57]

The dependence, finally, of the temple of Diana Aventinensis and of the myth of Servius Tullius upon that of Diana Aricina is clear. It results from the circumstance that, in a case of incest, Emperor Claudius believed it opportune to recall to vigor certain ancient laws of the Romans, and ordered that expiations be made according to the rite established by Servius Tullius for the grove of Diana Aricina.[58] The legend of Servius Tullius was closely related to the story of the incestuous love of his daughter

ARICIA AND THE LACUS TURNI

Tullia with the young Tarquinius. Similarly, the Greek story spoke of the love of the stepmother Phædra for Hippolytus, who later was brought back to life under the name and the figure of the aged Virbius. It is fully comprehensible, then, why the antiquarian Emperor Claudius should wish to reënforce laws attributed by the sacred annals to the sixth king of Rome.

From what has thus far been said we may conclude that religious tradition was not in error in affirming that the temple of Diana on the Aventine had relations with the Latins. It results that the legends referring to *Servius rex* are but the cults and the myths of the lake at Aricia, which, in 338 B.C., yielded its *sacra* to Rome. The circumstance that the remains of Orestes, when transported from Aricia, were not buried on the Aventine, but in the Forum, is to be explained by the fact that the officially recognized founder of the temple of Diana Aricina was not the Greek Orestes, but the Arician Egerius.[59] Hence, just as the myth of Egerius was inserted into the story of the deeds of Tarquinius, so the nymph Egeria (the goddess of the fountain near the temple of the Arician lakes) was united at Rome with the Ardeo-Arician Numa, and localized in the valley of the Camenæ along the Cælian and the Aventine.[60]

This localization of the cults connected with the grove and the lake of Aricia compels us to acknowledge as Latin and as Arician the legend of Servius Tullius. Instead of being the sixth *rex* of Rome, he was, originally, the *rex servus*, the priest of the cult of Diana Aricina transferred to the Aventine. He was the priest of the protecting goddess of fugitive slaves. Dionysius affirms that till his time there was preserved, in the temple of Diana Aventinensis, an inscription written in archaic Greek characters, stating the law of the temple and commemorating the names of the Latin peoples. It is, then, natural to believe in the change and in the erroneous interpretation of the *servus rex* for *Servius rex*.[61] By an analogous error of interpretation, the ancients thought to have in their possession the sepulchral stele of the mythical Hostus Hostilius, the ancestor of King Tullus Hostilius, and also the inscription written in archaic letters with which Romulus himself was supposed to have recorded his deeds.[62]

When the plebs, whose rallying centres were the temples of Diana on the Aventine and of Ceres (situated at the foot of the same hill), began to narrate the deeds of its members, it aimed at producing a history almost, if not quite, as ancient as that of the patricians. If Romulus had been the founder of the State upon the Palatine (by gathering, too, slaves and fugitives who in the end became patricians), Servius, on the other hand, had founded the community of plebeians on the Aventine and on the Cælian. The story of the cult of Diana, of Virbius, and of his priest, offered material for a pseudo-history. The religious legends referring to the cult of Ceres formed the basis of the story of the agrarian legislation. As the result of such a process, all the rites of the cult of Diana became metamorphosed into pragmatic and constitutional history.

On the ceremonies of the 24th of February (the *Regifugium*), the *rex sacrorum,* after completing his sacrifice, fled from the Forum. It is doubtful whether this reflects a ceremony connected with the legend of Servius Tullius rather than with that of Romulus or of some other king. Some ancient writers explained the ceremony with the flight of the Tarquins. Others affirmed that the Tarquins did not flee from the city, but merely went into exile. We would be led to assign such rites to Servius on account of the similar story of his flight from the Forum, when threatened with death by his son-in-law Tarquinius. This story reappears in a slightly different form in the case of a Tullius who was created consul in 500 B.C.

It is hard to admit that among the ceremonies performed by the *rex sacrificulus* there were some of plebeian character. On the other hand, we must remember that according to the Romans' conception of their constitution, the king, even if he had been a plebeian, became patrician by the mere process of his having been made king. The story of Tarquinius Priscus is a very clear example, and the same is true of the emperors in later ages. The 24th of February (on which day the above rites were performed) marked the end of the year in the most ancient solar calendar of the Romans. It is natural, then, that also Romulus should have been slain in the Forum on this day.[63] It is to be noted, moreover, that on the same day fell the feast of the Poplifugium, a feast similar to the Regifugium. The former, however, was explained either by the death of Romulus, by the invasion of the Gauls, or by that of the Fidenates.[64] The fact that the Poplifugium was placed in relation both with the patrician Romulus and with the slave maid-servants in the legend of Tutela, teaches us that the Regifugium, by some connected with the Tarquins, may also be related to Servius Tullius.

Clear, too, are other elements of the legend which have been transferred to history. The goddess Fortuna who, entering by the door Fenesta, secretly visited her lover Servius, was changed into the Etruscan Tanaquil, who from the *fenestra* (window) presents Servius to the people as the successor of the dying Tarquinius. Servius, finally, who, in origin and in substance, was a legendary character, was chronologically inserted into the series of Roman kings. And, whereas the most ancient annalists (as Dionysius affirms) related that Servius was miraculously sprung from the domestic Lar (the protecting god of slaves) and from a humble slave woman, later tradition presents him as the son of the king of a Latin city, and of a princess who gave him birth in the palace of the Etruscan Tanaquil.[65] Servius was the personification of all the reforms obtained through the revolution of the plebs. It was therefore natural that he should have been considered as one of the later kings. Since tradition (at bottom affirming the truth) stated that the end of the monarchy coincided with the expulsion of the Etruscans, Servius was made to succeed the reign of the Etruscan Tarquinius. The latter's wife, Tanaquil, was changed into the goddess Fortuna, or Gaia Cæcilia; and the Latin Servius Tullius was identified with the Etruscan Mastarna.

To sum up, then, we have seen that all that refers to the political and the constitutional activities of Servius Tullius is a web of falsifications; and that what pertains to his relations with the Etruscan domination is utterly unworthy of faith. The two Tarquins, or better, King Tarquinius, is a misty figure chosen to represent in a more or less exact manner the actual domination of the Etruscans over Latium. Servius is a Latin conception, and belongs to a solar cult and to that group of legends with which are to be connected, not only Virbius of Aricia and Hippolytus, but also Pelops and Hippodamia. We may, perhaps, better understand the meaning of this myth and its being localized at Rome by making certain other considerations. The valley situated between the Cælian, the Esquiline, the Velia and the Palatine was originally the *lacus fagutalis*.

Near this *lacus* and on the border of the Esquiline lived both Servius Tullius and Tarquinius Superbus. Near this same lake there were, on the side towards the Velia, the *Dianium* and the *vicus Orbius,* near which Servius was supposed to have been slain. It is, therefore, natural to suppose that the cults of the Arician lake were localized at Rome in a region quite analogous to their former homes, and similarly dedicated to the worship of the Sun and Moon.[66]

We do not marvel that a solar and river divinity should have been made king of Rome. Romulus, Tullius, Numa and Ancus Marcius were all solar deities. We find the same process operating not only in classical times, but also in the beginning of the Middle Ages. We find it in the case of Helen (the moon), queen of Sparta, and of Phalanthus (the sea), founder of Tarentum, and of Vodan, king of the Germans. It is worthy of note that Servius Tullius and the remaining Roman kings do not belong to the most ancient list of the hills of the Septimontium. The original list of kings was related to the eponymous divinities of the seven hills—divinities which, at the same time, represented the forces which produced vegetation, life and human beings. Jupiter Fagutalis, Ruminus and Viminalis, the god inhabiting the fig-tree and osiers were, surely, the most ancient gods and kings of the Romans. In the earliest lists there figure a king Palatinus and a king Aventinus. The names of the kings who were later received into the official records are in perfect harmony with the development of the city, due to the foreign elements which superimposed themselves upon the more ancient and indigenous ones. Tradition, though full of imaginary names and circumstances to which it endeavors to give the character of authentic history, nevertheless with reason affirms that the Cælian, the Aventine and the Capitoline, as well as the Oppian and the Cispian, were settled by foreign elements from the Alban Hills, by the Prisci Latini, by the Sabines and the inhabitants of Tusculum and of Anagnia. The name of the Esquiline, indeed, contrasts these foreigners with the natives.

The myth of Servius Tullius serves to mark the intervention of the Latin element, which, having penetrated into Rome as a conquered and captive force, later gave life to the plebs. The latter, by continual struggles with the

THE MONS VELIA

patricians, in the end became masters of the Latin State. At the same time the legend reveals to us the conditions of the earliest civilization of the Prisci Latini. From the slopes of the Alban Hills, however, there did not come to Rome only that cult which was to give origin to the legend of Servius Tullius, the founder of the plebeian history and of the Compitalia (the feast of the street Lares), and, finally, of the constitution which placed the consuls at the head of the State. From that soil, so rich in human energies, where flowers and forests grow in such wild beauty, there came to Rome also the legend of Juturna, and those of Numa, of Egeria and of Coriolanus. From that same region, too, in which the hardiness of its people is found together with the most odorous flowers of poetry, there was transported to Rome the beautiful episode of the fair and chaste maiden who, with her blood, was destined to assure liberty to the Romans.

CHAPTER VIII

THE LEGENDS OF THE HORATII AND THE CULT OF VULCAN

FEW families have furnished so much material for Roman legend as the Horatian *gens;* nevertheless, of few families have such scanty historic traces remained. If we scan the Fasti, which, according to the generally accepted opinion, contain the most authentic records of the Roman people, we shall find mention of only four consuls of this family, for the years 509-507 B.C., 477, 457, and 449 B.C. These are followed by three *tribuni militum consulari potestate* in 425, 386 and 378 B.C.; but it is vain to endeavor to discover traces of this famous family among the historic deeds of the Romans. If we examine the documents relating to the chronology of these years, we shall not be surprised to find that the Horatian tribunes of 425, 386 and 378 B.C. do not appear in the chronological list of Diodorus of Sicily. Beginning with Niebuhr and with Mommsen, all have recognized that the Fasti of Diodorus are, in many cases, far more reliable than those of Livy and of Dionysius. For the year 425 B.C. Diodorus gives three tribunes instead of six, and four instead of six for the years 386 and 378 B.C. We would decide, then, that the three Horatian military tribunes are spurious, adding that for the year 386 B.C. Diodorus does not recognize even a Valerian tribune— that is, a member of the family which was always united with the Horatii.[1]

An Horatius and a Valerius appear as consuls in 449 B.C., the year in which the Decemvirate was abolished, and in which the celebrated Horatio-Valerian laws were passed. But the passing of these laws was variously assigned by the annalists to the reign of Tullus Hostilius, to 339 B.C., and even to 300 B.C. In 457 B.C., when an Horatius was consul, there is mentioned the creation of ten tribunes; but other versions affirm that the ten tribunes were elected for the first time in the consulship of the better known Horatius of 449 B.C. A third Horatius was consul in 477 B.C., when he succeeded in defending Rome against the attacks of Etruscans advancing from the Janiculum. But it is a strange fact that the events of 477 B.C. are a mere duplicate of those of 480 B.C. Moreover, the deeds attributed to the Horatius who was consul in 477 B.C. have a strange similarity to those performed but a few years earlier by the more famous Horatius Cocles, against Etruscans coming (in this case also) from the Janiculum.

There remains the most ancient Horatian consul, Pulvillus, who in 509 and again in 507 is made the colleague of M. Valerius Publicola. It is, however, to be remarked at once that Livy ignores the existence of the second consulship, the Varronian year 507 not occurring in his Fasti at all. This is not surprising. We must remember that, according to other chronological computations, the year 507 is the first year of the Republic—the year in which Horatius was supposed to have dedicated the temple of Jupiter Maximus Capitolinus. I omit dwelling on the fact that such dedication was attributed to his colleague of this year, Valerius Publicola, and that it is regularly repeated for the Valerian and the Horatian consuls of 449 B.C. I shall affirm, instead, that nothing is so false as the pretended dedication of the Temple of Jupiter Capitolinus during the first years of the Republic. Polybius, indeed, states that Brutus and Horatius were consuls in the first year of the Republic, the year of the first treaty (he adds) between Rome and Carthage. But I unhesitatingly agree with Mommsen, who was the first to discover the falsity of this story. The first treaty between Rome and Carthage is to be assigned to about the year 348 B.C., in which it is recorded by both Livy and Diodorus. The error of Polybius must be connected with the fact that other Fasti entirely ignored the consulship of Horatius and Brutus in the first year of the Republic.

According to a well-known story of the Roman annals, Horatius Pulvillus was supposed to have dedicated the temple of Jupiter Capitolinus notwithstanding that in that very moment the death of his son had been announced to him. In this way he frustrated the hopes of his colleague, Valerius Publicola, who had himself aspired to the great honor of dedicating the principal temple of the Roman nation. That the story is a fruit of the imagination is proved absolutely by what I have set forth elsewhere.[2] It will be sufficient for me to show briefly that the temple of Jupiter Capitolinus was not dedicated in the first year of the Republic.

The tradition which was most widely diffused simply endeavored to make the origin of the nation's principal temple and the first treaty with Carthage coincide with the first year of the Republic. But this treaty was made only towards the year 348 B.C. Furthermore, it was only some decades after 386, and perhaps not earlier than 338 B.C., that the temple of Jupiter became the chief Roman sanctuary. Tradition relates that the erection of the temple of Jupiter was conceived by the Tarquins, who built the substructions after the capture of Suessa Pometia. In the earliest treaty between Rome and Carthage there is mention of the temple and cult, not of Jupiter Capitolinus, but of Jupiter Lapis—that is, of Jupiter Terminus. This god (as we learn from Cato) was expressly exaugurated to give place to Jupiter Capitolinus. When, in about 426 B.C., Cossus killed the king of the Veientes, Tolumnius, he did not dedicate the rich spoils to Jupiter Capitolinus; he consecrated them in the distinctly different temple of Jupiter Feretrius. And probably, when, after the departure of the Gauls in 386 B.C., Camillus reorganized the national cults, he established, for the first time, the worship of Jupiter Tutor on the Capitoline. However, he did not make of it the religious centre of the entire nation, but only of those who dwelt on the hill which had successfully resisted the invasion of the Gauls. The evident proof that the Temple of Jupiter Capitolinus as the religious centre of the nation did not arise in the first year of the Republic is that, in the absolutely historic period (in the last century of the Republic) there still existed on the Quirinal the *Capitolium Vetus*. This was dedicated to the same divinities as those of the Capitoline triad, and, as late as the time of Sulla, was honored with the same worship as the Capitol.

From this there results the truly recent origin of the principal cult of Jupiter Capitolinus. Only after the complete subjugation of the Peninsula in 338 B.C. did it acquire its paramount importance and character. In other words, it gained the ascendency only when, as I have demonstrated elsewhere, the Forum became the political centre of the city and of the Latin nation.

The corroboration of what has been said is found in the texts relating to the most ancient cults of the Capitoline. From a mass of religious references I would deduce that the most ancient god worshipped on that hill was called

PALAZZO CAFFARELLI, ON THE SITE OF THE TEMPLE OF JUPITER CAPITOLINUS

Tarpeius, just as Tarpeia was the principal female divinity of the citadel. Later he was considered the custodian of the citadel in the time of Romulus, and still later he became identified with King Tarquin. Tarpeia, likewise, was transformed into the maid who betrayed the citadel to the Sabines; or else, into the good vestal virgin Tarquinia, who donated to the Romans the Campus Martius. This, in turn, was said, by others, to belong to her contemporary, King Tarquin.

If we desire to sift to the bottom the information regarding the oldest cults of this time, we shall find, by the side of Jupiter Lapis and of Jupiter Feretrius, the lost divinities of Vulcan and Summanus—the first representing the diurnal activity of the Sun, the second the nocturnal. The cult of these deities gradually yielded, it is true, to that of Jupiter Tutor, who later became known as Jupiter Capitolinus. Nevertheless, Vulcan continued to adorn the façade of the temple of Jupiter. To him and to Summanus continued to be sacred the slopes of this hill. Here, till a late historic period,—that is, till the Empire,—was located the Vulcanal, adjacent to and, in earliest times, forming part of the Comitium. And precisely because Vulcan was the primordial god of ancient Rome, he was also (as I have shown elsewhere) the principal god of Rome's earliest colony,—Ostia, and of other Latin colonies of the third century,—as, for example, Æsernia.

If, therefore, the hypothesis is to be admitted that, in the time of the more or less mythical Tarquinii, or in the beginning of the Republic, a temple was indeed erected on the Capitoline, we must not think of the cult of Jupiter Optimus Maximus (which arose only after 386 B.C.), but of that of Vulcan. This conclusion agrees with the story of that Vulca Volcentanus to whom Tarquinius entrusted the task of raising into place the famous terracotta quadriga of Jove which adorned the Capitol, and which was put in position only in the first years of the Republic. The Etruscan artificer Vulca is Vulcanus himself, the primordial god of Etruria. He therefore erects a temple to himself, in the same manner as the god Hephaistos at Delphi and as the goddess Diana at Rome. Similarly, the smith Mamurius Veturius, the maker of the shields honored in the temple of Mars, was identical with the god Mamers Vetus.[8]

If we duly consider the non-historic character of the Horatii of the early Republic, we are drawn to conclude that our Horatius, the dedicator of the Temple of Jupiter Capitolinus, is a character entirely enveloped in the mists of legend. And this conclusion is strengthened when, on the one hand, the legend of the Horatii and the Curiatii is examined, and, on the other, that of Horatius Cocles.

The legend of the Horatii and the Curiatii has no historic value. It was connected, at various times, with the law *de provocatione,* with the Horatio-Valerian laws of 449 B.C., and with a Valerian law of 300 B.C. In fact, it refers to ceremonies in honor of Jupiter Tigillus and Juno Sororia. These were performed on a portion of the ancient Septimontium adjacent to the Forum, but on account of the growth of the city were later transported outside the Porta Capena. Likewise, the myth of Horatius Cocles, though embedded in the story of the war with Porsenna, is closely connected with the cult of Vulcanus. A more careful study will reveal to us that Cocles was a purely imaginary and divine character.[4]

I have shown elsewhere how many fantastic elements— (fruits of the elaboration of religious and topographical data) are to be found in the story of the war with Porsenna. Among others, we have the various myths of Horatius Cocles, of Clœlia, and of Mucius Scævola. Livy himself, in relating the story of Horatius, remarks that it was a deed that would receive more glory than belief from future generations, *rem ausus plus famæ habituram ad posteros quam fidei.* Florus rightly said, "And then there are those prodigies and marvels of the Roman name,—Horatius, Mucius and Clœlia,—all of whom would now seem mere myths were they not to be found in the annals" (*Tunc illa Romani nominis prodigia atque miracula, Horatius, Mucius, Clœlia, qui nisi in annalibus forent hodiæ fabulæ viderentur.*)[5]

Though modern criticism discards legends which, as has often been remarked, were invented by the Romans to hide their own defeats, nevertheless there still remains the desire to know what occasioned the formation of such legends. As regards Clœlia, it must be remarked that a statue representing an equestrian divinity (perhaps Venus Cloacina) was identified with her. The same conclusion is reached by examining the legend which substitutes for Clœlia a Valeria, sister of the consul Publicola and (according to infallible data) an ancient goddess of the Roman people. Again, a comparison of parallel traditions proves that Mucius Scævola, who, having failed in his endeavor to slay Porsenna, bravely thrust his hand into the fire, is an imaginary person similar to that Mucius, tribune of the plebs, who a few years later causes to be burned alive Spurius Cassius and his faithless colleagues. Even in the legend of Mucius Scævola there enters a sacred and topographical element—the worship of a divinity in the *prata Mucia*. A similar origin may be attributed to the legend of Horatius Cocles, who, according to a more ancient version known to Polybius, died beneath the waters of the Tiber.[6]

The origin of this story (like that of the dedication of the temple of Jupiter Capitolinus) is to be sought for in the worship of Vulcan. Plutarch, in his life of Publicola, states that two explanations were given for the name *Cocles*. According to the first, Horatius had been so named because he had lost an eye in war; according to the second, because his nose was of such a shape that no space was visible between the eyes, and because the two eyebrows joined and appeared as one. The result was, continues Plutarch, that the people, in endeavoring to say *Cyclops*, by faulty pronunciation called him *Cocles* instead.[7] The word *Cocles* was used also in the sense of cyclops or *unoculi*, among others by Ennius and by Plautus.[8] Plutarch adds that the Romans rewarded Horatius Cocles not only with gifts of land (as is recounted by Livy and by Dionysius of Halicarnassus), but also with a bronze statue erected in the temple of Vulcan, wishing thus to compensate him for the wound he had received in the thigh.[9]

This statement does not stand isolated. It was known also to Dionysius that Horatius Cocles had become lame as the result of his wounds. The source from which he drew added that on this account Horatius had to renounce all military magistracies.[10] And that a statue to Horatius was erected *in area Vulcani* above the Comitium is plainly related in the *Annales Maximi*.[11] These spoke of the Vulcanal which was established (according to tradition) by Romulus, who here pledged his faith to the Sabine Tatius, and here dedicated the quadriga won at the conquest of Cameria.[12]

Why should the Romans have erected a statue to Horatius, and, of all places, within the area of Vulcan? If we are to believe the statement of the *Annales Maximi*, because that region had been struck by lightning. Nevertheless, we must consider that the name Cocles means *the cyclopes*, that the cyclops, in Greek mythology were (at least after the fifth century) placed in relation with Hephaistos and later with Vulcan, and, finally, that in the Homeric epics and also in the most ancient monuments Hephaistos was represented as lame. We shall thus (I think) reach the conclusion that the statue in the area of Vulcan, supposed to represent the lame Cocles, rather than being the statue of a legendary hero, was that of Vulcan himself. In such a case, the god Vulcan became a man in consequence of the same process by which Lycurgus, the one-eyed god and hero of Arcadia, became Lycurgus, the famous lawgiver of the Spartans. Also Lycurgus had been rendered blind in one eye, according to tradition, by a blow from a club. Finally, it must be remembered that Vulcan was considered a cyclops in the same manner as Wòtan among the Germanic tribes and as Varuna among the Hindoos.

Vulcan is one of the most ancient Roman divinities. He is, indeed, neither more nor less than the protecting deity of the State. For this reason the area of Vulcan was supposed to have been established by Romulus; for this reason Servius Tullius, one of the founders of the Roman State, was called the son of Vulcan. Vulcan, too, is the protecting god of the armies. He appears as a primordial deity (as we have already said) on the summit of the temple of the Capitoline. There is nothing strange, then, in the fact that legend should have confused the hero who saved Rome by holding the bridge with the tutelary deity of the State

and, indeed, the very symbol of its life. It is very natural, moreover, that Horatius Cocles, admitting him to be an emanation from Vulcan, should have been placed in relation with the Tiber.

We shall put aside the Hellenic myths in which Hephaistos is constantly placed in relation with water. We shall limit ourselves to recalling the famous feast of the Vulcanalia on the 23rd of August, when the Romans threw into the fire *pro animis humanis* fishes from the Tiber obtained by fishermen of the *area Vulcani* near the river.[13] We shall add that at Ostia, a city situated at the very mouth of the Tiber, the highest magistracies were the *pontifex Vulcani* and *prætor Vulcani*—titles which recall the ancient wooden bridge defended by Cocles, whose preservation (as is well known) was entrusted to the *pontifices*.[14] Finally, we shall find still another point of contact in the legend of Cæculus, the mythical founder of Præneste, who, also, was considered the son of Vulcan and had been found by maidens not far from a spring.[15] It may be observed that *Cæculus,* the squint-eyed, is a name which has its origin in a cause similar to that which gave rise to the expression of *Cocles,* the one-eyed.[16]

Lightning flashing from the midst of clouds is the cause of these relations between water and fire—between Vulcan and the Tiber.[17] Legend rightly supposes the nymph Egeria to have taught Numa the art of performing expiations in cases of disasters caused by lightning.[18] Numa, the founder of the priesthood, is merely the eponym of the sacred stream Numicius. Likewise Egeria, his bride and counsellor, is the personification of the fountain on the shores of the lake at Ariccia. Some ceremony which was consecrated by religion caused the legend of Cocles, who defends the Sublician Bridge, and who hurls himself into the river, in which (according to the most ancient version) he meets his death. This legend has, perhaps, some relation with the ceremony of the twenty-four stuffed figures (representing the local heroes called *Argei*), which, on the Ides of May and in the presence of the pontiffs and of the vestal virgins—the guardians of the sacred fire—were thrown into the Tiber from the Pons Sublicius.

It is not in itself improbable that a valorous Roman should have sacrificed himself for the welfare of the State, and, against the whole of Tuscany,

Orazio sol contro Toscana tutta,

should have impeded the advance of the enemy. In the

age of the Gracchi such an event did actually occur. But the similarity noted above between our Cocles and Vulcan induces the belief that we have here a legendary story of the same class as that of Curtius and the famous vortex. It is in keeping with the tendency of the ancient annalists to ascribe this heroic act to one of the Horatii. For, to this family a conspicuous part in the history of the Roman people was often assigned, and they were connected (it must be remembered) with the worships of Jupiter Tigillus and Jupiter Vulcanus.

The statue of the lame Vulcan-Cocles that was mentioned by Dionysius, Plutarch and Pliny must have played a prominent rôle in the formation of the legend. It is clear, furthermore, that the more ancient version (according to which Horatius was drowned in the Tiber) could not speak of the injury received by the hero. This was not, however, the only statue or monument which gave origin to pretended historical events in the war with Porsenna. The annalists, as we have already said, recorded also a bronze equestrian statue on the Sacra Via. This statue, according to the majority, represented Clœlia, but others asserted it to be the statue of Valeria, daughter of Publicola. Finally, Plutarch relates that, after peace had been declared with Porsenna, the Romans honored their former enemy with a bronze statue, simple and archaic in style and situated near the Curia.[19] These words prove that he who first spoke of this monument judged of its antiquity even from its style. But that this statue actually represented Porsenna is incredible. Furthermore, it is beyond belief that the Romans should have honored him by whom they had been conquered and humiliated, and should have erected the statue in the Senate itself. No one would expect to find a statue of Barbarossa in Milan, or one of Napoleon in a public building or square at Berlin. The history of art, moreover, forbids our placing any faith in the statement that at Rome, and in the beginning of the fifth century, so many bronze statues were cast representing contemporary characters.

It is much more natural, in the meantime, to believe that it was through popular fancy, or, better, through that of some author, that a bronze statue was attributed to Porsenna—a statue which, though archaic and of a later period, in all probability represented a divinity, as did those of Clœlia and of Horatius Cocles. This supposition contains nothing strange or improbable. If legend often rendered mortal beings divine, it at times lowered to human level beings considered immortal. Phalanthus, in whom antiquity unanimously recognized the historic founder of Tarentum, and whose father and mistress even could be indicated, never really existed.[20] Still less did he go to Sparta, since he, as well as Æthra, his consort, is a purely mythological being. He is the personification of one of Poseidon's attributes,[21] whose adventures were soon partly referred to an historical character—the Lesbian Arion.[22] The statue of Aristæus Proconnesius (which was at Metapontum near the image of Apollo) was not the portrait of a mortal, as was thought in the times of Herodotus. It represented Aristæus, the well-known son of Apollo.[23] No one with any critical sense now believes that the Lycurgus to whom the Spartans erected a temple and paid divine honors was a mortal being.[24]

Those authors, whether Greek or Roman, who related the most ancient history of Rome, made use even of monuments as historical material. They questioned the statues, so to speak, and the interpretation of them suggested to their imagination facts and circumstances that were later retained as true. The legend of Mucius Scævola draws its origin from a monument, as does that of Hostus Hostilius, whose eulogy was supposed to be recorded on the archaic stele of the Forum.[25] It is now the common opinion that the cognomen Scævola gave origin to the famous anecdote. We must keep well in mind the age in which the Roman cognomen begins to be used, which, it must be admitted, was rather late. We must, too, remember what has been said in regard to accepting monuments as historic sources. It will not, then, seem to me too hazardous an hypothesis to assume that the legend of Scævola had its origin in a monument representing a person with his hand extended towards an altar, either in the act of adoration, or in that of scattering incense upon it.[26]

Whatever may be the value of this last hypothesis, it seems necessary to emphasize the fact that ancient historiography did, in fact, draw upon monuments as sources for the early history of the Roman people. Dionysius is wont to cite inscriptions and documents of the regal period. He, as well as Plutarch, speaks of the bronze statue crowned by victory which Romulus himself placed upon the bronze quadriga captured at Cameria.[27] The inscription, he says, was written in ancient Greek characters. But probably this was a monument of the fifth or fourth century, which, like the Forum stele, was misunderstood and dated in the eighth century. To be sure, Dionysius was not the first to direct his attention to this species of document; nor did he alone deduce from them interpretations entirely erroneous and fantastic. As early as the fifth century,—beginning, that is, with Herodotus and Thucydides,—Hellenic historiography had drawn material from sculptured monuments and from inscriptions. At times it made good use of them, but it often fell into error, either by attributing such monuments to an earlier age, or by assigning to them an erroneous signification.[28]

Many examples of this can be found. It will suffice to recall a few. The walls of the Acropolis of Athens, which, on account of their shape, were called the storks' nest τὸ πελαργικὸν), perhaps gave origin to the legend of the presence of the Pelasgians in Attica.[29] It is so recorded by Hecatæus. The statue of the Assyrian conqueror Sanherib, which was erected at Anchiale on the coast of Cilicia, and the position of its hands and fingers, occasioned the legend that it represented instead Sardanapalus, and that the inscription beneath it read " Eat, drink and be merry—the rest is worth nothing." [30] Likewise, the Egyptian monuments often gave origin to the most curious legends, which were at times related and recorded as true history. Herodotus is full of anecdotes suggested by the erroneous interpretations of monuments; and in his honor we shall here recall the story of the *colossi* with maimed hands. These, according to the professional guides of the day, represented the maid-servants who had been thus punished for having furthered the incestuous designs of Micerinus upon his daughter. But this was sheer nonsense, remarks Herodotus, inasmuch as the hands had broken off through great age, and he himself had seen them lying at the foot of the monuments.[31]

Without, however, going beyond the city of the Seven Hills, it will benefit us to consider how many legends came to life in the Middle Ages through false interpretation of ancient monuments. The statues of the Dioscuri on Monte

Cavallo became, in the Middle Ages, the two philosophers Praxiteles and Phidias, contemporaries of Tiberius.[32] A statue representing one of the subject provinces and prostrated at the feet of a Roman emperor occasioned the famous legend of the Arch of Pity and of the widow who begs Trajan for justice—a legend found also in a splendid episode of the Divine Comedy.[33] The statue of Marcus Aurelius furnished material for the strange story of the *caballus Constantini*.[34] And, finally, a late Roman statue even now to be seen at Pisa suggested the legend of Cinzica dei Sismondi, who saved the Pisan district of Cinzica from the Saracens.[35]

Between the Oriental guides, the Greek chroniclers and the Roman annalists on one hand, and the uncultured mediæval writers on the other, there are many points of contact. Errors of this kind, though of different measure and value, are not entirely avoided even by modern critical students. Similarly the ancient writers, even the learned ones, could not altogether escape them. Demetrius Phalereus himself, though a learned and careful pupil of Theophrastus, fell into grave error regarding Aristides, because he founded his arguments on a document which Panætius rightly referred to another Aristides, of an age later than that of the famous contemporary of Xerxes.[36] It is therefore easily understood how Roman annalists of the second and first century, and how Greek writers who studied the history of their conquerors, even though without deceitful aims, should have been led to misinterpret the age and the meaning of the monuments before them, which, after all, they were right in consulting.

From what has been said, it clearly results that not one of the Horatii recorded for the regal period and for the first centuries of the Republic is an historic character. They are either spurious, as the consuls and the military tribunes; or, as the Horatii (who were the enemies of the Curiatii), and Horatius Pulvillus and Horatius Cocles, they are fantastic creations related to the cult of Jupiter Tigillus and Jupiter Vulcanus.

The same result is obtained by examining the deeds of the Valerii, who were always connected by tradition with the Horatii. That first Valerius who established the worship of Dis at Tarentum is imaginary. Equally fanciful is that Valerius Publicola who is also traditionally placed in relation with Tarentum, or who was supposed to dwell on the Velia near the Temple of the Penates,—the home of Tullus Hostilius. Mythical, too, is Valeria, by some considered the sister of Valerius Publicola, by others indentified with Clœlia. She is simply that Valeria Luperca who, like Faunus, the god of the Lupercalia, had the virtue of curing those sick with the plague.[37] This Valeria, indeed, is the same one mentioned in the capture of the mythical Suessa Pometia in the legend of Coriolanus, and in the story of the foundation of the temple of Virtus Muliebris.[38] All the deeds, then, attributed to the Valerii have a legendary and divine character also.

It is clear, however, that a great part of the legends of the Valerii draw their origin from the deeds of the Valerii of a later historic age. Towards 300 B.C. we find a Valerius introducing the bill *de provocatione*, which we have seen attributed to the Valerius of the regal period, or of 509, or of 449 B.C.[39] This Valerius, too, was supposed to have pacified the rebellious Aretini in 302 B.C. in the same way as a Valerius, and not Menenius Agrippa, was said to have brought to an end the secession of the plebs.[40] Finally, Valerius Levinus, a contemporary of Hannibal, proposed in 216 B.C. those same reforms that are attributed to the Valerius of 508 B.C.[41] The ancients affirmed that, at the foot of the Velia, there was the tomb of Valerius Publicola, at which the Valerii customarily performed sacred rites before proceeding elsewhere to bury their dead.[42] There is no doubt that the Valerii (Sabines in origin) constituted one of the most ancient families taking part in the authentic history of the Roman people.

Far different is the case with the Horatii. Livy himself declares that the ancients doubted whether the Horatii, the enemies of the Curiatii, were Romans rather than Albans. Though he states that the cults of Jupiter Tigillus and of Juno Sororia were entrusted to the Horatii, no trace has come down to us of an authentic Horatius belonging to a patrician gens. Nevertheless, the mere presence of the *Horatia tribus* among the sixteen ancient rustic tribes is evidence that there must have been patrician Horatii, just as there were patrician Lemoni, of whom history makes no mention. The Sabine Valerii and the Roman Horatii, then, would seem to belong to those very ancient families whose early deeds were lost in the obscurity of time,—families which, because of their antiquity, were connected with the most ancient national worships.

The name of the Valerii is connected with the verb *valere*, and with the divinities of victory and of health. Therefore, just as Valeria was considered a deity who cured the sick, so Valerius Publicola lived in a place called *Vica Potæ*,— that is, *Victoria Potens*. This was near, or actually within, the temple of the Penates.[43] The Horatii, on their part, seem to be related to the god *Horatus,* who announced to the Romans the victory of Silva Arsia. They were, at any rate, the representatives of Jupiter Hastatus or Quirinus. Perhaps it is not inopportune to recall that Hora was the spouse of Quirinus.[44] It is evident that in these cults which, from the fifth and the beginning of the fourth century, yielded gradually to the new gods, we have the most sacred and legendary patrimony of the nation. The most ancient deeds of the Valerii and the Horatii fall within the period in which national history was not yet written. For this period the annals are alive with a long series of legends, whether of Spurius Cassius, of Virginia or of Coriolanus.

It is vain to insist on finding in all these legends an historic, rather than a religious, nucleus. The only conclusion to be drawn therefrom is that the continuance of the patrician family of the Valerii into the historic period gave a greater certainty to their deeds. The rapid disappearance of the patrician Horatii, on the contrary, caused merely the recollection of their participation in the deeds of the legendary kingly and early Republican period. If the Horatii are always placed in relation with ancient Valerii, the reason is not to be sought for in a story which appears false after careful examination. It is to be found exclusively in the relations between the cults of these two families. Indeed, if we consider a moment, we shall see that the Horatii are never mentioned unless in connection with sacred ceremonies, and then, too, only as accessory figures by the side of a Valerius.

It is impossible, at present, to trace with complete exactness all these various relations. It is to be observed, however, that the ancients represented Valerius Publicola as desiring to deprive his colleague, Horatius Pulvillus, of the honor of dedicating the Capitoline temple. Again the myth of Horatius, who slew his own sister, and the cult of Jupiter Tigillus and Juno Sororia were all located near the house of Valerius Publicola and the temple of Vica Potæ. Both these cults, then, were at the foot of the Velia,—at the furthermost limit of the ancient Septimontium. All, therefore, favors the belief that the more or less legendary and divine progenitors of the two families were related by those same topographical reasons through which, as we have seen elsewhere, the cult of Janus gave origin to the legend of his relations with Saturn, and through which Hercules was connected with Faustulus, Bona Dea and Acca Larentia.

Moreover, to understand perfectly the whole meaning of the cults originally connected with the Horatii and the Valerii, we must turn our thoughts to the most ancient period of Roman civilization. At that time the early conception of the divinities had not yet developed; at that time, as in Egypt, as in the earliest period of Greek civilization, and as later in many savage tribes, animal worship played a prominent part. We do not know under what form the earliest Romans conceived the course of the Sun. The legend of the Horatii and the Curiatii (which must be connected with the worship of Jupiter Tigillus) recalls the analogous myth of the solar god Janus, who, it seems, was connected with the gates.

At Lavinium Juno was originally worshipped under the form of a she-goat, and Acca Larentia (and, perhaps, Valeria Luperca, too) was honored under the form of a she-wolf. We have reasons for believing that in a similar manner the goddess of Victory was revered under the form of a bull and a cow. This might be proved by the term Vitulatio, which (according to an ancient annalist) signified Victoria,[45] and also by the fact that the ancient Romans and other peoples adored the goddess Vitellia.[46]

The bull and the cow were the national totems of several Italic stocks. On the coins of the Social War we see the bull overpowering the Sabellian wolf. Similarly, at the battle of Sentinum the Romans regarded the appearance of the *lupus Martius* as an omen of victory. It is obvious

THE ISLAND OF THE TIBER

A ROMAN DIVINITY. (MAGAZINO COMUNALE, ROME)

HORATII AND VALERII

then, that under the form of a cow were worshipped both the goddess Vitellia and the goddess Vacuna, the Sabine goddess of Victory.[47] And since Vitellia was connected with Evander and the Fauni, our thoughts naturally turn to the temple of Victory situated above the grotto of the Lupercal. The ancients, indeed, affirmed that the feast of Victory, as well as that of the Lupercal, had been founded by Evander.[48] It seems as though we should connect with these cults the statue of Valeria who, on the coins of that

family, was represented as riding upon a bull.[49] The Valerii, then, appear to have connected their origin with the cult of this animal. Finally, as we shall see in a subsequent chapter, it was from a bull that the Roman family of the Minucii traced their origin.[50]

CHAPTER IX

THE FABII AT THE RIVER CREMERA, AND THE SPARTANS AT THERMOPYLÆ

WHEN, in the second century before our era, the patrician Fabius undertook to write the annals of Roman history, a great part of the traditional material had already been elaborated. Fabius and his contemporary Cincius Alimentus were (as is told us) the first Romans to write the history of their own city. But the same author who offers us this notice also informs us that they were preceded by a long series of Greek writers beginning with the end of the fifth century. Antiochus of Syracuse made mention of Rome as early as c. 420 B.C.; and also Callias and Timæus, the celebrated Syracusan historians, spoke more or less extensively about it.[1] Timæus, indeed, towards the end of the fourth century or the beginning of the third touched upon the coast of Latium, went to Rome and to Lavinium, and left us various notices regarding the coinage of Servius, the feast of the October horse, and the Trojan vases. Even before Timæus, Aristotle had discussed the more important Roman customs. To these authors there succeeded a long series of Greek chroniclers and historians, who labored to give an Hellenic aspect to the Roman legends. These historians, together with the authors mentioned above, were the teachers of the earliest Roman annalists.

Fabius Pictor and Cincius Alimentus, surely, were not the first to express their thoughts through the medium of prose history. Everything favors the belief that (as I have elsewhere endeavored to show) they were preceded by Appius Claudius, Gnæus Flavius and Sempronius Sophus. The ancients speak of only the juridic and the linguistic activity of these men, it is true. Nevertheless, many notices regarding the last Samnite wars seem to have been preserved for us only through them. It is clear that Gnæus Flavius must have been abreast of historical researches, since he indicated upon the temple of Concord how many years had elapsed from the founding of Rome.[2] The large number of references, so strictly Roman in character and of a time anterior to the Punic Wars, must have had their origin in family records and in the unknown predecessors of Fabius and of Cincius. These latter, at any rate, taking part for both political and literary reasons in the culture then become general, not only wrote their histories in Greek, but even repeated the old Hellenic tales.

Cincius related the story that the Greek Evander had brought the alphabet to the Latins. Fabius, in discussing the origin of Rome, repeated (as is well known) a Greek story already related by Diocles of Peparethos. Under the influence of those unknown predecessors, who were neither few in number nor wanting in efficacy, the history of the regal period was rapidly elaborated. To this result, too, there contributed the priestly organizations, which raised to the dignity of history the sacred and religious elements of the temples and the native divinities. The eponyms of the Roman hills and streams, the gods and the heroes worshipped in the sanctuaries, all became historic characters, through the identical process which made the Teutonic tribes place a god at the head of their genealogy, and which made the ancient Greeks establish one at the head of each *genos.*

Meeting with an elaboration already so well accomplished, and with names of gods and of heroes already so generally worshipped, the ancient annalists must have found but a limited field for their inventive powers and for the claims of their function as historians. The Marci, the Pomponii and other families tried, indeed, to insert and to mingle their names with those of the legendary Roman kings. They did not dare, however, invent new kings, different from those already accepted in the sacerdotal lists and already recognized by public opinion. The Fabii, as well as the Valerii, made mention of their own private rites and cults, connecting them with the most ancient legends; but they did not venture to alter perceptibly the ancient religious material which had been preserved by the priesthoods. We note that the Fabii were connected with the nymph Tiberina, the progenitress of the family and the mistress of Hercules.[3] They are, too, the principal figures in the story of the companions of Romulus or of the Lupercal,—a story referring to the rites performed by these during the siege of the Capitol.[4] But this infiltration (so to speak) never was of sufficient importance, nor did it sink deeply enough to change materially the most ancient legendary tales.

There was still left an ample field for the pretensions of both the patrician and the plebeian families,—to narrate the deeds of their ancestors in the substantially historic period of the struggles with the neighboring Etruscans, Volscians, Æqui, and others. Further material for such amplifications was offered in the recounting of the internal struggles. In these the different patrician and plebeian families had fought, with the respective purposes of keeping intact the old constitution and the acquired rights of the ancient families, and of obtaining a victory in the name of more liberal and more democratic principles.

From this point of view, it may be said that the same course was followed, both by the earliest annalists of the third century (the contemporaries of Hannibal) and by those of the first century,—of the time of Sulla and Cicero. Cato the Elder declared himself scandalized at such inventions, and preferred to cite the name of the bravest elephant rather than that of an unfit and unwarlike commander. But it must not be forgotten that at the same time he lost no opportunity of praising his own work (comparing it, in fact, with those of the ancient Greeks), and that he adhered to the general rule of declaring the deeds of the Roman people equal to the most famous and glorious events of the ancient Hellenic people.[5]

Both these characteristics are easily recognized in the stories of the Fabii, whether represented as fighting against the Etruscans of the fifth and fourth centuries, or against the Volscians, the Aurunci, the Samnites, and others. The tendency to reproduce famous episodes of Hellenic history is especially marked in the story of their struggles with the Veientes, the Etruscans and the other confederated Italic peoples who were finally subjugated at the battle of Sentinum, in 295 B.C.

The beautiful legend of the three hundred Fabii who perished at the River Cremera is well known. To quote the very words of Livy, " three hundred and six soldiers, all patricians and all of one family " undertake as " a private enterprise " the war against the Veientes—the public enemy of the Roman people.[6] They departed from their fatherland; and, accompanied by their clients, four thousand in number (five thousand according to another version),[7] they established themselves in a fort not far from the Etruscan city of Veii. Here they managed to maintain themselves

THE FABII

superior to their enemies for nearly three years; but, in the end, fell into snares prepared for them by the enemy, and died fighting. And of all that glorious family, which had played, for a time, such great part in the public life of the Romans, and which, by its patriotic resolve alone to oppose the Veientes, had expiated its hostile bearing towards the plebs in the past, there remained alive but one child. This child, who had been left at Rome, was the seed of the Fabian race (observes Livy), destined to be of great aid to the Romans in their hour of need, both in peace and in war.[8]

This picture of heroism seemed to be deliberately overdrawn even to the ancients. Dionysius himself, who, as is his wont, appears to believe it, cannot refrain from remarking that it is altogether inadmissible that the 306 Fabii should have left at Rome one child only. In this regard he adds that there is in the tale a smack of the legendary and theatrical,—words which modern criticism can, perhaps, extend to the entire story.[9] Modern scholars are not agreed as to the value of this legend. Neibuhr and Schwegler have especially aimed at criticising its various details, and at drawing forth from it an historical nucleus. Others, like Mommsen, have endeavored to trace its didactic character, or, like Richter, have examined its meaning in respect to Roman topography.[10] Mommsen, who is anything but disposed to place faith in the most ancient Roman history, and who has often taught us the way in which its problems should be investigated, does not seem entirely averse to placing some belief in Diodorus.[11] According to this historian, the Fabian gens had not died alone, but in a great battle fought by the Romans near the Cremera. Ihne, on the contrary, in the second edition of his History of Rome, is more resolute. Using to good advantages the observations already partly made by Perizonius and by Beaufort, he emphasizes their value, and considers the entire story as pure legend, altogether lacking in historical truth.[12]

In my opinion, Ihne comes much nearer the truth in this case than Mommsen. Contrary to the latter's opinion, I do not consider the version of Diodorus more worthy of belief than that preserved for us by Livy and by Dionysius. In other words, I do not believe Diodorus to be more exact than the others, when he asserts that the Fabii perished with other Romans in a great battle. For, just as I deem him inexact (as far as can be judged) in placing their number at 300 rather than 306, he is likewise so in merging into one event the fall of the Fabii and the subsequent and sudden defeat inflicted by the Veientes upon the consul Menenius.[13] I shall not here insist on this point. It may be the object of a special study when the work of Diodorus will have been more carefully examined. I have, moreover, demonstrated elsewhere that, beginning with Niebuhr and Mommsen, too much importance has been attached to the statements of Diodorus. This author is not a better nor a more exact source for Roman history than that which he has proved himself to be for Greek history; and this, too, notwithstanding that in both cases he frequently drew upon primary sources, and always upon valuable ones.[14]

As regards the intrinsic credibility of the event, one cannot avoid thinking of another disaster which befell 307 Romans under the leadership of a Fabius, and ascribed to a period 114 years later,—a very analogous, not to say identical, case, and one which has not escaped the observation of Ihne. In 358 B.C. the consul C. Fabius Ambustus,—a descendant of the Fabii who perished at the Cremera,—fought a battle "thoughtlessly and inconsiderately" (even as his ancestors) against the Etruscans of Tarquinii. Nor, adds Livy, did he incur heavy losses in the line of battle only; for the Tarquinienses slaughtered 307 Roman soldiers who had been made prisoners.[15] Almost all critics, beginning with Perizonius, agree in denying that just exactly 306 soldiers died at the Cremera, and all belonging to the Fabian gens. It is also readily seen that the 307 prisoners of the Tarquinienses recall the 306 killed by the Veientes. The interval of almost 114 years between the two events is not an obstacle to their identification. We have abundant examples of the reduplicating of an event or deed attributed to the same family in different ages of the earliest Roman history. This story of the Fabii merely proves the general rule. In that same family, indeed, we have another conspicuous example of this process,—a story closely connected with the legend of the Cremera.

According to the more diffused, or we may say, the general opinion of Roman writers (an opinion, however, which

THE FABII

was not shared by Ovid's sources), the battle of the Cremera was fought on the 18th of July,—a day ever afterwards numbered among the *nefasti*. It was not for this reason alone that the 18th of July was considered *nefastus*. On that same day had occurred the defeat of the Allia,—a defeat sustained on the banks of another small tributary of the Tiber, distant from the Cremera by about two miles. It is to be remarked, moreover, that of the military tribunes who led the Romans against the Gallic invaders on the day of the Allia, three were the Fabii who had already been sent as ambassadors to Clusium,—then being besieged by the Gauls.[16]

Plutarch labors heavily in his endeavor to prove, by means of synchronisms partly authentic and partly false, that it is entirely possible that the battle of the Cremera and that of the Allia were fought on the same day. Even the most trusting critic cannot but see in this either a simple confusion, or else a deliberate mingling of the stories. If there were any doubt in this regard, it would be dispelled by the fact that Ovid, or (to be more exact) the source from which he drew, fixed upon the 13th of February, and not the 18th of July, as the day of the slaughter at the Cremera. The same process is to be noticed, for instance, in the history of Pisa, in which the great majority of the glorious deeds of the Republic are made to coincide with the feast of S. Sisto.

This repetition of dates and events (which is so common in the history of the wars against the Veientes and the Gauls) manifests itself also in other elements of our story. The Fabii, it is said, departed from Rome through the Porta Carmentalis; and, never having returned to Rome, this gate was afterwards called *scelerata*. No one ever ventured to pass through it. But the cult of Carmentis (who was there buried) was connected with that of Evander, or Lupercus, and the latter was worshipped on the 13th of February. The Lupercalia began on the immediately following odd day of the month. Furthermore, it is well known that in this celebration the Fabii played the most prominent part. The Porta Carmentalis was connected also with the Gallic invasion. Near it was the rock (*saxum*) on which the Gauls mounted when they endeavored to scale the heights of the Capitol.[17] Finally, it must be added that, according to other fantastic data, the 13th of February was the day on which Rome was liberated from the Gauls.[18]

It is not in the slightest degree probable that the Romans should have suffered three memorable defeats under the leadership of the Fabii,—those, namely, of the Cremera in 477 B.C., of the Allia in 390 B.C., and from the Tarquinienses in 358 B.C. On the contrary, everything causes the belief that one single event was, at various times, cast and recast according to the caprice of the annalists. Perhaps we would better say according to the fancy of the family historian. That this reduplication (in the case of the Fabian gens) was most strangely abused is proved by the absurd story of the 300 Romans under Fabius Maximus, who perished together in the war against Hannibal. It is clear that this fanciful tale (related by the novelist Aristides, the author of the Milesiaca) is merely a later and grotesque recasting of the better-known legend of the Fabii at the Cremera.[19]

In all probability the least ancient of these stories (with the exception, to be sure, of the last) has the greatest likelihood of coming near the truth. Moreover, the story that, through the bad leadership of a Fabius 307 Roman warriors fell into the hands of the Tarquinienses and were massacred in the principal square of their city has every appearance of truth. For, both the barbarous customs of the period must be considered and also the fact that the leader Fabius is in no wise glorified as in the legend of the Cremera. In fact, regarding his carelessness, which caused the ignominious death of 307 men, Livy remarks that " that foul massacre rendered more marked the ignominy of the Roman people."[20] This last story evidently does not spring from a family tradition of the Fabii, nor from a *laudatio funebris* of the *gens*.

Other elements of the legend of the Fabii seem to derive their origin from still more recent events. The seven Fabian consuls seem to be entirely hypothetical; but it is to be noted that Fabius Rullianus, the famous general of the fourth century, was supposed to have held the supreme magistracies of the State seven times,—five times as consul, twice as dictator. Fabius Rullianus, too, was accompanied by 4000 volunteers,—a number and a circumstance which recall the clients of the Fabii at the Cremera,—which were by some numbered at precisely 4000. According to

MAP OF ROME, FIDENÆ AND VEII

one version, the child of the Fabii who owed his life to his having been left at Rome had the *prænomen* Numerius. An author worthy of faith, however, declares that the first Fabius to be called Numerius owed such *prænomen* to a certain Ottacilius, a rich maternal grandfather from Beneventum.[21] It is sufficient to recall that only in 354 B.C. (according to tradition) did the Romans come into contact with the Samnites. The mention of the distant Beneventum, then, obliges us to think immediately of Fabius Rullianus.

From what has been said thus far, it does not necessarily and inevitably result that the entire story of a Roman defeat at the Cremera is false. The very confession of a Roman reverse, rather than the boast of a victory, should weigh in favor of its credibility. But even laying aside such considerations, the excellent topographical studies of Richter demonstrate, I think, that the legend has as a foundation real topographical conditions. These are that, between the valleys of the Valca (the Cremera) and the Valchetta (both of which rise near Veii and empty into the Tiber) there was, directly opposite the ancient Fidenæ, a strong strategic position. This position must necessarily have been chosen to interrupt communications between Veii and Fidenæ,—the common enemies of Rome. Richter rightly observes that these wars between Rome on one side, and Veii and Fidenæ on the other, must have numbered more than one; but that the dubious value of Roman annals prevents our determining exactly when they occurred. Whosoever, trusting in his own inspiration and critical talents, would think of even cautiously availing himself of material which, for this entire period, is almost entirely without historic value, and would hope thus to distinguish the true from the false, would be endeavoring the vain labors of Sisyphus. He would, furthermore, merely prove that he has not a clear conception of the material consulted, nor of the critical method with which it is to be examined.

The most prudent criticism establishes the fact that in the formation of the legend there have contributed vague notices of struggles with the Veientes, and also religious and topographical elements, such as the Porta Scelerata and the cult of the Lupercalia. Of these cults and ceremonies we have only incomplete notices. The ancients themselves were often unable to interpret them.[22] In a topographical way we can merely observe that the gates of various ancient cities were not considered sacred. Some indeed, were held to be ill-omened and impure. The cause for such opinion was a subject of discussion with the Roman antiquarians. They ascribed it to the fact that corpses and malefactors were led out through some of the city gates,[23] —a belief which accords with the story of the slaying of Horatia in the *vicus sceleratus* and at the gate later known as Porta Capena. Moreover, in certain districts of Umbria to-day the old houses have a special door through which the dead are carried out. The non-sacred character of some of the gates is to be connected, also, with the custom of affixing thereto the heads and the limbs of dead enemies and of executed criminals.

We shall not discuss, here, the question of the exact year in which the Romans were overcome by the Veientes at the Cremera. We shall rather turn to the investigation of what event must have been in the mind of the Roman historian in the composition of this legend.

No modern critic (to my knowledge) has observed that which did not escape the notice of an ancient writer— namely, that the legend of the Fabii at the Cremera bears a striking resemblance to the heroic defence of Thermopylæ by Leonidas and his 300 Spartans. The number of the 306 Fabii and 4000 clients (according to Mommsen and Ihne) was suggested by the strength of the legion and its cavalry. But it is more natural to observe that also Leonidas had with him, in addition to the 300 Spartans, 4000 Peloponnesians.[24] If the number of the Fabii at the Cremera is at times given as 300 rather than 306, it seems admissible to believe (as in the case of Calpurnius Flamma, to be cited below) that an attempt was made to bring closer together the two heroic events.[25] The similarity between the two events is not limited to the number of combatants. It extends to other particulars as well. Leonidas and his men perish because of their betrayal by Ephialtes; the Fabii die through the jealousy of the consul Menenius, who was less than four miles away (30 stadia), and who (like Ephialtes) was afterwards punished for his treacherous inactivity. Even that single Fabius left at Rome, who later became the propagator of his race, has a parallel in the Greek story. Herodotus tells us that the soothsayer Megistias of Acarnania (who had prophesied the battle), although dismissed by Leonidas, nevertheless remained on the field of battle, and instead sent home his only son.[26]

Regarding the chronology of the two events, as was already noticed by the ancients,[27] there is an almost perfect synchronism. In 480 B.C. Leonidas dies at Thermopylæ; in the Varronian year 477 B.C. (275 U.C.) the Fabii march to the Cremera. This slight chronological difference is easily smoothed over, when it is considered that also for the year 480 B.C. the Roman annals register a battle between the Veientes and the Romans, in which both the consuls perish. Of these two consuls, one belonged to the Fabian gens; and after this defeat (as after the battle of the Cremera) the Fabii renew their friendships with the Roman plebs.[28] It is evident that the battles of 480 and 477 B.C. represent two different versions of the same event, told in a slightly different manner. Both stories are recorded in the annals of Livy, for the reason that he, without having a clear understanding of the material, in collecting notices from various sources did not realize the parallelism of events more or less identical with those ascribed to other years. From all this there results a substantial resemblance between the two events, inasmuch as both Leonidas with his 300 Spartans and the 306 Fabii sacrificed themselves for the safety of their country.

Such a great similarity in the fundamental details and such chronological correspondence are surely not the result of chance. The most careful criticism (like that of Mommsen) has admitted the fact that the most ancient Roman history was merely a web of deliberate falsifications. Such conclusion very well explains this and other similarities between Greek and Roman history. In the present condition of critical studies, I deem it superfluous to demonstrate how, by the mere process of transference, a Greek event may have been reproduced and inserted into the pseudo-Roman deeds. It is common knowledge that this occurred on a large scale, not only in Roman history, but also in that of the nations in the Middle Ages. The process is but a phase of that same phenomenon through which the Greek myths of Thessaly and of Arcadia were localized in other Hellenic and barbarian regions.

The legend of the Fabii can, I think, be placed in the same category with the story of Tarquinius and of Gabii. It can be compared with what is related by Herodotus concerning Periander and Zopyrus, or with the pseudo-history of the wars fought by the Romans in the early years of the Republic. These latter are, in fact, versions taken more or less literally from the Iliad, or they are repetitions of more ancient battles fought between Greeks.[29] As regards chronology, the correspondence in time between the defence of Thermopylæ and the legend of the Fabii is to be numbered among those synchronisms that are so frequent in the histories of the two peoples. Of these it will suffice to recall the parallelism between Numa and his pretended teacher Pythagoras; of the Servian legislation assigned to the age of Solon; of the expulsion of the Tarquins, which was made coincident with that of the Pisistratidæ, and of the founding of Rome corresponding to the rise of the Babylonian Empire. It is not necessary to dwell on a phenomenon, which, if not evident thirty or forty years ago, is to-day clearly understood by all who study Roman history with objective methods. And, finally, considering the subject-matter of the legend, not many demonstrations are necessary to discover its author, and, at the same time, the author of this continued parallelism between the histories of Greece and of Rome.

Fabius Pictor immediately occurs to our minds. He was the first historian of Rome in order of time, and the author of a history written in Greek, and on Greek lines. To him the Fabian gens is doubtlessly indebted for such great prominence in the annals of the ancient Republic. In all probability it was from the history of Fabius Pictor, or, at least, from other domestic records of the Fabian family, that the tradition arose which made the progenitor of the Fabii a son of Hercules and of the nymph Tiberina. The Fabii, therefore, were Heraclidæ, as well as Leonidas and other Spartan kings,—a belief fully in keeping with the fact that the Fabii were considered of Sabine origin. For the Sabines (as was known even before Cato) believed themselves the descendants of Spartans. The origin of this belief, in turn, was the friendly relations of the Sabines with the Spartan Tarentum. The earliest Roman historians (beginning with Fabius) often narrated Roman deeds in imitation of Greek ones, and, to obtain still greater resemblance, established false synchronisms. It will appear anything but strange, then, that they altered what was perhaps an inglorious event of nearly a century earlier, and

ISOLA FARNESE, FROM THE WALLS OF VEII.
(AFTER DENNIS)

ROCK-CUT TOMB AT VEII. (AFTER DENNIS)

invented that, at the same time in which the Heraclides Leonidas sacrificed himself and his companions for the safety of his country, the Heraclidæ Fabii, at their own expense and with the sacrifice of themselves and their clients, should have similarly undertaken to free Rome from its war against the Veientes.[30]

Mommsen is of the opinion that the legend of the Fabii had, in the minds of the earliest annalists, a purely didactic purpose—to demonstrate the futility and the failure of a *bellum privatum* and of a *coniuratio* as contrasted with the success of the *militia legitima*. In fact (he says) the didactic aim of this story is to teach that the citizen must not perform heroic deeds on his own initiative, but, instead, must valorously repulse the enemy under the command of superiors to whom he voluntarily subordinates himself.

We shall not discuss, on this occasion, the observations of Mommsen, which are founded on a misconception of the constitution of the early Roman army. It seems to me that the principal aim of this legend is to glorify the merits of the family. It desires to teach that the Romans, and the Fabian family in particular, were not less brave than the Spartans, who were considered the bravest of the Greeks. The legend of the Fabii is not the only deed of arms which suggested to the Romans a comparison with the heroic Leonidas. A few decades after Fabius Pictor, Cato contrasted with the noble Spartan king the figure of an obscure military tribune, Q. Cædicius, who, in the neighborhood of Camarina and during the first Punic War (258 B.C.), rescued the Roman army with only 400 companions. To make the similarity still greater, some writers actually reduced these 400 to 300.[31] Cato himself, moreover, together with Manlius (just as the Persians led by Idarne and Ephialtes), scaled by night the hill overhanging Thermopylæ, and thus rendered possible the defeat of Antiochus, who had fortified himself there (191 B.C.). And, in the passage in which he so greatly praises his own deed, Cato confesses that the thought of undertaking such an enterprise had been suggested to him by the recollection of that famous episode of the Persian War.[32]

The parallelism between the Spartan and the Roman history was not limited to the legend of the Fabii. The race which for so long had held the political and the military hegemony of the Peloponnese, and had for some time imposed it upon the rest of the Greeks; the race which was considered to have given origin to the Sabines—such a race more than any other lent itself to furnishing pretended origins to the institutions of the Roman people. The Romans later treated the degenerate Spartans and Athenians with deference in virtue of their glorious past. Therefore, there have not been lacking scholars to maintain that the 300 *celeres Romani* were an imitation of the 300 Spartan *hippeis;* the senate, an imitation of the *gerusia;* the banquets of the curiæ, a derivation from the *pheiditia;* and the tribunes of the people, an institution entirely analogous to the Spartan Ephors. The number of five Ephors, indeed, seems to have been the origin of the false tradition that at first the representatives of the plebs were not two or four, but five.

The national tendency of likening Roman events to Greek, fostered by the Greeks themselves, reached the point of actually declaring the Roman constitution a pure imitation of the Spartan. Other tales, such as that of the embassy to Athens at the time of the Twelve Tables, tended instead to prove the Athenian origin of the Roman constitution.[33]

The repetition of the episode of the Spartans at Thermopylæ is not an isolated phenomenon. It is to be connected with a mass of traditions which, beginning with the second century (the earliest period of Roman historiography), were generally accepted by the most authoritative writers. Sparta, however, was not alone in furnishing material to be abundantly used by the Romans. Athens, with its story of Harmodius and Aristogeiton, the slayers of Hipparchus (who had become enamored of a fair maiden), suggested the legend of Lucretia, or of Brutus and Valerius, the liberators of their country. And, surely, it is not coincidence, but rather the result of deliberate falsification, that the expulsion of the Pisistratidæ falls in 510 B.C., and that in 509 B.C. should have occurred the expulsion of the Tarquins—the tyrants in both cases being the builders of the principal temple of their nation. The Roman historian undoubtedly had in mind the history of Athens, when, for the year 433 B.C., he relates an entirely imaginary pestilence, merely to establish a parallel with the celebrated plague described by Thucydides. With Aristides and Phocion were contrasted the Latin Fabricius and Curius Dentatus; and the ancients themselves recognized that the story of Coriolanus had been cast in such a way as partly to corre-

THE FABII

spond,—both in chronology and in other particulars,—with that of the Athenian Themistocles. Of all the stories of the Hellenic races which the Romans hastened to imitate and to reproduce we must here recall that of Alexander the Great.
The striving for imitation seems to have existed from very early times. It manifests itself in the fact that, in the story of M. Furius Camillus, there are elements taken bodily from the adventures of Alexander. From the very beginning of Roman annals Fabius Pictor seems to contrast with the great Macedon his own ancestor, Fabius Rullianus, who was the first to advance beyond Mount Ciminus, invade Etruria and penetrate as far as Perusia, and who later was supposed to have conquered the united Italic forces at Sentinum. In fact, the ancient annalists copiously discussed the question as to what would have occurred had Alexander turned to the west. They contrasted with the son of Philip the conquerors of the Samnite Wars. The desire to compare Roman deeds to those of the Macedonian hero is evident throughout the course of Roman historiography,—from Hannibal to Cæsar and Pompey,—or rather, from Hannibal through the Empire. It would be an easy matter to enumerate the long list of Romans whose conduct was inspired by their cult for the Macedon. We may recall Pompey, who, after having conquered and overrun Asia Minor, thought to possess the right of wearing the mantle of Alexander, and who, in like manner, caused men to call him *Magnus*. Indeed, if victory, instead of falling to the cause of the deified Julius and of Octavian, had, on the contrary, been won by the successors of Pompey, rather than a series of *Cæsares* and *Kaisers,* the world would have had a long succession of *Magni.*
Cæsar, however, was of too individual a character to deign to adapt his conduct and his bearing to that of Alexander, even though feeling himself urged to rival the latter's deeds. It was natural, however, that inferior men like Crassus, Caracalla and Alexander Severus should have endeavored to imitate the Greek conqueror. Considering, then, the freshness of the impressions and the conduct of the Diadochoi, it does not seem strange that the deeds of Alexander should have been imitated by so prominent a character as Scipio Africanus. We have just spoken of the Diadochoi—the successors of Alexander, who made it their study to imi-

tate the movements and the gestures of the great general, and who considered themselves fortunate if, in their physique, there was something resembling, and hence recalling, that of the Macedon. The motions and the bearing of Alexander the Great were assumed by his contemporaries in the same manner as the contemporary princes of Frederick of Prussia imitated his gestures and bearing. All may easily see that this propensity is strong in our own age.

The historical atmosphere in which the Romans lived at the time when they set out to conquer the world explains why they could not escape such influences. It is easily understood how Scipio Africanus (who, as is known, tried to create a personal government), in order to imitate Alexander the son of Zeus, by his very bearing caused men to spread similar reports regarding his own origin. Likewise, his historians affirmed that Scipio had captured Carthage with the aid of Neptune, his uncle, in the same manner as Poseidon had aided his nephew Alexander in the capture of Tyre. Finally, the generous behavior of Alexander towards Darius' wife (who had become his prisoner) was asserted, by some, to have been imitated by Scipio, who sent back undefiled the beautiful daughter of the Spaniard Indibilis.

Thus it is seen that the statesmen and the historians of the second century and of the succeeding ages sought for inspiration in the bearing of the great men of Greece and in its great events. Naturally this endeavor must have appeared also in the earliest history of Rome, in which are to be recognized the chronological precedents of the anxious imitation so firmly and so deeply rooted in the time of the earliest annalists. The Romans, in emerging from a degree of culture so inferior to that of Greece, felt the necessity of entering into line with the more civilized peoples, who, in turn, were their inferiors in physical training and in military education. The nation which, only a few decades after conquering Hannibal, had already subjugated the kingdoms of the Seleucidæ and Macedonia, felt humiliated in confessing itself less ancient and poorer in history than the conquered nations. It was natural that, during the period in which Greece and Macedonia had not yet been entirely subdued, and in which Athens was still a political State whose integrity was respected by all, the Romans should have been content with declaring their deeds equal to those of Greece. It is natural, too, that, writing within this period, Postumius Albinus should have excused himself for presenting a history written in bad Greek.

Cato, however, who began to write his history a few years after the battles of Cynoscephalæ and Magnesia had assured to the Romans the supremacy of the world, naturally did not limit himself to mere comparisons of Roman and Greek deeds. He endeavored, instead, to bring into special prominence the virtues of the Romans. In Cato's eyes Cædicius was superior to Leonidas himself—Cædicius, whose deeds were so insignificant that other annalists, instead of Cædicius, made mention of a certain Laberius or Calpurnius Flamma. This comparison recalls the more or less legendary centurion Siccius Dentatus, whom annalists styled the Roman Achilles.[34] In the mind of the Italian Cato the deed at Camarina assumed greater importance than that at Thermopylæ. And this feeling of contempt which Cato felt for the Greeks of his age (so different from the Greeks of the ancient Hellas), added to a very strong pride in his country's greatness, explains why, in writing his *Origines* in Latin, he disdainfully speaks of Postumius Albinus, who had excused himself to the Greeks for his lack of proficiency in their tongue.

Fabius Pictor, Postumius Albinus and Cato, whether writing in Greek or in Latin, or comparing Roman deeds to Greek ones in different languages and in different ways, had but one aim—to glorify Rome by contrasting her with the more ancient Hellenic civilizations. The annalist who conceived such comparisons was actuated, not so much by false pride, but by the conception that to defend and proclaim the glory of one's country was equivalent to performing the duties of good citizenship. To treat of the antiquity of Rome and of the valor and the prudence of its commanders and statesmen was to sustain the moral prestige of the nation and to inculcate the fact that Rome was worthy of commanding other races. This sentiment was gradually exaggerated. Poor and servile Greeks, who betook themselves to Rome in search of bread and position, flattered this sentiment of the Romans, and placed at its service both their renown and their pen. The day came when the Romans, disdaining all such comparisons, believed themselves in every way superior to the Greeks. In the first period, the Greek historical novelists modestly endeavored to transfer to Roman history the legends of the Babylonian Zopyros (who was compared with Sextus Tarquinius), and of Periander and Cypselus. Later annalists ventured to declare Roman institutions as ancient and as glorious as those of Greece. But between these two there fell still a third and intermediate period, in which the Romans attempted to compete by recounting those national deeds which they judged worthy of comparison with the most glorious ones of Greece. The legend of the Fabii at the Cremera, as all the traditional annals of the second century, belongs to the middle period; to it, too, belongs the history of Fabius Pictor.

The imitating of foreign history is, moreover, a frequent occurrence, and has manifested itself in every people and in every literature. The Romans reproduced the history of Athens, of Sparta and of Alexander; similar legendary stories are found in the annals of different Germanic races; and the Italian historians of the Renaissance repeated and copied literally situations and events already found in Livy and in th Roman writers. A study of this phenomenon, comprising all the modern histories, has already given, and will continue to give, interesting results. It will suffice to cite an example, very characteristic and suitable to our case—the legends, namely, of the Middle Ages and of modern times which draw their origin precisely from the story of the Spartans at Thermopylæ and of the Fabii at the Cremera. These legends must have been present to those who spoke of the Venetian Giustiniani in the Orient—all massacred with but one exception; and of the Pisans, annihilated by the Genoese. The old Greek and Roman legends must, likewise, have been present to him who first spoke of the 300 heroes of Pforzheim who were exterminated on the 6th of May, 1622, at Wimpfen. To-day, however, it is generally recognized that the deed of the Giustiniani is fictitious, and that it is false that the 300 heroes fell at Wimpfen. Dionysius of Halicarnassus, in his version of the legend of the Fabii at the Cremera (it will be remembered), said that it smacked of the legendary and the theatrical. And the story of the 300 of Pforzheim found its way into some German histories through the impression caused by a drama in which those heroes were mentioned for the first time—heroes that were literally reproduced from the old annals of Sparta and of Rome.

CHAPTER X

THE LEGENDS OF LUCRETIA AND OF VIRGINIA, AND THE
CULTS OF THE PRISCI LATINI

OF all the ancient Roman legends, that of the fair Virginia is certainly one of the most charming, and also one of the richest in poetic elements. Ardently desired by the wealthy and haughty Appius Claudius for her beauty, Virginia was on the point of falling a prey to the proud patrician. Vain had been the proofs of her free birth presented by her father and her fiancé, Icilius. Appius Claudius pronounced the sentence in his own interests; and the maid was about to be delivered to his client Claudius when she is unexpectedly snatched from impending dishonor by the avenging dagger seized by her father in a neighboring butcher's stall. The maid expires at the foot of the statue of Venus Cloacina, the protectress of virgin modesty; but her death becomes the signal for uprisings and revolutions. The plebeians destroy the tyranny of the Decemvirate, restore the former consular government, and, with it, the tribunate of the people. Liberty flourishes once again on Roman soil. I emphasize this fact because the blood of Virginia restored liberty to the Romans, just as that of Lucretia, the victim of the young Tarquinius, had already rescued it from servitude to the kings.

The similarity between the story of Virginia and that of the chaste Lucretia, the wife of Tarquinius Collatinus, extends even to minor details. In the legend of Lucretia (as in that of Virginia) the tragedy is preceded by an embassy to Greece, for the purpose of becoming acquainted with new and better laws.[1] On the death of the one (as on that of the other) there succeed the popular laws of the Valerii. In regard to the causes, Lucretia was dishonored by Tarquinius while the neighboring city of Ardea was being besieged; Virginia was wronged more or less in the same year in which there occurred at Ardea a similar secession on account of a maid. Finally, in both cases, there follows a political treaty between Rome and Ardea. Brutus vindicates the liberty of the Roman people by brandishing the knife with which Lucretia was slain, and swears revenge over the corpse which had been brought into the Curia near the temple of Venus Cloacina. Likewise, the father of Virginia, near that same statue, grasps a knife from those *tabernæ novæ* which had been inaugurated by a Brutus in 192 B.C.[2] In short, the two legends are, both in their general and their minor characteristics, so very closely related as to make it quite evident that they are two different versions of but one story—a story which connects the history of Roman liberty with the martyrdom of a woman. Lucretia causes the fall of the monarchy; Virginia, that of the patrician oligarchy.

What is related of the two women, however, is not of the slightest historical value. Lucretia, the most virtuous of the brides of the reigning house of Tarquinius, is but a differentiation of Gaia Cæcilia, and is surrounded with a series of quite fantastic stories relating to the pretended seven kings of Rome. Lucretia, the wife of Tarquinius, is not separate from the chaste Lucretia, spouse of Numa, nor, perhaps, from that wife of King Servius who committed suicide in consequence of the crime of another Tarquin. Likewise, the story of the maid Virginia is surrounded by a mass of historical and legal impossibilities referred to the fifth century and to the Decemvirate, impossibilities which I have elsewhere subjected to minute examination.[3]

From the psychological point of view, so to speak, the legends of Lucretia and of Virginia do not present anything uncommon. It has been often noted (beginning with Aristotle and even with Herodotus) that struggles over a woman have resulted in political revolutions. Aristotle, in enumerating the minor causes that provoke uprisings, mentions that of love in regard to political changes which occurred at Syracuse, at Mytilene and among the Phocians. Indeed, he actually cites examples of revolutions at Delphi and at Epidamnus on occasion of weddings.[4] Love (as Thucydides testifies) caused the death of Hipparchus, which was followed by the expulsion of Hippias from Athens. In about the same period that legend assigns to Lucretia, the love of Aristodemus for Xenocrite presented Cumæ with the occasion for regaining its lost liberties.[5] For less ancient periods, it will suffice to recall how the promise of marriage between Buondelmonte and a maid of the Amidei was, according to the Florentine historians, the cause which established also in that city the two factions of Guelph and Ghibelline. Examples could be multiplied indefinitely. Probability, however, is quite a different matter from reality; the former pertains to romance—the latter to history. Since, then, a long series of narratives and events proves the non-historic character of the beautiful episodes of Lucretia and of Virginia, it is behooving to investigate what causes were responsible for their formation and their insertion into the story of the earliest Roman deeds.

The answer to this question is readily obtained from an examination of what Livy narrates for the sixth year after the death of Virginia—a story by other annalists referred (as it seems) to the very year of her death.

In the year 311 of the city (443 B.C.) the Paduan historian says that there arrived at Rome ambassadors from the neighboring city of Ardea, to implore aid against the popular party which was then greatly endangering their fatherland. The following were the facts: There lived at Ardea a maid of humble origin (*virgo plebeii generis*), famous for her beauty. Two youths became enamored of her, the one a noble, the other a plebeian. A marriage with the latter was favored by the guardians of the maid, themselves plebeians; the mother, however, who looked kindly upon a union with the nobility, favored the young patrician. Since the guardians and she could not come to an agreement, they resorted to a judge, who decided that the marriage should take place according to the wishes of the mother. There arose thence a great tumult. The guardians, having bitterly complained in the square of the city, collected some plebeians, by whose aid they ravished the maiden from the maternal home. On the other hand, the Optimates espoused the cause of the young aristocrat, and moved upon the plebeians. A battle resulted, and the plebeians were expelled from the city; but, having fortified themselves upon a hill, they in turn devastated the lands of the aristocrats with fire and sword. At this juncture they were reënforced by those plebeians who had remained within the city, and together they prepared to besiege the city. When events had reached such a pass, the Optimates sadly found themselves obliged to entreat help from Rome.

The plebeians, in their turn, appealed to the arms of the

Volscians, who, on their arrival under the leadership of Æquus Cluilius, surrounded the city with a rampart. The Roman consul, M. Geganius, similarly enclosed the Volscians, who were consequently compelled to surrender. The Volscian leader graced the triumphal chariot of Geganius; and the Roman senate ordered that the leaders of the rebellion should be beheaded. On account of this civil war the citizens of Ardea were greatly reduced, and in the following year (442 B.C.) new colonists were led thither. There was thus decided, in a most practical manner, a dispute of the previous year concerning the territory of Ardea which had been seized by Rome.[6]

It is not necessary to enter upon a long discussion to demonstrate that this story of the *virgo* and of the secession from Ardea is, in substance (as also in many details), a mere repetition of the legend of Virginia. Both maids are plebeians. At Ardea the guardians insist upon a wedding with the plebeian suitor; at Rome the father and the relatives desire that Virginia should marry the plebeian Icilius. The magistrate at Ardea does not (as the judge at Rome) desire the maid for himself; but, as at Rome, he decides in favor of the Optimates. What is still more important is that in both cities a private quarrel gives origin to the same serious consequences—namely, to civil war and to the secession of the plebs, which in both cases occupies a hill outside the city walls and prepares to wage war against the fatherland. Livy, who clearly perceives the points of contact between this story and that of the first Roman secession, says that the defeated plebeians of Ardea were in no wise similar to the Roman plebs, because they left the city as an armed body, and, taking possession of a hill, made incursions upon the estates of the aristocrats with fire and sword. But it must be observed that, according to other traditions recorded by Livy himself, the Roman plebs, even in the first secession (which, when all is said, is a repetition of the same event), devastated the lands of the patricians.[7] Furthermore, in the story of the second secession, we see the Roman army encamped on Mons Algidus making common cause with the plebeians who had remained in the city, and, guided by the father of Virginia, moving hostilely against Rome.

The two stories are identical, not only in the main outline, but also in some minor details. It is evident that

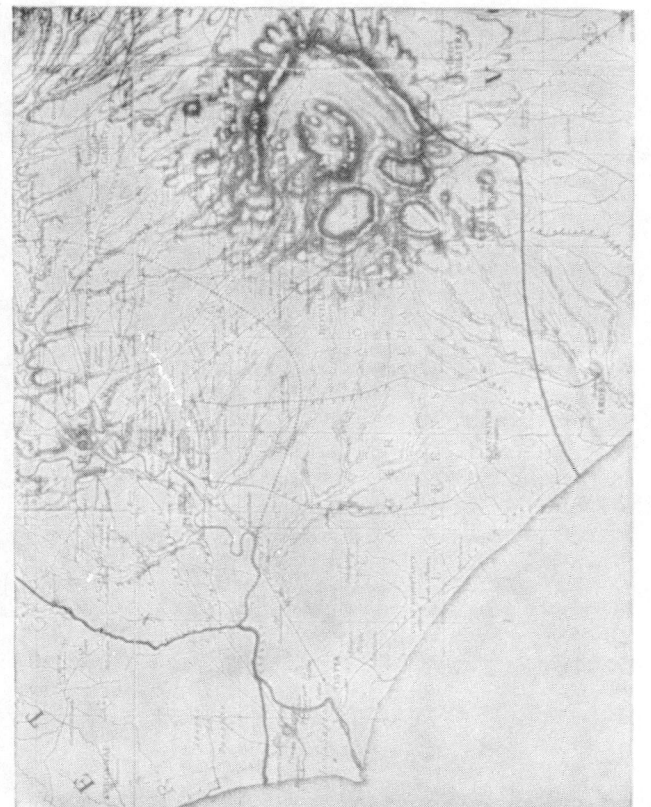

THE COUNTRY OF THE PRISCI LATINI

Æquus Cluilius, who leads the Volscians against the Optimates of Ardea and who surrounds the city with a *vallum*, is in no wise different from that Cluilius, King of Alba, who similarly advances against Rome and gives origin to the name *Cluiliæ fossæ*.[8] At about the same time in which Æquus Cluilius marches against Ardea. the Romans are engaged in war with the Æqui and the Volscians, who had taken advantage both of the secession at Ardea and of the one at Rome. Indeed, they had advanced as far as the Porta Esquilina in the hope of capturing the city divided against itself.[9] They do not, however, succeed in their attempt, being conquered by the legendary T. Quinctius Cincinnatus—that same person who, fifteen years earlier, was supposed to have conquered the same enemies, under the leadership (even then) of a Cluilius.[10] Though the two stories are practically identical, some slight discrepancies exist that have no great weight either one way or the other. The important variant that Virginia was motherless whereas the maid of Ardea was fatherless, and that the former was saved by her father while the latter was aided by her mother, do but confirm the general lines of the legend.

It is evident at first sight that the same event, accompanied by the same political consequences after a few years, or (according to other chronological computations) in the same year, has been repeated for different years.[11] This conclusion will appear still more evident if it be considered that the magistrate at Ardea declares valid a marriage between patrician and plebeian in 443 B.C., and that such a union had been legally recognized at Rome only two years before, as a result of the *lex Canuleia*. The passing of this law represents conditions different from those which others supposed to have been attained by the laws of the Twelve Tables.[12]

The undoubted similarity between the two stories naturally causes the question as to which of them is the more ancient and authentic, and which may have served as a pattern for the other. It is absurd to maintain that this extended story is of Roman origin, and that from Rome it penetrated into the annals of Ardea. This is contrary to the nature of Roman historiography, which very rarely gathers facts foreign to the Roman Fasti. An exhaustive study of the legend obliges us to accept the contrary view. Likewise, the legend of Lucretia does not belong to Rome, but to

Ardea and to Collatia, in which latter city Lucretia was supposed to have lived.

It is clear, therefore, that we have here one of the many infiltrations of the history of the Prisci Latini into the Roman annals.[13]

We have already had occasion (in speaking of Servius Tullius) of recognizing such borrowing from the legends and the myths of Aricia. We must now establish this phenomenon, and in even greater degree, in the case of Ardea. We find this city constantly connected with Rome, whether in the time of the Decemvirate or in that of the Gallic invasion, when it was from Ardea and at the head of the Ardeates that the liberator Camillus arrived. We shall shortly return to this question. We note, in the meantime, that, even conceding the story of Virginia to have originated in that of Ardea, we refrain from considering worthy of belief what is related of that similar secession at Ardea, or of the intervention of the Romans in 443 B.C. The history of the relations between Ardea and Rome after the fall of the Decemvirate is not, either historically or chronologically, by any means more certain or authentic than the history of the relations assumed for the period of the expulsion of the kings.

In the history of the struggles for the territory of Ardea and of Aricia in 446 B.C. there is found a certain Scaptius. As was already seen by Niebuhr, this is but the personification of the tribe Scaptia, to which belonged the territory under dispute, but which was formed only in 332 B.C. The struggles, moreover, are narrated in that part of Livy's history in which there are manifest traces of the annalist Licinius Macer. It is clear that in the history of the relations between Ardea and Rome, in the years between 446 and 442, there are many falsifications and repetitions of various kinds, whether in respect to chronology or to the name of the Roman magistrates who founded the colony.[14]

The *fœdus Ardeatinum* of 444 B.C. is to be thought of together with the founding of the Latin colony, which Livy himself dates two years later—that is, in 442 B.C. Similarly, the embassy sent by Ardea in 444 is a reduplication of that of 446, which visited Aricia after a war over the boundaries of the territory of Corioli.[15] The cause for the first embassy was a question of territory; that for the second, internal upheaval. At Rome these same events are referred

to the Decemvirate of 450-449 B.C., and the legend of Virginia must be connected either with this or with the passing of the *lex Canuleia* of 444 B.C., by which marriages between patricians and plebeians were declared legal.
Even the story of the siege of Ardea is not worthy of faith. We have seen that it resembles very closely the siege of Rome which the Volscians and the Æqui instituted after the fall of the Decemvirs, and that their leader, Æquus Cluilius, is forcibly reminiscent of the Alban King Cluilius. I omit discussing what degree of probability there may be in the statement that Ardea, a city which was besieged in 443 B.C. by an Æquus Cluilius, should have been turned the following year into a Latin colony by Cluilius Siculus, whom we find to be one of the supreme magistrates of Rome in that same year. We can scarcely consider this Æquus Cluilius, the leader of the Volscians, as different from that Cluilius, the leader of the Æqui who, in 458 B.C., was overcome by the legendary L. Quinctius Capitolinus in practically the same manner as the Volscians before Ardea had been conquered by M. Geganius.[16] In both cases the enemy are surrounded and are made to pass beneath the yoke. Both Æquus Cluilius and Cluilius, the leader of the Æqui, are made prisoners, and, to cap the climax, the colleague of the consul M. Geganius was none other than T. Quinctius Capitolinus.[17]
Likewise, it must be recalled that the deeds of the mythical T. Quinctius Cincinnatus were confused with those of L. Quinctius Cincinnatus, and that the various undertakings of Cincinnatus are narrated six or seven different times in the Roman annals. One of them is precisely in the year 440 B.C., that is, a few years later than the pretended events of which we have been speaking. Analogous remarks are suggested by the names of the triumvirs *coloniæ deducendæ*, Menenius Agrippa, T. Cluilius Siculus, and M. Æbutius Helva. T. Cluilius Siculus (according to Dionysius, who, in this case, follows the same source as Livy) is one of the military tribunes *consulari potestate* of the year 444 B.C., in which the *fœdus Ardeatinum* was established.[18] Æbutius Helva is, too, similar to the homonymous consul of 442 B.C., in which Ardea was transformed into a colony.[19] Consequently, it is not inappropriate to ask whether or not Menenius Agrippa is the consul of 439. It is true that, according to the custom of Roman constitutional law, it

was entirely possible, in the historic period, to bear at the same time the office of consul and of the magistrate presiding over the founding of a colony.[20] Nevertheless, such names cause some suspicion when it is considered that, according to Livy, those three magistrates remained in the colony which they founded; and when, in addition to the chronological contradictions, there are examined also other data relative to the history of Ardea and to the foundation of the Latin colony.

Even if there were no grounds for suspicion from the legal point of view, all the narratives would appear as little worthy of faith from the historical standpoint. If a careful examination be made of the frequent repetitions in the history of Roman magistracies and magistrates from 509 B.C. throughout the fourth century, it results that the same persons are at different times made consuls, dictators and tribunes of the people. The same persons, too, are many times assigned to ages so widely distant from each other that it would cause no surprise if our Menenius Agrippa is to be identified with that Menenius Agrippa who, according to other versions, played so conspicuous a part in the famous secession of 494 B.C. This same Agrippa (more or less altered) reappears in the agrarian agitations of 440, 439, 410 and 357 B.C. The same Valerius reappears (and on occasion of similar laws) at the time of King Tullus Hostilius, of the expulsion of the kings, of Menenius Agrippa, of Menenius of Ardea in 449 B.C., and again in 300 B.C. In our case, the suspicion that we have before us data of no historical worth is confirmed by the fact that the consuls supposed to have made the *fœdus Ardeatinum* of 444 B.C. were L. Papirius Mugilanus and L. Sempronius Atratinus. These consuls, whom Licinius Macer found mentioned in the *libri lintei* preserved in the temple of Juno Moneta, were (to the justification of Livy) unknown to the ancient Roman annals and to the records of the magistrates.[21] We have before us, therefore, false data. It is likewise false that these same persons were the censors for the following year, 443 B.C. Indeed, some traditions dated the origin of the censorship only in 435 B.C.[22]

In short, the serious doubts which pervade the entire Roman history of this period operate with still greater vigor for the less famous cities of Latium. We are compelled to believe, then, that the story of the maid of Ardea, though more ancient than that of the Roman Virginia, arose in an age comparatively late, and was adapted to conditions far later than those to which the original story referred. If, however, we should desire to find the origin, both of the story of Ardea and of the parallel Roman one of Virginia, we must necessarily resort to the most ancient religious legends of the Latin stock.

In the earliest history of the Roman Republic we frequently meet with legends whose origins were due to imported Greek myths. From such legends there are later developed events that are historical in appearance. It is certain that the cult of the Sicilian Demeter localized in Rome the legend of Telines of Gela, who was transformed into Menenius Agrippa or Valerius Maximus. The myth of Castor and Pollux gave life to the story of the Dioscuri at the battle of Lake Regillus, fought in about 494 B.C.

Finally, the temple of Pietas, which was vowed by Manius Acilius Glabrio for his victory over Antiochus of Syria at Thermopylæ and which was dedicated ten years later, in 181 B.C., transplanted to Roman soil the Attic legend of Xanthippe and Mycon.[23]

Ardea was not more backward than Rome, Tusculum or Aricia in thus harboring foreign cults. Ardea, too, maintained very close relations with Sicily.[24] Just as Siceliot artists decorated the temple of Ceres at Rome,[25] so a Greek artist ornamented at Ardea the temple of Juno Regina and was, in turn, granted the citizenship of the town.[26] At Ardea, finally, there was a very ancient temple of the Dioscuri, in which there was represented (in paintings equally old and surely the work of a Greek artist) the story of Capaneus.[27] But, in the temple of the Dioscuri, the story of Helen, their sister, could not have been omitted; for she was worshipped in equal degree and together with them, not only on the native soil of the Peloponnese, in Sicily and in Magna Græcia, but also at Rome.[28] The story, then, of the beautiful maid of Ardea who was loved by the two rivals and who was the cause of her city's ruin, is, at bottom, merely the story of the beautiful Spartan. Are we to think, therefore, that the more ancient and famous Greek legend, or, to be more exact, that the explanation of the painting in which this myth was represented, gave origin to the anecdote of the maid of Ardea?

I refrain from asserting this to be the case. I emphasize

the fact, however, that Ardea was the political and the religious home of that cult of Aphrodite or Lavinia-Vesta who, like Helen, was the cause of such bitter wars between the Rutuli and the Latins—between Æneas and Turnus. The temple of Aphrodite was situated in the Latin Lavinium. But surely, after the struggle between the mythical Turnus and Æneas (which legend placed in very early times), the management of the cult was in the hands of the Rutuli of Ardea, the most prominent community of that region.[29] As a result of the battle fought at the foot of Mount Veseris, as well as of the continued victories won over the Latini by the consuls C. Mænius and L. Furius Camillus, the Romans (tradition says) conceded citizenship to various towns of the Prisci Latini, with the understanding that the various cults should become the common patrimony of both the conquerors and the conquered.[30] With this influx of Latin cults into Rome are to be connected the legend of Tutela who saves the Romans, that one of the temple of Juno Caprotina at Lavinium, and that of Coriolanus who (as is implied in the very name) was connected with the ancient Corioli and with the spring of the goddess Ferentina. With this same introduction of foreign myths (as we have had occasion to establish in a preceding chapter) is related the cult of Orestes, which was transplanted to Rome from Aricia, and the legend of the sixth king of Rome, Servius Tullius, who is but the pale reflection of the cult of Diana Aricina and of the *servus rex nemorensis*—that is, the king of the Arician grove.[31] About 340 B.C. the Romans had established a special *fœdus* with the knights of Lavinium, and later, in 338 B.C., had punished the Laurinates for having entered upon an alliance with the rebellious Latini. It is natural, then, to believe that, particularly in this period, the cult of Vesta and of the Penates of the Lauro-Lavinians should have become entirely Romanized.[32] The cult of Vesta and of the spring Juturna, after having been transferred to Rome and located on the slopes of the Palatine, forced into oblivion Caca, the Vestal of the Palatine, as well as the cult of the Lares.[33] This latter cult, which was ascribed to King Ancus Marcius, was later restored to honor by Augustus.

It is obvious that the cults of Ardea must have had the same lot. In a more ancient period Ardea had had a great

MONTE CAVO (MONS ALBANUS) AND THE LAKE OF ALBANO

political importance; and this period (subsequent, perhaps, to the still more ancient glory of Lavinium) is the opening of the fifth century. Ardea, in fact, played a conspicuous part in the struggles with the Etruscans and the Gauls, at the time of Porsenna and of Camillus respectively. By Greek annalists she is placed in relation with Cumæ and with the tyrant Aristodemus Malaco. What is stated by Greek historiography is, in part, related also by the Roman annals of the fifth century, and is assigned by legend to the eleventh century B.C., in speaking of the mythical wars of Æneas against Turnus and Mezentius, king of the Etruscan Cære. Concerning the subsequent importance of Ardea, we obtain some small light from the Greek legend which considered Ardea, Rome and Antium (the largest maritime city of Latium and of the country of the Volscians) as the three daughters of Ulysses and of Circe.[34] Ardea passed as one of those cities which had transmitted to Rome some of their institutions. Some authors, indeed, derive from Lucerus, King of Ardea, the name and the institution of the Luceres—one of the most ancient Roman tribes, which, by others, was connected with Lucumo Tarquinius and the Etruscans.[35] Likewise there were not lacking Roman annalists who asserted that the institution of the Fetiales was borrowed by the Romans, not from the Æquicoli, but from Ardea.[36] Even in the time of Cicero Roman priests performed sacred ceremonies at the Ardeatine temple of Natio [37]—namely, of that divinity which presided over births.

Surely, that people which, as was asserted by its own writers, appropriated the territory of Ardea without any claims whatsoever, similarly seized upon the episode of the maid of Ardea.[38] It is to be remarked that the Romans who, as the result of *deditio,* made themselves masters of *divina humanaque omnia,* could very well and with full legality appropriate even the history of the subject peoples.[39] This is not mere hypothesis and probability, but historical reality. It is proved by the fact that (as we have already noted) the Romans appropriated the cult of Lavinium after historical wars which we cannot determine with precision, but which could not have been waged without the direct or indirect participation of Ardea. The close religious connection between Ardea-Lavinium and Rome is proved by the fact that Roman priests and magistrates yearly betook themselves to those cities to perform sacred ceremonies.[40]

These ceremonies (as all know) were those of the Aphrodite or Venus who answered to the native name of Lavinia or Ferentina. We have already seen that the legend of Virginia, whose origin was that of the maid of Ardea, was in close topographical relation with the sanctuary of Venus Cloacina.[41] It is natural to believe, then, that there is a similar sacred and topographic element in the story of Ardea. Nor will it be difficult to discover the original tale, if it be considered that the story of the maid of Ardea who, according to the desires of her guardians, was to have married a plebeian, but who, in obedience to her mother's will, became, instead, the bride of a patrician, is simply a version of the legend of the goddess Lavinia. In this latter legend, her father Latinus bestows Lavinia upon Æneas the foreigner, whereas Amata, the mother, desires her to be the bride of Turnus. In the more ancient legend it is Vesta-Amata, and not her daughter Vesta-Lavinia, who commits suicide; in the later versions Lucretia and Virginia perish. But in this we see only a slight variation of the fundamental conception.[42] Thus, what was at first the subject-matter of legend and of religious ceremonies became, in the end, the material for history, just as, for instance, the myths and the cults of Ceres gave occasion to the formation of the history of the agrarian agitations in those same years.

With due consideration of the date ascribed to the *foedus Ardeatinum*, bearing in mind, also, that, according to annalists like Licinius Macer, a copy of this *foedus* was preserved in the temple of Juno Moneta on the Capitoline citadel, it is rather tempting to believe this myth to have penetrated into Rome at least as early as the fifth century. The narratives of the secession at Ardea and of the Roman secessions of the fifth century are false, and only in 332 B.C. was the tribe Scaptia formed, to which reference is made in the story of the contest between Ardea and Rome. These facts teach us that the introduction of the legend of Virginia must be ascribed to a more recent date. The *foedus Ardeatinum* ascribed to 444 B.C. cannot be earlier than 345 B.C., in which year the temple of Juno Moneta was erected, since the treaty was said to have been preserved in that temple. Moreover, we have seen that the information regarding the magistrates mentioned therein does not appear in the earliest annals.[43] In the story of Roman intervention in the affairs of Ardea we have a false exposition set forth by the jurist-annalists of the end of the Republic, such as Licinius Macer. On the other hand, with due consideration of the fact that only in 340 B.C. did the Romans become the representatives of the cults of Lavinium, we find no reason for attributing to a more ancient period the influx of the myths of Ardea. For, though this city had, up to that time, held a special position towards Rome, she must have lost such position after the important victories over the Latins in 340-338 B.C., and after Rome's alliance with Capua.

There still remained a trace of the former importance of Ardea in the myths and the cults referred to. It is revealed, also, by the fact that Rome ever makes mention of this city on occasion of the crises in Roman life—such as the expulsion of the Etruscan kings, the fall of the patriciate, the establishment of the plebeian State, and, finally, the coming of the exiled Camillus from Ardea when Rome was burned by the Gauls.

The stories of Lucretia and of Virginia are, then, but late elaborations of legends related to the cults of Ardea—cults which were transplanted to Rome in the second half of the fourth century. The cults of all the neighboring Latin cities were, at different times, similarly transferred to the capital of Latium. Therefore, it is fully intelligible how, in adapting itself to new soil, the myth should have been enriched with new elements of local color, and how various touches, historical in character, were added by the annalists of the second and first centuries B.C.

We can still trace some of these later additions. In a fragment of the twentieth book of Livy it is narrated that the patrician Publius Clœlius, contrary to all precedent, had wedded one related to him by blood, though removed to the seventh degree. She had already been betrothed to M. Rutilius, a plebeian. This one, publicly grieving at the violation of an ancient law (which, at the same time, robbed him of his bride), fomented an uprising of such formidable proportions as to compel the senators to flee from the curia and to seek shelter in the Capitolium. The fragment is so mutilated that it would be vain to endeavor anything beyond establishing whether or not this episode (assigned to 241-

218 B.C.) actually contributed to the later literary casting of our legend.[44] Towards the localizing of the myth in the Forum, however, the cult of Venus Cloacina must have greatly contributed. With this sanctuary, indeed, the death of Virginia was connected; and with it, too (I believe), must be joined another tale preserved in Livy, when he speaks of the origin of the cult of Pudicitia Plebeia.

In narrating the events of 296 B.C., Livy affirms that there occurred a serious disturbance at Rome near the temple of Pudicitia Patricia, situated in the Forum Boarium, near the round temple of Hercules. Virginia, daughter of Aulus (a man of patrician ancestry), was thrust away from the temple by patrician matrons because she had wedded L. Volumnius, an illustrious man, but a plebeian. In vain did Virginia proclaim her patrician birth, her chaste life, her single marriage. She asserted that, rather than feeling any sense of shame, she was proud that her husband was not a patrician, but a plebeian. She seconded her words with deeds. In the house on the vicus Longus (where she lived) she cleared a space in which she set up an altar to Pudicitia Plebeia; and, having gathered therein the plebeian matrons, she expressed the prayer that it might be said of this goddess that she was more religiously and more chastely honored than Pudicitia Patricia.[45]

In strong contrast with this version of Livy,—that it was from the temple of Pudicitia Patricia in the Forum Boarium that Virginia had been removed,—there is a fact of paramount importance. Aside from the fact that in this area (situated as it was, outside the ancient *pomerium*) it would be difficult to discover traces of an ancient patrician cult, we actually know that there did exist in that region a temple of Pudicitia—but it was of Pudicitia Plebeia. It was that temple which (as we have had occasion to see in the legend of Servius Tullius) was by some reputed to be the seat of the goddess Fortuna.[46] From this error, however, it does not by any means result that the story in Livy should be discarded as a whole, without further consideration. The difficulty is easily removed if the scene which Livy places in the Forum Boarium is, instead, referred either to the temple of Fortuna Seia near the Velia, or to the Forum Romanum, and particularly to the Sacra Via at that precise spot where was the sacellum of Venus Cloacina.[47]

Tradition, in fact, dated this monument as early as the

REMAINS OF THE BASILICA ÆMILIA, ON THE SITE OF THE TABERNÆ NOVÆ

times of Tatius. At this place, as a result of the intervention of the Sabine women, had the fathers and the husbands formed the fundamental compact of the united nations. Venus Cloacina thus became recognized as the goddess of chaste and holy matrimony. The cult of Venus Cloacina is strictly patrician; and, if it is related that the plebeian Virginius slew his daughter near the statue of that goddess, such a statement proves still further that the legend of Virginia was connected with the patrician cult of Venus Cloacina, and demonstrates the foreign origin of the tale localized in the Forum Romanum. The transference occurred only after the neighboring *tabernæ* had been altered

in 192 B.C. by the plebeian M. Junius Brutus and had consequently been called plebeian. In other words, it occurred only after alterations made by a member of that plebeian family which aspired to trace its origin to L. Junius Brutus, the pseudo-patrician recognized as the first consul of the Republic.[48] From the *macellum,* therefore, that had thus been repaired by the plebeian Brutus sprang the characteristic element of the butcher's knife with which Virginius slew his daughter. At any rate, it is a very significant coincidence that both the myth of Virginia and that of the maid of Ardea refer to loves or unions between plebeians and patricians. Similarly, the legends of Æneas and of Turnus spoke of the maid Lavinia, whose hand was sought for both by a prominent native and by a foreign leader.

The annalists of the third to the first century enriched the story of the earliest deeds with a wealth of details. The writers of the last centuries distorted the legends which constituted the first-hand material for the earliest political history. This does not, however, prevent us from tracing and discovering the first origins of such stories. An accurate examination of data will enable us to establish the character and the significance of those cults from which, rather than from any historical facts, such legends were derived.

We know that Æneas, who aspired to the hand of Lavinia, was merely an ancient Latin god. Lavinia is Vesta; and Æneas, who falls into the Numicius and becomes the god of those waters honored under the name of Jupiter Indiges, is, at the same time, a solar and river divinity.[49] For this reason that fountain at Laurentum was sacred to the Sun, which was said to have sprung up on the arrival of the Trojan hero.[50] Turnus, also, is a river deity,—Turnus, whom Vergil represents as the brother of the fountain Juturna, which flowed in a region not distant from Lavinium and from Ardea. From the river deity Turnus, finally, was named a lake in the neighboring territory of Aricia.[51] The sacred traditions said that Vesta-Lavina was beloved by two streams, just as the fountain Juturna and the goddess of the springs, Venilia, were said to be loved by a river and solar divinity at the same time as by Janus. In like manner, we must recognize as river divinities both Egeria and Numa or Numicius, who were originally worshipped in the grove at Aricia and who later became, respectively, the well-known king of Rome, and his faithful counsellor in founding the State and the Roman religion.[52]

With this group of legends must be correlated King Servius Tullius, originally connected with Diana Vesta of the Arician grove, and whose name of Tullius seems to be derived from *tullius*, an old Latin word meaning a spring. Numa and Tullius, kings of Rome, were merely river and solar divinities. The same is true of Ferentina, whose springs, situated near Ardea and Aricia, were the gathering places of the Prisci Latini. To comprehend fully the meaning of the myth, it is necessary to place ourselves, in thought, in those times in which mankind did not interpose between itself and other living things so great a barrier as at present; in which the metamorphosis of a human being into a tree or a rock was considered as natural as the attributing to them of human sentiments. The loves of Janus for Juturna, and of Turnus for Lavinia, fall into the category of those myths which narrate the story of the young stream Acis, enamored of the beautiful sea-nymph Galatea, or of the stream Achelous which, flowing beneath the sea, strove to rejoin in Sicily his mistress Ortygia.

The Greek race, whose authentic political history ante-

VALLEY OF THE LACUS TURNI

dated that of Rome by many centuries, assigned such narratives to a period preceding the so-called Trojan War. The young Latin civilization similarly endeavored to attain to this great antiquity in its myths, and made Turnus and Lavinia contemporaries of the Trojan Æneas. But the lack of historical material compelled it to people with legendary characters even the subsequent periods as late as the fifth century, in which at last there flashes the first spark of national life. As the result of this process, not only Numa and Servius became kings of the earliest centuries of Roman history, but also the stream Egerius and the lake Turnus were inserted into the history of the deeds of the fifth century. Egerius, the founder of the temple of Diana Aricina, was transformed into a dictator of Tusculum, or into a relative of Tarquinius and an inhabitant of Collatia.[53] In like manner, the stream Turnus, the rival of Æneas, was changed into that Turnus Herdonius, either of Aricia or of Corioli, who vainly strove to prevent Tarquinius Superbus from becoming master of the Latin league, and who in consequence was drowned in the spring Ferentina.[54]

The process of transforming religious myths into pseudo-history is not confined to the regal period. It continues throughout the greater part of the fifth century. Lucretia and Virginia, in origin two goddesses, became mere mortals; Vulcan was changed into the lame and one-eyed Horatius Cocles; and, as we shall see in the following chapter, the god Minucius was transformed into a tribune of the people, or a *præfectus annonæ* of the end of the fifth century.

The study of the political and the constitutional history destroys and impairs those legendary tales which give to the development of Roman history a false and fantastic turn. On the other hand, the study of the evolution of the historical and the literary forms lovingly examines the legends which reconstitute for us the moral and the social conditions in which such tales were fashioned. We have no knowledge whatsoever of the religious ceremonies performed in the cults of Lavinium. It was a mystery which the annalists themselves hesitated to investigate.[55] Again, we still lack exact topographical researches as to the site of the lake of Turnus, of the fountain of Juturna near Aricia and of the various local elements which caused the formation of the love legends of these different divinities. The emptying of springs and of streams into a lake formed doubtlessly positive elements of the myth, and sacred rites, processions, and pilgrimages from one temple to another surely furnished material for varied stories and comments.

The loss of the more ancient Greek historical literature referring to the Romans, as well as that of the earliest Roman writers, prevents our following (as we would desire) the gradual development of this building up of legends. It prevents our verifying how, in consequence of successive transformations, river and solar deities gradually became either the types of legends indefinite in time, or characters connected with the developed political history. It is granted us to trace in a sufficiently exact manner only the general and fundamental lines of such phenomenon,—to understand the character and the moral conscience of the times in which such myths were transformed.

The study of law pervaded every part of the Roman people, and rendered it less fit to study other problems of the human soul. Beginning especially with the age of the Gracchi, the social and agrarian problems gave the aspect of party-struggles to all the early history, which, in reality, consisted only of myths and divine personages. Even before these annalists, who looked upon the primitive history only from the standpoint of class struggles, and who applied to it the rigid forms of a later procedure and constitutional law, the subject-matter had been treated by Greek authors and by Roman poets. Timæus and Antigonus, Ennius and Nævius set forth these stories according to the rules of an already developed art. This explains the many points of contact between such myths and Hellenic culture. But, at the same time, Nævius and Ennius represent the nobility of the Roman sentiments and the morality of their own age. The myths of Lucretia and of Virginia, when stripped of the coverings and of the legal and constitutional atmosphere in which later annalists enveloped them, reveal to us the sentiments of the Romans of the end of the fourth and the beginning of the third century.

The legends are noble and conspicuous examples of the power wielded by woman in the life and the domestic education of the golden age of the Roman people. If, indeed, Virginia and Lucretia are entirely legendary, it is all very well. But if the sacrifice of a chaste bride and of a similarly chaste maiden form a fundamental part of the history of the city,—of its rescue from the tyranny of the kings and that of the oligarchy,—then the legends are to be correlated both with the power of woman and with the respect with which she was surrounded at Rome,—a sentiment which modern criticism wrongly denies to ancient society. It is true that history, in speaking of the virtues of Roman women, draws at times upon Greek examples, and copies literally particulars pertaining to the more ancient history of Athens or of Sparta. The anecdote of Cornelia, mother of the Gracchi, who opposes her two sons to the jewels shown her by the proud Campanian matron, is but a bare repetition of the story of Phocion's wife, who extolled her husband, twenty times *strategos* of Athens, above the baubles of the wealthy Ionian.[56] But the daughter of Scipio was undoubtedly a woman of noble sentiments, and worthy of being compared with the wife of the Athenian, just as the Roman Fabricius was deserving of comparison with Aristides.[57]

Lucretia did not escape dishonor with the knife, as had the wife of the first Dionysius, or the Thessalian Theossena; Virginia was not slain by her father, the zealous guardian of her virgin chastity. The freshness and the honesty which breathe forth from this story, as well as the nobility which reigns in that of Lucretia, are a proof that Roman historical prose arose in the time when Greek historiography had fully flourished. The perpetuity of these legends does not depend only upon the excellence of such poets as Nævius and Ennius, to whom the mind recurs whenever we encounter a noble legend, such as that of Coriolanus. The skill of neither poet nor chronicler could have had the power of rendering popular such delicate types among a corrupted people, just as among a righteous people there is but little field for an unchaste muse. The legends of Lucretia and of Virginia, as well as that of the Sabine women who established peace, and of Veturia and of Volumnia, who conquered the fierce spirit of Coriolanus, could not possibly have become popular had not patriotism, respect for family life and love been held in the highest estimation. These myths, that were so dear to the earliest Latin poets, testify, at the same time, to the purity of the Romans,—the rivals and the conquerors of Pyrrhus and of Hannibal, and the destined masters of the world.

CHAPTER XI

THE LEGEND OF SPURIUS MÆLIUS, SERVILIUS AHALA, AND LUCIUS MINUCIUS

THE legends hitherto examined have led us to establish the fact that the recognized narratives relating to the first decades of the Republic are not, in any way, worthier of belief than those referring to the seven kings of Rome and to the arrival of Æneas on the shores of Latium. The external history assigned to the fifth century is, in general, an anticipation of what occurs during the fourth century. For instance, the story of the battle of Lake Regillus clearly contains elements derived from the cult of Castor and Pollux. The constitutional history and the record of internal events are rich in many and varied statements, which, particularly for such a period, are to be found in the history of no other people of classic times. But, alas, such wealth is comparable to the gilt lead which Hannibal was supposed to have deposited in the temple of Juno Lacinia in place of the golden treasure.

The passages relating to the agrarian struggles and to the turbulent tribunes of the plebs are, unfortunately, the product of an extensive falsification accomplished in the period extending from the third to the first century. Above all, they reflect the contests of the era of the Gracchi, and of the revolution of Sulla. The Licinian laws which, towards the middle of the fourth century, conceded to the plebs the right of participating in the supreme magistracies of the State are enveloped in legends and in falsifications; and the same may be said of the Publilian laws of a few decades later, by which the plebs were finally rescued from the usurers. Only towards the end of the fourth century, in the censorship, namely, of Appius Claudius and the ædileship of Gnæus Flavius, and only in the contests over the Ogulnian and the Hortensian laws (312-287 B.C.) have we before us those struggles and those victories of the plebeians which tradition persistently transferred to the first century of the Republic. In this falsified annalistic tradition, however, there appear, at times, traces of more ancient elements that are worthy of examination. But such examination reveals to us merely religious or topographical elements, arbitrarily interpreted in order to attain to a history of greater antiquity, to justify the plebeian pretensions with tales of the past, and to legitimize and give authority to the dispositions contained in the laws. With the cult of the Sicilian Demeter (which was fused with that of the Italic Ceres) are connected the episodes of Spurius Cassius, of Coriolanus, and, especially, of Menenius Agrippa. The last, indeed, was supposed to have reminded the Roman plebs of the similar and contemporaneous revolution of the Kyllyri of Syracuse against the " gamoroi "—the patricians. Likewise (as we have seen) with the cult of Ardea is connected the legend of the chaste Virginia.

A study of the years subsequent to the Decemvirate demonstrates that that period is still far removed from the field of non-legendary history. And if, on the one hand, the stories of the plebeian secessions and of the institution of the tribunate are related to the cult of the Greek Demeter, on the other hand the history of the later plebeian agitations is to be explained with the cult of the Greek Hercules. This clearly results from the tale of Spurius Mælius, who, like Spurius Cassius, aspired to sovereignty, but who was killed at the denunciation of L. Minucius and by the arm of Servilius Ahala.

This story was variously given by the different traditions, —traditions that were partly fused and partly distinct, and that are recorded in the annals of Livy and of Dionysius of Halicarnassus. In the year 315 or 314 of the city (440-439 B.C.) Rome was visited with a famine. In order to facilitate relief from such straits, the plebs elected to the office of *præfectus annonæ* L. Minucius, who, notwithstanding the sale of the corn received from Etruria, failed to relieve the plebeians. Consequently, many of these, finding it impossible to resist longer the pangs of hunger, threw themselves into the Tiber.

At this juncture a second attempt was made by a wealthy Roman knight named Spurius Mælius. Having procured great quantities of grain from Etruria and from Campania, he sold it at very low prices,—in fact, donated it sometimes to the poorest citizens. Though he won the favor of the populace by agitating for political equality, he incurred great danger. The citizens whom he had aided thought of nominating him consul, or of bestowing upon him even greater honor. There was not the slightest doubt that Spurius Mælius aimed at becoming the ruler of his fatherland. In the doings of Mælius, his rival, the patrician Minucius, naturally took a great interest,—Minucius, who, being vested with legal authority, alone had the right of distributing grain, and who, consequently, could ill endure that a private citizen should sit in the Forum and should assume the bearing proper to a magistrate only. In the meantime he silently collected the proofs of the steps by which Spurius Mælius aspired to rise to power, and presented his denunciation to the senate. This body elected dictator the venerable L. Quinctius Cincinnatus, who, in turn, appointed C. Servilius Ahala master of the horse.

The seriousness of the danger did not permit the observance of the customary forms of procedure; and, moreover, the mere fact of a magistrate's election in such a contingency authorized more summary methods. Therefore, Servilius Ahala, followed by a number of knights, approached Spurius Mælius, who was distributing grain, and urged him to visit the dictator. Spurius Mælius endeavored to escape from the impending peril, and fled towards his house. He was overtaken by Servilius Ahala in a shop of the neighboring *macellum;* and, his arm having been severed, he was left to perish miserably. The dictator Cincinnatus approved the deed of Servilius, who, from *ahala* (arm), received the cognomen of Ahala for himself and his posterity. The house of Spurius Mælius was razed to the ground. No edifice was ever erected on that spot; and the area became known as the *æquimælium,*—that is, the area of Mælius. Lucius Minucius, who had saved his country by presenting the accusation, was honored by the senate with a statue representing a golden ox, erected near the Porta Trigemina. The populace, who had dearly loved Mælius, was easily reconciled to his death when Minucius distributed the grain which had been gathered by Spurius Mælius, —to each one a measure for a coin. According to other versions the *populus* itself erected a statue of Minucius.[1]

Dionysius of Halicarnassus, after presenting this narrative (briefly reported also by Livy), acknowledges having borrowed it from those annalists whom he considered most worthy of faith. He thereupon adds a more ancient version,—one preserved by Cincius Alimentus, the contemporary of Hannibal, and (together with Fabius Pictor) the earliest Roman historian. The version of Cincius (as we learn from Dionysius) was accepted also by L. Calpurnius Piso, the well-known annalist of the Gracchan era. According to these, the murder of Spurius Mælius was not committed at the order or with the approval of the dictator L. Quinctius Cincinnatus, nor at the hand of the *magister equitum*, Servilius Ahala. Of these regular magistrates the two annalists made absolutely no mention. Lucius Minucius, on discovering the aims of Spurius Mælius, had (according to this second version) denounced him to the senate; and, since one of the senators had said that the only remedy was to remove the demagogue, he (Minucius) had turned to the vigorous youth Quintus Servilius, and had entrusted to him the task of killing the conspirator. Servilius then concealed a dagger under his arm and approached Mælius as if to converse with him. After he had treacherously slain him he betook himself to the senate, bearing still wet with gore that knife which was a proof of his deed,—a deed which assured to him and to his posterity the surname of Ahala.[2]

To the main discrepancies in these two versions there are to be added still others. From the version of Livy it is evident that this story was, by the different annalists, variously assigned to the years 314 or 315 of the city. Again, while some spoke of the famine as caused by an evil season, others attributed the scarcity of grain to the fact that the plebs, distracted by political struggles and allured to listen to the harangues of popular orators, had not paid any attention to the fields.[3] It is easily understood, therefore, how such a famine was said to have occurred in the consulship of a Menenius Agrippa, a character connected with the classic secession of the plebs. The divergency of the sources in regard to the magistracy of L. Quinctius Cincinnatus is in keeping with the killing of Mælius, which (according to other authors) occurred in the consulship of L. Quinctius Capitolinus.[4] Likewise, the following two statements are in strong opposition,—that Lucius Minucius was honored by the senate with a statue representing a golden ox, and that he was similarly honored with a column surmounted by a statue erected with the spontaneous offerings of the *populus*.[5] But of all these contradictions surely the greatest is that which aroused the quite legitimate doubts of Livy.

According to some traditions (says the Paduan) Minucius had not been content with reconciling the plebs to himself by distributing at very low prices the grain gathered by Mælius; he had, indeed, himself become a plebeian by means of the *transitio ad plebem,* and had been chosen eleventh tribune of the plebs. The error of such a statement is quite obvious. Livy himself observes that the tribunes of the plebs never exceeded the number of ten, and that only a few years before (according to tradition) it had been explicitly established by the Trebonian laws that the tribunes could not coöptate their colleagues.[6]

On examining all the details of the stories of the demagogue Spurius Mælius, and of his rivals L. Minucius and Servilius Ahala, we are irresistibly led to the conclusion that those data which are less credible and are of a legal aspect originate with the annalists of the time of Sulla, such as Licinius Macer,—the glorifier of the deeds of the Licinii (his ancestors) and also of those of other plebeians. With an historian of the age of Sulla there fully agrees the creation of a *præfectus annonæ,* an office which (as Mommsen rightly observed) arose for the first time in the last century of the Republic.[7] Of such an office (as we learn from Livy) there would have been no mention in the *libri lintei,* which spoke merely of a *præfectus,* without any further designation.[8] With writers of the age of Sulla, too, there very well accords the late invention of an eleventh tribune and of the pretended patricianship of the Minucii. Hence we are inclined to believe that only in a very late period, when the Fasti and the chronology of early Rome were being reconstructed, was the story of Mælius and Minucius crystallized and inserted among the events of the year 440 or 439 B.C.

If, however, we make a thorough examination of all the tradition relating to the agrarian agitations, we shall discover that Spurius Mælius, Minucius, Servilius, and the legendary L. Quinctius Cincinnatus not only oscillate between 440 and 439 B.C., but are also represented under various forms for years far more widely separated. Agrippa, who is at one time represented as a patrician of plebeian origin, and at another as a plebeian, plays a great part (as we have seen) in the agrarian disturbances of 440, 410, and 357 B.C. In discussing the myth of Virginia we have met him in the fantastic story of the Roman colonization of Ardea. Spurius Mælius, in our story, is styled a knight,—that is, patrician,—and consequently (as Dionysius observes) he could not aspire to plebeian offices.[9] But in 436 B.C. we meet a Spurius Mælius, *tribunus plebis*, as the accuser of Servilius Ahala.[10] And, finally, it is surely worthy of note that the famine of 492 B.C., which was caused by the abandoning of the crops in Sicily, occurs in the consulship of a Minucius; and that another Minucius is consul for the following year, when the foreign grain arrived which Coriolanus had not wished should be distributed to the plebs.[11]

After an examination of the traditions concerning the agrarian laws of the fifth century, not only do we conclude that the story of the more recent annalists is false, but there also arises the suspicion that the data of not even the safest tradition,—that of Cincius and of Piso,—are entirely deserving of belief. Such suspicion is confirmed by the examination of certain elements which belong to the more ancient version. The later version declared that Minucius had been honored with a statue; and such version was accepted by the plebeian Minucii Augurini on the coins issued by them, on which a human figure appears upon a column.[12] The more ancient version, however, asserted that Minucius had been honored with a gilt statue representing an ox. I shall not discuss the question of the gilt statue; for, according to the statements of the ancient authors, it was only in the last years of Cincius Alimentus that the custom arose at Rome of gilding metal statues.[13] Nevertheless, the odd fact remains that a man should have been honored with a statue representing an ox; and the question naturally arises, why should such statue have been erected outside one of the gates of the city and not in the Forum? Rather than dwelling upon the hypothesis of Mommsen,—namely, that a vague statement relating to a demagogue was arbitrarily referred to one year of the national chronology rather than to another,—we shall, instead, endeavor to ascertain whether or not our story does not originate in three distinct topographical elements closely connected with one another.

Let us begin with Spurius Mælius. It was said that he was a knight (*eques*), and that his house was leveled with the ground. This area, which was still pointed out in the times of Dionysius, was therefore called *æquimælium*. We leave aside the fact that the title of *eques* given to Mælius is in relation with a different mode of pronouncing the word *æquimælium,* deriving its etymology from *equimelion.* We shall affirm, on the other hand, that the area in question was situated at the foot of the Capitoline, not distant from the porta Carmentalis, and on the side facing the Tiber. The *æquimælium* (as we learn from Cicero) was a market-place where, among other things, meats were sold.[14] Not very far from the *æquimælium,* beyond the porta Carmentalis (and still near the Tiber), were situated two other market-places,—the *porticus Minuciæ,*—one called the *porticus Minucia vetus,* and the other the *porticus Minucia frumentaria.* The erection of both was assigned to a L. Minucius Thermus, the conqueror of the Scordisci in 110 B.C.[15]

Tradition related that Spurius Mælius fled from the place

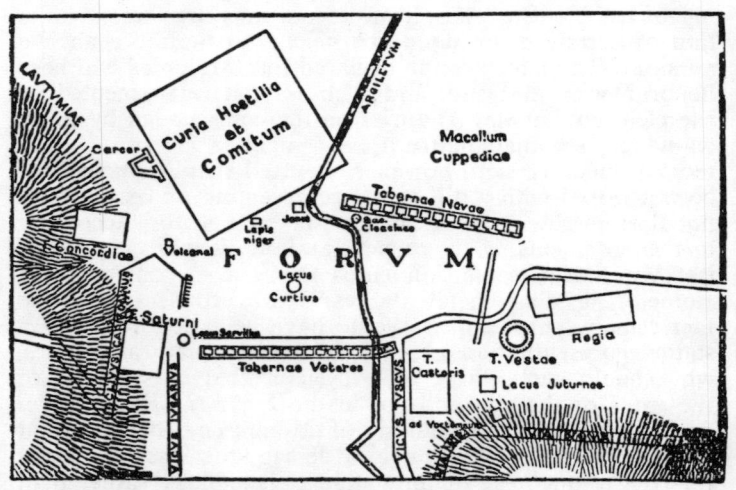

THE FORUM ROMANUM IN THE FIRST CENTURIES OF THE REPUBLIC

where corn was distributed and sought refuge in a neighboring butcher shop. There he was overtaken by Servilius Ahala and was maimed in one arm by his pursuer. Tradition adds, in this case, topographical details which very closely correspond with the truth. Directly in front of the *æquimælium* were the *tabernæ veteres,* and hard by these was the *lacus Servilius*,—a spot famous in history for the proscriptions of Sulla. For in this place the heads of the proscribed fathers had been exposed to view.[16] Admitting, then, that our legend originated in data offered by these monuments, it becomes clear how the eponym of an area so near to the Capitoline should have been transformed into a demagogue aspiring to sovereignty. In like manner, Gnæus Manlius, whose house was on the Capitoline, became considered a popular leader having similar ends in view.

We must bear in mind the meaning attached to the various parts of edifices and of monuments. In a preceding chapter many elements of the legend of Acca were seen to spring from the vicinity of the temple of Hercules. We can now easily perceive that the eponyms of the market-place Mælius and of the *Porticus Minuciæ* were transformed into two rivals,—rivals in selling corn at the lowest price. It also results that one of them, Minucius, supplants and forces into oblivion the other, and that both were placed in close relation with the alleged eponym of the monument where the bodies of the guilty were hung. The custom of thus exposing the corpses of the executed was a common one in Rome, as, for that matter, throughout the classical world. Indeed, it flourished in certain parts of Italy as late as the last century. That condemned persons were executed in the Forum appears from other data besides the mention of the *lacus Servilius*. Our explanation of the legend of Mælius, Minucius and Servilius gains still greater value and significance when we study the history of the other *macella* situated along the borders of the Forum Romanum.

The site of the *macellum* and the market-place of the *cuppediæ* (pastries or sweetmeats) had, according to ancient writers, been leveled with the ground only a few years before the erection of those buildings, in 179 B.C., by the censors Fulvius and Æmilius.[17] The reason for such procedure was the apprehension and the execution of the two robbers Macellus and Equitius Cuppedius. It is needless to say that these men were not authentic characters of the years preceding 179 B.C. They are merely the eponyms of the area devoted to the sale of the *cuppediæ*, and of that of the *macellum*. They correspond in every respect with the eponyms of the *æquimælium*, of the *lacus Servilius* and of the *Porticus Minucia*. The analogy between the two stories appears still greater from the detail of the knife with which C. Servilius slew Spurius Mælius. This was snatched, presumably, from the *tabernæ* situated on the southwest side of the Forum, and near the *lacus Servilius*. In other words, the particular of the knife plays the same important part in this legend as in that of Virginia, with the difference that, in the latter, the knife is taken by the father from one of the *tabernæ* on the northeast side of the Forum. The tabernæ were, indeed, back of the *macellum* and market-place for *cuppediæ,* of which we have already spoken. On account of their barbarity and their lack of sympathy, butchers are even to-day, in common speech, called thieves by the Italians. The fact serves to explain the legend of the two robbers Macellus and Cuppedius. In a similar manner, then, the competition and the vicinity of the two market-places, and the fact that one was so close to the *lacus Servilius,* gave origin to the story of the jealousy and the rivalry between Mælius and Minucius, and to the tale of the arm (*ahala*) which was severed by Servilius.

The existence of statues representing the eponyms of these markets may have contributed towards the speedier formation of the stories. At Sparta, in the street called Hyacinthus, and in the " pheiditia " (the dining-halls) there were to be seen the statues of Matton and of Keraon, that is, of the heroes personifying bread and wine. We meet with this custom throughout Greece. At Cyprus were worshipped the images of Zeus 'Ειλαπιναστής ; at Epulone, that of Zeus σπλαγχνοτόμος, or cutter of entrails; in Achaia was worshipped Deipneus, the eponym of dinners and of banquets; and for Attica, it will be sufficient to recall that at Munychia, near Athens, there was honored the statue of Acratopotes, who symbolized the unmixed wine.[18] As the result of similar statues representing divinities, which, in time, sank to the level of historical characters, there arose (as we have seen) the legends of Clœlia and of Horatius Cocles. We do not know what relation the *lacus Servilius* bore to a statue of a hydra there erected by Agrippa. In compensation, however, we have explicit information concerning a statue of Minucius.

This statue was approximately near the Porta Carmentalis and the Capitoline, though situated outside the Porta Trigemina at the northern extremity of the Aventine.[19] The more ancient version of the honors conferred upon Minu-

THE SITE OF THE TABERNÆ NOVÆ

cius asserted that they were obtained through the favor of the senate, and not of the plebs. Furthermore, it made mention, not of a column surmounted by the statue of a man, but of a golden bull. Some authors have thought to recognize a picture of Minucius in the coins of the Minucii, which, in fact, represent a column at whose base are two persons. The column itself is surmounted by a human figure. We must, however, duly consider the lion-heads that are to be seen by the side of the column. By so doing, we shall recognize that the human figure represents Hercules, whose temple was near the Porta Trigemina. The statements relating to the statue of Minucius give us, therefore, a new topographical element, somewhat different from those hitherto examined. They provide us, indeed, with the most ancient elements of the myth.

In the later versions of the story it is said that it was Minucius who was rewarded for the denunciation of Spurius Mælius, and not Servilius, who had actually slain a probable tyrant. Cincius Alimentus already connects the names of Servilius and of Minucius, the former of whom had been urged to kill Mælius. It is, consequently, permissible to believe that Minucius Thermus, in 110 B.C., did not lay the foundations of the *porticus Minucia frumentaria,* but merely enlarged and modified the *porticus Minucia vetus.* This latter we must consider as having already existed in the times of Cincius and of Fabius Pictor. On the other hand, the mention of a statue outside the Porta Trigemina representing a bull, and erected in honor of a Minucius, leads to a primitive element of the myth quite distinct from that of Servilius. This new element we can easily discover if we examine the cult of Hercules at Rome.

There is a legend which, under Roman dress, preserves an old solar myth already localized in Sicily and in Magna Græcia by the poet Stesichorus. It told that Hercules, on his arrival at Rome, had been robbed of a part of his herd by Cacus, who, in this version, replaces the Gerion of Stesichorus. Cacus hid the stolen oxen in a cave; but Hercules, by their bellowing, was put on their track, and in a short time slew Cacus. Later he was supposed to have erected an altar in honor of the temple of Jupitor Inventor or Invictus and to have sacrificed to him an ox.[20]

The myth of Hercules was not localized only on the Aventine. Other legends connected Hercules not only with the Aventine and the Porta Trigemina, but also with the neighboring Forum Boarium. In this latter Forum, indeed, were the celebrated temple and altar consecrated to this solar deity. And since the story of the stolen oxen constituted a fundamental element of the myth and the cult of Hercules, a celebrated bronze statue (supposed to have been brought from Ægina) adorned the Forum Boarium. Similarly, a gilt statue of a bull adorned the Porta Trigemina.[21] The connection between Hercules and the bull was so close that one of the most ancient series of Roman coins represents on one side the image of this animal and on the other that of the Argive hero. The golden bull with which the

senate was said to have honored Minucius was that of the Porta Trigemina and near the temple of Hercules. This connection with Hercules is proved, not only by the column represented on the coins of the Minucii, but also from the fact that there was, near the *Porticus Minucia,* a third temple dedicated to Hercules.[22] The question, therefore, arises spontaneously, What relation could there have been between the god Hercules and the gens Minucia?

Verrius Flaccus offers a satisfactory answer to this question. He affirms that there was at Rome a gate Minutia, or even Minucia, called thus from a certain Minucius or Minutius, whose altar and shrine were near by.[23] Granting that the god Minutius was identical with the divinity worshipped near the Porta Trigemina, we shall come to the conclusion that the Minucii believed themselves to be the descendants of a god Minutius. In a similar manner (it will be remembered) did the Horatii connect their origin with the statue of Horatius Cocles, that is, of the lame Vulcan; and the Valerii with that of the mythical Valeria, situated near the Porta Mugonia. However, this is not sufficient for determining why the mythical ancestor of the Minucii should have been represented under the form of a bull.

What constitutes for us to-day an insurmountable difficulty was, on the contrary, a most natural phenomenon for the ancients, who believed in the metamorphosis of gods into men and animals and rocks, and who assigned their origin (as the savage tribes of America and of Africa) to the sacred totems of their clans and nations. The study of comparative mythology is too well developed for me to state that the ancient Greeks originally worshipped Athena or Æsculapius under the form of a serpent, and Aphrodite under that of a bird. It is sufficient to recall that the Arcadians believed in the transformation of wolves into men; and, vice versa, that the Romans worshipped Jupiter under the form of an oak and of an osier, that they believed the god Faunus a goat, and made the she-wolf the originator of their race.

The family names of many Roman families are easily explained with the conception that human races sprang from totem animals. The Roman families of the Asinii, the Porcii and the Suilli considered themselves descended from *asini* and from *sues*. We can readily understand, therefore, why the Minucii should judge themselves the offspring of the god Minucius, worshipped under the form of a bull. Surely the Roman goddess Vitellia, the ancestress of the Vitellii, was worshipped under the form of a cow. And in conclusion, it must be added that the bull was generally connected with all the Sabellian and the Italic races.[24] There is, hence, nothing strange in that the god Minucius, or Minutius, near the Porta Trigemina, should have assumed the figure of a bull. It remains to be asked why the bull should have been called Minutius. The answer is again proffered by the cult of Hercules.

The Roman legend assumed that Hercules found the stolen oxen by means of their bellowing. We would expect the creation from this fact of a deity Mugonius or Mugonia. Indeed, from the bellowing of the oxen kept on the Palatine, Roman legend named the Porta Mugonia, as well as a hero Mugonius, on that part of the Palatine facing the Forum Romanum, and not on that facing the Forum Boarium.[25] In order to obtain the form Minucius, it is necessary to bear in mind the fact that the first writers of

Roman legends were Greeks, such as Timæus and Callias; also, that the first Roman annalists who, like Cincius Alimentus, narrated these legends, wrote in Greek. In addition, we must remember that the cult of Hercules was Greek, and that the ancient annalists (like Acilius) placed the origin of Rome in relation with this cult.[26]

We have already shown how, from false etymologies of the Latin words *æquimælium* and *ahala* there arose, in our legend, the elements of Mælius the knight (*eques*) and of Servilius Ahala (*ahala*, the arm). It is natural to think that similar varying stories may have been derived from Greek words. We know that false etymologies from the Greek gave life to many incidents in the Roman legends. For instance, the story of the renewal (*instauratio*) of the Latin games (*ludi Latini*) in the time of Coriolanus is explained by the ’ἀπὸ σταυροῦ, that is, from the story of a slave who was to be crucified. Without wandering far from our subject, however, I shall recall that the Greek cult of Hercules in Rome originated in the identification of Evander, the good man, with Faunus,—the beneficent god,—who was contrasted with Cacus, no longer the god of fire (from καίω), but the evil god (κακός). The rites of the Pinarii, who, for religious reasons unknown to us, never assisted at the beginning of the sacrifices to Hercules, were explained by the false etymology from πεινᾶν, that is, to suffer hunger.

Bearing these facts in mind, it will not be difficult to discover the reason why the bull near the Porta Trigemina was called Minutius, and why the god Minutius was transformed into Minucius, the enemy of Mælius. In examining the legend of Spurius Mælius we saw that Minucius was not awarded a statue by the senate (nor by the plebs) because he had slain the demagogue. The credit for this (as we have already pointed out) belonged to Servilius Ahala. And, whereas tradition speaks of a reward given to Minucius, it does not mention (as we would expect) any reward given to Ahala. The merit of Minucius consisted in having denounced the aims of Spurius; and, in the version of Cincius (who wrote in Greek), as well as in the more recent ones recorded by Dionysius, this fact is referred to by the noun μήνυσις and by the verb μηνύω. Minucius, or Minutius (as he was called by the sources known to Verrius Flaccus), had been the μηνυτής, or informer, denouncer of Mælius, just as μηνυτής had been the bull who had revealed to Hercules the hiding place of Cacus.[27] In the same way, the old Greek legend derived from the verb μηνύω the name Motye, the woman who revealed to Hercules the place in which the oxen had been hidden. A Roman reproduction of this Greek legend stated that Cacus was betrayed by his sister Caca, who revealed to Hercules the hiding place of the oxen. In this case the name of Caca is no longer derived from καίω, but from κακή,—hence we have Caca, the evil woman. Moreover, we again find in the Latin text a reference to the verb μηνύω in the expression *fecit indicium*.[28]

The similarity of the etymology is due to the original unity of the stories. The myth of Hercules at Rome is drawn from those same authors who had already localized it in Sicily and on the coast of Campania. The statue of a bull and the etymology of the name of the Minucii were, therefore, closely connected with the cult of Hercules. Furthermore, they gave origin and actually formed the nucleus of the legend of Minucius.

The horned head of a divinity situated on a high portion of the Aventine gave rise to a similar phenomenon. As we saw in the legend of Servius Tullius, the Aventine was the seat of the temple of Diana, which extended protection to fugitive slaves. Such fugitives were also called stags, *cervi*.[29] Indeed, it was natural that a cult which was identified from the earliest period with that of the Greek Artemis should have been placed in relation with the animal sacred to that goddess, and that a gate leading to the sanctuary should have been adorned with a statue of Actæon, who was transformed into that animal.

In a story known to Pliny this circumstance gave origin to a legend concerning the prætor Cipus Gænucius that was deemed quite authentic. It was related that Cipus, clothed in the solemn robes worn by a general in time of war, went forth against the enemy from the Porta Raudusculana, and that, on having passed through the gate, horns immediately grew from his head. The miracle was explained to the prætor by the priests as a sign of future sovereignty, whereupon Cipus Gænucius chose for himself perpetual exile. This generous resolution was deemed worthy of commemoration, and above the gate, which was on this account called Raudusculana, there was subsequently erected a statue of bronze, or *raudus*. The name Cipus (which at the same time, means both chief and rex) explains the connection of the strange story with the cult of Diana.[30] The name Gænucius recalls the fact that the gens was plebeian, and that the establishment of the plebeian power is closely connected with the Aventine. We therefore reach the conclusion that the story of Minucius is, in origin, composed of religious and topographical elements connected with the cults of the various gates of Rome. To the same class belong the legends of Cipus Gænucius, of Tarpeia, of Horatia (slain by her brother near the Porta Capena), and of the three hundred and six Fabii who left Rome by the Porta Scelerata, and who were destined never to return to their homes.

The more ancient legends regarding Rome's origins do not connect Rome with Æneas, but, rather, with Hercules. From this cult the early Roman annalist Acilius (who wrote in Greek) deduced the Greek origin of Rome. From one of the most ancient series of Roman coins, upon which are represented Hercules and the bull, we gather that Acilius did not express a merely personal opinion, but, indeed, a version which, in the end of the fourth and the beginning of the third century, had already received official sanction. We can comprehend, too, why the plebeian Minucii should have connected themselves with this foreign cult, situated for this very reason outside the patrician boundaries. For, by false genealogy, they claimed descent from a Minucius who had brought safety to the Roman people in the first years of the Republic. Indeed, they considered as the divine author of their race that bull μηνυτής, which had been consecrated by the god Hercules outside the Porta Trigemina and at the foot of the plebeian Aventine.

The group of myths belonging to the region at the base of the Capitoline hill and near the Porta Carmentalis had, originally, nothing in common with the legend of the bull Minutius. In all likelihood that group spoke only of the demagogue Spurius Mælius and of his slayer, Servilius Ahala. But, when there arose, in the vicinity of the Porta Carmentalis, the older of the two *porticus Minuciæ* (which was itself related to the cult of Hercules), the two groups became fused, and gave life to new elements which were duly registered in the later versions. Thus, there arose the story of the rivalry between the representatives of the

THE AVENTINE AND THE PORTA TRIGEMINA

market place called Minucius and that called *æquimælium*. If, in the new form of the myth, Minucius is not presented as the slayer of Mælius, this fact is due to the former version, which had already assigned the rôle to the eponym of the *lacus Servilius*. Minucius, who, in the myth of Hercules, had been connected with the bull, became, in the latter story, the denouncer or μηνυτής, the author, that is, of the μηνυσις. The bull, considered as their sacred totem by the Minucii, now yielded its place to a magistrate. And since, by a long series of falsifications, the agrarian agitations of the times of the Gracchi and of Sulla were assigned to the first decades of the Roman Republic, imaginary ancestors were created for the builders of the porticus Minucia. Similar was the procedure in the case of the more important plebeian families of the Sicinii, the Trebonii and the Duellii, and in the case of the ædilis Seius of the times of Cicero. This last, who also procured grain for the plebs, was given as imaginary ancestor another Seius, also an ædilis who had performed similar deeds in the decades to which were assigned both Coriolanus and our Minucius.[31]

The tendency thus to create imaginary ancestors, and to attribute to them deeds performed in later ages, does not constitute a special characteristic of the Roman people. It is a phenomenon which the historian discovers in all nations. Both Cicero and Livy deplored the fact that, as the result of such pretended genealogies, the sincerity of the early Roman history had become doubtful.[32] The famous Arabian writer, Ibn-Kaldûn, later made the same complaint regarding the various tribes of Berbers. It has, finally, been often noted in the story of mediæval and of modern Europe. The historic Assyrian King Sargon considered himself a descendant of the very ancient Sargon, who was enveloped in the mists of legends; and both were said to have performed the same deeds. A similar falsification is to be recognized in the case of Hiero II. of Syracuse, born of an humble mother, who was said to have been a descendant of the more ancient and more famous Hiero. Likewise, finally, Cen-Shin, son of a driver, was (like Confucius) supposed to be descended from the most ancient kings of China.

The rich and fertile plain of Latium, watered by the largest stream of central Italy and broken by the beautiful Alban Hills, was, more than any other, sure to attract human races and to allure them to establish their permanent homes there. Let us grant for the moment that here, as in the rich valley of maritime Etruria, there already flourished advanced forms of civilization when, in the eighth century B.C., Greek colonists began to arrive. From this, however, it would not result that the political history of Etruria and of Latium began thus early. History is not merely the production of vases and of bronzes; it is not merely a warlike or a commercial intercourse between different races. By history we understand noteworthy events,—events that go beyond the common sphere of life, that follow the development in the formation of political organisms and in the evolution of religious and of moral ideas. Above all, history is to be derived from facts determined in time and space, and from the authenticity of events guaranteed by the writings of a contemporary author. History cannot truly begin except after a long continued political and artistic development of nations. If, therefore, Herodotus estimated at five centuries the interval between himself and Homer, the *primo pittor delle memorie antiche,* it is quite natural that four centuries should have intervened between Fabius and Cincius, the first Roman annalists, and the beginning of the fifth century,—the period in which it was affirmed that the kings had been expelled, and that the free Roman Republic had had its origin.

Surely, those who, from the discovery of mere pottery and of bronzes in the classic soil of Rome, have derived a confirmation of the fantastic legends of the regal period and of the beginning of the Republic are greatly in error. The Paduan Livy showed himself to be much more prudent in declaring that only when Rome was liberated from the Gauls (c. 387 B.C.) did the truly historic period of Rome begin.[33] For, in the preceding age (he says), rare and unusual was the art of writing; and even if public and private monuments had existed they were, for the most part, destroyed by the burning of Rome. But if history did not survive, there remained faint traces of monuments; there survived, above all, cults and ceremonies whose explanation was handed down by word of mouth; there remained, finally, the war songs which the national bards sang in honor of whomsoever should invite them to the banquet. In various parts of Italy, and on certain occasions, stereotyped sonnets of praise are similarly employed.[34]

Contact with other historic peoples largely augmented the legendary material. The conquered cities of the Prisci Latini surrendered their cults to Rome together with the legends that had been built up around them. Several Greek scholars (as, for instance, Timæus), in writing the history of the western nations, called attention to the parallelism and the synchronism between the histories of Lavinium and of Troy, of Rome and of Carthage. The Roman annalists who followed in their tracks searched for further parallelisms and synchronisms with the history of Athens, of Sparta and of Syracuse. The stories of the gods, as already in Greece and later among the German peoples, were transformed into the stories of the first kings of the nation. The list of Alban kings serves to give Latium an origin at least as ancient as the warriors battling at Troy; the origin of Rome and that of the Sabine Titus Tatius (considered of Spartan stock) were made to coincide with the creation of the Ephors at Sparta; the expulsion of the kings was fixed in the same year in which the Pisistratidæ were expelled from Athens; the organization of the plebs at Rome was made contemporary with the similar occurrence at Syracuse; and, finally, the Fabii were supposed to have perished at the Cremera in the very year in which Leonidas and his Spartans were betrayed at Thermopylæ.

On the other hand, events of a more recent period were attributed to a much earlier age. At Athens there was assigned to the times of Theseus that maritime hegemony which was possible in the fifth century only after the victories over the Persians. Mention of the Athenian Mnestheus was inserted into the epic of Homer. Athens, which, from the beginning of the fifth century, was the most brilliant State of Greece, blushed at not having as ancient a history as her older rivals. Rome, which, at the end of the fourth century and especially at the beginning of the third, had become the most powerful State of the Peninsula, could not tolerate and would not concede being younger than the cities of Magna Græcia and of the Hellenic East with which she then entered into relation. It was not a question of mere erudite falsification. It was a question of moral ascendency, analogous to that which made the kings and the representatives of France discuss their prerogatives and titles of nobility against the claims of Spain.

We have seen how legends originating in Campania, in

Sicily and in Greece were transformed into political history. As has already been said, this characteristic is not peculiar to the Romans. It is common to all the peoples of history. The Arabians presented as a national production material borrowed from the literature of the conquered Persians. In a similar manner the ancient Persians reproduced monuments of the Assyrian age, and the Æthiopians literally copied, and considered as their own historical patrimony, both the monuments and the events of ancient Egypt. The same situation was reproduced in more recent times. Everyone knows that characters of the Renaissance are often but pale imitations of Roman ones. Piccinino was likened to Scipio Æmilianus, as Alphonso of Aragon to Philip of Macedon. Again, mediæval characters are made to deliver speeches partly borrowed from Livy and from Cicero, just as the Latin historians copied the situations and the addresses which they read in their Athenian authors.

A critical and exhaustive examination reveals the legendary character of what is presented to us as the history of the first four centuries of Rome. Nevertheless, the interest and the charm of this old literary patrimony is not by any means diminished. By it we become acquainted with the most ancient beliefs of the early Latin races. By carefully studying its cults we can follow the development of the political relations of Rome, and the elevation of its moral ideals. We can follow, step by step, the successive elaborations of the myths at the hands of the poets and of the historians, till we reach tha' period when legend is transformed into pretended constitutional history, when the annalists, having lost all conception of the historical sense, transport to th regal period and to the first century of the Republic the political views and opinions of their own age. The artificial manner of annalists of the stamp of Licinius Macer and Valerius Antias finds its perfect counterpart in the vain and incapable effort of those scholars who endeavor to keep alive what Vico justly called "the vanities of nations," *borie delle nazioni*.

In stripping, therefore, from the strong and powerful tree of Roman history the dry and withered branches that do not belong to it, the proper duty of the historian is fulfilled, —namely, to search for and declare the truth. By speaking the truth, the following fact is brought into strong relief:

that Rome, within a comparatively short period, arose from a condition of very humble civilization to one which made her the mistress of the world. This was, in great part, the fruit of the Italian arm and sword; but it also depended from the unerring observation of political events, and from the wisdom of her political and her legal administration. The Anglo-Saxon races are justly proud of the development particularly natural to them—namely, the development of the individual. But no collective and universal organism can properly develop and unfold itself unless it have a due regard for that which Rome either created or experimented. To every ideal of faith and of truth the young land of America is sacred. But no nation presents such numerous instances of the love of justice and of country as Rome.

Rome has sanctified patriotism and liberty with the tales of both the legendary Coriolanus and Cincinnatus, and of the historic Scipio and Gracchi. She has related her Fasti of science and the pure joys of the contemplation of nature in the verses of Lucretius and of Vergil. Love of liberty breathes from the immortal pages of Cicero, of Livy and of Tacitus. May the tongues of Vergil, of Livy, of Cicero and of Tacitus, together with that of Dante, reëcho throughout this youthful country, and may the study of the genuine glories of Rome contribute to the formation of the character of young and great nations like that of America.

CHAPTER XII

ON THE TOPOGRAPHY OF THE EARLIEST ROME

I. ROMA QUADRATA

IN the legends already examined, we have established the fact that topography and religion furnished the principal material for such stories. I deem it necessary, however, to add to the preceding chapters one strictly topographical in character—the more so that (if I be not mistaken) various problems either have not been properly investigated or have not received satisfactory solutions. If the reader finds that this chapter is somewhat more austere than some of the preceding, he may omit it, at least casting a glance at the topographical maps in which I embody my conclusions.[1]

The question of the earliest *pomerium* of the Palatine forms, in the words of Theodore Mommsen, "the most difficult problem of Roman topography." [2] To me it seems possible to reach some conclusion if only we take into consideration an entire series of facts, either new or not as yet examined—if we trace to their sources the contradictory statements of the authors, and thus establish the meaning of the expression *Roma Quadrata*.

To-day the opinion prevails that the famous words of Ennius,—*et quis est erat | Romœ regnare quadratœ*,[3]—refer to the entire Palatine Hill, which, with its natural outlines (so it is said), forms a square. Such opinion has the approval of Dionysius and of Plutarch, who clearly state that Rome with its walls formed a square.[4] With these there is commonly connected (though wrongly, as we shall see) a passage of Solinus. In speaking of the *Roma Quadrata* of Romulus the author says that it extended from the Porta Mugonia to the steps of Cacus (*Scalœ Caci*), and that it was thus called because *ad æquilibrium foret posita*.[5] The testimony of Gellius, too, is evoked, the burden of which is that the *pomerium* of the Palatine of Romulus extended to the base of the hill;[6] and, finally, that of Tacitus, who bounds the city of Romulus with the famous statue of the bull in the Forum Boarium and the altar of Hercules (which is placed within the *pomerium*), the altar of Consus, the *curiæ veteres* and the shrine of the Lares.[7]

It is clearly evident that these references to *Roma Quadrata* are related to the legend of Romulus, who founded his city according to the auspices of the vultures. They are also related to the *lituus auguralis,* which was for so long preserved by him on the Palatine, and to the theory of the square *templum*. We can readily understand how the seeming harmony of texts has induced the majority of scholars to affirm that the Rome of the Palatine was truly square in form. Nevertheless, if these passages be examined somewhat more closely, it will be found that the resemblance is only apparent. It will, indeed, result that some of these texts either exclude the idea of a square city, or suggest a far different area.

From extant texts we learn that Romulus, strongly preoccupied with the idea of defending his city, fortified it with a wall and a ditch.[8] Precisely on account of this endeavor to give the city a strong defence, it is said that he included within the walls that part of the Palatine which offered an easy approach to the enemy.[9] The texts of Dionysius and of Plutarch fully agree with this idea. The statements of Gellius and of Tacitus, however, are greatly in opposition to it. These authors speak of the *pomerium* established by Romulus at the foot (*per ima, radicibus*) of the Palatine. It is not necessary to refer to the theory of the *pomerium* accepted by Livy, according to which the word *pomerium* meant not only the space behind the wall towards the city,—separating the *urbs* from the *mœnia,*— but also the land surrounding the wall on the outside. In fact, according to Livy it was established that *extrinsecus puri aliquid ab humano cultu pateret soli*.[10] We know, however, of many sepulchres of later age, situated between the earliest walls of Rome (which were built midway up the slope of the Palatine) and the foot of the hill. Even aside from this fact, the space is too large to which to apply the words of Livy.

But this is not all. It is the general opinion (and it has recently been defended by one of the best Roman topographers) that the boundaries indicated by Tacitus really form a square. If, however, we cast a glance upon the map, we shall see the original outlines of the Palatine. We shall observe that the elevations constituting the entire hill,—the Cermalus and the Palatuar,—did not form a square. Still less is the mention of the shrine of the Lares compatible with the idea of a square. For, though this shrine was by some located on the northern angle of the Palatine, it was in fact situated *in summa sacra via,*—that is, near the Velia and the Porta Mugonia.[11] The limits, therefore, given by Tacitus,—the altar of Hercules, the bull in the Forum Boarium, the *curiæ veteres* and the temple of the Lares,—do not include an exact square. Even granting that they did, an examination of these passages will show that Tacitus followed very late sources absolutely unworthy of faith.

In speaking of the *pomerium* of the Palatine, Tacitus says that Romulus began to mark out the furrow at the place where the bronze statue of the bull was, because that was the animal customarily yoked to the plough,—*quia id genus animalium aratro subditur,*—and in order that he might include also the altar of Hercules,—*magnam Herculis aram complecteretur.* The statue of the bull in the Forum Boarium and the altar of Hercules are not in any relation with the myth of Romulus. In studying the legend of Minucius we have seen that these monuments were closely connected with the myth of Hercules, the slayer of Cacus and the guest of Evander. The latter was considered the ancestor of the Palatine kings. The bull of the Forum Boarium, moreover, was a Greek work from Ægina, and was originally connected with Greek myths.[12] In a similar manner, the Hellenic myth of Evander is related to the neighboring statue of Hercules, which Evander himself is said to have dedicated.[13]

The legend of Hercules as founder of Rome had been told as early as the second century by the Sicilian historian Silenus.[14] Thus, at the foot of the Palatine and of the Aventine there were established the cults of Mercury, of Hercules and of Ceres; and on the island of the Tiber the god Æsculapius was worshipped. The statement of Tacitus, then, that Romulus included within the *pomerium* the bronze statue of the bull and the altar of Hercules is, in its religious aspect, an absurdity.[15] Furthermore, such declaration is contrary to the most elementary laws of military science, and does not well accord with the fact that the earliest walls of the Palatine are situated much higher up the slope.

It is possible that Tacitus accepted the doctrine of the marking out of the *pomerium* according to the common interpretation given to the ancient Etruscan rites, in which the bull and the cow drew the plough. These had already been cited by Cato.[16] In addition, however, he clearly followed a recent source, in which the exotic character of the ancient divinities at the foot of the Palatine had been lost sight of. Instead of adhering to facts that could be confirmed and verified, Tacitus preferred to adopt the conjectures of scholars and of priests of a later age. This is proved unquestionably by his affirming as an opinion (*credidere*), and not as a fact, that the Forum and Capitolium were afterwards added to the city by Titus Tatius.[17]

Furthermore, there was great difference of opinion as to the limits of the city founded by Romulus. According to Solinus the square city of Romulus extended from the grove of Apollo Palatinus, where the *mundus* and the area of the Palatine were situated, to the Cermalus, where the *tugurium Faustuli* and the *scalæ Caci* were.[18] Pliny and the sources of Varro affirmed that Romulus provided the city with only three gates; still others spoke of a more extensive wall, having a greater number of gates.[19] According to a widely diffused version (which was accepted by the sources of Ovid), the city of Romulus included the area of the Forum defended by the Porta Janualis even earlier than the war against Tatius.[20] From these indications we obtain anything but a square. There were some, too, who declared that Romulus occupied the Palatine and the Cælian;[21] and, finally, others placed the *casa Romuli* on the Capitoline.[22] From all this it is difficult to derive the idea of *Roma Quadrata* as meaning or representing a square city. For there does not correspond with such a conception even what the authors tell us concerning the form of the ancient Latin cities.

As we have already remarked, it is customary to connect the expression *Roma Quadrata* with the shape of the *templum* marked out by augurs. One may think, too, of the camps from which Roman colonies so frequently sprang, and which were built in the form of a square according to the rites prescribed by the augurs. At the same time, however, we must consider that when Varro speaks of ancient Roman cities marked out according to augural rites, and with a plough drawn by the bull and the cow, he does not speak of a square, but indeed makes distinct mention of an *orbis,* or circle.[23] A glance at the form of the early Septimontium, as well as at the more recent one, shows that the Romans, in fixing the boundaries of their city, took no thought of the abstract theories of the priesthood. They were guided by strategic reasons, and consequently often gave their cities the shape of a circle.

The shape of some of the more ancient Roman colonies (as Anxur and Minturnæ) shows that even in such cases the square form was not employed.[24] That the square was to be avoided in founding a city is most clearly urged by Vitruvius for military reasons.[25] In keeping with this is the fact that, although the boundary stones (*cippi terminales*) of the Gracchi bear the lines of the *cardo* and the *decumanus,* they nevertheless are not square, but circular in form. The circular form is reproduced also in the drawings annexed to the text of the Gromatici Veteres. If, then, these authors (who cite Varro) declare that the boundaries were fixed according to Etruscan rites or to the theory of the *mundus,* we must not forget that, according to the drawings which illustrate their declarations, the *mundus* was not necessarily square.[26] Therefore, we cannot offhand (as has often been done) declare Plutarch guilty of a gross error when he says that the *mundus* of Romulus in the Comitium was circular in form.[27] The conception of the *templum,* moreover, does not conflict with the circular form of the temple of Vesta. The conception of the square does not consist in the exterior lines, but in the intersection of the *cardo* and *decumanus* which marked the cardinal points of the *mundus.*[28] It is clear that the Romans were not exclusively influenced by abstract reasons in defending their city, but followed the dictates of military exigencies. This we notice in the case not only of Syracuse, of Volsinii and of Præneste, but also of all the ancient and the modern peoples.

Consequently, all that is said in regard to the *Roma Quadrata* of the Palatine to the effect that Romulus founded a square city is contradictory both to religious and to military theory, and to fact. This will become still more apparent by recollecting that originally the Cermalus was distinctly separate from the Palatinus. These elevations

formed two separate hills of the earliest Septimontium, and
still appear as two distinct hills in the official records (*acta*)
of the sacrifices of the Argei.[29]

All the indications of the authors agree in locating the
primitive Rome upon the Cermalus,—to be exact, precisely
on the site of the *ficus Ruminalis,* the Porta Romana and
the Lupercal. In other words, they located it on the site
where Romulus was supposed to have lived.[30] There is
absolutely no proof that the earliest encircling wall of the
Palatine was square.

In order to solve our problem it is necessary to examine
more closely those passages of the authors which refer to
Roma Quadrata more specifically.

Solinus (as we have seen) declares that *Roma Quadrata*
had been placed *ad æquilibrium,* and that it extended from
the grove of Apollo Palatinus to that crest of the hill upon
which were the *scalæ Caci* and the *tugurium* of Faustulus.
Furthermore, he states that it was called square *quod ad
æquilibrium foret posita.* By examining these topographical
data we shall conclude that a far smaller area is in question than the entire Palatine, but we shall by no means
reach the solution of our problem. Nevertheless it is to
be noted that Solinus mentions the grove of Apollo Palatinus and the *scalæ Caci.*

He thus refers to two distinct localities, in each of which
there is an area called *Roma Quadrata.* As regards the
Roma Quadrata in front of the Palatine temple there is no
need of demonstrations. Every one is acquainted with the
famous passage in Festus, in which it is said that in front
of the temple of Apollo Palatinus there was an area paved
with square stones, and thence called *Roma Quadrata.* It is
likewise well known that this locality is mentioned in official
documents of the Empire. From the passage in Festus
just cited,[31] as well as from other data, we deduce that *Roma
Quadrata* was the *mundus* sacred to the gods of the dead,—
dii manes.

We are justified in assuming the existence of a second
Roma Quadrata near the Lupercal from another passage
in Festus,—an assumption confirmed by a new Pompeian
fresco. In speaking of the Porta Romana Festus emphasizes the fact that it was made square by means of steps,—
gradibus in quadram formatus.[32] The new Pompeian fresco
represents the *ficus Ruminalis* as bursting through a large

rock (*saxum*) near which are the Twins suckled by the she-wolf. We have already had occasion to note that the name *Roma* is not derived from *rumon* (current), but from *rumis*, which signified both the fig-tree and the breast of the she-wolf. We have seen, too, that the name of Porta Romana or Romanula was closely connected with that of the *ficus Ruminalis* or *Romularis* and that of Romulus. Finally, we have learned that, according to an essential particular of the official legend, the cradle containing Romulus and Remus was set adrift at the foot of the Palatine, and would have been carried away by the waters had it not been overturned by striking a rock.[33] The safety of the Twins, therefore, and the subsequent founding of the city were due to this rock. This corner-stone of the city, this *saxum quadratum* which was the very beginning of Rome (just as the *saxum* of the Aventine which gave origin to the city of Remus[34]), is brought into special relief in our fresco. It is placed by the side of the *ficus Ruminalis*,—that is, by the side of the primordial cult of the earliest Rome.

We must bear in mind the purpose to which the *Roma Quadrata* of the Palatium was devoted, and also the meaning of the square stone by the side of which the *ficus Ruminalis* grew. It might at first sight be thought that the *Roma Quadrata* of the Porta Mugonia and that of the Lupercal had nothing in common. That this is not so, however, will appear from an examination of the fundamental character of Roman religion.

The fundamental conception pervading the earliest religion of the Romans (as well as that of so many other primitive peoples) is the transition from life to death, from light to darkness. In another portion of this volume I have shown how Acca Larentia, the mother of the Lares and a sepulchral deity worshipped at the end of the year (on the Brumalia), was placed in relation with Jupiter,—or better, with Vulcan, the god of light. This conception may explain why Vulcan was associated with the cult of the Lares (or Larvæ and Lemures), and why the *mundus* of the Palatine was open on the even day following the feast of the Vulcanalia. As a result of this conception, too, the Lupercalia,—a feast related to the fecundity of human races and of animals,—occurred in February, the last month of the ancient Roman year, a month which was conspicuously sepulchral in character.

ON THE TOPOGRAPHY OF ROME   231

By examining carefully the topographical evolution of Rome we shall observe that it had three successive centres; the first was on the Cermalus,—that is, on the Lupercal; the second was situated on the Velia; the third, in the Forum Romanum. We shall hereafter return to the question of the time in which this transformation took place. For the present we shall affirm that in all three places we discover traces of the same cults. Near or in the Comitium of the Forum Romanum we find the Vulcanal, the tomb of Romulus, the *ficus Ruminalis,* the *mundus* and the *niger lapis.* On the extremity of the Velia and on the edge of the Palatine we see the temple of the Lares by the side of the *mundus.* And near the Lupercal we meet with the *ficus Ruminalis* side by side with the cult of Romulus and Remus, whom the ancients connected with the cult of the Lares, and who were said to have been nursed by Acca Larentia, the mother of the Lares.

We have already seen that the *ficus Ruminalis* of the Forum Romanum was an offshoot of the one on the Lupercal.[35] It is natural, then, to assume that the *mundus* close by (of which Plutarch speaks[36]) was transferred from the Palatine also, and that to the Palatine, too, belonged the earliest cult of Vulcan,—the god of the city-hearth. According to the earliest form of the legend, Romulus disappeared in the temple of Vulcan near the marsh of the *caprificus,* which originally must have been localized on the Velia at the foot of the Cermalus.[37] We naturally conclude that here, where the sepulchre of Acca Larentia was situated, there existed also the original cult of the Lares.

The transference of the cults of the Cermalus to the Comitium of the Forum Romanum must have occurred in an epoch later than the existence of the cults on the Velia and in the adjacent region of the Palatium. There is no doubt that the Velia was, for a longer or shorter time, the home of many of the most ancient Roman cults. Here, in fact, were the temple of the Penates and the palace of Ancus Marcius and of Tarquinius Priscus. The latter was situated in that part which was adjacent to the Palatium,— in other words, to the Porta Mugonia. Here, too, were the temples of the Lares and of Orbona, and the palace of Servius Tullius, situated on the side towards the Esquiline. A glance at the position of the Velia proves beyond question that it attained such great importance only when (as the legend of Servius Tullius presupposes), the Esquiline was added to the two hills forming the Palatine. All the evidence warrants the assumption that at that time the Velia became the religious centre of Rome. Hither was transferred the cult of the Lares Præstites from the Cermalus; and to the Caca or Vesta of the Cermalus, to whom the vestal virgins continued to offer sacrifices, there succeeded the temple of Vesta at the foot of the Palatine and in the Roman Forum.[38]

From what has been said, it results that the cult of *Roma Quadrata* (that is, of the locality marked by a *saxum quadratum*) does not originally belong to the *mundus* of the Palatine, but rather to the Lupercal,—that region which was called Rome before all others. Here were the *ficus Ruminalis*, the goddess Rumina, the Porta Romana built of *saxum quadratum*, and the *saxum quadratum* that first marked the site of Rome. This conclusion is confirmed by the fact that, whereas Remus wished to found the city upon the Aventine, Romulus determined that it should be established on the site where he had been exposed, where he had been reared by the she-wolf and by Faustulus, and where he continued to have his *casa*.[39]

Religion preserved the memory of the most ancient Roman versions. According to these the earliest Rome arose on the southwest corner of the Palatine, the home of Cacus, who, like Vulcan, represented the god of fire (καίω). There is no proof that this most ancient city was square in form. On the other hand, the configuration of the Cermalus, considered in connection with the statements of the authors regarding the circle (*orbis*) in which the ancient city (*urbs*) was built, does not exclude the idea of the circle. Thus, nothing proves—indeed all the evidence refutes the hypothesis—that the phrase *Roma Quadrata* referred to the more or less rectangular boundary of the Palatine. It signified the square stone (*saxum quadratum*) near the Porta Romana. Later it was explained as referring to the square wall of the Palatine, or to the *pomerium,* which became square only by the addition of localities which originally could not have belonged to it. This transference resulted from the explanations of scholars of the ages of Sulla and of Augustus,—scholars who had lost sight of the original meaning of the expression, or who allowed themselves to be influenced by elements of later origin.

To this result there doubtlessly contributed the square form which the Palatine gradually assumed in the last century of the Republic and in the beginning of the Empire,— a form due to the magnificent palaces erected along the edge of the hill and concealing the primitive roughness of the cliffs.[40] There contributed, too, the rigid application of the theory of the *templum* (said to have been employed by Romulus), and the belief that the city (*urbs*) and the *pomerium* were marked out in the same manner as the camps from which sprang so many Roman colonies. Perhaps the idea of *Roma Quadrata* as a square city may have originated in the square wall of the Palatine, of which we still see some traces. We must not forget, however, that this wall is situated on a part of the hill higher than that where tradition supposes the Lupercal to have been. Finally, it must be considered that this wall belongs, not to a very remote age, but only to the fourth century, and that it is not earlier than the invasion of the Gauls in 387. In other words, it is not earlier than the years in which (according to legend) the god Aius Loquens (Faunus) counselled the Romans to rebuild the walls of the Palatine. Indeed, it is precisely on account of the lack of strong walls on the Palatine that the Romans entrenched themselves on the stronger Capitoline Hill, and that the Gauls captured the former without difficulty and set fire to it.[41]

The fact that these ancient walls surrounded the Palatine from the fourth century on did not give origin to the expression *Roma Quadrata*. Ennius, who, if not the earliest, surely (according to Verrius Flaccus) was one of the earliest inventors of ancient national history, employed this expression in reference to the *mundus* of the Palatine. From a well-known passage in Tacitus we deduce that the expression *ficus Ruminalis* was wont to be applied, not to the ancient *ficus Ruminalis* of the Palatine, but to the more recent one of the Comitium. We learn, too, that this latter *ficus Ruminalis* was considered to be the one which actually protected Romulus and Remus.[42] There is nothing strange in the fact that Ennius, in speaking of the *Roma Quadrata*, should have had in mind the *saxum quadratum* of the Palatium rather than of the Cermalus. It is the latter, however, that is represented in our Pompeian fresco. The expression *Roma Quadrata* did not arise in the Palatium, but rather in that part of the Cermalus in which the name

Roma first arose. Finally, it may well be that, just as the *ficus Ruminalis* of the Cermalus was transferred to the Comitium, so was the *Roma Quadrata;* and that we are to recognize it in that rectangular area situated above the tomb of Romulus,—an area which the ancients called *niger lapis in Comitio,* and which the excavations in the Forum have now restored to light.

II. THE EARLIEST SEPTIMONTIUM

Another important problem of the most ancient Roman topography is that relating to the earliest Septimontium. It does not seem to me that the most eminent Roman topographers have examined all the data preserved by the authors in regard to the ancient Septimontium, its extent and its gates. A brief examination of this question, therefore, may not be amiss.

We are informed by Antistius Labeo (and it has often been observed) that the hills of the original Septimontium were the Palatine, Cermalus, Velia, Oppian, Cispian, Fagutal and Cælian.[43] The Sucusa (indicated by SVC in the inscriptions) must, as was seen by Wissowa, be placed on the Cælian. Varro erroneously identified it with the Subura. It is a strange fact, however, that from the pages of Varro it results in a most explicit manner that there belonged to the fourth region both the Subura (*eidem regioni attributa Subura, quod sub muro terreo Carinarum*) and the pagus Succusanus (*quod succurrit Carinis*).[44] The pagus Sucusa was south of the Velia, whereas the Subura was north of both it and the adjacent Carinæ. But these localities appear as only one administrative district,—as one of the four regions; which fact evidently proves that both were suburbs of the ancient Septimontium.

In the earliest times the suburb of the Palatine (that is, of the primitive Rome) consisted of the ridge of the Velia and of the Esquiliæ. The latter is indicated to be a suburb from its very name, and included the Fagutal, Cispian and Oppian,—all parts of the Esquiline Hill. When the city, in its growth, embraced also these regions, new suburbs sprang into existence. These were, on the one hand, the Subura, which bounded on the Forum Romanum and the dwellings of the Sacra Via; and on the other, the Cælian

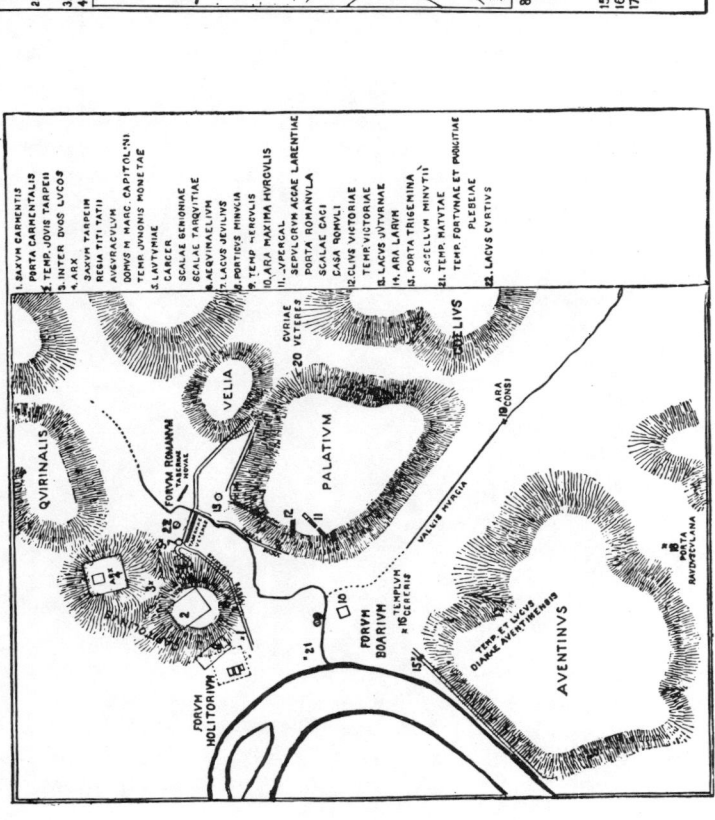

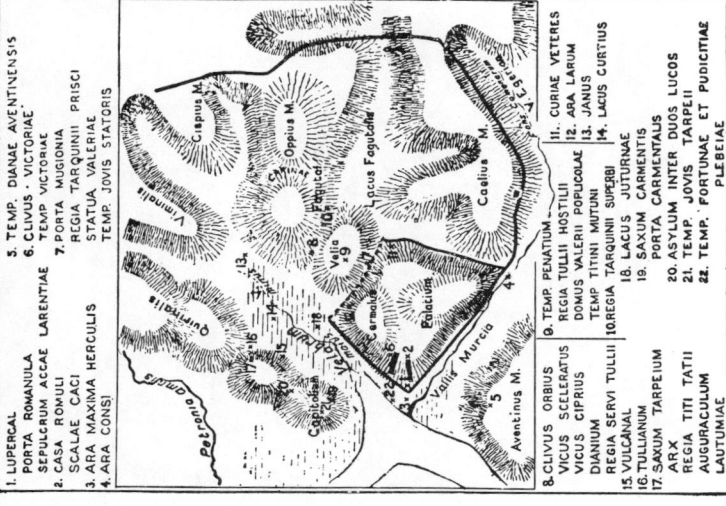

1. SAXVM CARMENTIS
   PORTA CARMENTALIS
   SEPVLCRVM ACCAE LARENTIAE
2. TEMP. JOVIS TARPEII
   INTER DVOS LVCOS
3. ARX
   SAXVM TARPEIVM
   REGIA TITI TATII
   AVGVRACVLVM
   DOMVS M. MARC. CAPITOLINI
   TEMP JVNONIS MONETAE
4. LAVTVMIAE
   CARCER
   SEPVLCRVM ACCAE LARENTIAE
   SCALAE GEMONIAE
   SCALAE TARQVITIAE
5. AEQVIMAELIVM
6. AEQVIMAELIVM
7. LACVS JEVILIVS
8. PORTICVS MINVCIA
9. TEMP. HERCVLIS
10. ARA MAXIMA HVRCVLIS
11. VPERCAL
    SEPVLCRVM ACCAE LARENTIAE
    PORTA ROMANVLA
    SCALAE CACI
    CASA ROMVLI
12. CLIVVS VICTORIAE
    TEMP VICTORIAE
13. LACVS JVTVRNAE
14. ARA LARVM
15. PORTA TRIGEMINA
    SACELLVM MINVTII
16. TEMP. MATVTAE
    TEMP. FORTVNAE ET PVDICITIAE
    PLEBEIAE
17. LACVS CVRTIVS

1. LVPERCAL
   PORTA ROMANVLA
   SEPVLCRVM ACCAE LARENTIAE
2. CASA ROMVLI
   SCALAE CACI
3. ARA MAXIMA HERCVLIS
4. ARA CONSI
5. TEMP. DIANAE AVENTINENSIS
6. CLIVVS - VICTORIAE
   TEMP VICTORIAE
7. PORTA MVGIONIA
   REGIA TARQVINII PRISCI
   STATVA VALERIAE
   TEMP. JOVIS STATORIS
8. CLIVVS ORBIVS
   VICVS SCELERATVS
   VICVS CIPRIVS
   DIANIVM
   REGIA SERVI TVLLII
9. TEMP. PENATIVM
   REGIA TVLLII HOSTILII
   DOMVS VALERII POPVCOLAE
   TEMP TITINI MVTVNI
10. REGIA TARQVINII SVPERBI
15. VVLCANAL
16. TVLLIANVM
17. SAXVM TARPEIVM
    ARX
    REGIA TITI TATII
    AVGVRACVLVM
    LAVTVMIAE
18. LACVS JVTVRNAE
19. PORTA CARMENTIS
20. ASYLVM INTER DVOS LVCOS
21. TEMP. JOVIS TARPEII
22. TEMP. FORTVNAE ET PVDICITIAE
    PLEBEIAE
11. CVRIAE VETERES
12. ARA LARVM
13. JANVS
14. LACVS CVRTIVS

PLANS OF THE MOST ANCIENT ROME

or Sucusa, which we know to have been, originally, the *Martialis Campus,*—the area devoted to military exercises when the Forum itself was flooded.[45] The Cælian, indeed, sloping as it did towards the south, offered in great part those elements necessary for a strong defence; on the side of the Carinæ, instead, a *murus terreus* (of which Varro speaks) was needed to join the Subura with the city.[46]

Before this time the Velia was the central point of the city, for it joined the Palatine, the aristocratic region, with the popular quarters of the Esquiline. At the foot of the Velia, too, were both the *Vicus Orbius* or *Sceleratus* and the *Vicus Cyprius* or *Good*. Here was the shrine of *Strenia*, perhaps identical with the temple of *Vica Potæ*, where Tullus Hostilius had had his palace, and later Valerius Publicola. Here, finally, was situated the gate connected by legend with Horatia, who was slain by her brother; and also the spears beneath which Horatius passed in expiation of his crime.[47]

When the city had expanded to such a degree as to enclose the Subura on one side and the pagus Sucusa or Cælius on the other, the Velia continued to be the centre of the cults identified with the Horatii and the Valerii, and with the royal abodes of Tullius and of Tarquinius Priscus. As late as the time of Augustus, in fact, there continued to be worshipped on this ridge Mutunus, the Roman Priapus. However, the gates which had previously been at the foot of the Velia were, for purposes of defence, transported to the confines of the Cælian and of the Subura. With the gates, of course, were also transferred the myths which had been connected with them. Thus the worship of Jupiter Tigillus and of Juno Sororia,—both of them cults related to the Horatii,—continued to be held at the Velia as late as the time of Dionysius. Notwithstanding this fact, however, there was pointed out at the Porta Capena (the new gate of the enlarged Septimontium) the sepulchre of the Horatii, who were said to have been buried on the spot where they had been killed.[48]

As a result of the city's expansion, also the entrance on the northern side of the Velia was removed; and the new gate of the Septimontium became the famous gate, and later temple, of Janus. About this gate both Ovid and Macrobius have recorded a charming legend, very probably given also by Varro. It was said that Titus Tatius and the Sabines, having descended from the Quirinal and the Capitoline citadel, endeavored to force an entrance into the city of Romulus through the *porta Ianualis*. This gate miraculously flew open, and the Sabines quickly rushed in. Thereupon Janus himself very astutely caused to flow down upon them such a quantity of boiling waters that they were all burned and drowned.[49]

This interesting legend, in all probability, is explained by the presence near by of a hot spring. It explains, moreover, why the temple of Janus was closed in time of peace, and open when war was raging. It is likely, too, that the cause of the phenomenon must be sought for in still another fact,—namely, that when the Sabine city of the *Collis* (that is, of the Quirinal) became fused with that of the Palatine and the Esquiline, the temple of Janus was found to be an entirely useless passageway from a military standpoint,— quite as useless as the *murus terreus* had become.

Macrobius, who recounts the story told above, adds a circumstance worthy of note. He affirms that the temple of Janus was situated *sub radicibus collis Viminalis*.[50] It would seem that we should deduce from these words that also the Viminal formed part of the ancient Septimontium. Nevertheless, not only the fact that Antistius Labeo excludes it is against this hypothesis, but also the circumstance that Varro, in speaking of the third region (the Collis or Quirinalis), adds to it both the *Collis Latiaris* (or Capitoline) and the Viminal.[51] Unless I be mistaken, the less hazardous conclusion is that the Viminal originally extended much more to the south. In like manner we may venture the hypothesis that the Cælian extended much further towards the extremity of the Esquiline, and in particular towards that portion where the Carinæ were situated. Only on such an assumption can we clearly comprehend the very obscure words of Varro, who says that the Cælian was connected with the Carinæ; and again, that the Ceroliensis interposed itself in that place whence the road from the Cælian led towards the Carinæ.[52]

From the passage in Macrobius cited above, it may be deduced that the outline of the Septimontium towards the north has not been rightly imagined by modern scholars. It is conceded by all that two successive extensions of the Septimontium took place, the former city having its gates at the foot of the Velia, the second having extended them to the suburbs of the Cælian and the Subura. In like manner, it is obvious that the Cloaca Maxima, the stream collecting the waters descending from the valley between the Quirinal and the Viminal (and partly also from the Cispian), must have been by the side of the gate of Janus—the northern boundary of the city. This character of the temple of Janus in the Forum as a boundary of the second Septimontium explains why it was deemed worthy of so important a worship, and why it was made the boundary of two *fora*.[53]

From what has been said it results that the various phases of the earliest Roman city were the following:

1. The Palatine Hill (the Palatinus and the Cermalus), with the Velia as a suburb.
2. The Palatine with the Velia, and the suburb Esquiliæ.
3. The Palatine (Palatinus and Cermalus), Velia and Esquiliæ (Fagutal, Oppius, Cispius), and Cælian,—that is, the first Septimontium.
4. The same seven hills, with the addition of the Pagus Sucusa and the Subura.

To these successive enlargements must be added the fusion of the Palatine-Esquiline city with the Quirinal-Viminal-Capitoline city; a fusion which resulted in transforming the slopes of these hills (formerly the suburbs of the two separate cities) into the Forum Romanum,—the political centre of Rome.

From arguments presented in various chapters of this volume, we conclude that such fusion was accomplished in the fourth century. We are not in possession of elements sufficient for determining previous conditions. The necropolis of the Forum Romanum, which chronologically extends to the sixth century (if not to the beginning of the fifth), makes it clear that the two suburbs at the foot of the Velia were included within the *pomerium* and formed part of a second extension in relatively recent times. Confirmation of this statement is received from the examination of the tradition relating to the feast of the *Equus October*. For, this story proves that, in the fourth century, the Sacra Via and the *Turris Mamilia*, to which the head of the winning horse was affixed, were still suburbs.[54]

The archaic necropolis of the Esquiline, on the other hand, tends to prove that towards the sixth century a population had already established itself on this hill, whether they formed part of the Palatine-Esquiline city, or whether they belonged to the suburb of the Palatine city.

Excavations may some day yield elements for the formation of more accurate judgments. For the present we shall limit ourselves to affirming that all the tales of the development of the city, and particularly of its gates, are based upon legend and religion. The utter lack of chronological value in these myths is evident. The road at the foot and near the gate of the Velia, which legend connected with Servius Tullius (whence its name *scelerata*), was, at the same time, related with the myth of the expiations of Horatius, the slayer of his sister. When all these facts are attentively considered, it will be seen that the myth must have originated in ceremonies and in worships similar to those on account of which the appellation of *scelerata* was given to the *porta Carmentalis*,—the gate from which went forth the three hundred Fabii destined never again to return to their fatherland.

III

In conclusion, we must admit that we cannot decide when Rome arose. Still less can we determine with chronological precision how many generations or how many centuries passed before the shepherds who first led their flocks to pasture upon the heights of the Cermalus spread over the entire Palatine. Similarly, we cannot declare when, becoming a political organism, they extended over the Velia, and thus united the most ancient city with the hills of the Esquiline. We grant that the earliest occupation of the hills of Rome by human races reaches back into the prehistoric ages,—ages that are beyond the control of chronology and of history. On the other hand, we can establish with certainty that, as regards the Palatine, as well as the remaining portions of the city, those structures and edifices which represent the complete development of civilization belong to Republican times.

The walls of the Palatine do not seem to be earlier than the invasion of the Gauls, nor than those walls of the Esquiline known as the *agger* of Servius Tullius. The abodes of the ancient inhabitants of the Palatine, moreover, continued for a long time to be humble dwellings of wood and straw. Upon this point the evidence of the texts is so clear as not to admit of doubt. We leave aside the fact that, for reasons of rite, some sacred buildings on the Palatine and on the Capitoline continued to be humble huts as late as the historic age.[55] We insist, however, on the fact that, according to Cornelius Nepos, the houses were still covered with shingles in the age of Pyrrhus.[56] This state of affairs did not disappear at once, but continued later than the age of Pyrrhus and of Hannibal. A clear proof is offered by the events narrated for the year 178 B.C. In that year a conflagration arose in the temple of Venus, which was so thoroughly destroyed that not a trace of it remained,—*sine ullo vestigio*.[57] This shows that the temple must have been built entirely of wood.

That the Roman houses of the fifth century were built of wood results, too, from the well-known legend of Valerius Publicola, whose house was transported from the summit of the Velia to its foot in one night.[58] Such structures were still common throughout the third century, as is proved by the declarations of Cornelius Nepos, by the burning of the temple of Venus in 178, referred to above, and by the conflagrations which in 241, 213, 210 and 192 B.C. destroyed so great a portion of the city.[59] Such fires were considered in Rome as a normal calamity even in later ages, which proves that even later than the third century wood constituted a large proportion of the building material.[60]

I called attention elsewhere to these building conditions in ancient Rome. My statements aroused the indignation of a number of local investigators, who do not clearly conceive the development of the history of civilization in the ancient world. These men consider it the duty of good citizenship to maintain intact the prestige of the original and uninterrupted greatness of Rome, even if such position be not in harmony with historical truth.

The study of ancient society in Western Europe shows that the conditions at Rome had also obtained in the East, and that similar conditions continued in the West till the establishment of the Roman Empire. As late as the time of Augustus the houses of the Gauls and of the Iberians were huts of wood. It was to the credit of the Romans that they gradually substituted for such humble dwellings built of stone and of bricks.[61] According to the Roman official tradition, bricks (*tegulæ*) were distributed among the Roman citizens after the Gallic fire. In this statement, then, we have the first indication of the substitution of bricks for wood. It naturally follows, too, that after the burning of Rome the citizens undertook to girt the city with walls of *saxum quadratum*.

This statement does not exclude the fact that even before this time Rome may have had foundations or public buildings partly or entirely constructed of stone. Nevertheless the passage from Cornelius Nepos already cited, regarding the use of wooden roofs as late as the age of Pyrrhus, shows that, even if the statement is deserving of belief, it should not be accepted as depicting a new and universal characteristic.

The exclusive, or nearly exclusive, use of wood in construction offers data for forming a conception of the abundance of the forests covering the plains and the mountains of ancient Italy. The foreigner who visits our country to-day, while admiring the infinite beauties of nature, notes the lack of those woods which constitute, at times, the most beautiful ornament of his native country. That Italy and, particularly, Latium were once covered with woods results from countless well-known texts which it is unnecessary to repeat. It will be useful, on the contrary, to emphasize that such conditions obtained till a very late historic age. The long continuance of forests and of houses partly built of wood explains why Varro, Ovid and others refer to the woods covering the Roman hills and the Forum. In late historic ages, therefore, there still remained traces of former conditions which permitted scholars of the school of Varro to reconstruct a picture of the ancient times.

The building conditions of the most ancient Rome, and the rapid development of the city in the fourth century after the conquest of southern Etruria and after the Samnite Wars, reflect (in this respect) the development in the United States of America. All know, for instance, that in 1803 Chicago consisted of only one small wooden fort, that thirty years later it had about one hundred inhabitants, and that in 1837 it had a few thousands still living in wooden houses. After the fire of 1871 rapid progress was made in rebuilding a city of stone and brick. To-day Chicago is well on the way towards a population of two millions of inhabitants. The unsurpassed abundance of American forests explains why the custom of building wooden houses has continued for so long a time. Similarly, the rapid disappearance of forests and the frequent fires explain why in Boston, New York and Chicago brick and stone have been gradually substituted for the former material. In California and in some cities of the South (as New Orleans) the transformation has still to take place, in spite of the wealth and the prosperity of those regions.

The examples of Rome and of America show how carefully we must avail ourselves of data furnished by monuments in reconstructing with historical truth a picture of the wealth and the power of a people. To-day, in fact, it behooves us to be very prudent in accepting the statements of mere archæologists. Archæological data, if not explained by the texts and interpreted by historical criticism, may lead to deplorable errors, as in fact is often the case. The deep insight of Thucydides clearly saw this truth, and, in establishing the standards of universal historical criticism, he drew the attention of the reader thereto. He remarks how greatly deceived would be that person who would endeavor to trace the wealth and the greatness of Sparta and of Athens from their monuments. If Sparta had been destroyed (he observes) no one could have deduced, from the unimportant remains of the houses and the temples, that Sparta had once ruled two-thirds of the Peloponnese, and had spread its hegemony over the remaining portions. On the other hand, from the glorious ruins of Athens he would have been led to conclude that this city had had twice the power which it had actually wielded.[62]

EXCURSUS I

THE STIPS VOTIVA OF THE NIGER LAPIS, AND THE FALISCAN MUSEUM OF VILLA GIULIA

I

In May, 1899, the archaic stele of the Forum that had been discovered beneath the *niger lapis* was published for the first time. It was then emphasized that a series of objects had simultaneously been found, placed around the monument, in which it was thought that a *stips votiva* should be recognized. They were examined both by those authors to whom the official publication of the inscription was entrusted and also by other scholars. And from the age of certain objects therein contained, it was concluded that the stele itself necessarily belonged to the sixth and perhaps to the seventh century B.C.

A few months after the discovery I was invited to publish my views on the subject, which I did in one of the most widely circulated Italian periodicals. I there brought to notice the fact that, in the official report of the excavations made by Boni, as well as in the subsequent interpretations of the inscription, it was declared that in the loose earth of the lower strata some small pieces of *giallo antico* had been found, also some smooth chips of Pentelic marble, and, finally, chips of black marble identical with that of the *niger lapis*.

Pentelic and colored marbles but ill agree with a *stips votiva* at Rome of the seventh or even sixth century B.C. I could, therefore, justly write in November, 1899: " Much importance, however, has been given to the circumstance that many of the *terre cotte* might belong to the sixth century, and that a fragment of an archaic Greek vase might date as early as the seventh. But no conclusion can be drawn from this, because such objects were found side by side with others that are to be ascribed to the last centuries of the Republic."[1]

Notwithstanding the circumstantial evidence produced by me, several scholars continued to speak of a *stips votiva* of the sixth century. The truth became known more

than one year after the discovery, when, as a consequence
of the general outcry of the scholars of the world,—an
outcry demanding a full knowledge of the details of the
excavations,—a report was finally published in the official
Notizie degli Scavi for April, 1900. In this report it was
said that "a full knowledge of the material is necessary,
in order that judgments may not be misdirected, as has
already occurred in part." The information was then given
that some of the objects composing the so-called *stips votiva*
belonged to the seventh, the sixth and the fifth centuries
B.C., while others could be assigned to the fourth century
and even to the end of the Republic. It concluded with the
words that it was not a question of a *stips votiva*, but "of
an accumulation gradually formed, transported thither from
some other place, and at one time, and used for the purpose
of filling in the empty space." We hope that after this
official communication, whoever discusses the age of the
monument will no longer insist on the value of this pre-
supposed datum.[2]

In the second chapter of this volume I have discussed the
age of the archaic cippus,—endeavoring to decide whether
it is to be assigned to the fourth or to the fifth century B.C.,
or rather to an age later than the burning of Rome, and
contemporaneous with the stratum on which it was found
resting. Here, instead, I deem it necessary to emphasize
with how little sincerity these particular excavations were
conducted. I have before me a double purpose,—firstly,
that I may establish the truth; secondly, that, with a full
knowledge of what has occurred in the past, it will be less
practicable to deceive scholars hereafter.[3]

The architect Giacomo Boni was persuaded that the archaic
cippus was surrounded with a *stips votiva*, and was disposed
(if I be not mistaken) to assign to it a very great age. In
the fulfilment of his duty he necessarily spoke also of the
fragments of ancient marble. It was this statement which
made it possible for the world to realize that the so-called
stips votiva was anything but archaic. Such reserve was
not maintained by the other publishers of the monument.
One of them, basing his arguments precisely on the *stips
votiva*, affirms that the cippus truly belongs to the sixth
century.[4] Other scholars were not allowed to see all the
material, which would readily have guided them towards
the truth. It is only thus that I can explain the strange fact

that Professor Comparetti, in an interpretation of the stele (accurate, indeed, but not at all commensurable with his worth and fame as a Greek scholar) has spoken of potsherds of the fourth century, of which Boni made no mention in his first report. At the same time he proves himself to be entirely unaware of the existence of the archæological strata surrounding the cippus—strata of material that was transported thither and containing a mixture of objects dating anywhere from the seventh to the first century B.C.

Professor Von Duhn, of Heidelberg, for instance, was not informed of the real state of affairs. For, referring to the affirmation of a "most trustworthy eye-witness" of the excavations, he declares the *stips votiva* a product of the seventh century, and, furthermore, a proof of the great antiquity of the cippus.[5]

Bearing in mind all these circumstances, and considering that scholars, through the authoritative voice of Huelsen, called for a resolution of all doubts,[6] it is possible, I believe, to formulate some questions. Why was it that the administration of antiquities, or the Commission charged with the preparation of the *Notizie degli Scavi,* did not immediately publish the facts relative to the excavations? Why did they wait an entire year to publish the report of April, 1900, in which it was said that complete information was given in order to avoid the formation of wrong judgments, as had already partly been the case?

II

The answer to the above questions is readily found. We must merely remember that the discovery of the *niger lapis* occurred at a time when certain men were searching with great avidity for proofs of the authenticity of the ancient Roman legends. For this reason those scholars were prevented from making a copy of the monument who might have given of it an interpretation unwarped by certain desired tendencies. For this reason, too, its publication was entrusted, in a special manner, to one who was disposed to defend a theory which he was then preparing to maintain. And thus it was thought both opportune and prudent to delay a year in the publication of all the facts relative to the excavations.

Justice compels us to state, however, that these conditions did not come about through the will of only one person, or of a few men, who aimed at using the glories of Rome as a mere means in their political career. Two were the elements which forced such a state of affairs. On the one side were ranged those politicians who wished that only so much should be made known as would strengthen the old and rhetorical conception of the origins of Rome; on the other were drawn up men closely affiliated to the former by poverty of soul and of intellect—a band of worthless archæologists and amateur scholars. These had for years watched with unkindly eye the strengthening of that modern criticism which, searching only for the truth, and unfettered by patriotic or by political aims, seemed to them to be despoiling Rome and Italy of their traditional glories.

This critical tendency draws its origin and its lustre from such men, particularly, as Niebuhr and Mommsen. It seemed a timely and fortunate event that a monument should have been discovered which would cause to be thrown into the flames the works of these historians, and also of those others who more or less freely followed a critical and objective tendency. The limits of the problems expounded by Niebuhr and by Mommsen were not clearly understood. It was natural, therefore, that certain theories should have been ascribed to those authors which, in all likelihood, they would have quite disavowed. We are not surprised that the cry of *fuori d'Italia i barbari* should have been hurled against those Italians and foreigners who, urged by their love of truth and of Italy, had dedicated their labors to a loving examination of authentic facts, and to the lopping of the withered branches.

Patriotic sentiments give life to historical researches; but at the same time they may dim the clear view of the truth. Whosoever clearly understands these sentiments will realize without surprise how scholars of scanty culture and of narrow scientific horizon should have seized the opportunity offered by the discovery of the cippus. They have used it to combat opinions which they judged insufficiently respectful to recognized tradition. In so doing they have unburdened themselves of the necessity of studying works which, for lack of critical preparation, they were unprepared to understand.

The earliest legends and the historical traditions of a

people constitute part of the sacred patrimony of a nation. Whosoever shakes belief in these matters lays himself open to censure; sometimes even to the persecution of those who have embraced the various confessions of faith and the religious dogmas. The scientific historian is well aware of the fact that the works of historical and political reformers have, throughout the world, been burned by the hand of the executioner as often as those works charged with heresy. Scientific arguments against scientific reforms have been lacking; resort has been had to the casting of discredit and of dishonor upon the reformers.

With these dark and obscure phases of the question we must contrast others worthy of our just consideration and respect. We must not forget that, if patriotism at times darkens the minds of scholars and prevents their seeing national defects and failings, it also produces and fosters those noble sentiments that urge to historical researches. The love for ancient Rome has caused the patient searching of the archæological soil of the city. Surely he is worthy of our highest esteem who, through such explorations, believes and hopes to trace out the real elements of the earliest legends.

The defence of the historical patrimony of a nation, the defence of sentiments of patriotism, may pardon defects in critical method and in historical training; but they do not authorize a resort to subterfuge and to deceit. We can readily comprehend how the discovery of the *niger lapis* might cause inexperienced and narrow-minded writers to believe that a monument had finally been discovered with which to beat down the critical tendency. This tendency is part of the serious and calm students of all nations. Certain ones in Italy, however, foolishly style it as the German school, as if G. B. Vico were a German, or as if it were the exclusive patrimony of the Teuton to investigate the truth without any preoccupations of party or of nationality! They have cried out loudly against the hypercritical school; but they have thus clearly shown themselves to belong (if I may use the word) to the acritical school.

It is neither admissible nor in any way justifiable that, to strengthen their own convictions and to flatter the views and the tendencies of men powerful in politics, they should have resorted to the shameful expedient of publishing only certain elements of the discoveries. These elements were such as were considered of very great age, and which were compatible with their own views. Those particulars, however, that would have offered arguments to scholars who maintained opposite views. were deliberately kept secret.

III

I do not think that I need dwell longer on the so-called *stips votiva* and its antiquity. The insincere method adopted by the concealers of truth passes its own judgment on their affirmations. It reveals the conscience and the doctrines of some of those who pose as the defenders of national tradition. I deem it necessary to establish that what was thus attempted in regard to the excavations in the Forum Romanum does not constitute an isolated phenomenon. It is, indeed, in perfect harmony with the facts regarding the Faliscan Museum of Villa Giulia.

The facts of the case are well known, and consequently it is not necessary to dwell long upon them. An official report was rendered by the Ministry of Public Instruction, drawn up by Professor L. Pigorini, the Director of the Italian School of Archæology. This report proves false the statements of Pasquale Villari, the Minister of Public Instruction. Basing his statements of information furnished him by Professor Felice Barnabei (who was then General Director of Italian Antiquities), Villari declared that the excavations made in the territory of Narce had been conducted under the supervision of government officials and with strictly scientific methods.

On the contrary, the report of Pigorini on the Museum established by Professor F. Barnabei contains the following statements:

"The first count to be made concerns the method according to which the ancient burial places in the Faliscan territory were excavated. The report of the Hon. Boselli, which is prefixed to the royal decree of February 7, 1899, referred to the material found at Falerii. It furthermore gave it to be understood that the excavations had been continually under the surveillance of government officials, and that, to the tombs explored by private individuals, others were to be added that had been explored under the direct supervision of the State. Later, the Hon. Villari (even this has been recorded), in inaugurating the collection of the antiquities of Narce, represented it as the fruit of the labors performed by the Museum officials, without making the slightest mention of the participation of private individuals. However, in the volume illustrating those objects of antiquity he limits himself (page 22, notes) to making *honorable mention of Signor Annibale Benedetti, who conducted excavations in the territory of Narce, and who gave constant proofs of his great interest in our studies and in our Museum.* The truth is, instead, that, with the exception of the *tombe a pozzo* (well-like tombs) at Pozzo S. Angelo and of a few others found here and there, the many sepulchres of the necropolis of Narce which yielded the material for the Museum were excavated by private citizens and on their own account. The directors of the Museum merely made a selection, and purchased those funeral ornaments which they deemed worthy of notice." [7]

I shall pay no attention to other facts brought forth by the Commission, whether in regard to the surveillance of the excavations, or to the manner in which the sepulchral ornaments were arranged in the Museum, or to the justifications of the expenses incurred in acquiring those objects. Surely such facts cast a somewhat unfavorable light on the scientific value of the Museum. On this point a positive and final word will be spoken only when the entire question will have been examined by persons free from bonds of obligation to the Commission on antiquities. And such examination must naturally be conducted with purely objective and scientific ends in view.

It is worthy of note that the official report of Professor Pigorini shows the greatest forbearance towards the work of Barnabei, the general director, whereas it contains bitter censure for Professor W. Helbig, who was the first to call the attention of scholars to the facts deplored by Professor Pigorini himself. From this it results in the clearest possible fashion that the official publication regarding the Museum of Villa Giulia (written by Professor F. Barnabei) is far from being a sincere and scientific document. It is truly unfortunate that in these latter years we are obliged to register the publications on the Museum of Villa Giulia and on the archaic stele of the Forum, those on the alleged forgery of the Etruscan tegula from Capua, and those on the pretended *terramara* of Tarentum.

IV

In examining the early history of Rome the critical historian is ever brought face to face with the falsifications of the ancient annalists; in investigating the researches of certain modern critics and archæologists of the Peninsula he likewise,—alas! too frequently,—finds himself in the presence of inaccuracies and sometimes even of misrepresentations. That beautiful portion of Italy which extends from the Tronto and the Tiber to Sicily is very rich in ancient monuments and in imaginative men. In this region, then, which has produced that bright luminary, G. B. Vico, rather than in central Italy or in the valley of the Po, have such men flourished as Ligorio, Pratilli, Antonini and their followers.

If we seek the cause of the forgeries in the ancient annals, we shall find them to be national pride and family ambition. If a glance be given to the more recent ones, we shall see that they are likewise to be accounted for by political ambition and by personal aims. Such forgeries crop up in countries less thoroughly educated to the rigid cult of truth; they are, generally speaking, the fruit of scanty scientific development. But there is not the slightest doubt concerning the scientific future of Italy. There is no doubt that in the management of the great national institutions the unfit and the unscrupulous will be replaced by others more learned and sincere. Surely it is to be hoped that the day will soon come when no one will have reason to doubt the sincerity of the data in the official publications. No doubt is ever entertained concerning the laboratory experiments of a scientist of great and indisputable merit. But the data furnished by even the most eminent scientist must be subjected to exacting comparison, and must be confirmed by experience. The data of the official publications relative to scientific matter must be similarly compared and contrasted. No science is complete if only one part of the truth is told, the other concealed. And it is an essential part of the truth to know the various subterfuges and frauds, as well as the circumstances which gave rise to them.

EXCURSUS II

THE AUTHENTICITY OF THE ETRUSCAN TILE FROM CAPUA AND THE SUPREMACY OF THE ETRUSCANS IN CAMPANIA

I

Fingebant simulque credebant.
—TACITUS.

THE ancients, through Cato and Polybius, inform us that the Etruscans had colonies also in Campania, and that they founded the towns of Capua and of Nola. These data are given by authorities of the highest value. They are, too, in perfect accord with the information relative to the expansion of the Etruscans throughout Latium and the territory of the Volscians in the end of the sixth and the beginning of the fifth century. Some historians have, without reason, doubted these statements, and their doubts have been reëchoed by some archæologists who have allowed themselves to be prejudiced by certain facts. The latter argue that in Campania no traces of Etruscan monuments have been found, with the exception of a few graffiti on local vases made in imitation of Greek ware. Even these graffiti, they continue, employ the Oscan alphabet.

The lack of Etruscan monuments at Capua, however, was not sufficient to impair the strength of the explicit declarations of ancient authors. For, the lack of Etruscan inscriptions and monuments at Rome does not brand as false the statements of the ancients regarding Etruscan supremacy in Rome and in Latium. In the one case as in the other, such domination was not of long duration. At Capua, indeed (according to the testimony of Cato and of Livy), it continued throughout half a century only—namely, from 471 to 424 B.C.

The weakness of the arguments employed to invalidate the declarations of Cato and of Polybius has been most clearly shown by the discovery of the *tegula* of which we present a copy. It was found at Capua, in the early part of the year 1898, not far from the Roman amphitheatre which is

THE ETRUSCAN TEGULA FROM CAPUA.
(BERLIN MUSEUM)

known under the name of *Quattordici Ponti*. Like other Etruscan inscriptions, our *tegula* refuses to reveal its secret. This was immediately recognized by Buecheler, the illustrious philologist at Bonn, who first edited the inscription. To but small results, too, did the laborious efforts of Elia Lattes lead. The latter, however, deserves the credit of having more minutely examined the inscription from its palæographical side. On the one hand, Buecheler, giving due weight to the affirmations of the ancients relative to Etruscan domination at Capua, assigned the tegula to the fifth century—the time when such dominion came to an end.[1] Lattes, on the other hand, has brought into relief the more recent palæographical character of the monument. We are therefore obliged to date it a century or two later.[2]

Tradition tells us that towards 438 B.C. (or, perhaps, 424) Capua was wrested from the Etruscans by the Samnite peoples who had descended from the plateau of the Apennines. It does not follow that the Etruscans disappeared from Campania immediately. According to Livy, the Samnites were at first welcomed by the Etruscans, and were permitted to share in the citizenship; but later the Etruscans were killed in the midst of the banquetting and sleeping of a festal day.

I know not whether these latter indications permit us to coördinate and to harmonize the two different traditions of Livy and of Diodorus. We would then be obliged to suppose that the Samnites were welcomed at Capua by the Etruscans in 438 B.C., and that nearly fourteen years later they became absolute masters of the city. At any rate, the Samnites did not at once expel the Etruscans, but had to resort to snares. Likewise, it is more than probable, nay, it is certain (as our *tegula* proves), that a certain number of Etruscans continued to live in Campania, either as subjects of the Samnites or as the priests of special cults that could not be entrusted to another race.[3]

This custom (to which also Lattes calls attention) was widely diffused in ancient society, and it is attested by so many declarations of the ancient authors that there is no necessity of a special proof on this occasion. It is sufficient to recall the Greek and the Phrygian priests who were continually summoned to Rome for the cults of Ceres and of the Mater Deum. Moreover, we must not forget the great care of the Etruscans and the Romans in entrusting certain cults to special families—families which alone were considered entitled to have relations with certain divinities.

Consequently, there is nothing strange in finding at Capua an Etruscan inscription of the end of the fourth or the beginning of the third century. Similarly, we should not marvel that the relatively late Campanian statues representing female fecundity show, in their style, such strong contact with the art of Etruria. The palæography of our Etruscan *tegula*, when joined with the Campanian vases bearing Osco-Etruscan graffiti, forms a most valuable document for the understanding of the development of the local alphabet.

II

The Etruscan *tegula* found at Quattordici Ponti is not valuable only in confirming the statements of the ancients regarding the Etruscan supremacy. It serves, also, in studying the power which this people exercised over the region directly administered by them for half a century—an influence extending as far as Pompeii and the sources of the modern Tusciano and Silaro.

Cato and Polybius affirm that the Etruscans established themselves at Capua and at Nola. The Italic names of these two cities, meaning, respectively, the *city of the plain* and the *new city,* have furnished arguments for those who maintain the Italic character of the Etruscan language—a thesis defended in ancient times by Varro. To others, however, the names have suggested manifold doubts regarding the value of such affirmation. We must not by any means exclude the possibility that the Etruscans occupied towns already inhabited by Oscan races.

In the case of Capua, it must be noted that the Etruscans did not settle at S. Maria di Capua Vetere,—the Capua of the ancient Romans,—but, indeed, at Volturnum, that is, at the place where, in Roman times, stood the city of Casilinum—the *old city.* This town was situated upon the banks of the Volturnus, and corresponds to the modern Capua.[4] All the evidence is in favor of the belief that the Etruscans were not successful in establishing themselves as masters of Volturnum-Capua. Surely this could not have happened before 524 B.C., in which year (according to the annals of Cuma, known also to Roman tradition) Aristodemus Malacus hurled them back some distance from his city. It must have occurred after 504 B.C., in which year the latter defeated the Etruscans at Aricia.

Though the intervention of Hiero of Syracuse prevented the Etruscan fleet from capturing Cuma in 474 B.C., we may well suppose events to have had a different issue on land, and the Etruscans to have become masters of Capua. According to Cato, this dominion was established in 471 B.C.; Polybius assigns it to the same period in which the Etruscans established themselves in the valley of the Po. In the latter case the texts would be in full harmony with the monuments. For the most ancient traces of the Etruscans in the valley of the Po belong to the end of the sixth and the beginning of the fifth century.

Finally, the beginning of Etruscan domination in Campania is later than that which they exercised over Latium by a few decades only. The legends with which Cato was acquainted spoke of the Etruscan Mezentius at Ardea, of the Etruscan King Metabus at Privernum, of the Etruscan Tarnus, and of others. There is no reason for concluding from all this (with some modern historians) that the Etruscan domination is to be referred to the seventh or the eighth century. We can derive therefrom merely that there were assigned to the mythical period events which occurred in the historic period. Similarly, there was referred to the legendary age also the arrival of Æneas, the enemy of Mezentius,—Æneas, who, like Camilla, daughter of Metabus, may, indeed, belong to legend and to religious cults, but not to history proper.

III

The clear and positive conclusions to which we have arrived would be somewhat impaired,—indeed, would be entirely destroyed,—if the observations made against our *tegula* by a certain critic were true.

The authenticity of this monument was never for a moment questioned by Buecheler, its first publisher. Indeed, it was and is recognized by Pollack and Kekule von Stradonitz (who procured it for the Berlin Museum), by Von Duhn and Lattes, and by many other archæologists and philologists who have had occasion to examine and to study it.

Professor Giulio de Petra, however, has declared against the authenticity of the *tegula*.[5] He was the first to be asked to state his opinion on the subject. He refused to acquire it for the Museum of Naples, his arguments being the following: He emphasizes, in the first place, the existence at Capua of a workshop (so to speak) for counterfeit *tegulæ;* and, secondly, the contemporaneous presence in our *tegula* of more recent graphic forms with other more archaic ones. Professor De Petra considers it strange to find the boustrophedon order in such a long document; and, also, has his suspicions aroused by the presence of one, two and three diacritic points.

I do not deem it worth while to dwell on such weak arguments. Indeed, the falsifying of Campanian *tegulæ* implies imitation of authentic documents—the result being but a bad and ill-made reproduction. We have already set forth the arguments of Lattes, which prove that the Etruscan *tegula* from Capua may be assigned to a period even later than the fifth century. This is not a case for basing arguments of fraud upon the peculiarity of some letters—for our Campanian *tegula* is the only Etruscan monument of considerable length. It awaits other discoveries which will some day permit of broader and more certain observations,—observations based on comparison. Moreover, as is known to De Petra himself, other inscriptions from Etruria and those from Lemnos present similar characteristics,— namely, the boustrophedon order and the presence in one and the same inscription of the one or two or three points as diacritic marks.

We are, then, utterly destitute of the means of comparison by which we might explain the inscription on the *tegula*. But, surely, there would not result from this fact any arguments against its authenticity. In Roman epigraphy (not to speak of Italic inscriptions) a new monument very often has its own peculiarities. But why discuss the pretended falsity, using arguments based upon peculiarities which we cannot explain, when all the external evidence, such as the material and the form of the monument, have declared its authenticity to those who have examined it?

But it is even against the external characteristics that Professor De Petra hurls his attack. To the above arguments, which are of no scientific value, he adds: *io credo alla sincerita dell' assicurazione datami, cioè che la terracotta venne seppellita ai Quattordici Ponti, perche sapevasi che là si doveva fare uno scavo.* To this same declaration are to be referred the words in the *Bulletino Ufficiale del Ministero della Pubblica Istruzione: Il dott. Prof. Paolo Orsi, attualmente direttore del Museo, incaricato del Museo Nazionale di Napoli afferma di aver presso di se un documento col quale gli scavatori della terracotta dichiarano di averla essi sotterata per dar credito alla scoperta.*[6]

That the pretended falsifiers should have confessed to their fraud proves that there was unusual interest in the case. No scoundrel will acknowledge himself a scoundrel without the pressure of powerful external forces, or that of special interest in the matter. As all know, scoundrels assume the bearing of gentlemen. Consequently, the suspicion came into my mind that the document referred to above, believed to be sincere by Professor De Petra and presented by Professor Orsi, was itself a fraud. All the greater did my suspicion become when I reflected that, according to the unanimous opinion of those German archæologists who had seen the monument, and according to the publication of Buecheler, the *tegula* was absolutely authentic.

The authenticity of one of the most precious documents of ancient Italic history was at stake. As a student of ancient history, and as director of the Museum of Naples (in whose province falls the surveillance of the whole of Campania), not only was it for my interest, but, indeed, it was my bounden duty, to ascertain the truth, and to declare it to all scholars.

In the meantime, I betook myself to S. Maria di Capua Vetere, and afterwards sent also some fellow-students to investigate that strange confession of fraud. The result obtained in both cases was the following.

The *tegula* in question was excavated without any fraud whatsoever at Quattordici Ponti by two illiterate men,— Gaetano Paolella and Domenico Santoro,—with the help of two other workmen. Signor Bartolomeo Formichelli, an expert and intelligent excavator, offered to sell it to the Museum of Naples. After having been declared false by Professor De Petra and by his collaborator, Professor A. Sogliano (who but glanced at a squeeze of the inscription), the *tegula* was offered to the Berlin Museum. And thus the *tegula,* a treasure for early Italic history, was acquired at the price of two hundred francs.

The news of the loss of this monument produced a certain stir in official circles. Professor De Petra was convinced of the falsity of the inscription. An officer of the Museum was sent to Capua to obtain the final proofs of the forgery of the *tegula.* I shall omit mentioning names and circumstances that would be of greater interest to the magistrate than to the student. The result was that another official found means of procuring an unsigned statement, in which the four workmen were made to declare that they themselves had buried the *tegula.* The peasant Gaetano Paolella, one of the workmen, was led into the tobacco store of Raffaele Monaco, of S. Maria di Capua Vetere. There he was made to affix his cross to the above declaration, which he, as an illiterate person, was not in condition to read. He could not, therefore, realize the importance of making his sign to such a document. The remaining three workmen were absent; nevertheless, three more crosses were affixed to the document; and thus it was represented that they, too, had been present.

Such is the document which Professor Paolo Orsi deemed worthy of mention in the *Bulletino Ufficiale del Ministero della Pubblica Istruzione.* Such is the document which Professor De Petra considered sincere.

The document, then, with which it was attempted to impair the authenticity of the precious *tegula,*—a monument spurned by the Museum of Naples and now tenderly cared for at Berlin,—is a forgery. On the other hand, the *tegula* which was declared a forgery is absolutely authentic. It is, indeed, one of the most important monuments for the ancient history of Italy.

The story thus briefly told of the discovery of the Etruscan *tegula* of S. Maria di Capua Vetere causes us to think sadly of *testis Campanus pro nullo habetur,* and of the many other falsifications with which the history of Campania has been constantly marred. The soil of this region still conceals many precious documents for the history of Italy. In the meantime let us hope, in the interests of science and of the Italian name, that a moral reformation may take place, and that such frauds either will no longer be possible, or else will be mercilessly revealed and condemned.

EXCURSUS III

THE RELATIONS BETWEEN THE SQUARE PALATINE, THE SQUARE PALISADES IN EMILIA, AND THE PRETENDED TERRAMARA OF TARENTUM

IN speaking of the *Roma Quadrata* of the Palatine I referred to the errors of both the ancient and the modern topographers in regard to the meaning of that expression. The belief that Rome was a square city induced several scholars to consider the square as the fundamental principle of every Roman organism. Indeed, a special volume on this subject has been written by a student of Roman law.

New theories have been added to the old. An examination of some *terramare* in the regions of Emilia has revealed that the palisades are square. In these latter years, Professor L. Pigorini and several students of primitive archæology, or (to use their own term) *paletnologia,* have found not merely a resemblance, but indeed an absolute identity in form between such palisades and the *Roma Quadrata.* This identity was corroborated (in their opinion) by the discovery of similar household articles in the palisades and at Rome. Thus the further conclusion was reached of the ethnographic identity between the inhabitants of the ancient valley of the Po and those of Latium, and of the derivation of the latter from the men of the palisade region.

The formulating of such a theory must have been partly due to a learned German having a truly deep knowledge of the texts and of the monuments. We must state at once, however, that its ulterior development is mainly due to a numerous group of students, who at first called their science primitive history (*preistoria*), and then entitled it *paletnologia* and primitive archæology. Such studies Mommsen, as is well known, was wont to style " the science of the *analfabeti."* And, when asked for the meaning of his biting remark, that keen critic would scornfully answer that in the studies of such archæologists he had ever failed to find traces of an alphabet. Professor Pigorini himself, in speaking of the most ancient civilization of Italy (*Le più antiche civiltà dell' Italia,* in *Rendiconti Lincei,* 1903, p.

67), remarks: *Caratteristica è la mancanza assoluta di segni che accennino a scrittura e di ogni indizio di arte figurata.* Mommsen was right in affirming that these are the characteristics also of many followers of the school of *paletnologia.*

In fact, the scanty knowledge of the Greek and the Latin texts is, in general, the fundamental characteristic of such researches. These are based on arbitrary interpretations of potsherds and of other articles—dumb material for him who is not in a position to give it life with the proper interpretation of the texts. At times one of these students (a *rara avis*) supplements the so-called "palæotnological" material with a knowledge of the written texts. But his inexperience reveals such a lack of method and of technique as to produce a sense of profound discomfort.

L. Pigorini, the director of the *Bullettino di Paletnologia,* abstains from such use of the Greek and the Latin texts. He does not conceal his complete inexperience in matters of classical culture. And though his theories have not received the approval of the most authoritative archæologists, they have, nevertheless, found a follower in Professor F. von Duhn of Heidelberg.

It would be extraneous to the purpose of this volume to enter upon a minute and ready confutation of the doctrines emanating from this "palæotnological" school. Because of their official character, and for reasons of professional advancement, these theories now constitute a conspicuous portion of that science which some would wish to be the ritual (so to speak) and the compulsory patrimony of the pupils of the School of Italian Archæology. If need be, such refutation will be presented elsewhere. For the present it will suffice to recall that Sergi, Professor of Ethnography in the University of Rome, has already proved indisputably that, in the square palisades of the region of Emilia (which are attributed to the earliest times), there are elements which must necessarily be referred to a much more recent period.[1]

No confirmation of the above theories has been obtained from the *terramara* of Tarentum. From the information given concerning the excavations at Scoglio del Tonno (near Tarentum), Pigorini immediately concludes that there was, in that place, a palisade built by races that had emigrated from Emilia. Dr. L. Foglia, however, proves in a recent work that this result was obtained either through superficial and inexact observations, or through the neglect and non-publication of material discovered. He proves, on the contrary, that it is merely a question of fishermen's huts which continued to the fully historic ages.[2] In a similar manner, no corroboration of the doctrines of Pigorini has been received (as that author has too hastily affirmed) from the excavations of the Sarno, which have not been brought to a close, and the results of which have not been published. Assuming that such excavations actually reveal the existence of palisades, and also clear traces of contact with the Greeks of southern Italy, there would not thence result any confirmation whatsoever of the ritual and the symbolic theory of the square.

It is readily understood how archæologists who arrive in Rome equipped with the limited knowledge of the excavations in their native Emilia, should have seen, in Latium, an extension of the civilization of their own regions. It is far nearer the truth, however, to see in the civilization of Emilia a late expansion of the culture of southern Italy and of Latium. Surely, the evidence of the archæological monuments discovered in the *terramare* of the valley of the Po points rather to the South than to the North. In other words, it points to that region of Italy which to-day is inferior to the others in moral and in economic development, but which in ancient times transmitted to central and to northern Italy the civilization of the Greeks, the Italiots and the Siceliots. This culture then disappeared from the Ægean and from southern Italy, but continued to flourish in the valley of the Po, among races having fixed abodes. This fact resulted from the same causes for which monuments of the Mycenean type continued in the same region as late as the sixth or even the fifth century, and for which types of archaic Greek art were long preserved among the Veneti, and continued till the Roman period in the Alpine regions. A proof of the last statement is offered by the decorative ornaments of the arch of Augustus at Susa.

On the other hand, it is a recognized fact that similarities in the shape of vases and in the decorations denote, sometimes, rather a necessary evolution of human laws than ethnic identity. Even if there exists some real historical connection, it will be found true, in many cases, that the resemblances are due to commercial relations and not necessarily to ethnic kinship. If from identity of form we were to derive ethnographic conclusions, by considering the geometric decorations on the vases of primitive American races we would reach the conclusion of an ethnic kinship between the American Indians and the stocks of Ægean and of Greece.

The students of "palæotnology" have abandoned themselves to strange notions. They attribute a special importance to the so-called horned vases (*vasi ad anse cornute*)—vases which they consider ritual in character and a characteristic of the primitive Italic civilization. The most superficial comparison with archaic forms preserved in the necropoles of the eastern Alps will show, instead, that what has by some been considered a special proof of chronology and of ethnography is but a poor and unsuccessful imitation of vases ornamented with the horns of a bull. It will show, too, that such imitations were the products of a people inexperienced in the plastic arts.

I deem it a waste of time to dwell upon all the strange hypotheses sustained by various followers of the school of *Paletnologia*. If necessary, I shall do so in the interest of science. Meanwhile I may be permitted to observe the strange hypothesis that two peoples belong to one and the same race because in both there are found palisades and wells trapezoidal in form. Pigorini himself (*op cit.,* p. 66) recognizes that this shape was due to hydraulic reasons, in order that the angle might separate the water which was to flood the ditch. Why, then, does he exclude the possibility that the same principle may have been adopted in different places and by different peoples? What have such wells to do with the casual coincidence that the Palatine came to have a more or less trapezoidal form? Likewise it is strange that he should call those wells mysterious (*misteriosi pozzetti,* p. 67), whereas other authoritative archæologists have recognized in them a purpose not merely *Italic*, but common to all peoples—namely, that of draining off the waters.

Many *paletnologi,* moreover, find traces of the Ligurians in all those primitive tombs of Italy in which bodies were found in a crouching position. Crouching, however, is not an ethnographic characteristic, but is common, for instance, to the peasants and the sailors of the entire world. It is a position assumed that warmth may not be lost when

THE TEMPLE OF CASTOR AND A CORNER OF THE PALATINE

sleeping in the open air,—a position assumed even by cats and by dogs. Skeletons thus crouched have been found in Africa, in Asia and in America; and, not to wander far from our subject, it will suffice to recall that there were found at Pompeii two reproductions of a statuette representing a fisherman sleeping in this manner.

According to Professor Pigorini (p. 63) this crouching, which recalls the *attitude del feto,* was chosen by the makers of the primitive sepulchres *quasi per esprimere la fede in una risurrezione.* It would result, then, that " in order to express faith in a resurrection " also the mariners of the world assume this crouching position. We would, furthermore, be obliged to acknowledge them all as Ligurians. The satire is not in my observations; it results from the theories themselves!

The followers of this school further affirm that the Italic races built their palisades in square form even on dry land, and that they did so, not because of the character of the soil nor the nature of the material at their disposal, but in observance of religious rites and traditions. The circle and the square are figures determined by nature, and form the inheritance of no particular race. The Romans possessed the circular hut and the square house. The mere presence of palisades, then, is insufficient ground on which to base the radical theory of peoples belonging to one stock and spreading throughout Europe from a common centre. We must recollect that palisades have been used, and are used to-day, among all peoples where it is necessary to defend oneself from inundations, or from dampness of soil, or from reptiles. They are common, too, wheresoever there is an abundant supply of wood.

The theories referred to need neither lengthy nor painfully elaborated confutations. It will be sufficient to note our conclusions—namely, that the earliest city of the Palatine was not originally square in form, that *Roma Quadrata* was an expression closely connected with the square form of the *Saxum,* and that neither the Palatine nor *Roma Quadrata* is in any relation with the palisades of Emilia. Finally, I shall note that analogies, and even strong resemblances, between the archæological material of Latium and that of the valley of the Po do not point to an ethnographical derivation from the *terramare* dwellers of the Po valley, but suggest, rather, a common source of civilization.

Some of the archæologists so often referred to by me have not deduced from the square form of the palisades the evident application of normal forms as determined by the nature of the material. They have seen in it, indeed, proofs of ritual observances dating back to very ancient times. If there were any truth in this, the very advanced character of some of the palisades would, perhaps, oblige us to believe them to have some connection with the Etruscans. The Etruscans, in fact, claim the merit of having drained and rendered habitable the valley of the Po, which had been covered by forests and by marshes. In such a region, therefore, the inhabitants necessarily resorted to the system of palisades. The Romans acknowledged that their cities were founded according to Etruscan rite. As we have already seen (Chapter XII) this fact does not necessarily lead us to the conception of the square, and consequently I do not desire to investigate whether or not this statement is to be applied to the palisades of Etruria. Even if such prove to be the case, we shall not arrive to prehistoric ages nor to any mystic origins of the Italic races. We shall but reach a period not far distant from 500 B.C.—the time when, as far as we can judge to-day, the dominion of the Etruscans began in the valley of the Po.

In the present state of our knowledge any conclusion would be premature. It is to be hoped that the studies of primitive Italian archæology, so nobly founded by Bartolomeo Gastaldi and Gaetano Chierici, may be continued by prudent and conscientious students. It is to be earnestly desired that such researches may be conducted, not only with careful and extensive excavations, but also with deep knowledge of philology, of ethnography and of historical criticism. Through their herald, Professor von Duhn, various *paletnologi* have complained that their researches were taken in absolutely no account by H. Nissen, in his *Italische Landeskunde*. I find that Professor Nissen was right in being so prudent. He was right in saying that in the work of the local archæologists, it was difficult to find the pearl in the mire. The students of *paletnologia* and of local archæology cannot pretend that their studies be considered by the critical historian until they will have given proofs of the thoroughness of their investigations and of their culture. Surely no one can to-day consider seriously the puerilities spoken by many *paletnologi*. No one,

THE ÆMILIAN PALISADES

finally, is encouraged to have any regard for the studies of "the mere archæologists" when, within a few years, he meets with the insincere publications on the Museum of Villa Giulia, on the *terramara* of Tarentum and on the *stips votiva* of the Forum, and, finally, with the clearly forged declarations of the falsity of the Etruscan *tegula* from Capua.

EXCURSUS IV

CÆLIUS VIBENNA, THE FRIEND OF ROMULUS; SERVIUS TULLIUS, AND CELER, THE SLAYER OF REMUS

I HAVE spoken, in a preceding chapter, of Cælius Vibenna and of the Etruscan supremacy in the times of the Tarquins, and of Servius Tullius. The thought was there expressed that this person, described at one time as the lly of Romulus and at another as the friend of Servius ullius, was none other than Celer, the commander of the Roman cavalry and (according to tradition) a contemporary of Romulus.

This statement is based on the ease with which the ancient annals modified the names of the characters who lived in the reigns of the various kings. The purpose in view was to obtain etymologies and etymological tales. Lucumo is made a contemporary of Romulus or of Ancus Marcius; and Ascanius is assigned to the age of the Alban kings, or to that of the Tarquins. Similarly, the *æquimælium* was derived from *æquare*, or from the *eques Mælius;* and, finally, the square of the *macellum* gave life to the imaginary *Cuppes eques*.[1]

If anyone should purpose to entrench himself behind the formal difference between Cœlius, Cælius and Celer, I shall call to notice that all these different forms were employed by Varro. In fact, he says: *Cælius mons a Cele Vibenna*.[2] A further proof of the arbitrary manner in which names and events were invented is offered by the detailed examination of Celer or Celerius, the captain of the three hundred knights of Romulus.

Annalistic tradition affirms that Romulus, in imitation of the Spartans, created a body of three hundred horsemen and appointed Celer in command of them.[3] However, it has been observed time and again that Celer is merely the personification of the *tribunus celerum,* who figures also on other occasions in the regal period as the commander of the Roman cavalry.[4] This Celer, whom Dionysius called also by the name Celerius,[5] I suspect to be that same Cælius who came from Etruria to the aid of Romulus. Some authors, indeed, assigned to Celer a principal rôle in the

ANCIENT WALLS OF THE PALATINE

slaying of Remus. The most widely diffused tradition (given also by Livy) stated that Romulus himself had killed Remus, exclaiming: "Thus shall it befall all who will venture to leap over the walls of my city."[6]

To this tradition Livy prefixes another version, in which it is stated that Remus fell in the combat with the slaves and the companions of Romulus. Dionysius, as is customary with him, is more extended and explicit in his narrative. He first refers the version of a personal contest between Romulus and Remus. Then he adds the story that Remus was slain by a certain Celerius, who had been standing on the city-wall and who, in fact, had uttered the words: "Anyone of ours would readily remove such an enemy."[7]

This latter version is given also by Verrius Flaccus.[8] Ovid, too, refers to it in speaking of the Parilia (the 21st of April), the anniversary of the founding of Rome; and again, in discussing the feast of the Lemuria (May 9, 11, 13), a worship of the spirits of the dead Lemures. The terms *Lemuria* and *Lemures* were, as the result of etymological manipulation, placed in relation with *Remuria*—that is, with that locality in which Remus was supposed to have been buried.[9] A pathetic description of the grief of Romulus and of the comfort he received from his nurse Acca Larentia is found both in Ovid and in Dionysius. This fact naturally suggests a common source. We may think either of Varro or of some annalist like Licinius Macer or Valerius Antias. Perhaps, too, unless I be deceived, the very fact that such version was received by Ovid may refer to a tradition preserved in religious annals that are earlier than the age of Sulla.

A third story told by Dionysius in the same place (but regarding Faustulus) bears the stamp of a late tradition. He says that, when the combat arose between the brothers Romulus and Remus, Faustulus (the shepherd who had reared them) endeavored to separate them. Being unsuccessful in this attempt, he thrust himself between the brothers, though unarmed, and thus attained his desire of dying "quickly," $\theta a \nu \acute{a} \tau o \upsilon$ $\tau o \~{u}$ $\tau a \chi \acute{\iota} \sigma \tau o \upsilon$ $\tau \upsilon \chi \varepsilon \~{\iota} \nu$.[10]

It is clear that these words of the Greek historian are but a rendering of a Latin text—a text in which, instead of the *mors* inflicted upon Remus by *Celer,* there was mention of the *celeris mors* of Faustulus. How and why this substitution took place,—whether it resulted from a false interpretation of a Latin text translated into Greek by a Roman or a Greek author, or whether, instead, it is due to some other reason,—we have no way of deciding. A thousand different hypotheses might be made on the subject. It is more to our purpose, however, to prove that this last form of the legend is connected with a final explanation, which precludes the possibility of an error or a blunder on the part of Dionysius.

This author affirms that, according to some writers, the stone lion situated in a conspicuous part of the Forum (near the Rostra) covered the body of Faustulus, who was supposed to have been buried on the spot where he had fallen. We have no means of understanding why in this passage only one lion is spoken of, whereas elsewhere two are mentioned. I do not venture to decide whether we are to infer the existence of two lions and of two separate tombs, one of Faustulus, the other of Romulus; or whether one of the lions had already disappeared when the legend arose. It is fitting, rather, to note that this story is readily explained by recollecting what I have elsewhere proved in this regard—namely, that the cults and traditions of the Lupercal were removed to the Comitium in 338 B.C., when this locality had become the centre of the Roman community, and of the two cities of the Quirinal and the Septimontium (Palatine—Velia—Cælian—Esquiline).[11]

The ancient legend stated that Romulus had disappeared in the marsh called *Caprea* or *Caprificus*—that is, near the *caprificus* or *ficus Ruminalis*, where he had been born. Near that same *ficus Ruminalis* was to be seen the tomb of Acca Larentia,—the she-wolf which had nursed Romulus. It was natural, then, that the tomb of the shepherd Faustulus (or the god Faunus) should have been situated in the same locality. Similarly, on the opposite extremity of the Capitoline was seen the tomb of Carmenta, the mother of Evander—that is, of Faustulus. It is natural, therefore, that when, by a miracle of the augur Attus Navius (as the sacred traditions relate), the *ficus Ruminalis* was transferred to the Comitium, and was replanted near the Rostra, also the tomb of Romulus should have been transported thither. Consequently, the shepherd Faustulus, too, was thought to be buried there.

But the tomb of Romulus is, as we have seen, a monument of comparatively recent age; and the cippus, which is more ancient than the tomb, belongs to a period earlier than 338 B.C. We have seen, moreover, that the archaic cippus was already in the area of the Curia Hostilia when the so-called tomb of Romulus was built. Dionysius elsewhere gives the tradition that, in this portion of the Forum, a monument to Hostus Hostilius was to be seen. Such tradition, after all, contains elements of a more sacred and, perhaps, more sepulchral character than the tomb of Romulus. The archaic inscription of the Forum surely does not contain a eulogy of this imaginary character, Hostilius; but it may well be related with the **Curia Hostilia**,—in other words, the Curia of the *hospites*.[12]

To return to our argument, then, we can, I think, conclude with remarking that the story of Celer, the eponym of the *celeres* or horsemen (compare the Greek κέλης, horse), offers a series of anecdotes which serve to determine the etymology of the word. In like manner, the name of Larunda, the mother of the Lares, gave occasion to its derivation from λαλεῖν, and also to the odd tale of the prattling of Lara, that is, of the goddess Tacita or Muta.

The history of the regal period abounds in such etymologies, as also the first century of the Republic. Thus Brutus, the *tribunus celerum*, is etymologically transformed into *brutus*, the dullard; Cocles (the god Vulcan), who had but one eye, becomes a warrior whose eyebrows were so knit together as to give the impression of his having one eye only. We have seen, furthermore, how the stories of Minucius and of the *æquimælium* were formed partly for similar reasons. For my part, I am certain that an extensive examination of the topographical and the etymological data will furnish the solutions of very many other legends—myths which tradition presents to us under the garb of austere and serious history of the Roman people.

EXCURSUS V

SERVIUS TULLIUS AND THE LEX ÆLIA-SENTIA

DIONYSIUS gives an interesting account of the Servian regulations regarding the manumission of slaves. He then considers it necessary to make a digression, in which he recounts the abuses deriving from such law, and the ease with which slaves were emancipated in his day.[1]

In earliest times,—those subsequent to the reform of Servius Tullius,—such manumission was granted only to those slaves who were considered worthy of it. The majority (he continues) were granted their freedom in virtue of their valor and their honesty ($καλοκαγαθία$); only a few, after having rendered righteous and just service, were freed for pecuniary considerations. To-day, however (Dionysius says), the greatest confusion has arisen. And slaves who have been punished for robbery and for every species of crime obtain freedom, by means of money, from the very mines to which they have been condemned. Moreover, they are immediately granted the rights of citizenship. The very masters, though conscious of the great perversity of their slaves, nevertheless aid them to become citizens, in order that the latter may participate in the free monthly distributions of grain.

Furthermore, Dionysius records (as an eye-witness) cases in which masters manumitted their slaves through mere vanity,—that is, in order that their funeral processions might be rendered pompous from the number of emancipated slaves attending. He bewails the serious dangers resulting from the perversion of the good and pious institution of Servius Tullius; and concludes with the hope, not that the ancient law may be abolished, but that it may be modified to meet existing conditions.

He proposes, therefore, that the censors and the consuls examine yearly, and with the greatest care, the number and the quality of those citizens who have been emancipated; and that fully as great a care be taken as in the case of the knights and the senators. He expresses the opinion that, as the result of such a law, the above-named officers should inscribe on the lists of citizens, should distribute among the tribes and permit to live within the city, only those men who appear worthy of so great an honor. And he further proposes that the dishonest multitude of slaves, even though already emancipated, be removed from the city under the pretext of founding colonies.

Dionysius, as we have seen, refers to testamentary manumission and to funeral pomp. This fact suggests that he writes of what he saw with his own eyes, and that he is giving vent to mere personal feelings. But it is a noteworthy fact that the modifications of the law invoked by him actually come into operation a few years later.

Indeed, in the year 4 B.C. the *lex Ælia-Sentia* was passed—a law restricting, in many ways, previous laws on the subject. To be more exact, this law recalled to vigor the ancient ones, and removed precisely those abuses indicated by our author. The *lex Ælia-Sentia* declared null and void manumissions of slaves under thirty years of age by masters who had not yet attained their twentieth year. The right of manumission was placed under the control of a *concilium,* with legal powers in reference to the *vindicta.* It was established that no emancipated slave could become a Roman citizen if he had ever been convicted of a serious crime. It was furthermore provided to limit the preceding testamentary manumissions, and to punish those freedmen who were ungrateful towards their previous masters. Finally, the *lex Ælia-Sentia* offered a remedy for the political evils deplored by Dionysius, and for the purity of Roman citizenship; it ordered minute investigations into the parentage of each citizen, to ascertain whether there had been intermarriage with Latins or with *peregrini;* and it ordained that persons recognized as *dediticiæ* should dwell beyond the one-hundredth milestone from Rome.[2]

This perfect correspondence between the modifications desired by Dionysius of Halicarnassus and the provisions actually made by the *lex Ælia-Sentia* is readily explained. It must be remembered that Ælius Tubero was a friend of Dionysius. He is the man to whom Dionysius dedicated his writings on Thucydides, and who is praised, in the preface to his history, as a δεινὸς ἀνήρ and ἐπιμελής. Moreover, in a fragment of Tubero preserved by Gellius,[3] there is mention precisely of the establishment of the censorship by Servius Tullius. This institution, as we have already remarked, was closely related to the inscribing of freedmen in the various tribes. By duly considering the above facts, then, we shall come to the conclusion that, in this part of his Roman History, Dionysius not only drew largely upon the historical work of Ælius Tubero, but even reflected the aims and the political and legislative aspirations of his protector.

The traditional history of the constitution and the reforms of Servius Tullius have not been influenced only by the political conditions and views of the second century annalists, as is generally stated to-day. As Mommsen has already shown, Dionysius does not ascribe to the king of the sixth century only the constitution in force in the second century,—that is, in the times of Fabius Pictor. Nor does he limit himself with drawing also upon Piso and upon Cato. For, as Mommsen has proved in reference to another passage in Dionysius, there were attributed to Servius Tullius words which were actually spoken by Julius Cæsar.[4] We may therefore better understand why Dionysius, in the passage under discussion, broke out so bitterly against the existing corruption. We need but recollect that the Ælii-Tuberones vaunted of being the representatives of the old and stern national customs. In fact, the historian Tubero carried this admiration for the past to such a degree as to write his books in archaic Latin,—a procedure which did not at all please the majority of his readers.

From what has been said, two conclusions may be drawn. The first is, that it is necessary to examine with greater attention similar passages of Dionysius of Halicarnassus,—passages which some modern critics (such as Niese and others) consider vain prattling of our author. I have shown, in regard to the capture of Naples by the Romans,[5] that, what is to-day judged to be mere prolixity on the part of Dionysius, is a reproduction and a *résumé* of those authors who were his principal sources. The second conclusion is a confirmation of what has been said by others and by myself on individual occasions,—namely, that the Roman annalists, in writing the history of the earliest times, did not purpose to be mere scholars and to describe past events for the use of the learned. Attending, as they did, to existing historical situations and to transactions of public and of private law, they set forth in their annals their

ANCIENT GATE OF REPUBLICAN TIMES ASSIGNED TO THE AGE OF KINGS

own opinions on the political conditions of their times. The condition of affairs is readily understood,—it is evident from an infinite series of events. It is that the annalists, though describing the institutions of past centuries, did not forget those of their own age. Similarly, the Venetian annalists, in discussing the prerogatives of the ancient doges, were wont to ascribe to them powers with which they were only later invested.

EXCURSUS VI

THE TOPOGRAPHY OF THE VIA NOVA, THE VICUS ORBIUS OR SCELERATUS, AND THE VICUS CYPRIUS, OR GOOD

I

One of those problems of the earliest Roman topography which has received various solutions is that of the Via Nova. Although this road was called Nova, it was indeed (as Varro already observed[1]) old enough. I note that the direction of this road has not been entirely marked out by all topographers. Some mark with the name Via Nova only that part which ran from the corner of the Palatine to the Porta Mugonia, and neglect thus to designate the portion which led from that same corner to the Velabrum. It may, therefore, be permitted to me to recall that the data of the ancient authors enable us to trace the course of this road with full certainty.

The Via Nova entered the Velabrum at that point where the Porta Romanula, the sepulchre of Acca Larentia, and the *sacellum* of the goddess Volusia were situated. This is clearly evident from Varro.[2] From passages of other authors we gather that it reached as far as that corner of the Palatine which hung above the temple of Vesta and contained the altar of the god Aius Loquens.[3] The road, however, did not stop at this point (as some topographers have supposed), but turned to the northeast and reached the Porta Mugonia. This is proved by Livy, where he speaks of Tanaquil recommending Servius to the people, addressing them from a window which looked out on the Via Nova. It results, also, from a passage in Solinus, in which it is said that Tarquinius Superbus had his palace *ad Mugoniam portam supra summam novam viam*.[4]

The Via Nova, then, consisted of two parts,—one extending from the Porta Romanula to the temple of Vesta (where it was connected with the Forum[5]), the other reaching to the very ancient Porta Mugonia. The road thus connected the two most ancient parts of the city of the Palatine. From

the name Via Nova given to this road it is natural to assume
the existence of a Via Vetus,—a still more ancient road
serving probably the same purpose.

We are not told when the Via Nova was established. If
conjecture were permitted, I would advance the hypothesis
that it was marked out after the Gallic fire, when the Palatine was surrounded with those walls of *saxum quadratum*
which contributed so largely to give life to the expression
Roma Quadrata.

II

Concerning the topography of the Vicus Orbius or Sceleratus I think I have given precise indications elsewhere.[6]
But, inasmuch as *Italica non leguntur* and the more authoritative Roman topographers continue to give erroneous indications on this subject, I may (I hope) reproduce my
arguments in this place.

When Servius Tullius was threatened by his son-in-law
Tarquinius Superbus, he fled from the Curia; and, on arriving *ad summum Cyprium vicum, ubi Dianium nuper fuit,
flectenti carpentum dextra in Urbium Clivum ut in collem
Exquiliarum eveheretur,* he was overtaken and slain.[7] Up
to that time the road had been called Urbius or Orbius;
after that crime it was named Sceleratus.[8] The ancient
authors, moreover, tell us that the palace of Servius Tullius
was upon the Esquiline and on the clivus Urbius, and that
also Tarquinius Superbus lived on that hill *supra clivum
Pullium ad Fagutalem lacum*.[9] The name Pullius recalls
the analogous etymology which suggested the name of Vicus
Sceleratus.

An entirely different conception is reflected by the name
of the Vicus Cyprius,—that is, the "good road."[10] This
path ended at the base of the Velia, at that point where the
tigillus sororius of the legend of Horatius was situated.[11]
At the foot of the Velia, moreover, and near the temple
of the Lares (where both Ancus Marcius and Tarquinius
Priscus had lived[12]), there was the altar of the goddess
Orbona,—a name which is clearly in close connection with
the Vicus Orbius or Urbus near by. This, in turn, naturally
suggests the neighboring temple of Mala Fortuna on the
Esquiline.[13]

A thorough consideration of all these elements will lead

T

to the conclusion that the Vicus Orbius-Sceleratus was not between the modern Via Cavour and the Via del Colosseo, as, for instance, it is shown to be in the Nomenclator of Huelsen. On the contrary, it was situated in the immediate vicinity of the Vicus Cyprius and near the Velia, at the point where this elevation unites with the Esquiline.

This is confirmed by that passage in Pliny which says that the *prætextæ* of Servius Tullius (with which had been covered the statue dedicated by him) continued to exist as late as the death of the famous Seianus.[14] From another passage in the same author we learn that when Nero built his golden house (extending from the Esquiline to the Velia) he included also the temple of Fortuna that had been consecrated by Seianus. Some, indeed, called the temple that of the Fortuna of Seianus.[15] It is, therefore, evident that the Vicus Orbius or Sceleratus is to be sought for near the Vicus Cyprius, or Good. The opposition in meaning in the names of the two roads was remarked even by Varro. It was suggested, indeed, by the proximity of the one road to the other.[16]

NOTES

NOTES TO CHAPTER I

THE CRITICAL METHOD

[1] My theories regarding the false tradition of the embassy of the Twelve Tables, and my views concerning the more recent character of this legislation, have given origin to an extensive literature in both France and Germany. These works have often been favorable to my views. Some students of Roman law, however, have defended the ancient traditions with great acrimony, or rather that which was considered in the schools to be the canonical tradition. This fact proves that I but probed the wound, and that I pointed out the sad necessity of renewing the critical foundations of their conventional culture. I shall return in good time to this and to other problems of paramount importance in the history of Roman law, which are indeed deserving of revision.

[2] POLYBIUS, VI. 3.3: περὶ δὲ τῆς Ῥωμαίων οὐδ' ὅλως εὐχερὲς οὔτε περὶ τῶν παρόντων ἐξηγήσασθαι διὰ τὴν ποικιλίαν τῆς πολιτείας, οὔτε περὶ τοῦ μέλλοντος προειπεῖν διὰ τὴν ἄγνοιαν τῶν προγεγονότων περὶ αὐτοὺς ἰδιωμάτων καὶ κοινῇ καὶ κατ' ἰδίαν.

[3] For these and similar questions, I refer the reader to the first chapter of my *Storia di Roma* (Torino, Clausen, 1898), where I treat of the development of Roman historiography. It is well known that both Fabius Pictor and Cato drew upon Greek historians. For the detailed stories of the annalists in regard to Romulus, see, for instance, CALP. PISO, in GELLIUS, *N.A.*, XI. 14 = fr. 8* P.

[4] DION. HAL., I. 6.

[5] B. NIESE strangely exaggerated the ideas of Mommsen. Believing authentic only what was related by Diodorus, Niese did not become aware of the fact that this author is frequently a capricious compiler who at times gives the less exact traditions. In rejecting whatever was not narrated by Diodorus, Niese discarded some precious portions of Roman History because they were given only by Dionysius of Halicarnassus. I have, however, already expressed my opinions concerning such erroneous theories and the insecure results attained through prejudice.

[6] See the passages in PETER, *F.H.R.*, pp. 3 sqq. The only large fragment there given (= GELLIUS, *N.A.*, IV. 5) contains much prattling that is derived from recent sources. Surely such talk was not registered in the most ancient records of the Roman people. This fact is proved, furthermore, by the Greek metre of the verses there cited.

[7] A careful examination of the problems relating to the *Fasti* requires a special volume which I hope to publish before long. I trust I may be allowed to recall here that LIVY, in referring to authors (as is his wont) and to documents regarding the *Fasti* of the first years of the Republic, declares (II. 21.4, *ad a.* 496 B.C.) *tanti errores inplicant temporum aliter apud alios ordinatis magistratibus, ut nec qui consules secundum quos[dam], nec quid quoque anno actum sit, in tanta vetustate non rerum modo sed etiam auctorum digerere possis.* (Compare II. 8.5; II. 18.4.) That this condition of affairs continued to the second half of the fourth century results from the strange confusion of what is related concerning the consuls and the military tribunes

of 444 and 443 B. C. (See LIVY, IV. 7, 8.) It results, too, from what is said of the consuls for 434 B. C. After citing the different traditions given by Valerius Antias, Licinius Macer, Aelius Tubero and the most ancient authors, LIVY says (IV. 23.3): *Tubero incertus veri est: sed inter cetera vetustate cooperta hoc quoque in incerto positum.* This proves that not even Tubero possessed documents on which he could unhesitatingly draw. The confusion of the *Fasti* throughout the fourth century is proved in the clearest manner by the annalist CALPURNIUS PISO. This author does not give the consuls for 307 and 306 B. C.; and LIVY (IX. 44.4) does not venture to decide whether this was due to mere carelessness, or to the fact that those consulships were spurious, — *falsos ratus*. If there had been official and genuine *Fasti*, LIVY would not have been in doubt. In the legend of Minucius (Chapter XI. of this volume), we shall bring into relief the fact that, according to the declaration of DIONYSIUS himself (XII. 4), the dictator of 439 B. C. was lacking in the lists of the ancient annalists. Livy informs us of the uncertainty of the *Fasti* of the dictators for the first year in which such office was established (II. 18.4, *ad a.* 501). From him, too, we learn that certain annalists gave false consuls for the years 361 and 342 B. C. In each case, then, Livy is not led to discover the proof of the falsity by a comparison with authentic documents of the *Fasti*, but merely by the failure of such indications in the most ancient annalists, — *vetustiores annales*, and again, *antiqui rerum auctores* (LIVY, VII. 9.5; 42.7).

Even DIONYSIUS (XI. 62), in accepting the magistrates for 444 B. C. that were not recorded by all the writers, does not refer to documents or to monuments, but to the *annales maximi* and to the private records of the magistrates, — πιστεύοντες δὲ ταῖς ἐκ τῶν ἱερῶν τε καὶ ἀποθέτων βίβλων μαρτυρίαις. It is fortunate that in all such questions Livy may, indeed, be accused of having neglected to make a minute critical examination that was foreign to his purpose; but surely he cannot be charged with dishonesty. From him (IV. 7.10) we learn, in fact, that those consuls whom Dionysius recorded were mentioned *neque in annalibus priscis neque in libris magistratuum*, but that they were recorded by Licinius Macer, who refers to the *foedus Ardeatinum* and the *libri lintei*. From the subsequent remarks of LIVY regarding the magistrates of 444 B. C. (IV. 8.7; cf. 22.7), and from the data of the *libri lintei* on the magistrates for 434 B. C., which neither Aelius Tubero nor LIVY (IV. 23.2) trusted, we learn that the source of Licinius Macer (which after all is the source of Dionysius too) was more than open to suspicion. (For the *foedus Ardeatinum*, see Chapter X. in this volume.) If Dionysius drew directly upon the *annales maximi* rather than upon a source like Licinius Macer, we would have a proof of the very recent character of that official compilation.

From what has been said we deduce that there were no genuine and official *Fasti*. With this conclusion there agrees the great divergence found between the various *Fasti* which we possess, — a divergence both in the *nomina* and in the *praenomina*. As far as concerns the matter treated in this volume, it will suffice to recall the *praenomen* Numerius for the Fabii who appear in the *Fasti Capitolini*, for the consuls of 421 and for the military tribunes of 407 and 406 B. C. Livy, instead, has the *praenomen* Gnaeus. (For the historical importance of these *praenomina*, see the chapter on the Fabii in this volume.) The attempt to harmonize *nomina* and *praenomina* in the *Fasti* which are so very discordant represents (it seems to me) a wrong tendency and one that must be abandoned, even though to-day accepted by the most prominent scholars. I have amply discussed the value of the *Fasti* in the various chapters of my *Storia di Roma*, and particularly in I. 1, pp. 598 sqq. New material and new observations on the *Fasti* will form the subject of a volume which I have been preparing for a long time.

THE CRITICAL METHOD

[8] DION. HAL., I 74. For the lack of historical value in the ancient census, see my *Storia di Roma, passim*.

[9] CIC., *Brut.*, 16.62; LIVY, VI. 1; VIII. 40.

[10] MOMMSEN, *Röm. Forsch.*, II. pp. 58 sqq.

[11] CATO, in CIC., *Brut.*, 19.75; *Tusc.*, I. 2, 3; IV. 2; VAL. MAX., II. 1.10; TAC., *Ann.*, III. 5; cf. my *Storia di Roma*, I. 1, pp. 8 sqq.

[12] Compare DION. HAL., VIII. 62, with I. 79. See, too, in this volume, Chapter XI., n. 34. There were tales of the deeds of the smith Mamurius Veturius also. But, as we learn from VARRO, *L.L.*, VI. 49 (45), these were religious tales and were related by the priests known as Salii.

[13] Compare the end of Chapter XI. in this volume, and notes thereto; for the historical value of Livy, *Storia di Roma*, I. 1, pp. 82 sqq.

[14] OVID, *Fasti*, III. 433.

NOTES TO CHAPTER II

EXCAVATIONS IN THE FORUM

[1] It is not necessary to report here all the worthless literature that has sprung up around this remarkable monument. The *cippus* was edited for the first time in the *Notizie degli Scavi*, 1899, pp. 151 sqq. The official interpretation there presented by L. CECI is pitiful. However, other scholars have contributed really important and weighty observations. It will be sufficient to mention : HUELSEN, in the *Röm. Mittheilungen*, 1902, p. 22, and in the *Beiträge zur alten Geschichte*, II. (1902), pp. 228 sqq.; THURNEYSEN, in *Rhein. Mus.*, LV. p. 484; and STUDNICZKA, in *Jahres. d. Oesterr. Inst.*, VI. (1903), pp. 129 sqq. MOMMSEN discussed the meaning of only the word *iouxmenta* in *Hermes*, XXXVIII. (1903), pp. 151 sqq.

[2] For the *rex* of the *dies agonales*, see VARRO, *L.L.*, VI. 12 ; FESTUS, *ep. Paul.*, s. v. *Agonium;* for the feast of the *Consualia*, *Fasti Praenestini*, s. d. 15 Dec.

[3] That at Rome the *hostiae* had to be *iniuges*, that is, untamed by the yoke, is a well-known fact. See, for instance, MACROB., III. 5.5. In certain cases, however, even those animals which had drawn the chariot were sacrificed. This is evident from the sacrifice to Mars of the right-hand horse on the victorious chariot. FESTUS, s. v. *October equus*, p. 179.

[4] See *Tab. Iguv.*, VII. A. 40 ; I. B. 40 : *postquam tertium populum lustraverit, iuvencam opimam fugato super comitio flamen, legati duas fugato infra forum seminarium capiunto.* Compare BUECHELER, *Umbrica*, p. 115 ; MACROB., III. 2.14. To the examples cited by Buecheler there can be added, I believe, the somewhat different ceremony performed at Hermione, in regard to the oxen sacrificed to *Ceres Chthonia*, PAUS., II. 36.7.

[5] Regarding the *iumenta* on the day of the *Vinalia*, see FESTUS, p. 289, M ; on the day of the *Septimontium*, see PLUTARCH, *Quaest. Rom.*, 69. The injunction forbidding the yoking of draught-animals on that day is to be connected with the statement of CATO (*de Agr.*, 138), where he speaks of the *feriae* of the oxen. The *rex* appeared on his chariot, LYD., *de Mag.*, I. 18 ; on the coins of the Vettii, however, the *interrex* appears mounted on a horse, — see BABELON, *Monn. d. l. Rép. Rom.*, II. p. 532.

[6] See note 51.

[7] The circumstance that the Vicus Iugarius led from the Forum to the *porta Carmentalis* is with difficulty separated from a statement concerning the feast of the Carmentalia, — namely, that on that feast it was permitted to the matrons to ride in carts drawn by oxen. OVID, *Fasti*, I. 619; FESTUS, p. 245, M, s. v. *pilentis ;* PLUT., *Quaest. Rom.*, 56. The *niger lapis* has suggested to some the cult of the *termini* (boundaries), which no one could move without becoming *sacer*, — a penalty extended even to the oxen. See FESTUS, *ep. Paul.*, p. 368, M, s. v. *Termino Sacra.* In regard to this cult see also SIC. FLACC., *de cond. agr.*, p. 141, L. Compare the collection of *Gromatici Veteres*, p. 347, L.

[8] MILANI, in *Rendiconti dei Lincei*, 1900, p. 303 ; cf. SERV., *ad Aen.*, XI. 785: *Sorani vero a Dite: nam Ditis pater Soranus vocatur.*

[9] WISSOWA, *Religion und Kultus der Römer*, München, 1902, p. 191 ; and also in ROSCHER, *Lex.*, I. col. 2693 sq.

EXCAVATIONS IN THE FORUM 281

[10] Concerning the Luperci and the Hirpini of Mount Soracte, see the chapter on Acca Larentia.

[11] AUG., *de civ. dei*, IV. 23 : *Romani veteres nescio quem Summanum ... coluerunt magis quam Iovem ... sed postquam Iovi templum insigne ac sublime constructum est, propter aedis dignitatem sic ad eum multitudo confluxit, ut vix inveniatur qui Summani nomen, quod audire iam non potest, se saltem legisse meminerit.*

[12] GELLIUS, *N.A.*, IV. 5.

[13] VARRO, *L.L.*, V. 157 ; FEST., *ep. Paul.*, p. 169.

[14] VARRO, in Scholiast to HOR., *Epod.*, XVI. 13, 14.

[15] VARRO, *l. c.*

[16] To Verrius Flaccus (p. 177, M) the *niger lapis in comitio* was a *locus funestus*, which was, according to some, *Romuli morti destinatus*, while according to others it was the tomb of Hostus Hostilius. The former version agrees with the statement that Romulus was struck by a missile in the war against the Sabines, DIONYS., II. 43 ; PLUT., *Rom.*, 18.10. The latter version, instead, is connected with the story that Hostus Hostilius, the grandfather of King Tullus Hostilius, died on that spot. He had been wounded in the battle, and by order of Romulus and Tatius had been buried ἐν τῷ κρατίστῳ τῆς ἀγορᾶς τόπῳ, στήλης ἐπιγραφῇ τὴν ἀρετὴν μαρτυρούσῃ, DIONYS., III. 1. Furthermore, DIONYSIUS (I. 87) makes mention of only one lion, where he says that Faustulus, having placed himself between Romulus and Remus, was slain, and was buried τῆς ἀγορᾶς τῆς τῶν Ῥωμαίων ἐν τῷ κρατίστῳ χωρίῳ παρὰ τοῖς ἐμβόλοις. VARRO, instead, speaks of two lions, in SCHOL. CRUQ., *ad Hor.*, p. 289: *nam et Varro pro rostris sepulcrum Romuli dixit, ubi etiam in huius rei memoriam duos leones erectos fuisse constat, unde factum est ut pro rostris mortui laudarentur ;* cf. PORPHYR., *ad Hor., Epod.*, XVI. 13. Horace in saying *quaeque carent ventis et solibus ossa Quirini — nefas videre — dissipabit insolens*, clearly refers to the common belief that behind the *rostra* there truly existed the tomb of Romulus.

The statement of an Italian scholar, DE SANCTIS (*Riv. di Fil. Class.*, XXVIII. p. 4, extr.), that in Festus the words *morti destinatum* are "undoubtedly" corrupt because "they are not Latin," is proved false by the following passage in VAL. MAX., I. 1.19: *imperio Caesaris morti destinatum Turullium.*

[17] The value of the fundamental observations of STUDNICZKA is not impaired by the recent study of E. PETERSEN, *Comitium, Rostra und Grab des Romulus* (Rom, 1904), pp. 27 sqq. Without valid reasons (as appears to me) the author believes that the tomb of Romulus is earlier than 338 B. C., and that perhaps it dates as far back as the fifth century B. C. For the *stips votiva*, see Excursus I.

[18] LIVY, V. 55.3 ; DIOD., XIV. 116.8.

[19] For the statues of the orators sent to Fidenae, see CIC., *Phil.*, IX. 2.4 ; LIVY, IV. 17 ; PLINY, *N.H.*, XXXIV. 23. For the *foedus Cassianum*, consult CIC., *pro Balbo*, 53 ; LIVY, II. 33 ; DIONYS. HAL., VI. 95 ; FESTUS, p. 166, M, s. v. *nancitor*. For a discussion of these data, see my *Storia di Roma*, I. 1, pp. 504 sq., and I. 2, pp. 24, 324, 604 sqq.

[20] LIVY, VI. 1.9.

[21] The three points : are to be found in the Attic inscription *I.G.A.*, n. 5, and in the laws of the *Hypoknemiadai* Locrians (*ib.*, 321), the dates of which are known. The boustrophedon order and the three points are found in *I.G.A.*, 492.

[22] *I.G.A.*, 510.

[23] See PAULI, *C.I.E.*, 3763.

[24] MOMMSEN, *Hermes*, XXXVIII. (1903), p. 153.

[25] *I.G.A.*, 512.

[26] I shall refer here to the well-known publications of ZVETAIEFF and

PAULI. For the Venetian inscriptions, in addition to those published by GHIRARDINI in the *Notizie degli Scavi*, 1888, see also the bilingual Veneto-Latin inscription edited by me in *Suppl. Ital.* to *CIL.*, V. No. 513. I hardly deem it necessary to recall that certain archaic letters, such as ꟼ and Ɛ, continued till the end of the Roman Republic, particularly in Etruscan inscriptions. I believe it worthy of note that the characters ⋜ for S and Π for P appear in the regions of Central Italy as late as the second and even first century B. C. See, among others, the inscription from Amiternum, *CIL.*, IX. 4204. PRAIFECTO⋜, the one from Ortona, *CIL.*, IX. 3812 VIITIV⋜A· ⋜A, and 3827, ΠAMΠILA· ANAIA· Π·

[27] See Excursus II.

[28] See GARRUCCI, *Mon. d. ant. Italia*, tav. 77 *no.* 21, ONAMOᖴ. Likewise at Tarentum there are found coins with letters in the direct and in the retrograde order, *op. cit.*, tav. 97 *no.* 27; at Aquinum, *ib.*, 82 *no.* 31; at Teanum, *ib.*, 83 *no.* 8; at Akudunniad, *ib.*, 90 *no.* 25. For Etruria, see Volsinii, *ib.*, 77 *no.* 21.

[29] Rome was called πόλις Ἑλληνίς by Heraclides Ponticus, a contemporary of Aristotle and of Plato. See PLUTARCH, *Cam.*, 22.

[30] A characteristic example of the persistence of archaic forms in Roman writing is offered by the letters OVF. — the official indication of the Oufentina tribe. This archaic abbreviation began in 318 B. C., the year in which the Oufentina tribe was created (LIVY, IX. 20.6), that is, six years earlier than the censorship of Appius Claudius.

[31] This information (given by PLINY, *N.H.*, XXXIV. 139) is worthy of consideration, because it occurs in a passage which affirms that the Romans were subdued by Porsenna.

[32] The statement of LIVY, II. 2, is very explicit. It would be a waste of time to examine the many modern attempts (vain attempts, indeed) to prove that there existed at Rome, at one and the same time, both the political *rex* and the *rex sacrorum*. Tradition itself is absurdly ignorant on this point.

[33] The priestly hierarchy among the Romans is given by FESTUS, p. 185: I. Rex; II. Flamen Dialis; III. Flamen Martialis; IV. Flamen Quirinalis; V. Pontifex Maximus.

[34] In ASCONIUS, *in Milon.*, 25. there appear *interreges* for the years 702 and 711 of the City (52 and 43 B. C.). This magistracy, then, formally continued to exist during that time. But such a state of affairs is not in contradiction with the fact that in the Roman annals *interreges* are not mentioned after the Punic Wars. Moreover, I would not be surprised if the same phenomenon occurred in the case of the *interreges* as in that of the dictators. These end in 202 B. C., to return to vigor only with Sulla and with Caesar, — a truth confirmed by the fact that from Augustus on, there is again no mention of *interreges*.

[35] For Tarentum, see HEROD., III. 136; for Veii, LIVY, V. 1; for the Etruscan Kings, VARRO, *R.R.*, II. 4.9. The Cilnii were kings of the Etruscan Arretium, and from them (as is known) Horace traced the lineage of Maecenas. Again, the Cilnii figure as the ruling clan of Arretium, and as the opponents of the plebs in 300 B. C. (LIVY, X. 5.13.) For those kings of the Sabellian races of Southern Italy who were elected in time of war, see STRABO, VI. p. 254, C.

The *rex sacrorum* continued as a magistrate at Rome till the period of the Samnite Wars. In a similar manner the βασιλεύς (king) — the priest at Byzantium and at Samothrace — continued to have the character of the eponymous magistrate. See *CIL.*, III. 7371, *add.*; cf. LIVY, XLV. 5.6.

[36] Our stele, perhaps, furnishes important data for the history of the *reges* at Rome. The *calatores* of the last centuries of the Republic, though having their seat in the Regia (like the *pontifex maximus*) were nevertheless officially styled *calatores pontificum et augurum*. It may be that in our inscription the

calator is mentioned as the immediate subordinate of the *rex*. If this were the case, we would have some information concerning a phase of the authority of the *rex sacrorum* of which we find no traces in the texts.

[37] The true date of the foundation of the temple of Saturn was known to the annalist GELLIUS, who is cited by MACROBIUS, I. 8.1.

[38] I have given the individual proofs in my *Storia di Roma*, I. 2, pp. 708, 737.

[39] DION. HAL., I. 87 ; cf. II. 43.

[40] See the passages quoted in my *Storia di Roma*, I. 1, pp. 292 sqq.

[41] PROC., in VARRO, *L.L.*, V. 148 : *tum quendam Curtium . . a Concordia versum cum equo eo praecipitatum*. It does not seem to me that this element of the legend has always been properly considered by modern students of the topography of ancient Rome.

[42] I refer to what I wrote concerning the stele, shortly after its discovery, in the *Nuova Antalogia* (Rome), November 1, 1899, and January 1, 1900.

[43] Even Manius Curius, the Conqueror of the Samnites in the time of Pyrrhus, made use of ware of such poor material. (PLINY, *N.H.*, XVI. 185.) This humble pottery, to which tradition often refers (e. g. CIC., *N.D.*, III. 17.43; DION. HAL., II. 23; VAL. MAX., IV. 4.11 ; IUVEN., VI. 343 ; SERV., *ad Aen.*, VIII. 278; ATHEN., √I. 229 c) is mentioned as late as APULEIUS, *de Mag.*, 18.

[44] See the chapter on the *Horatii* in this volume, and notes.

[45] LIVY, VII. 6 ; cf. VARRO, *L.L.*, V. 150.

[46] Concerning the Valerii, see PLUT., *Val. Pupl.*, 23, and *Quaest. Rom.*, 79 ; for Fabricius, PLUT., *Quaest. Rom.*, 79. For the restricting laws in this regard, in the time of Duillius, see SERV., *ad Aen.*, XI. 206, and my *Storia di Roma*, I. 1, p. 573.

[47] For Acca, see following chapter ; for the Servilii, VARRO, *L.L.*, VI. 24 ; regarding the Cincii, FESTUS, s. v. *Cincia ;* regarding the Claudii, SUET., *Tib.*, 1.

[48] VITRUVIUS, I. 7.1.

[49] Concerning the temple of Mars at Porta Capena, see LIVY, VI. 5.8 (388 B. C.). I speak of the cult of Horatia in that vicinity, in my *Storia di Roma*, I. 1, p. 297.

[50] As is well known, the marsh called *Caprea* was, in the end of the Republic, localized in the Campus Martius. However, I think I have demonstrated that originally it was situated in the Forum Romanum, where the *Caprificus* or wild fig tree was, near the *puteal* of Navius and the tomb of Romulus. See my *Storia di Roma*, I. 2, p. 741. Indeed, as I have stated in the chapter on the " Origins of Rome," all the evidence favors the belief that the *Palus Caprea* was at the foot of the *ficus Ruminalis*, — that is, in the *Velabrum Maius*.

[51] Traces of the fact that the ancient character of the Forum was that of a region outside the Pomerium are found in a famous ceremony. In the month of October, horse races took place in the Campus Martius. (See FESTUS, s. v. *October equus*, p. 178, M.) At the end of the races, the right-hand horse of the winning chariot was immediately slain. Thereupon followed a lively struggle for the possession of the horse's head between the inhabitants of the Via Sacra and those of the Suburra. If the *Suburanenses* succeeded in capturing it, they hung it from the *turris Mamilia ;* if the *Sacravienses*, from the Regia in the Forum. The tail of the animal was quickly carried to the Regia, so that a sacrifice to Mars might be made with its blood.

If the sacrifice of horses was, in the Republican period, performed in the same locality as under the Empire, — that is, in the modern Via Ripetta (*ad nixas*) (cf. Calendar of PHILOCALUS, *ad loc.*), it is difficult to understand how it was possible for the animal's blood to be still dripping in the sacrifice to

Mars in the Regia. It is more natural to believe that the sacrifice took pl..e in a locality far nearer to that temple.

Furthermore, the mention of the *Suburanenses* and of the *Sacravienses* produces the impression that the latter (like the former) were the inhabitants, not of the most aristocratic and central way of the city, but, indeed, of some suburb. In fact, the Forum Romanum must have been originally the suburb of the Palatine, just as the Suburra was the suburb of the Esquiline. The mention of the *turris Mamilia* shows that the ceremony is connected with the time in which the Tusculani established themselves in Rome. This leads us, if not to the year 327 (which I am inclined to favor), at least to 381 B. C., the year in which the Tusculani were conquered by Camillus. In the neighborhood of that year, then, the Forum Romanum was still outside the Pomerium.

The suburban character of the Forum results, moreover, from still another fact. When in 48 B. C., Caesar wished to subdue a revolt of the soldiers, he caused two of them to be slain in the Campus Martius, and had their heads fastened to the walls of the Regia in the Forum Romanum. Evidently Caesar thus called to life an ancient ceremony. The story also proves that the early Romans decorated their houses with the skulls of the conquered, in precisely the same manner as the Liguri and the Celts, as several Germanic tribes, and as, even to-day, various barbarous peoples. But the fact that Caesar did not cause the heads of the two soldiers to be fastened to the temple of Mars near the Porta Capena, nor to the altar of Mars (which was placed in the Campus Martius as early as 138 B. C.), clearly proves that he re-established the ancient ceremony in every particular, and also that the earliest Campus Martius was situated in the vicinity of the Regia.

[52] Concerning the monument of Romulus, see DION. HAL., II. 54: καὶ ἀπὸ τῶν λαφύρων τέθριππον χαλκοῦν ἀνέθηκε τῷ Ἡφαίστῳ καὶ παρ' αὐτῷ τὴν ἰδίαν ἔστησεν εἰκόνα, ἐπιγράψας Ἑλληνικοῖς γράμμασι τὰς ἑαυτοῦ πράξεις. Cf. PLUT., *Rom.*, 24. Regarding the monument of Servius, see DION. HAL., IV. 26: αὕτη διέμεινεν ἡ στήλη μέχρι τῆς ἡμῆς ἡλικίας ἐν τῷ τῆς Ἀρτέμιδος ἱερῷ κειμένη, γραμμάτων ἔχουσα χαρακτῆρας Ἑλληνικῶν, οἷς τὸ παλαιὸν ἡ Ἑλλὰς ἐχρᾶτο. This second monument is discussed in the lecture upon Servius Tullius. For that of Brutus, see POSID., in PLUT., *Brut.*, I.

[53] In regard to Tatius and the temple of Flora, see VARRO, *L.L.*, V. 74, who cites the authority of the *annales*. For the pretended dedication by T. Quinctius Cincinnatus after the capture of Praeneste, see LIVY, VI. 29.9. Livy gives even the text of the dedication.

[54] See Excursus I and II.

NOTES TO CHAPTER III

THE ORIGINS OF ROME

[1] DIONYSIUS, I. 76, speaks of the killing of Aigestos, son of Numitor, while attending a hunt ordered by King Amulius; LIVY, I. 3.11, on the other hand, simply says: *stirpem fratris virilem interimit* (i. e. Amulius). A comparison here (as in all the parts of the two works relative to this period) shows that both authors drew upon the same sources. Livy, however, hastens to reach a later period which he will describe at length; and consequently, for the earlier period, his aim is to be as brief as possible. Dionysius, instead, gives the substance of his sources in full detail. Quite erroneous is the theory of B. Niese (accepted by other German scholars), that Dionysius expatiates on the sources of Livy, and that Livy himself was one of his sources.

In the hunter Aigestos, brother of Rhea Silvia, it is easy to recognize the friend of Ascanius, son of Aeneas, and the chief of the priests who from Alba return to Lavinium its *sacra* (DION. HAL., I. 67). This same person is Aigestos, the founder of the temple of Diana Aricina at the foot of the Mons Albanus, and the grandson of one of the Tarquins and an inhabitant of Collatia. We shall return to this subject hereafter in this volume.

[2] The facts thus briefly stated are given, among others, by Livy, Dionysius, and Plutarch. The last two authors are more copious in their particulars, and PLUTARCH, *Rom.*, 3, confesses that Diocles of Peparethos is his source. DIONYSIUS, I. 79, briefly refers to the Roman authorities which he followed in the various particulars. Such were Fabius Pictor, Cincius Alimentus, Cato the elder, Calpurnius Piso, and others whom he refers to in general.

[3] See my *Storia di Roma*, I. 1, pp. 200 sqq.

[4] See, particularly, JUST., XLIII. 1.7. sq.

[5] The characteristic form of the story in which Cacus and Pinarius extend to Heracles an honorable reception is preserved by DIODORUS SICULUS, IV. 21. Diodorus declares that, for this period of Roman History, he followed national sources that had been preserved for a long time. These sources are not Fabius Pictor, as Mommsen believed in his paper on this subject, but, indeed, the Annales Maximi. Nor is it surprising that in those documents special mention should have been made of the Pinarii, the well-known falsifiers of Roman history. For this family pretended to have given the first priest of Hercules, and to be the direct descendants of Numa. (CIC., *de domo*, 52.134; PLUT., *Numa*, 21; SERV., *ad Aen.*, VIII. 270.)

[6] I deem it unnecessary to refer to the infinite variations of this myth. In our case it is pressing, instead, to note that the myth of Pallas was already related by the Sicilian author, SILENUS of Calacte, a contemporary of Hannibal. See SOL., I. p. 5, M; PAUL., *ep. Fest.*, p. 220, M; cf. POLYB., in DION. HAL., I. 32 and 43.

[7] I think I have proved this in my *Storia di Roma*, I. 1, pp. 205 sqq.

[8] Judging from extant sources, the first to speak of the Trojans in Latium was DAMASTES of Sigeum. The passage, however, has been sus-

pected for various reasons; we can with full certainty, instead, refer to Aristotle. See DION. HAL., I. 72; PLUT., *Quaest. Rom.*, 6; FESTUS, s. v. *Romam*, p. 269, M; SERV., *ad Aen.*, I. 273; SOL., I. 2, M.

[9] LIVY, XXIX. 14, 37; XXXVI. 36; cf. DION. HAL., I. 32.

[10] SOLOMON REINACH has clearly brought into relief the fact that among the Gauls and the Romans geese were considered totem animals. I fully agree with this view. I do not, on the contrary, share the opinion of ED. MEYER, who denies any value whatsoever to the famous passage in Strabo, in which the *ver sacrum* of the Sabelli is spoken of. Similar traditions and customs are to be found in all primitive and savage peoples. According to Arabian traditions, even Mahomet would have accepted hospitality from that house to whose door his steed should have led him.

[11] JUST., XLIII. 1.7: *ipsum dei simulacrum nudum caprina pelle amictum est, quo habitu nunc Romae Lupercalibus decurritur*; cf. LIVY, I. 5; PLUT., *Rom.*, 21.

[12] For the Lupercalia and Acca Larentia, see the fourth chapter of this volume.

[13] According to DIONYSIUS, I. 79, Faustulus merely chanced to pass in that vicinity. With this version there is to be contrasted a more rational one, — namely, that Faustulus (or Faunus) was a dweller of the Palatine (JUST., XLIII. 2.6; cf. SOLIN., I. 17), and that in this place was situated the *tugurium Romuli* which, in all probability, is identical with the *casa Romuli*.

[14] CIC., *de div.*, I. 17.30; DION. HAL., XIV. 2; VAL. MAX., I. 8.11; PLUT., *Rom.*, 22; *Cam.*, 32; LUTAT., *apud Fast. Praenest.*, *ad diem* 23 *Mart.*

[15] See VITRUVIUS, I. 7.1.

[16] ANT. LAB., in FEST., s. v. *Septimontio*, p. 348, M; cf. *ep. Paul.*, p. 341, M.

[17] VARRO, *L.L.*, V. 53 sqq.: *Quartae regionis Palatium ... huic Germalum et Velias coniunxerunt; quod in hac regione scriptum est: GERMALENSE QUINTICEPS APUD AEDEM ROMULI ... Germalum a germanis Romulo et Remo, quod ad ficum ruminalem et ii ibi inventi cet.*

[18] DION. HAL., I. 79; PLUT., *Rom.*, 20. When the Capitoline Hill was added to the city and when it was supposed that Romulus had been buried in the Comitium, the hut of Romulus was located on the Capitoline. See VITRUVIUS, II. 1.5; SEN., *Contr.*, II. 1.4; CON., *Narr.*, 48.

[19] PLUTARCH, *Rom.*, 20, says that the tree was carefully preserved, and that it was surrounded by an enclosure.

[20] DION. HAL., I. 77.

[21] LIVY, I. 16.2; DION. HAL., I. 56.

[22] DION. HAL., I. 79; PLUT., *Rom.*, 3.5.

[23] DION. HAL., I. 79.

[24] OVID, *Fasti*, II. 237; PLUT., *Fab. Max.*, 1; SIL. ITAL., II. 627; PAUL., *ep. Fest.*, p. 87, M., s. v. *Fovii*.

[25] DION HAL., *l. c.*

[26] LIVY, X. 23.12.

[27] VERG., *Aen.*, VIII. 631 sqq.; cf. SERV., *ad. loc.*: *sane totus hic locus Ennianus est.* LIVY, I. 4.6: *eam submissas infantibus adeo mitem praebuisse mammas, ut lingua lambentem puero magister regii pecoris invenerit.* DION. HAL., I. 79: καὶ τῇ γλώττῃ τὸν πηλὸν ᾧ κατάπλεοι ἦσαν ἀπελίχμα.

[28] LIVY, I. 4.5: *ubi nunc ficus Ruminalis est.* OVID, *Fasti*, II. 411: *arbor erat, remanent vestigia, quaeque vocatur Rumina nunc ficus, Romula ficus erat.*

[29] OVID, *Fasti*, II. 597. See also the chapter on the Fabii.

[30] Concerning the Alexandrine character of Pompeian art, I shall refer the reader to the learned exposition of Helbig. The contrary arguments of A. SOGLIANO (*Atti della Accademia di Napoli*) with which he endeavors

to prove an independent and national character for Roman art, reveal an utter lack of critical power and of knowledge of the development of classic civilization.

³¹ OVID, *Fasti*, II. 615 sq.
³² For the meaning of the Lares and of Acca Larentia, see the chapter on Acca Larentia in this volume.
³³ TAC., *Ann.*, XII. 24. See also Chapter XII. in this volume.
³⁴ CASS. HEM., in DIOM., I. p. 384, K = fr. 11., PETER.
³⁵ VARRO, *L.L.*, VI. 23. Compare this passage with V. 164.
³⁶ *Fasti Praen.*,'*ad d.* 21 *Dec.*; PLINY, *N.H.*, III. 65; cf. SOL., I. 6; MACR., I. 10.7 sq.; III. 9.4.
³⁷ For the *statua Cinciae*, see FESTUS, s. v. *Romanam portam*, p. 262, M; cf. s. v. *Cincia*, p. 57, M. VARRO, *L.L.*, VI. 25, says that, near the sepulchre of Acca Larentia in the Velabrum, the priests sacrificed *manibus servilibus*. If I be not mistaken, this statement can be placed in relation with the epigram and the scene described therein, — that, in the temple of Apollonides, the mother of the princes of Pergamum (who died between 166 and 159 B. C.) represented *Servilia*, the mother of Romulus and Remus. See *Anth. Pal.*, III. 19. We shall not here discuss the very involved question of the origin of this particular phase of the myth. At any rate, we know that it was officially received in the second century B. C. by the Roman annalists. I advanced the hypothesis, some time ago, that the explanation of this legend was related with the power of the plebeian family of the Servilii, one of whom was sent as ambassador to Attalus in 192 B. C. (LIVY, XXXV. 23; cf. my *Storia di Roma*, I. 1, p. 208, n. 4.) I have noted, moreover (*ib.*, p. 324), that this version may have drawn its origin from the fusion of the legend of Romulus with that of Servius Tullius, who was often confused with Romulus, even in many details of the legend.
³⁸ VARRO, *R.R.*, II. 11.5; PLUT., *Rom.*, 4; *Quaest. Rom.*, 57; AUG., *de civ. dei*, IV. 11; VI. 10; VII. 11.
³⁹ DION. HAL., I. 32.
⁴⁰ See Excursus III.
⁴¹ SERV., *ad Aen.*, VIII. 63, 90.
⁴² LIVY, I. 4.5; OVID, *Fasti*, II. 412 sqq.
⁴³ VARRO, *R.R.*, II. 11.5; PLUT., *Rom.*, 4; AUG., *de civ. dei*, IV. 11, 21; VII. 11.
⁴⁴ PLINY, *N.H.*, XV. 77; DION. HAL., III. 71; FESTUS, p. 169, M, s. v. *Navia*; TAC., *Ann.*, XIII. 58; CON., *Narr.*, 48. Compare, also, my *Storia di Roma*, I. 1, p. 708, n. 2.
⁴⁵ ENN., in *Charis.*, p. 128, K = fr. 41, B.
⁴⁶ PLINY, *N.H.*, XV. 77: *Colitur ficus arbor in foro ipso ac Comitio Romae nata, sacra fulguribus ibi conditis magisque ob memoriam eius, quae nutrix Romuli [ac Remi] conditoris imperii in Lupercali prima protexit, ruminalis appellata, quoniam sub ea inventa est lupa infantibus praebens rumim, ita vocabant mammam, miraculo ex aere iuxta dicato, tamquam in Comitium sponte transisset Atto Navio augurante.* VARRO, *R.R.*, II. 11.5: *non negarim, inquam, ideo aput divae Ruminae sacellum a pastoribus satam ficum. ibi enim solent sacrificari lacte pro vino et [pro] lactentibus. mamma enim rumis [sive ruminare] ut ante dicebant: a rumi etiam nunc dicuntur subrumi agni, lactantes a lacte.* FESTUS, s. v. *Ruminalem*, p. 270; LIVY, I. 4.5; OVID, *Fasti*, II. 412. A different opinion is expressed in FESTUS, s. v. *Romulum*, p. 266, M. Compare, too, the texts cited above in n. 36.
⁴⁷ PLINY, *N.H.*, XIV. 88: *Romulum lacte, non vino, libasse indicio sunt sacra ab eo instituta, quae hodie custodiunt morem.*
⁴⁸ PLINY, *N.H.*, XV. 77; DION. HAL., III. 71; FESTUS, p. 169, M, s. v. *Navia*; TAC., *Ann.*, XIII. 58; CON., *Narr.*, 48. Compare also my *Storia di Roma*, I. 1, p. 708, n. 2.

[49] Even among the ancients there were not lacking those who denied a connection between Romulus and the *ficus Ruminalis*. This, however, was due to the more flattering derivation of the names of Romulus and Remus from ῥώμη, — strength. See FESTUS, s. v. *Romulum*, p. 266, M.

[50] FESTUS, p. 262, s. v. : *Romanam portam vulgus appellat, ubi ex epistylio defluit aqua. qui locus ab antiquis appellari solitus est statuae Cinciae, quod in eo fuit sepulcrum eius familiae. sed porta Romana instituta est a Romulo infimo clivo Victoriae, qui locus gradibus in quadram formatus est. appellata autem Romana a Sabinis praecipue quod ea proximus aditus erat Romam.* VARRO, *L.L.*, V. 164: *alteram* (i. e., *portam*) *Romanulam ab Roma dictam.* The water which ran from the epistilium naturally makes us think of the spring in the adjacent Lupercal. Compare DION. HAL., I. 79; VARRO, *L.L.*, VI. 24.

[51] STEPH. BYZ., s. v. συκαί.
[52] PLINY, *N.H.*, XV. 78.
[53] LYDUS, *de mens.*, III. 52.

[54] In my *Storia di Roma*, I. 2, pp. 741 sq., I have brought to notice that Plutarch has rightly translated the *palus Caprea* by αἰγὸς ἕλος, and that this neighborhood was, originally, not in the Campus Martius (in which it was placed only when the boundaries of the Pomerium were extended), but, indeed, in the Velabrum. Perhaps it indicated from the very beginning that marsh which extended from the Palatine towards the Capitoline, and was situated in that part of the Velabrum (or Velabrum minus) which encircled the Vulcanal, near which Romulus was killed. PLUT., *Rom.*, 27. It must be added that the Vulcanal was adjacent to the tomb of Romulus.

[55] DION. HAL., II. 56; PLUT., *Rom.*, 29.

[56] VARRO, *L.L.*, VI. 18: *Nonae Caprotinae quod eo die in Latio Iunoni Caprotinae mulieres sacrificantur, et sub caprifico faciunt : e caprifico adhibent virgam ;* cf. CALP. PISO, in MACR., III. 2.14; PLUT., *Coriol.*, 33. For the meaning of the ceremony, see my *Storia di Roma*, I. 2, p. 125.

[57] HERACL. PONT., *fr.*, 25, in MUELLER, *Frag. Hist. Graec.*, II. p. 219; DIOD., VIII., 23.2; DION. HAL., XIX. 2.

[58] DIOD., VIII. 21; DION. HAL., XIX. 1.2, gives also the legend of Rhegium.

[59] See my *Storia della Sicilia e della Magna Grecia*, Torino, 1894, I. p. 612.
[60] ATHEN., III. p. 74.

[61] PLINY, *N.H.*, XV. 68, not only says that *e reliquo genere pomorum ficus amplissima est*, but explicitly states, *ib.*, 77, *colitur ficus arbor in foro . . . sacra.*

[62] TAC., *Ann.*, XV. 23, *ad a.* 63 A. D.
[63] CIC., *de leg.*, II. 8.20; cf. *ib.*, 12.29.

NOTES TO CHAPTER IV

ACCA LARENTIA

[1] Both these versions are accepted by PLUTARCH, *Rom.*, 4 sq.; *Quaest. Rom.*, 35. Cato (in MACROB., I. 10.16) already was acquainted with the legend of Acca, the hetaira, and of the fields donated by her. The words of Licinius Macer (*ib.*), relative to the feast established in honor of Acca, are to be compared with the story with which the same annalist explained the feast of the *Brumalia*. See JOH. MAL., *Chr.*, VII. p. 179. Concerning the will of Acca, see VAL. ANT., in GELL., *N.A.*, VII. 7.6. The two versions are to be found also in VERR. FLACC., *Fast. Praen., ad d. 23 Dec.*: *Fer]iae Jovi. Accae Larentin[* . . .] *Hanc alii Remi et Rom[uli nutricem, alii] meretricem Herculis scortum [fuisse dic]unt; parentari ei publice, quod p(opulum) R(omanum) he[redem fece]rit magnae pecuniae, quam accepe[rat testame]nto Tarutilli amatoris sui.* As to Acca and the Arval brothers, see MASUR. SAB., in GELL., *N.A.*, VII. 7.8; cf. PLINY, *N.H.*, XVIII. 6; FULG., *Serm. Ant.* 9. p. 114. Helm.

[2] BAEHRENS, *Neue Jahr. f. Philol.*, 1885, p. 17; cf. PASCAL, *Studi di Antichità e Mitologia*, Milano, 1896. p. 138. I attach no importance to the difference in quantity between *Lăres* and *Lărentia* as against the statements of the texts; cf. *Fŭria* with *Fŭrrina*. The *Larentia* of the Fasti has a parallel in the feast of the *Larentinal*. See VARRO, *L.L.*, VI. 23, who says in addition, *diem Tarentini Accas Tarentinas*. Whether there is here an error in the text, which should be corrected to *Larentini* and *Larentinas*, or whether there is a reference to the Tarentum which originally was adjacent to the Velabrum rather than to the Campus Martius, I do not venture to decide.

[3] MOMMSEN, *Die echte und die falsche Acca Larentia*, in *Röm. Forschungen*, II. pp. 1 sqq.

[4] PAUS., II. 2.8.

[5] See JUSTI, *Geschichte d. alt. Persiens* (Berlin, 1879), pp. 67 sqq.

[6] PAUS., III. 10.6.

[7] PAUS., II. 15.2.

[8] WISSOWA, *Religion und Cultus der Römer*, pp. 188, 230.

[9] The text of MACROBIUS, I. 10.11, is very explicit: *decimo Kalendas feriae sunt Jovis quae appellantur Larentinalia*.

[10] VARRO, *R.R.*, I. 1.5. Likewise PLUTARCH (*De Superst.*, 8) recommends the invocation to Zeus Chthonios and to Demeter.

[11] VARRO, in GELL., *N.A.*, XVI. 16.4.

[12] For the Pythagorean doctrine on the value of the uneven days, as, for example, at Cuma, see LIVY, XXIII. 35.

[13] VARRO, *R.R.*, I. 34; PLINY, *N.H.*, XVIII. 204.

[14] I do not agree with those critics who, like H. PETER (in ROSCHER, *Lex.*, II. col. 1890, s. v.), deny the sepulchral character of the Lares, already recognized by VARRO (in ARNOB., III. 41; cf. GRANIUS FLACC., in CENS., *De die natali*, III. 2), and who forget that in the *tutela* of the hearth is to be found a fact related to the worship of the dead.

[15] It seems to me that one need not take into consideration the doubts of WISSOWA (in ROSCHER, *Lex.*, II. col. 2323, and *Religion und Cultus der Rö-*

mer, p. 230), as against the explicit statements of VARRO, *L.L.*, IX. 61: *videmus enim Maniam matrem Larum dici* (cf. ARNOB., *adv. nat.*, III. 41); of AELIUS STILO (in FESTUS, p. 129, s. v.); and finally of ALBINUS CAECINA (in MACROB., I. 7.34), who state that Mania, the mother of the Lares, was worshipped on the *Compitalia*, a festival sacred to the Lares.

16 See OVID, *Fasti*, II. 570 sqq., where he speaks of the *Feralia* sacred to Tacita, that is to say, to Muta or to Larva, mother of the Lares. By this means it was explained why Maia became considered mother of the Lares, and why she was worshipped on the 1st of May, a day sacred also to Bona Dea (OVID, *Fasti*, V. 129 sqq.). Lactantius, too, speaks of the Dea Muta, *Inst. Div.*, I. 20.35 : *hanc esse dicunt ex qua sint Lares nati et ipsam Laram nominant vel Larundam*. WISSOWA (ROSCHER, *Lex.*, s. v.) supposes that in this there is merely to be seen the influence of later traditions. He seems to follow the version that placed this divinity in relation with Camena and Numa. But I fear he is mistaken. Plutarch (*Numa*, 8) believed that she was called Tacita in honor of the Pythagorean silence, and by so doing proves the recent origin of his version. Moreover Tacita (as is evident from OVID, *Fasti*, II. 596 sqq.) had nothing in common with the Camenae worshipped by Numa, who were south of the Caelian and outside the Porta Capena. Tacita had her sacrarium near the Vicus Tuscus, not far from the fountain of Juturna, where was also the sacellum of Larentia and of Angerona.

17 VARRO, *L.L.*, VI. 23 : *Angeronalia ab Angerona cui sacrificium fit in curia Acculeia*. MACROB., I. 10.7 : *duodecimo vero feriae sunt divae Angeroniae, cui pontifices in sacello Volupiae sacrum faciunt*. I. 10.8 : *Masurius adicit simulacrum huius deae ore obligato atque signato in ara Volupiae propterea collocatum, quod qui suos dolores anxietatesque dissimulant perveniant patientiae beneficio ad maximam voluptatem*. For the *sacellum Volupiae* near the Porta Romanula, see VARRO, *L.L.*, V. 164. From the Fasti we learn that the same day was sacred to Dea Dia.

18 CORNEL. LAB. (in MACROB., I. 12.21) : *Auctor est Cornelius Labeo huic Maiae, id est terrae, aedem Kalendis Maiis dedicatam sub nomine Bonae Deae et eandem esse Bonam Deam et terram ex ipso ritu occultiore sacrorum doceri posse confirmat. hanc eandem esse Bonam Deam Faunamque et Opem et Fatuam pontificum libri indigitari*. For Mania, the mother of the Lares, see VARRO, *L.L.*, IX. 61 ; PAUL., *ep. Fest.*, p. 129, 145, M ; ARNOB., *adv. nat.*, III. 41.

19 This state of affairs is not particularly Roman, but was to be found also in Greece, PAUS., I. 34.3; I. 31.4; VIII. 36.1. Moreover, it is sufficient to think of the worship of the Catholic believer, — a worship which, in the various chapels of a church, represents different phases of the life of a saint. In a similar manner, in a single Greek temple one might have seen different statues of Aphrodite, represented under various aspects. PAUS., VIII. 37.12.

2) For the seeds which were scattered upon the Roman people on the day of the *Floralia, quando Terrae ludos colebant*, see Scholiast to PERS., V. 178. For the relation between the *Sementiva* and the *Brumalia* see above. All that we are here stating would become far clearer if we could explain the passage in PLUTARCH, *Quaest. Rom.*, 35 : τῇ δ' ἑταίρᾳ (ἱτέρᾳ) Λαρεντίᾳ Φαβόλαν ἐπίκλησιν εἶναι λέγουσιν. To Mommsen it seemed that the word *Fabula* was equivalent to *Schwatzmaul*. He may be right ; and one might then think of the epithet Μῦθος applied to Demetrius Poliorcetes when he became enamored of Lamia. (PLUT., *Demetr.*, 27.) It must be noted that, according to Plutarch, sacred offerings were made to Larentia in April by the Flamen Martialis. This is doubly true because the 23rd of December was sacred to Larentia. (VARRO, *L.L.*, VI. 23 ; CIC., *ad Brut.*, I. 15.8.) Perhaps in Plutarch there is confusion with other divinities. The 1st of April was sacred to Venus, but it seemed fit to Macrobius not to state why this was so. (MACROB.,

ACCA LARENTIA 291

¹ I. 12.15.) To Venus, the protectress of hetairae, was sacred also the 23rd of April (OVID, *Fasti*, IV. 865. sqq.; *Fasti Caer.*, *ad d. 23rd Apr.*) The 23rd and 25th of April were sacred to the *Venalia* and *Robigalia*, in which, probably, the *flamines* were engaged; on the 28th was the *Floralia*. To Flora, perhaps, is to be referred the passage in Lactantius (*Inst. Div.*, I. 20.5, p. 72, Br.), where, after having talked of Acca, it is said: *nec hanc solam Romani meretricem colunt, sed Faulam quoque, quam Herculis scortum fuisse Verrius scribit;* and shortly after there follows the story of Flora, so that in place of *Faula* there might be substituted the name *Flora*. The word *Fabula* perhaps refers to a version of the myth which referred to the progenitress of the gens Fabia, who was courted by Hercules at the foot of the Palatine. (OVID, *Fasti*, II. 237; PLUT., *Fab. Max.*, I. 1; SIL. ITAL., II. 627, *et passim*; PAUL., *ep. Fest.*, p. 87.) But I do not think it behooving to insist upon such an hypothesis. Still less do I think that the passage in Horace should be referred to our myth (HOR., *C.*, I. 4.16.) : *iam te premet nox fabulaeque manes.* A. KIESSLING rightly remarks on this passage that it is a reminiscence of the ψεῦδος μῦθος of Callimachus.

What I shall say in this lecture will exonerate me from the task of confuting the hypothesis of Zielinski (*Quaest. com.*, Petersburg, 1887, pp., 113 sqq.) accepted also by WISSOWA (*Religion u. Cultus d. Römer*, p. 230), — namely, that *Fabula*, in being referred to Acca Larentia, proves, not the sacred, but the comic and burlesque character of the legend of the temple-warden. I deem it fitting, rather, to bring into relief the characteristic touch of the idle sacristan who plays. Even to-day, in Italy, playing at cards is considered the favorite pastime of priests.

²¹ VARRO, *L.L.*, V. 164, VI. 23; PLUT., *Quaest. Rom.*, 34.

²² To this same locality and worship were referred the coins of P. Accoleius Lariscolus (BABELON, *Monn. d. l. rép. Rom.* I. pp. 98 sqq.) upon which there is a nymph, identified (rightly or wrongly) with Acca Larentia ; on the reverse are to be seen three nymphs.

²³ OVID, *Fasti*, II. 603 sq.

²⁴ OVID, *Fasti*, V. 421 sq. : *ritus erit veteris, nocturna Lemuria, sacri. Inferias tacitis manibus illa dabunt ;* cf. *ib.*, 483 : *mox etiam lemures animas dixere silentum.* Why Angerona was represented with a closed mouth is not known. Some thought that she was the goddess of silence, and that she kept secret the true name of Rome (PLINY, *N.H.*, III. 65). Others referred her name to *angores*, and still others to *angina*. (See MACROB., I. 10.7 ; PAUL., *ep. Fest.*, p. 17.) MOMMSEN (*CIL.*, I. ed. 2, p. 337) deduces from the Fasti Praenestini that she was connected with the dying year and with its new birth. The words of the Fasti, *aiunt ob an* [*num . . . mani*] *festum esse* [. . .]*m* [*a*]*nni nov*[*i*], suggest to me a feast connected with the end of the year, rather than with the beginning.

²⁵ MARQUARDT-WISSOWA, *Röm. Staatsverwaltung*, III. ed. 2, pp. 452 sqq.

²⁶ For Volusia as the *Dea Voluptatis*, see TERTULL., *Ad Nat.*, II, 11, p. 115; cf. AUG., *De civ. dei*, IV. 8, 11.

²⁷ CIC., *de Nat.*, II. 23.61; cf. VARRO, *L.L.*, VI. 47 ; cf. in NON., p. 64, where there is mention of a grove sacred to *Venus Lubentina*, also mentioned by FESTUS, p. 265. s. v. *Rustica vinalia ;* DION. HAL., IV. 15.

²⁸ I refer in this place, also, to the belief of Wissowa (ROSCHER, *Lex.*, II. 2. col. 2035), who is followed by AUST, *Die Religion der Römer* (Berlin, 1899), p. 144. Almost without any arguments they deny the real relation between the worships of Cloacina, Libitina, etc.

²⁹ PLUT., *Quaest. Rom.*, 23 ; cf. PLAC., *Corp. Gloss.*, V. 30.14. sqq.

³⁰ CASS. HEM., in DIOM., I. p. 384, K = fr. 11 P.: *pastorum vulgus sine contentione consentiendo praefecerunt aequaliter imperio Remum et Romulum . . . monstrum fit : sus parit porcos triginta, cuius rei fanum fecerunt Laribus Grundilibus.* For the Lares Grunduli, see ARNOB., *adv. nat.*, I. 28, and FULGENT.,

Serm., 7. p. 113, Helm., where we read *suggrundaria antiqui dicebant sepulcra infantium qui necdum quadraginta dies implessent.* The custom of burying the little bodies of abortions beneath the eaves is still extant in the country round Pisa in Tuscany. In this, it seems to me, there is the remnant of a belief relative to the Lares of the *grondaie*, or eaves. Our Lares Grunduli recall the Lares Praestites, worshipped on the 1st of May *in Summa Sacra Via.* See, *Act. div. Aug.*, IV. 7; OVID, *Fasti*, VI. 791.

[31] OVID, *Fasti*, I. 233 sqq.; MACROB., I. 7.21.
[32] DION. HAL., I. 38; MACROB., I. 7.27.
[33] MACROB., III. 11.10.
[34] The relations between the worships of Herakles and Demeter are well known. See PAUS., III. 20.5; VIII. 31.3.
[35] It is sufficient to mention the legend of the love of Hercules for the nymph Pallas, mother of Latinus (SILEN., in SOL., I. 15; DION. HAL., I. 43; PAUL., *ep. Fest.*, p. 220, s. v. *Palatium*), or for Fauna, the daughter of Faunus (JUST., XLIII. 1.9; CASS. DIO, fr. 4.3), or for the nymph Tiberina, the progenitress of the Fabii (OVID, *Fasti*, II. 237; PLUT., *Fab. Max.*, I.; cf. PAUL., *ep. Fest.*, s. v. *Fovii*).
[36] VARRO, in MACROB., I. 12.28; PROPERT., V. 9.53 sqq.
[37] PROPERT., V. 9.5: *qua Velabra suo stagnabant ftumine.* Evander was localized on the Aventine, it seems, as we learn from the myth of Faunus, of Picus, and of Numa. See OVID, *Fasti*, III. 295.
[38] CORNEL. LAB., in MACROB., I. 12.21.
[39] PROMATH., in PLUT., *Rom.*, 2 extr.
[40] See above, note 30.
[41] OVID, *Fasti*, II. 303 sqq.
[42] OVID, *Fasti*, II. 357 sqq.
[43] OVID, I. 390 sqq. The story of Ovid is explained by both Latin and Greek rites. For the fact that *Deus inter sacra Romana a Vestalibus colitur,* see PLINY, *N.H.*, XXVIII. 39. Satyrus was to be seen in the temple of Vesta at Tarentum, CIC., *in Verr.*, II. 4.135; cf. CALLIXEN. RHOD., in M. *F.G.H.*, III. p. 65. The myth of Priapus among the nymphs is well known in tradition and upon monuments. ARNOB., *adv. nat.*, III. 10.
[44] SILEN., in Sol., I. 15; DION. HAL., I. 43; JUST., XLIII. 1.9; PSEUDO-PLUT., *Parall. Min.*, 38. Other myths spoke of good relations between Hercules and Evander, that is to say, Faunus. Accordingly, the statue of Hercules in the Forum Boarium, which was carried about in triumph, was said to have been dedicated by Evander. PLINY, *N.H.*, XXXIV. 33.
[45] With the story of the sacristan who leads a courtesan to the temple of the god, one may obviously contrast that of the woman whom the priests were accustomed to lead to the Babylonian god, Belus. (HERODOT., I. 181.) Similarly, it is well known that the wife of the archon βασιλεύς had, once a year, to lie with the god Dionysos. A similar custom existed in Egypt, because the wives of Pharaoh were considered brides of the god; and the custom has been noted by Cameron also in central Africa. The characteristic touch of the god's imposing upon his concubine to kiss the first man she might encounter, finds a parallel in the legend of Cephalus, ruler of the eponymous island of Cephallena. See ARISTOT., in *Etym. Magn.*, s. v. Ἀρκείσιος.
[46] SERV., *ad Georg.*, I. 10: *Cincius et Cassius aiunt ab Evandro Faunum deum appellatum; ideoque aedes sacras Faunas primo appellatas postea fana dicta, et ex eo qui futura praecinerent Fanaticos dici.* With this, one may join the fragment of ENNIUS (fr. 155 B), where he speaks of *Fauni, vatesque* (cf. VARRO, *L.L.*, VII. 36), as well as the texts in which it is said that *Fenta* or *Fauna* was called also *Fatua.* See, for example, JUST., XLIII. 1.8: *Fauno uxor fuit nomine Fatua, quae assidue divino spiritu inpleta veluti per furorem futura praemonebat. Unde adhuc, qui inspirari solent, fatuari dicuntur.* PAUL., *ep.*

ACCA LARENTIA 293

Fest., s. v. *Fanum*, p. 88; cf. s. v. *Saturno*, p. 325; CORN. LAB., in MACROB., I. 12.21; GAV. BASS., in LACT., *Inst. Div.*, I. 229; ARNOB., *adv. nat.*, I. 36. With such correspondence between *Faunus* and *Fatuus*, one may join also the strange story of the well-known god, Aius Loquens, who, shortly before the arrival of the Gauls, gave warning to Caedicius on the Via Nova to repair the walls. CIC., *de divin.*, I. 45; LIVY, V. 32, 50. Aius Loquens, whose temple was near that of Vesta, seems to be a divinity analogous to Silvanus and to Pan, who made similar predictions to the Athenians (HERODOT., VI. 106), and to the Romans, LIVY, II. 7.2.

[47] It is well known that, at Rome, all the temples of Venus were situated outside the Pomerium. From VITRUVIUS, I. 7.1, we learn that this was fixed by law also in the books of the *haruspices*.

[48] For the connection of Acca Larentia with the Arval Brothers, see MASUR. SAB., in GELL., VII. 7.8; PLIN., *N.H.*, XVIII. 6. For the *ager Semurium*, see CIC., *Phil.*, VI. 14: *iis quoque divisit Semurium, Campus Martius restabat*. Also from Cicero, we learn (*Phil.*, V. 20) that Anthony had destined for his followers even the city territory; and, from *Phil.*, VI. 15, in which L. Anthony is spoken of as *a Jano medio patrono*, it may be deduced that the confiscations extended to the Vicus Tuscus.

The *ager Solinium* is, by Baehrens and others, identified with the *ager Solonium* near Laurentum, on the assumption (which is not at all warranted) that the word *Solinium* was a corrupted form. If the argument of false texts be admitted, then one may think also that instead of *Lintirium*, *Latinium* should be read, — a well-known field near Rome. (CIC., *de har. resp.*, 28.62.) But it is dangerous to insist on such hypotheses.

[49] PLIN., *N.H.*, XXXIV. 25: *invenitur statua decreta et Taraciae Gaiae sive Fufetiae virgini Vestali, ut poneretur ubi vellet* . . . *meritum eius ponam annalium verbis: quod campum Tiberinum gratificata esset ea populo*. GELL., *N.A.*, VII. 7: *Accae Larentiae et Gaiae Taraciae, sive illa Fufetia est, nomina in antiquis annalibus celebria sunt. Earum alterae post mortem, Taraciae autem vivae amplissimi honores a populo Romano habiti* . . . *ius ei potestasque exaugurandi atque nubendi facta est munificentiae et beneficii gratia, quod campum Tiberinum sive Martium populo condonasset*.

[50] It is sufficient to recall that the legend itself presupposes that the Lupercal was bathed by the waters of the Tiber. (LIVY, I. 5; DION. HAL., I. 79; PROMATH., in PLUT., *Rom.*, 2; PROP., V. 9. See also the Pompeian fresco here reproduced.) That the Velabrum extended not only to the Porta Romana or Romanaula, but, indeed, as far as the Janus Bifrons, is clear from VARRO, *L.L.*, V. 156. The Roman Forum, as is well known, was a marsh often flooded by the Tiber (HOR., *C.*, I. 2; OVID, *Fasti*, III. 520; cf. PAUL., *ep. Fest.*, s. v. *Martialis Campus*). The same was true, of course, for the base of the Aventine. See VARRO, *L.L.*, V. 43.

[51] CIC., *de rep.*, II. 18.33; LIVY, I. 33; DION. HAL., III. 44 sqq.

[52] MACROB., I. 10.16.

[53] TIMAEUS, in DION. HAL., I. 67, and in POLYB., XII. 4, 6.

[54] Timaeus described several sacred festivals and Roman customs, as is deduced from his story of the "October horse." See POLYB., XII. 4.b. = fr. 151, M.

[55] It is not necessary to demonstrate that the god Innus was the *goat* Inus, who later was represented *caprino pede* and leaping *caprino more* (DIOM., *Ars gramm.*, III. p. 476, K). To him the Lupercalia were sacred (LIVY, I. 5.2.); he was the husband of Pales (ARNOB., *adv. nat.*, III. 23, 4c) and is identical with the *hircus* worshipped under the name of *Faunus bicornis* in the feast of the Lupercalia (OVID, *Fasti*, II. 268). He is the same *hircus* invoked on that feast: *Italidas matres, inquit, sacer hircus inito* (OVID, *Fasti*, II. 441). The ceremony of those women who, being desirous of bearing children, were beaten by goat-straps during the feast of the Lupercalia, sym-

bolized the *inito* of Innus or Faunus. And the etymology of Inus from *inire* was already recognized by the ancients. SERV., *ad Aen.*, VI. 775.

[56] I allude to the myth of Faunus and Omphale given above.

[57] CIC., *pro Cael.*, 11.26 : *sibi in Lupercis sodalem esse Caelium dixit. Fera quaedam sodalitas et plane pastoricia atque agrestis;* cf. *Phil.*, II. 85.

[58] In the passage of SERVIUS, XI. 785, relative to the custom of the Hirpini of Mount Soracte of *vivere raptu*, there is a valuable element which has not been well understood by some modern critics, as, for example, by WISSOWA, in ROSCHER, *Lex.*, I. col. 2694. Such customs can be understood only through the study of comparative ethnography. The custom of the Hirpini, who endeavored to imitate the ferocity of their totem, the wolf, is to be found also among the ancient customs of the Indians and of other savage peoples.

[59] Even the nuptial ceremonies in which *Talassio* was invoked had an obscene signification. See my *Storia di Roma*, I. 1, p. 273.

[60] ARNOB., *adv. nat.*, IV. 7 : *etiamne Perfica una est . . . quae obscenas illas et luteas voluptates ad exitum perficit . . . etiamne Pertunda, quae in cubiculis praesto est virginalem scrobem effodientibus maritis? etiamne Tutunus cuius immanibus pudendis horrentique fascino vestras inequitare matronas et auspicabile ducitis et optatis?* Compare AUG., *de civ. dei*, VII. 24 : *in celebratione nuptiarum super Priapi scapum nova nupta sedere iubebatur;* cf. VI. 9 ; LACT., *Div. Inst.*, I. 20.36; TERTULL., *Ad nat.*, II. 11, end. From FESTUS, s. v. *Mutini Titini*, p. 154, M. we learn that the cult of Tutunus Mutunus, the ancient Priapus of the Palatine community, lasted till the time of Augustus.

[61] PLUT., *Quaest. Rom.*, 20; SEXT. CLODIUS, in ARNOB., *adv. nat.*, V. 18; LACT., *Div. Inst.*, I. 22, p. 89 Br.

[62] FAB. PICT., in PLINY, *N.H.*, XIV. 89.

[63] PLUT., *Rom.*, 14.9 ; 19.13. As results from DIONYSIUS, II. 47, such data are, chronologically, of dubious worth. Of the concession made to women of riding in vehicles, there is mention also at the time of the Gallic fire (LIVY, V. 25.9; DIOD , XIV. 116, end). The true reason of such concession is to be sought for, not in any historical motive, but rather in the attentions necessarily due to pregnant women. Therefore this custom was connected with the Carmentalia, in which such women betook themselves to thank the goddess.

[64] DION. HAL., II. 24.

[65] It is hardly necessary to recall that *familia* and *pater familias* included the conception of movable property. The ancient *proletarius* (rich in children) sold his children, just as the poor mountaineer of southern Italy sold his (as late as the beginning of the 18th century), to whomsoever would take them to distant regions.

[66] The meaning of the formula *ubi es Gaius tu ibi Gaia* is well known ; and from Cato (in SERV., *ad Aen.*, V. 755) we learn of the custom of the bull and the cow, who were yoked, the former on the right and on the outside, the latter on the left and on the inside, when the ceremony was performed of cutting the first furrow to mark a new city. They symbolized, respectively. external and warlike deeds, and the domestic cares of the couple.

[67] This observation had already been made by LACTANTIUS, *Div. Inst*, I. 20.2. Observe, also, that Phaia, on account of her bad morals, was called *sus* (PLUT., *Thes.*, 9); and that Leaena, in the story of Harmodion and Aristogeiton, is represented in the shape of a lion (PLINY. *N.H.*, XXXIV. 72).

[68] Regarding the goats and lambs, see OVID, *Fasti*, II. 361 ; PLUT., *Rom.*, 21 ; SERV., *ad Aen.*, VIII. 343 ; for the dogs, see PLUT., *l. c.* The wolves in such feasts were represented by the Luperci themselves, as was the custom also among the Hirpini of Mount Soracte.

[69] For the *lupus Martius* or *Martialis* as the symbol of the nation, see LIVY, X. 27, XXII. 12 ; VERG., IX. 566 ; HOR., *Carm.*, I. 17.9. Likewise,

ACCA LARENTIA 295

lupa is called Martia, CIC., *de divin.*, I. 12.20; PROP., V. 1.55; PLUT., *Rom.*, 4.

[70] In regard to the origin and the meaning of the Roman legend of Rhea Silvia, see my *Storia di Roma*, I. 1, pp. 205 sqq. Romulus was born in the grove of Mars (DION. HAL., I. 77; TROG. POMP., in JUST., XLIII. 2.7). By admitting that Mars and the wolf were contemporaneously worshipped in the cave of the Lupercal, it will be better understood why the *lituus* of Romulus should nave been found in the temple of Mars (DION. HAL., XIV. 2). It results from these texts that the temple of Mars was simply the house of Romulus. Also the meaning of LIVY, X. 27.9, *hinc victor Martius lupus, integer et intactus, gentis nos Martiae et conditoris nostri admonuit*, will then become clear.

[71] PLUT., *Numa*, 8.9.
[72] PLINY, *N.H.*, XXXV. 152.
[73] PLINY, *N.H.*, XXXV. 157; cf. my *Storia di Roma*, I. 1, p. 352.
[74] PLINY, *N.H.*, XXXIV. 23.33.
[75] NAEV., in FEST., s. v. *penem*, p. 230, M.
[76] CASSIUS HEMINA, in DIOMED., I. p. 384, K; DION. HAL., I. 79.
[77] VARRO, *R.R.*, II. 4.18.
[78] DION. HAL., I. 59, end.
[79] MACROB., I. 12.25.
[80] For the cippi of the ancient Palatine, see TACITUS, *Ann.*, XII. 24. That they were considered sacred images of Jupiter Terminus is explicitly stated by DION. HAL., II. 74.
[81] VARRO, in NON., p. 547; SERV., *ad Aen.*, III. 175; there was a similar superstition in Boeotia.
[82] SERV., *ad Aen.*, VIII. 190; LACT., *Div. Inst.*, I. 20.36.
[83] For Jupiter adored under the form of an oak on the hill Querquetulanus (later the Caelian), and of an osier (whence the name of Collis Viminalis), see VARRO, *L.L.*, V. 51.
[84] ENN., in CIC., *de divin.*, I. 107.
[85] AUG., *de civ. dei*, VII. 11.
[86] PLINY, *N.H.*, XVII. 50: *quae regi suo Stercuto Fauni filio ab hoc inventum immortalitatem tribuit.* For the relations and ancestry of Picus, Faunus, and Stercutus, kings of the Palatine and of Laurentum, see VARRO, in AUG., *de civ. dei*, XVIII. 15; SERV., *ad Aen.*, X. 76. For the identification of Stercutus with Saturnus, see for example, MACROB., I. 7.25. For the cult of Stercutus by the Senate, see PRUDENT., *Peri St.*, II. 449 sqq.; cf..TERTULL., *Apol.*, 25; *Ad nat.*, II. 9.
[87] SERV., *ad Aen.*, IX. 4: *Pilumnus et Pitumnus fratres fuerunt dii: horum Pitumnus usum stecorandorum invenit agrorum, unde et Sterculinius dictus est;* cf. SERV., *ib.*, X. 76; VARRO, in NON., p. 528, considered them the *dei coniugales* to whom *in aedibus lectus sternebatur.*
[88] VARRO, *L.L.*, VI. 34: *Lupercis nudis lustratur antiquum oppidum Palatinum graegibus humanis cinctum.*
[89] CIC., *pro Caelio*, XI. 26: *fera quaedam sodalitas et plane pastoricia atque agrestis germanorum Lupercorum, quorum coitio illa silvestris ante est inst'tuta quam humanitas atque leges cet.*
[90] VERG., *Aen.*, VIII. 314 sqq.
[91] For Caca, see SERV., *ad Aen.*, VIII. 190.
[92] GELLIUS, in SOLIN., I. 7.7, M.
[93] STRABO, after having narrated the legend of Herakles and Evander, says (V. 3.3, p. 230 C): καὶ ὅ γε Κοίλιος, ὁ τῶν Ῥωμαίων συγγραφεύς, τοῦτο τίτεθαι σημεῖον τοῦ Ἑλληνικοῦ εἶναι κτίσμα τὴν Ῥώμην, τὸ παρ' αὐτῇ τὴν πάτριον θυσίαν Ἑλληνικὴν εἶναι τῷ Ἡρακλεῖ.
[94] See my paper on *Elementi Sicelioti nella più antica Storia di Roma.*
[95] The fact that the principal feast of the Palatine Palatuar was connected

at one time with the youth Pallas (POLYB., in DION. HAL., I. 32; cf. also the version in Vergil), and at others with the nymph Pales (SERV., *ad Aen.*, II. 351), proves that there must have existed some doubt as to the sex of the divinity which they invoked with the formula *sive mas sive femina*. The fact that Lucilius (fr. 30.128, Müll.) mentions the nymph *Pallantina* rather than *Palatina* causes us to believe that he, too, had in mind one of the two well-known myths.

[96] PLINY, *N.H.*, XXXIV. 33.
[97] OVID, *Fasti*, III. 339 sqq.
[98] MACROB., I. 7.34, 35.
[99] VARRO, in MACROB., I. 7.28; DION. HAL., I. 38.
[100] Accordingly, the myth of the altar of Saturn, dedicated by Hercules and spoken of, among others, by EUXENUS (in DION. HAL., I. 34), acquires a new signification.
[101] CIC., *pro Balbo*, 24.55.
[102] OVID, *Fasti*, III. 55 sqq.
[103] PROP., V. 1.55 sqq.

NOTES TO CHAPTER V

THE MAID TARPEIA

[1] For the connection of the myth of Tarpeia with other Roman legends, see my *Storia di Roma*, I. 1, pp. 268 sqq. (Torino, Clausen, 1898).
[2] This is the version given in LIVY, I. 11.5. sqq.
[3] These authors flourished at the end of the third, and the beginning of the second century B. C. See *Hist. Rom. Frag.*, pp. 6, 31 sq.
[4] FAB. and CINC., in DION. HAL., II. 38 sqq.
[5] For example, in DION. HAL., IV. 7, in regard to the Tarquins.
[6] Lived in the time of Augustus. CALP. PISO, in DION. HAL., II. 38 sqq.
[7] DION. HAL., II. 40.
[8] LIVY, I. 11.9: *sunt qui eam ex pacto tradendi quod in sinistris manibus esset derecto arma petisse dicant, et fraude visam agere sua ipsam peremptam mercede.* This is precisely the opinion of CALPURNIUS PISO, who, moreover, is directly quoted by LIVY in other passages: I. 55.7; II. 32.3; IX. 44.3; X. 9.12; cf. FLOR., I. 1.12: *dolose puella pretium rei quae gerebant in sinistris petiverat, dubium clipeos an armillas.*
[9] See the coins of P. Petronius Turpilianus, of the age of Augustus. BABELON, *Monn. d. l. Rép. rom.*, II. p. 301; and of L. Titurius, *op. cit.*, II. p. 498, nn. 4 sqq.
[10] PROP., V. 4, verse 32: *et formosa oculis arma Sabina meis*, might give ground for the supposition that the poet had in mind also that version which made Tarpeia desirous of the rich arms. But the verse is to be explained like the preceding, *obstupuit regis facie et regalibus armis*. Tatius simply appeared still more handsome to Tarpeia because of his splendid weapons.
[11] NIEBUHR, *Röm. Geschichte*, I. p. 255 = p. 188; Isler, n. 632. SCHWEGLER, *Röm. Geschichte*, I. (ed. 2), p. 485, n. 10.
[12] PLUT., *Röm.*, 17.11. Concerning Antigonus, see SUSEMIHL, *Geschichte der griech. Litt. in d. Alexandrinerzeit*, I. 640, n. 628.
[13] SIMYL., in PLUT., *Rom.*, 17.13 sqq. Unfortunately, we cannot completely and clearly understand how Simylos pictured the story to himself, Plutarch quoting only the beginning and the end of his version.
[14] PLUT., *Rom.*, 17: ἀπίθανοι μέν εἰσιν οἱ Τατίου θυγατέρα τοῦ ἡγεμόνος τῶν Σαβίνων οὖσαν αὐτὴν κ τ.λ. . . . Σιμύλος δ' ὁ ποιητὴς καὶ παντάπασι ληρεῖ.
[15] FESTUS, s. v. [*Sa*]*xum Tarpeium*, p. 343, M.
[16] VAL. MAX., I. 1.13.
[17] VARRO, *L.L.*, V. 148; LIVY, VII. 6. The confusion between 445 and 362 B. C. was probably caused by the fact that a Genucius was consul in 362, and also in 445, in which year he had as colleague a certain Curtius.
[18] POLYAEN., VIII. 25.1.
[19] FEST., s. v. *Tarpeiae*, p. 363; PAUL., s. v. *Pandana Porta*, p. 220, M; ARNOB., *adv. nat.*, IV. 3, p. 128; cf. VARRO, *L.L.*, V. 42; SOL., 1.13, p. 8, M. The Porta Pandana forms one of the most confused questions of ancient Roman topography.
[20] CLEITOPH., in STOB., *Flor.*, X. 71, and in [PLUT.], *Par. Min.*, 15. Brennus is the warrior at Ephesus too; the name of the maiden who becomes enamored of him and who was buried beneath the weight of Gallic gold is,

however, not mentioned. Those acquainted with the Pseudo-Plutarch know that, at times, the Greek stories are but imitations of legends already attributed to the Romans.

[21] SCHWEGLER, *Röm. Geschichte*, I. (ed. 2), p. 487, although not at all disposed to give weight to the unofficial tradition, is forced to say: *Dieser Zug der Sage stammte ohne Zweifel aus der gallischen Belagerung des Capitols.* However, instead of believing in the existence of a more primitive form of the legend, — a form which would refer Tarpeia to the Gallic age, — he is inclined to believe in the fusion of two different and distinct legends. In this case it did not occur to him that the *armillae* befit not only the Gauls, but also the Samnites who, in 310 and 293 B. C. fought with shields, weapons and dress that were resplendent with gold and silver (LIVY, IX. 40; X. 39). The gold of the Samnites was famous (PLUT., *Cat. Maior*, 2.2). In regard to the Sabines proper, Plutarch relates that, according to Fabius Pictor (in STRABO, V. p. 228, C), the Romans became acquainted with wealth only after the conquest of that race, — that is to say, towards the end of the fourth century and in the time of Curius Dentatus (290 B. C.). The use of *armillae* among the ancient Romans was not unknown. Indeed, while the *torques* (even when made of gold), was conceded to the allies, the *armillae* were reserved to the citizens. (PLIN., *N.H.*, XXXIII. 37.) The use of jewelled rings, on the other hand, can in no wise be attributed to the Gauls. The custom was a Greek one (PLIN., *N.H.*, *ib.* 10; cf. XXXVII. 3 sqq.), and found its way into Rome only at a very late period. It was natural, instead, to suppose the Sabines to be thus adorned, who, owing to their relations with the Italiots (above all, with Tarentum), were more familiar with Greek customs.

[22] DION. HAL., II. 66; PLUT., *Numa*, 11; SOL., I. 21, p. 10, M.

[23] LIVY, I. 33.2; DION. HAL., II. 50; PLUT., *Rom.*, 20.8; SOL., I. 21, p. 10, M.

[24] DION. HAL., II. 65. In like manner the temple of Fides, which, according to the generally accepted tradition, was dedicated by Numa (LIVY, I. 21.4; DION. HAL., II. 75; PLUT., *Numa*, 16), was, according to others, founded by Aeneas. (AGATH. CYZIC., in FEST., s. v. *Romam*, p. 269).

[25] LIVY, VI. 20.13: *cum domus eius (i.e. M. Manlius Capitolinus) fuisset ubi nunc aedes atque officina Monetae est.* SOL., I. 21, p. 10: *ceteri reges, quibus locis habitaverint, dicemus. Tatius in arce, ubi nunc est aedes Iunonis Monetae.* For the worthlessness of the story of Marcus Manlius, defender of the Capitol, see MOMMSEN, *Röm. Forschungen*, II. 179 sqq., and my *Storia di Roma*, I. 2, p. 378.

[26] LIVY, I. 24.1, after having said that the truth is uncertain, declares his preference for the version that the Romans were the Horatii, because this was the story told by the majority of authors, *plures tamen invenio*. This was a very singular criterion, and does not agree with the fact that Livy, when in doubt, usually followed the more ancient sources. It is clear that even the best sources were uncertain upon the question.

[27] Titus Tatius is particularly indicated on another coin of L. Titurius. BABELON, *op. cit.*, II. p. 497, no. 1.

[28] I am aware that this standard of judgment did not seem a just one to SCHWEGLER, *Röm. Geschichte*, I. (ed. 2) p. 485, and that it was not accepted by MOMMSEN, — for example, in regard to the legend of Remus, *Hermes*, XVI. p. 23, no. 4. Nevertheless, I believe that I have already proved its efficacy elsewhere, and note with pleasure that C. TRIEBER (in his article on the legend of Romulus, *Rhein. Mus.*, 43 (1888), pp. 369 sq.) adopts a similar method.

[29] The stories of Medea, of Ariadne and of Amphiaraus are well known; for that of Scilla see [APOLL.,] III. 15.82; PROP., V. 4.39; PAUS., II. 34.7; of Arne, OVID, *Met.*, VII. 465 sq.

[30] For the Acrocorinthus and the widow Nicea, who was deceived by the wedding of Demetrius, see PLUT., *Arat.*, 17; for the woman who brought about the capture of Tarentum, LIVY, XXVII. 15; PLUT., *Fab.*, 21. Likewise, Ira was captured through a woman, PAUS., IV. 20.9 sqq.; a similar intrigue delivered Sestus into the hands of the Abydeni, POLYAEN., I. 37; and the love of a Spartan for the wife of Epaminondas aided the Thebans in recovering Cadmea, according to the isolated account in POLYAEN., II. 3.1, in which, among other things, the name of Phebiades seems corrupt. Also JUSTINUS, XXIII. 1.12, speaks of the castle which Bruttia surrendered to the Bruttii, — but this seems to be a legend.

[31] PROP., V. 4.39. This has already been observed by NIEBUHR, and by A. G. SCHLEGEL, in SCHWEGLER, *ll. cc.*

[32] This, perhaps (notwithstanding the mutilated condition of the text), may have been the version which connected the name of L. Tarpeius with the Saxum Tarpeium. See FESTUS, s. v. p. 343, with the supplements of C. O. MÜLLER.

[33] APP., *De reg.*, 4: Κελεύσαντος δὲ Τατίου τὸν χρυσὸν ἐς τὴν παῖδα ἐλίθαζον, ἔστε τιτρωσκομένη κατεχώσθη. According to SIMYLOS, instead, the Gauls adorned the corpse of Tarpeia with their *armillae*.

[34] PLUT., *Rom.*, 17 seq.

[35] I have given, in general, the tradition of the Naxian historians. This story, too, was given many different versions. According to some, Polycrita, having been made a prisoner, had become the spouse of Diognetus. According to others (among whom Aristotle), Diognetus saw her in a temple. The manner of death ascribed to her must have seemed but little natural to Aristotle, who, instead, related that she died of joy. According to some versions, Diognetus was killed; according to others, his life was saved by Polycrita. (PARTH., *Erot.*, 9, 18; PLUT., *De mul. virt.*, 17; GELL., *N. A.*, III. 15; POLYAEN., VIII. 36.) Such differences are to be found in the legend of Tarpeia also. Thus, for example, while the majority said that she had gone outside the walls for the purpose of drawing water (as a vestal), others (as DIONYSIUS, II. 38), asserted that Tarpeia saw Tatius from the summit of the citadel; while DIO CASSIUS (fr. 4.12, Melber) affirmed that, having been made prisoner, she was conducted into the presence of Tatius.

[36] PARTH., *Erot.*, 21. Parthenius refers to the poet who sang the κτίσις of Lesbos, and quotes some verses that may, in part, be compared to those of Propertius, *l. c.* This unknown poet is undoubtedly (according to MÜLLER, *F.H.G.*, IV. p. 314) the celebrated Apollonius Rhodius, author of other κτίσεις (cf. SUSEMIHL, *op. cit.*, I. pp. 392, 900). One may think of others also, such as THEOLYTUS of Methymna, author of ὧροι Λεσβίων. (ATHEN. XI. p. 470 b; cf. MÜLL., *op. cit.*, p. 515.)

[37] That the Greeks possessed many similar legends is proved by the story of Mandrolytos, who, through love for Leukofrie, betrayed the city; and of Nanis, who betrayed the city of Sardeis and her father Croesus in the hope of becoming the wife of Leukofrie. (PARTH., *Erot.*, 5, 22.)

PAULUS DIACONUS (*Hist. Langob.*, IV. 37) narrates a similar story. At the siege of Forumiuli by the Avari, their leader rode round the citadel, and *hunc Romilda* (the wife of the prince) *de muris prospiciens, cum eum cerneret iuvenili aetate florentem, meretrix nefaria, concupivit eique mox per nuntium mandavit ut si eam in matrimonium sumeret ipsa eidem civitatem cum omnibus qui aderant traderet.* The leader of the Avari promised to wed her; but, when the city was captured, *nocte una quasi in matrimonio habuit, novissime vero duodecim Avaribus tradidit,* and ended by having her impaled, saying, *Talem te dignum est maritum habere.* The Longobardian chronicler closes with the words: *Igitur dira proditrix patriae tali exitio periit.* Even this episode, which is to be joined with various other events of legendary character, seems to be an imitation of the myth of Tarpeia. Soon after, Paulus Diaconus, in endeavoring to fix the origin of the story, relates another one of a wolf, which appears to be an imitation of the *ver italicum*.

We see traces of the tale of Tarpeia also in the legend of Clovis who, with bracelets of counterfeit gold, gained the affections of Bagnacarius.

Paulus was well acquainted with German as well as with Roman affairs. Whether he had in mind, not Roman legends, but those Germanic sagas with which he begins his history, and which, in such case, would be the origin of these stories, — I leave to those who 'like Prof. Raina) make a special study of this author and his age.

[38] *Chron.*, *a.* 354, p. 113, FRICK.

[39] FEST., p. 363, M. *Tarpeiae esse effigiem ita appellari putant quidam in aede Iovis Metellina, eius videlicet in memoriam virginis, quae pacta a Sabinis hostibus ea, quae in sinistris manibus haberent, ut sibi darent, intromiserit eos cum regi Tatio, qui postea in pace facienda caverit a Romulo, ut ea Sabinis semper pateret.*

[40] PLUT., *Rom.*, 18: Τῆς μέντοι Ταρπηίας ἐκεῖ ταφείσης ὁ λόφος ὠνομάζετο Ταρπήϊος, ἄχρι οὗ Ταρχυνίου βασιλέως Διὶ τὸν τόπον καθιεροῦντος ἅμα τε τὰ λείψανα μετηνέχθη καὶ τοὔνομα τῆς Ταρπηίας ἐξέλιπε. *Numa*, 7; cf. preceding note, FESTUS, s. v. [*Sa*]*xum Tarpeium*, p. 343; VARRO, *L.L.*, V. 41; DION. HAL., III. 69; IV. 60. The Capitoline games established by Romulus were called also *Tarpeii*, according to CALPURNIUS PISO, in TERTULL., *De spect.*, 5. = fr. 7.* P.

[41] Compare the Latin *quis* and the Umbro-Oscan *pis*, *Papius* = *Paquius*, etc.

[42] Tarpeia is expressly called a Vestal by VARRO, *L.L.*, V. 41; PROP., V. 4.18 sqq., and is considered as such also by those authors who say that she went outside the walls to draw the water (LIVY, *l. c.*; VAL. MAX., IX. 6.1; [AUREL., VICT.] *De vir. ill.*, II. 6; DIO CASSIUS, fr. 4.12, Melber). Finally, she is called Vestal also in the Chronographus of the year 354, *l. c.* SANTARELLI (*Rivista di Filologia Class.*, XXXI. 1903) has absolutely no arguments to prove that the conception of Tarpeia as a vestal is a recent one, and that it is not earlier than Varro.

Whosoever will duly consider the question will see that, after all, the particular of Tarpeia's going outside the walls to draw water is but a variant of the story of the Vestal Ilia. For, also the latter was rendered mother (of the Twins) while going forth to draw water. (See DION. HAL., I. 77.) The legend which makes Tarpeia a Vestal, seems to be in a certain relation to that according to which Tarpeia saw Tatius ἀπὸ τοῦ μετεώρου (DION. HAL., II. 38), that is to say, from the Capitol. This last element is, perhaps, borrowed from some Greek legend, for in a like manner do Peisidike and Scilla see Achilles and Minos from the summit of the citadels which they betray.

[43] PLUT., *Publ.*, 8, refers this Vestal Tarquinia to a period later than the expulsion of the Tarquins, in spite of the fact that he little believes in her actual existence (καὶ ταῦτα μὲν οὕτω γενέσθαι μυθολογοῦσι). PLINY, *N.H.*, XXXIV. 25 (who draws upon the Annales), calls her *Taracia Gaia sive Fufetia*. The name *Taracius* is, perhaps, in the same ratio to *Tarquinius* as *Tarquinia* is to *Tarracina* (cf. PLUT., *Quaest. Rom.*, 30; GELL., *N.A.*, VII. 7). Likewise Taracia was confused with a certain Fufetia, just as Tanaquil (wife of Tarquinius Priscus) was confused with a Gaia Caecilia (VARRO, in PLIN., VIII. 194; FEST., s. v. *Praedia*, p. 238, M) and also with a Gegania (DION. HAL., IV. 7). This fact proves that she is connected with the myth, and that the *Annales* cited by Pliny, perhaps the *Annales Maximi*, were wrong also in this case.

[44] PLUT., *Numa*, 10. The first four Vestals were Gegania, Verenia, Canuleia and Tarpeia. Gegania is surely the one whom certain authors, quoted

but not mentioned by DIONYSIUS (IV. 7), made the wife of Tarquinius Priscus in place of Tanaquil (see preceding note). About her, however, Dionysius declares οὐδεμίαν παρειλήφαμεν ἱστορίαν. Compare PLUT., *De fort. Rom.*, 10. For the number 4 of Vestals, DION. HAL., II. 67.

[45] PLUT., *Rom.*, 17.4, who believes true the official version of the treachery of Tarpeia, thinks those to be in error who believed that Tarpeia, and not her father Tarpeius, was the guardian of the Capitol; and shortly later he says, on the authority of Juba and of Sulpicius Galba, that also Tarpeius was punished by Romulus.

[46] See MOMMSEN, *Die echte und die falsche Acca Larentia*, in *Röm. Forschungen*, II, pp. 1 sqq. Plutarch gives, one after the other, the stories of two persons called Acca Larentia, believing them to be entirely distinct and belonging to different ages (*Rom.*, 4 sq.; *Quaest. Rom.*, 35). In the same manner he speaks of two, or rather, of three *Tarpeiae*, as of persons living in different ages.

[47] This has been remarked several times, for example by PRELLER-JORDAN, *Röm. Mythol.*, II. p. 351, where (in n. 1) there is reference to a dissertation by L. KRAHNER, *Die Sage von der Tarpeia* (Friedland, 1858). This last I have not been able to procure.

Among the various examples of traitors hurled from the Tarpeian Rock (in addition to the escaped hostages of the Tarentum and of Thurii, LIVY, XXV. 7.14, 212 B. C.) there may be cited that of the traitorous slave Sulpicius. This historic case can, in a certain way, be compared with the legendary one of Tarpeia. LIVY, *Ep.*, 77; PLUT., *Sylla*, 10.

[48] FAB., and CINC., in DION. HAL., II. 39.

[49] From this point of view it is logical for the chronographus of 354 (*l. c.*) to represent Tarpeia as buried alive by Tatius.

[50] To believe with SANTINELLI, *l. c.*, that Propertius has invented this tradition, is not to understand the historical poetry of Propertius, nor the fundamental character of Roman legends.

[51] That Piso, contemporaneous with C. Gracchus, was acquainted with the Greek sources of ancient Roman history is not proved merely by his etymology of the word *Italia* from *vituli* (in VARRO, *R.R.*, II. 1.9). This had already been seen by Hellanicus and then by Timaeus. It is proved, rather, by the mention of the god Lycoreus in connection with the *asylum* of Romulus. (SERV., *ad Aen.*, II. 761.) It is clearly evident that, had Piso admitted the element of love, his legend of Tarpeia would have been very much similar to that of Polycrita given above.

[52] LIVY, I. 11.7: *accepti obrutam armis necavere, seu ut vi capta potius arx videretur, seu prodendi exempli causa, ne quid usquam fidum proditori esset.* PLUTARCH, too (*Rom.*, 17.7) makes similar considerations upon the reward which treachery deserves. PROP., V. 4.89: *neque enim sceleri dedit hostis honorem.* And, finally, it is natural for Dionysius in this case to give merely a long and dry narrative of the event.

NOTES TO CHAPTER VI

THE SAXUM TARPEIUM

[1] See the authors cited by BECKER, *Handbuch d. röm. Alterth.*, I. p. 411. It is hardly necessary to observe that the epithet *sub Tarpeio* as applied to a mediæval church might be accounted for both by the *Saxum Tarpeium* and by the *templum Iovis Tarpeii*. It results from the texts that the cult of Jupiter Tarpeius, which preceded that of Jupiter Optimus Maximus Capitolinus, continued throughout the Empire.

[2] DUREAU DE LA MALLE, *Mémoires d. l'Acad.*, 1819.

[3] JORDAN, *Topogr. d. Stadt Rom*, I. 2, p. 130; GILBERT, *Geschichte und Topographie d. Stadt Rom*, II. pp. 426, 453; RICHTER, *Beiträge zur röm. Topographie*, Berlin, 1903, p. 30; HUELSEN, *Formae urbis Romae antiquae*, tab. I. III.

[4] DION. HAL., VII. 35: ἐπὶ τὸν ὑπερκείμενον τῆς ἀγορᾶς λόφον. And VIII. 78: ἐπὶ τὸν ὑπερκείμενον τῆς ἀγορᾶς κρημνόν, ἁπάντων ὁρώντων ἔρριψαν κατὰ τῆς πέτρας

[5] GILBERT, *op. cit.*, p. 426, n. 1, draws an argument in favor of his hypothesis from VARRO, *L.L.*, V. 41 : *e quis Capitolinus dictus quod hic, cum fundamenta foderentur aedis Iovis, caput humanum dicitur inventum. hic mons ante Tarpeius dictus a virgine Vestale Tarpeia.* He also draws upon DIONYSIUS, IV. 60 sq., in which it is stated that the hill upon which the temple of Jupiter Capitolinus was erected was called Tarpeius. But what is there in these passages which precludes that also that part of the Capitoline on which the *arx* was situated was called Tarpeius? Marcus Manlius was called *Capitolinus* because he lived on the Capitolium. (See MOMMSEN, *Röm. Forschungen*, II. pp. 179 sqq.) And yet, his home was on the *arx*. The same extension of meaning, therefore, must have held for the term *Tarpeius*; (cf. *Tarpeiae arces*, OVID, *Fasti*, I. 79).

[6] *deae Virgini (sic) Caelestis praesentissimo numini loci montis Tarpei, Not. d. Scavi*, 1892, p. 407. The *Virgo Caelestis*, who is addressed as the presiding deity of the *mons Tarpeius*, is, as Gatti clearly saw (*Atti d. Accad. Pontif. d. nuovi Lincei*, 1896, pp. 331 sqq.), a Carthaginian divinity which was imported to Rome, and to which, in time, there succeeded the worship of *S. Maria in Ara Coeli*.

[7] TAC., *Hist.*, III. 71 : *tum diversos Capitolii aditus invadunt iuxta lucum asyli et qua Tarpeia rupes centum gradibus aditur.*

[8] FEST., p. 363, M : *Tarquitias scalas, quas res Tarquinius Superbus fecerit, abominandi eius nominis gratia ita appellatas esse ait volgo existimari.* Modern students of Roman topography have not, to my knowledge, made use of this passage. Moreover, I do not find mention of these *scalae Tarquitiae*, either in the very extensive index of GILBERT, or in the *nomenclator* of HUELSEN.

[9] FEST., p. 340, M : *sepultum m]orte moroque † cum ait . . . d]e L. Terentio, Tusci vici [magistro, significat,] vivum de saxo Tarpeio [desiluisse cum eo v]enisset commissatum, quod [vini vi facere es]set coactus.* As has already been noted, there is mention of a *Terentius Tuscivicanus* in LIVY, XLV. 17.4, for the year 167 B. C.

[10] PROPERTIUS, V. 1.7, says : *Tarpeiusque pater nuda de rupe tonabat.* SILIUS ITALICUS, III. 623 : *aurea Tarpeia ponet Capitolia rupe ;* and LUCAN,

III. 154, reads: *tunc rupes Tarpeia sonat;* (cf. CLAUD., XXVIII. 44 sq.). These statements are clearly understood, by keeping in mind the more ancient name of the Capitolinus, — that is (as the ancients themselves affirmed), *mons Tarpeius;* (cf. n. 5). The claim of some modern topographers, — namely, that the epithet *Tarpeius* is the invention of an ancient scholar, — is without foundation. In the first place, we find the expression *ludi Tarpeii* employed by the annalist CALPURNIUS PISO, in TERTULL., *De Spect.*, 5. Moreover, there is the still more remarkable fact that ULPIAN, 22.6, mentions *Iovis Tarpeius* among those divinities which could be appointed as heirs. Surely Ulpian did not employ the term *Tarpeius* in place of *Capitolinus* for the sake of mere antiquarian erudition. This passage, instead, proves that the cult of Jupiter Tarpeius preceded that of Jupiter Capitolinus. The latter I believe to have been established in the time of Camillus. For the relations between *Tarpeius* and *Tarquinius* see my *Storia di Roma*, I. 1, pp. 370 sqq.; I. 2, pp. 763 sqq.

I shall, at some future time, discuss the value of the passage from Ulpian in establishing the chronology of the testamentary powers in Rome.

[11] It has been often emphasized by JORDAN (*op. cit.*, I. 2, p. 127, n. 125), that the technical designation was *Saxum Tarpeium. Rupes* and *Saxum* were interchangeable terms. VARRO, *L.L.*, V. 41; TAC., *Hist.*, III. 71.

[12] See n. 10. We obtain the same results from FESTUS, p. 363 : *Tarpeiae esse effigiem ita appellari putant quidam in aede Iovis Metellina* †, *eius videlicet in memoriam virginis, quae pacta a Sabinis hostibus ea, quae in sinistris manibus haberent, ut sibi darent, intromiserit eos cum rege Tatio, qui postea in pace facienda caverit a Romulo, ut ea Sabinis semper pateret.*

In the last words there is a reference to the *Porta Pandana*, VARRO, *L.L.*, V.42; PAUL., *ep. Fest.*, p. 220, M. This gate figures in the legends of the Sabine Appius Herdonius (DION. HAL., X. 14) and of the Gauls who besieged the Capitoline (POYLAEN., VIII. 25). The fact that the *Porta Pandana* was originally called *Saturnia* (VARRO, *l. c.;* cf. SOL., I. 13, M), and that it was not distant from the *porta Carmentalis* (DION. HAL., *l. c.*), would not, in itself, prove that Tarpeia lived on the southern portion of the Capitoline, — that is, where later rose the temple of Jupiter. It would prove merely that the only gate leading to the *arx* which she betrayed was originally situated in the region where the temple of Saturn was later erected. Indeed, even in this story there seem to be traces (as I have elsewhere pointed out) of two different versions regarding the burial-place of Tarpeia.

[13] FESTUS, p. 343, M: *Sa*]*xum Tarpeium appel*[*latam aiunt partem mon*]*tis, qui ob sepultam Ta*[*rpeiam ibi virginem quae*] *eum montem Sabinis* [*prodere pacta erat, ita*] *nominatus est. vel* [*ab eo, quod, quidam nomine*] *L. Tarpeius Romulo* [*regi cum propter rap*]*tas virgines adversa*[*retur, in ea parte, qua sa*]*xum est, de noxio poena* [*sumpta est. Quapropter*] *noluerunt funestum locum* [*cum altera parte*] *Capitoli coniungi.* JORDAN (who is followed by GILBERT and HUELSEN) supposes that the *Saxum Tarpeium* was in the vicinity of the Capitolium. He therefore supplies [*cum parte sacra*] *Capitoli coniungi*. I suspect that in place of the *quidam nomine* substituted by Mueller, one should supply *praefectus arci.* Nor is there any hindrance in the fact that the father of Tarpeia is called Spurius (LIVY, I. 11.6). Such confusion is common, not only in regard to legendary persons, but also, as we see from the *Fasti*, in regard to the *praenomina* of the earliest consuls.

[14] LIVY, VI. 20.12: *locusque idem in uno homine et eximiae gloriae monumentum et poenae ultimae fuit.*

[15] CIC., *de domo*, 38, 101 : *M. Manlius cum ab ascensu Capitoli Gallorum impetum reppulisset.*

[16] The words of Livy are almost literally translated by PLUTARCH, *Cam.*, 36.8, who actually cites Livy as one of the sources for that life (see 6). In ZONARAS it is said that Manlius was hurled from the identical precipice

from which he had repelled the Gauls. But Zonaras, in respect to this story of the Manlian plot, follows an entirely different version (cf. CASS. DIO, fr. 25.10, p. 82, Boiss.). Therefore it is not clear whether he alludes to the region of the *arx* or to that of the *Capitolium*.

[17] LIVY, V. 47.1: *dum haec Veiis agebantur, interim arx Romae Capitoliumque in ingenti periculo fuit.*

[18] LIVY, VI. 20.13: *cum domus eius fuisset ubi nunc aedes atque officina Monetae est;* V. 47.8: *ad aedes eius (i. e., of Manlius), quae in arce erant;* VII. 28.5: *locus in arce destinatus (i. e., the temple of Juno Moneta), quae area aedium M. Manli Capitolini fuerat;* cf. CIC., *de domo*, 38.101.

[19] The bad custodian of the *ad Carmentis Saxum* was (according to LIVY, V. 47.10) precipitated *de saxo*. In the version of DIODORUS (XIV. 116.) it is said that, since no one was bold enough to make front against the attacking Gauls, Manlius came to the rescue: ἐκβοηθήσας ἐπὶ τὸν τόπον.

[20] Compare LIVY, VI. 20.14, with CASS. DIO, fr. 26.1, p. 83, Boiss. The restriction of 384 B. C. in regard to dwelling on the Capitolium is contradictory to legend itself, which assumes that that place had been consecrated by King Tarquinius.

[21] PLUT., *Rom.*, 18.1: τὰ λείψανα μετηνέχθη.

[22] The version which speaks of Tarpeius, father of the traitorous Tarpeia, is recorded by both JUBA and SULPICIUS GALBA, in PLUT., *Rom.*, 17.10. We do not know the exact relation between this version and the one preserved by FESTUS, p. 343, M: *vel [ab eo, quod, quidam nomine?] L. Tarpeius Romulo [regi cum propter rap]tas virgines adversa[retur, in ea parte, qua sa]xum est, de noxio poena [sumpta est.* Compare n. 13.

MOMMSEN, *Röm. Strafrecht*, p. 993, n. 6, believes that in this version there is reference to an illegal procedure on the part of Romulus, who caused various citizens to be hurled from the rock. (See DION. HAL., II. 56.) Nevertheless, it must be observed that in the same passage Dionysius refers to Roman citizens who were punished for having preyed on neighboring lands.

[23] PLUT., *Rom.*, 20.9; SOL., I. 21, M.

[24] See preceding chapter; also, my *Storia di Roma*, I. 1, pp. 274 sqq.

[25] LIVY, I. 11; PROP., V. 4.1. The element of the fountain is lacking in the version of DIONYSIUS, II. 38, and also in the shorter account of PLUTARCH, *Rom.*, 17.

[26] PROP., V. 4.11 sqq.

[27] DION. HAL., II. 38: μεταξὺ τοῦ τε Κυρινίου καὶ τοῦ Καπιτωλίου τίθησιν ἐν τῷ πεδίῳ τὸν χάρακα.

[28] That the Tullianum was, originally, a reservoir, or, in other words, the public fountain, is not unreasonably maintained by JORDAN, *op. cit.*, I. 1, p. 453. For the *Porta Fontinalis* see LIVY, XXXV. 10.12.

[29] It is clearly stated in the *Epitome* of FESTUS, p. 117, M., that from the quarries of the *Lautumiae* had been *excisi lapides ad exstruendam urbem*. Compare VARRO, *L.L.*, V. 151.

[30] TAC., *Hist.*, III. 71.

[31] FAB. PICT., and CINC. ALIM., in DION. HAL., II. 38 sqq.

[32] CALP. PISO, in DION. HAL., II. 39 sq.

[33] I have discussed this question in the preceding chapter.

[34] DION. HAL., VII. 35, inde PLUT., *Coriol.*, 18.

[35] DION. HAL., VIII. 78.

[36] VARRO, in GELLIUS, *N.A.*, XVII. 21.24; LIVY, VI. 20.12.

[37] For the various accounts of the death of Spurius Cassius, see LIVY, II. 41; DION. HAL., VIII. 79; of M. Manlius, see CORNEL. NEP., in GELL., *l. c.*; cf. my *Storia di Roma*, I. 1, pp. 2, 504 sqq.

[38] MOMMSEN (*Röm. Strafrecht*, p. 933, n. 6) rightly deduces from DIONYSIUS (XI. 6) that the power of death from the Tarpeian rock was an

attribute of the tribunes of the people even under the Empire. I doubt, however, if he is right in characterizing the execution of L. Tarpeius as an example of abuse of power by Romulus. (FESTUS, p. 343.) This passage is too mutilated to permit of drawing positive conclusions. If I am not mistaken, the story of Lucius Tarpeius might have referred to an hypothetical case of *imminutae maiestatis*. The same may be said of the slave who succeeded in becoming praetor in the year 39 B. C.

[39] LIVY, XXIV. 20.7.
[40] LIVY, XXV. 7.14.
[41] LIVY, *Ep.*, LXXVII.; VAL. MAX., VI. 5.7; PLUT., *Sylla*, 10.
[42] APP., *B.C.*, III. 3. In this class belong the more or less authentic cases recorded by DIONYSIUS. The account in XI. 6, refers to an usurpation by the decemvirs of the powers of the tribunes of the people.

It is not quite so easy a matter to decide the case of the tribune Atinius, who, in 131 B. C., ordered the censor Q. Metellus to be hurled from the rock. (CIC., *de domo*, 47.123; LIVY, *Ep.*, LIX.; PLINY, *N.H.*, VII. 143.) The versions which give as the motives of Atinius that *in senatu legendo praeteritus erat*, or that Metellus *e senatu eicerat*, may very well be explained by the *crimen imminutae maiestatis tribuniciae* (cf. MOMMSEN, *Röm. Strafrecht*, p. 538, n. 1), and also by the *sacratio* of the possessions of Metellus. Indeed (as was already seen) this fact could be placed in relation with the *plebiscitum Atinium*, which confirmed the right of the tribunes to form part of the senate. Other arguments, however, have caused some scholars (WILLEMS, *Le Sénat d. l. Républ. rom.*, I. 2, pp. 689 sqq., and MOMMSEN, *Röm. Staatsrecht*, III. p. 862, n. 1) to assign the plebiscitum to a period later than 123 B. C. and earlier than 102 B. C. A state crime (if not one *imminutae maiestatis tribuniciae*) must have been the cause or the pretext for an execution from the Tarpeian rock in the year 84 B. C. In that year Popilius Laenas, the tribune, meted out such death to Sextus Lucilius, the tribune of the preceding year. See LIVY, *Ep.*, LXXX.; VELL., II. 24; PLUT., *Mar.*, 45.

[43] It does not seem to me that Mommsen is right. (*Röm. Strafrecht*, p. 933, n. 1.) Regarding this passage, he says: *Senecas Worte* (*de ira*, I. 16.5) *sind nur exemplificirend*. For the variety of penalties for the crimes of *perduellio* and of *lèse majesté*, see MOMMSEN, *op. cit.*, pp. 590 sqq., 915 sqq.

[44] Tab. VIII. 14, Br. = GELL., *N.A.*, XI. 18.8: *ex ceteris autem manifestis furibus ... servos ... verberibus affici et e saxo praecipitari; ib.*, 23 = GELL., *N.A.*, XX. 1.53: *si nunc quoque ... qui falsum testimonium dixisse convictus esset, e saxo Tarpeio deiiceretur.*

[45] TAC., *Ann.*, II. 32. We cannot determine why L. Pituanius should have been hurled from the Tarpeian rock, whereas P. Marcius was crucified outside the Esquiline gate. (Cf. MOMMSEN, *Röm. Strafrecht*, p. 918, n. 5.) Nor can we establish whether this difference was due to the variety of penalties for the crime of witchcraft (MOMMSEN, *op. cit.*, p. 643), or to the greater or lesser degree of guilt, or to the different social conditions of the two culprits. (See PAUL., *Sent.*, V. 23.15 sqq.)

It is far more difficult to understand why the Spaniard Marius, guilty of incest with his daughter (in reality envied by Tiberius for his extraordinary riches), should have been hurled from the Tarpeian rock. (TAC., *Ann.*, VI. 19.) For, under the Empire, those guilty of such crime were, in general, deported. See PAUL., *Sent.*, II. 26.15; cf. MOMMSEN, *Röm. Strafrecht*, p. 688. The latter justly remarks that there must have been precedents of this kind in the Republican period.

The punishing of incest with death from the *saxum* would be less obscure if it were true that vestal virgins were thus punished. (SEN., *Contr.*, I. 3; QUINT., VII. 8.3 sqq.) But to MOMMSEN (*op. cit.*, p. 928, n. 4) this last appears to be the vain imaginings of rhetoricians. In fact, everything favors such a conclusion, because the story of the punishment of the Vestals in the

Campus Sceleratus is quite contradictory to such an hypothesis. Nevertheless, we should bear in mind a fact to which Mommsen does not here refer, — namely, that on the 13th of February the Vestals made *inferiae* to Tarpeia. (PHILOCAL., *ad diem ;* cf. CALP. PISO, in DION. HAL., II. 40; LYD., *de mens.*, IV. 24; MOMMSEN, *ad CIL.*, I. (ed. 2) p. 309.)

TACITUS (*Ann.*, XII. 8, *ad. a.* 49. A. D.) makes mention of *piacula* performed *apud lucum Dianae* in the time of Claudius, *ex legibus Tulli regis*. MOMMSEN (*Röm. Strafrecht*, p. 913, n. 6) is quite right in affirming that Tacitus refers to Tullus Hostilius and to the lake at Aricia. But I do not think that he ought to be followed further, when he believes that there is reference to expiations made for the death of Horatia, who was slain by her brother. If at all, I should be inclined to think of the *sponsalia* between the cousins, — the sons of the two Siciniae. (DION. HAL., III. 13.)

However, I believe that in Tacitus we are to see one of the many cases of confusion between Tullus Hostilius and Servius Tullius. I think I have proved that Servius Tullius is merely the *servus rex* of Nemi, — the priest of Diana Aricina, whose worship he was supposed to have transported to the Aventine. That expiations for incest should have been offered by the priest of the virgin Diana is most natural. For, it must be remembered that Virbius-Hippolytus fled from the incestuous love of his step-mother. (For one of the Latin forms of the legend, see DOSITHEUS, in PSEUD. PLUT., *parall.*, 34.) In fact, incest appears in the legend of the marriage of the sons of Tarquinius Priscus with the daughter of Tarquinia, wife of Servius Tullius. In other words, we have, in that story, a union between uncles and nieces. To this we must add the killing of the good Tullia and of one of the two Tarquins. LIVY (I. 46.9), in speaking of this wedding, says: *iunguntur nuptiis magis non prohibente Servio quam adprobante*. From the point of view of the law in force during the last centuries of the Republic (cf. TAC., *Ann.*, XII. 6), DIONYSIUS (IV. 30) is more correct. He asserts that Tarquinius Superbus married Tullia against the will of Servius, who did not approve of the marriage, and that he had first performed τὰ προτέλεια τῶν ἀνοσίων γάμων. It remains to be proved whether, according to the ancient Roman law and legend, such *nuptiae* were *nefariae* only on account of the killing of Aruns Tarquinius and of the good Tullia, or also because they had been contracted between uncle and niece.

From this point of view, it is clearly seen that Roman legend (as, also, many Greek myths), reflected the legal and moral conditions of a period anterior to the historic age. In a speech to induce the Senate to recognize as legitimate unions between uncles and nieces, it was observed that *aliis gentibus* they were *solemnia, neque ulla lege prohibita* (TAC., *l. c.*). This fact was brought into relief from a spirit of adulation. But, at bottom, it corresponded with the truth. (In this regard compare the law of Egypt, Macedonia, etc.) LIVY (XX. p. 134, W) affirms: *P. Cloelius patricius primus adversus veterem morem intra septimum cognationis gradum duxit uxorem*. This fragment, indeed, proves that such legal restrictions were already enforced before the third century; it does not prove that they belonged to the earliest Roman law. From some passages, as from ULPIAN, IV. 5, it may be deduced that in regard to marriages there occurred under the Empire an evolution of a non-restrictive tendency. It does not follow, however, that such restrictions (so to speak) were not the fruits of an evolution following a contrary course to that which must have occurred in the first centuries of the Republic. I hope to give the proofs of this statement on another occasion.

I am undecided whether or not I should add that another memory of the Republican period is preserved in the anecdote given by the PSEUDO-PLUTARCH, *Parall.*, 19. Under the name Aristides, he speaks of the maid Medullina who killed her incestuous father upon the altar of Ἀστραπή, — that is, of the goddess of the thunderbolt. We are in complete ignorance as to the location of the βωμὸς τῆς 'Αστραπῆς at Rome. (Compare the goddess *Fulgora*, SEN., in AUG., *De civ. dei*, VI. 10.) It is, however, very characteristic that, according to FESTUS (p. 363, M), there was to be seen an image of Tarpeia *in aede Iovis Mettellina*. Is there any relation between the Medullina of the story given by the Pseudo-Plutarch and the name Metellinus? Is this latter name, in turn, derived from Metellus? The latter opinion is generally accepted. I have elsewhere preferred to place it in relation with Medullinus, the cognomen of the Furii.

[46] MOMMSEN, *Röm. Strafrecht*, pp. 898 sqq.

[47] See my *Storia di Roma*, I. 1, pp. 577 sqq.; 2, pp. 632 sqq. The penalty of the Tarpeian rock could not, originally, have had any connection with the crimes of slaves. A proof of this is to be found in the account of the disturbances of 44 B. C.; the citizens were hurled from the rock by the soldiers of Anthony; the slaves, instead, were crucified. See APPIAN, *B.C.*, III. 1.3.

[48] For this matter I shall refer the reader to the masterly remarks of MOMMSEN, *Röm. Strafrecht*, pp. 940 sqq.; cf. pp. 59 sqq.

[49] It has been often asserted that there is some close topographical connection between the temple of Fides Publica on the Capitolium and the fact that it was from the *arx* that traitors were sent to their death (e. g., JORDAN, *Top. d. Stadt Rom*, I. 2, p. 128). I do not venture to decide the question. It is, however, worthy of note that the temple of Fides Publica on the Capitolium was erected by a certain Atilius, and, in all likelihood, in expiation of a state crime, — that is, of the betrayal of the citadel of Sora. (See my *Storia di Roma*, I. p. 398.)

[50] The first mention of the *Scalae Gemoniae* is found in the story of the execution of M. Claudius, — the author of a shameful peace with the Corsi in 236 B. C. See VAL. MAX., VI. 3.3; cf. VI. 9.13; PLINY, *N.H.*, VIII. 145, *gradus gemitorii*; TAC., *Ann.*, III. 14; VI. 4,31; *Hist.*, III. 74,85; SUET., *Tib.*, 53,61,75; *Vitell.*, 17; CASS. DIO, LVIII. 5. (the passage which fixes the topography, JORDAN, *op. cit.*, I. 2, p. 324).

[51] See above, n. 8.

[52] For the *Lautumiae*, see VARRO, *L.L.*, V. 151; PAUL, *ep. Fest.*, p. 117, M; LIVY, XXVI. 27.3; XXXII. 26.17; XXXVII. 3.8; XXXIX. 44.7. It is generally conceded that they were situated in the vicinity of the *carcer Tullianum*, and on the slopes of the citadel which faced the Forum. PROPERTIUS (V. 4.1) describes the *Tarpeium nemus* and the *lucus* . . . *hederoso conditus antro*, which was *Silvani ramosa domus*, and in which was the source of the fountain of Tarpeia. (Was it the *tullius* of the Tullianum?) We are led, by this passage, to think of the Lautumiae. Indeed, we should recall that vegetation was most abundant in the quarries at Syracuse and at Surrentum.

The mention of the god Silvanus brings to mind the statue of this god, which was situated on the slopes of the Capitolium, and by the side of which grew the *caprificus*. PLINY, *N.H.*, XV. 77.

[53] MOMMSEN, *Röm. Strafrecht*, p. 949: *Die Zwangarbeit ist dem republicanischen Strafrecht unbekannt und unter dem Principat aufgekommen, vielleicht zusammen mit der Deportation im J. 23 durch Tiberius eingeführt worden.* And, after having noted that the penalty *ad metalla* was borrowed from Egypt, he remarks (p. 950, n. 2): *Uebrigens begegnet die Zwangarbeit in den Steinbrüchen auch in früher Zeit in Sicilien und Italien.*

[54] LYD., *De mens.*, IV. 24: πρῶτος γὰρ αὐτὸς ὄργανα ποινῶν καὶ μέταλλα ἐξεῦρεν.

[55] SUID., ed. Berh., II. p. 831, s. v.: Σούπερβος . . . δεσμά τε καὶ μάστιγας κλοιοὺς ξυλίνους καὶ σιδηροῦς, πέδας, ἀλύσεις, μέταλλα καὶ ἐξορίας ἐφευρών. Cf. s. v. Ταρκύνιος, p. 1085, B.

[56] IOH. ANTIOCH., fr. 36, in M. *F.H.G.*, IV. p. 553 (*Exc. d. virt.*, p. 786). Old is the observation of Valerius, — that the words Johannes Antiochenus are to be found in Cedrenus. Those of the chronographus, moreover, are repeated in the so-called *Historia Miscella*, and in ISIDORUS, *Orig.*, IV. end.

[57] CASS. HEM., in SERV., *ad Aen.*, XII. 603 = fr. 15* P; *cum cloacas populum facere coegisset, et ob hanc iniuriam multi se suspendio necarent, iussisse corpora eorum cruci affigi.*

[58] PLINY, *N.H.*, XXXVI. 107: *cum id opus Tarquinius Priscus plebis manibus faceret, essetque labor incertum maior an longior, passim conscita nece Quiritibus taedium fugientibus, novum et inexcogitatum ante posteaque remedium invenit ille rex ut omnium ita defunctorum corpora figeret cruci spectanda simul civibus et feris volucribusque laceranda.*

[59] LIVY, I. 38.5; 56.2; 59.9; DION. HAL., IV. 44. For the usual confusion between the two Tarquins, see my *Storia di Roma*, I. 1, pp. 347 sqq.

[60] LIVY, I. 49.4 sq.: *cognitiones capitalium rerum sine consiliis per se solus exercebat, perque eam causam occidere, in exilium agere, bonis multare poterat.* . . . Compare DION. HAL., IV. 43: τιμωρίαι . . . πικραὶ καὶ ἀπαραίτητοι.

[61] LIVY, I. 59.9: *victores omnium circa populorum, opifices ac lapicidas pro bellatoribus factos.*

[62] CIC., *pro C. Rabirio perd. reo*, 4.13 sqq. In *Phil.*, III. 4.10, he presents a different version, — indeed an entirely contradictory one: *supplicia vero in cives Romanos nulla Tarquinii accepimus.* But it is clearly evident from the contents of the latter passage that Cicero deliberately exaggerates in order to render still more odious the contrast of Anthony with that king.

[63] There are two versions regarding the *duoviri perduellionis*. In one case, the *duoviri* figure in the trial of Horatius; in the second, in the trial of C. Rabirius, which was carried on under the procedures established by Tarquinius. The *duoviri*, therefore, are represented as the creation of two different kings. But MOMMSEN himself admits that the two versions are one and the same thing. (*Röm. Strafrecht*, II. (ed. 2) p. 598, n. 2.) The identical formula, *caput obnube . . . arbore infelici suspende*, is found in the text of LIVY, I. 26.11. In regard to the contradiction that a crime of parricide should have been represented as one of *perduellio*, see MOMMSEN, *Röm. Strafrecht*, pp. 527 sqq.

[64] I have endeavored to explain the origin of this legend in my *Storia di Roma*, I. 1, pp. 297 sqq. I shall shortly have occasion to demonstrate it in still greater detail from its religious and its legal aspects.

The words of LIVY, I. 26.11: *verbera vel intra pomerium, modo inter illa pila et spolia hostium, vel extra pomerium, modo inter sepulcra Curiatorum*, refer to expiatory and funeral sacrifices. The words *vel intra . . . vel extra pomerium* have led MOMMSEN (*Röm. Strafrecht*, p. 913) to affirm that, according to the ancient custom, there was a free choice (on occasion of a crucifixion) of a site either within or without the city limits. But, unless I be greatly mistaken, those words suggest the fact that the legend of the death of Horatia was originally connected with the gate of the Septimontium which was situated at the base of the Velia; and that later, when the boundaries of the city were extended, it was connected with the *porta Collina*. (See my *Storia di Roma*, I. 1, p. 297.) It does not seem to me that those words lend themselves to the generalization for which Mommsen has used them. On the contrary, I believe that for this there is available a passage in TACITUS (*Ann.*, II. 32) in which it is said that P. Marcius was *more prisco* crucified *extra portam Esquilinam*. With this fact is to be connected the very general custom, throughout the classical world, of exhibiting the heads of the condemned on the gates of the town-walls. Recall, for instance, the famous reliefs of the gate at Volterra; see also Chapter XI.

[65] Compare my *Storia di Roma*, I. 1, p. 373; I. 2, pp. 182. sqq.

⁶⁶ Compare *ib.*, I. 1, pp. 350 sqq.

⁶⁷ LIVY, XXXII. 26.17, *et triumviri carceris Lautumiarum intentiorem custodiam habere iussi.* The constant theory of the ancients placed the names *Lautumiae* and *carcer* in close relation with the terms employed at Syracuse. (VARRO, *L.L.*, V. 151; cf. SERV., *ad. Aen.*, III. 500.) This connection is to be explained by the paramount influence of the Syracusan, and in general, of the Siceliot civilization upon the coasts of Latium, particularly after 480 B. C. I have elsewhere given the proofs of this.

⁶⁸ MOMMSEN, in his *Strafrecht*, discusses only those questions which bear the stamp of authenticity. He justly avoids recalling or dwelling upon these earliest legends. But I deem some of these ancient stories worthy of examination, especially if one endeavor to discover the most ancient phase of the Roman penal laws. I shall not tarry in a discussion of the penalty visited upon Mettius Fufetius, inasmuch as such account may be an imitation of a Greek tale. But I do not by any means believe that the story of Turnus Herdonius should be passed over in silence. Ferrini (*Diritto penale romano*, Milano, 1899, p. 244) has justly noted that in this story there are preserved traces of a penalty to be found also in the Teutonic laws, and that the story must be referred to that stage of material imperfection which must have existed in the earliest period of Roman law.

In my opinion there is still another fact which renders the story even more noteworthy, — a fact which, to my knowledge, has not yet been observed. This form of punishment, which LIVY (I. 51.9) styles *novum genus leti*, reappears in LIVY himself (IV. 50.4, 414 B. C.), in regard to the more or less authentic killing of Postumius, *tribunus militaris consulari potestate.* Even this story is not free from serious suspicions. (See my *Storia di Roma*, I. 2, pp. 31 sq.) Nevertheless, it is quite natural that the early annalists of the third and second centuries B. C. should have still made mention of this penalty, — a penalty which, in their time, had but lately been abandoned, but which appeared to Livy altogether new and unusual.

Moreover, in the legend of Turnus Herdonius I would recognize the memory, not of a very ancient and authentic event, but of religious rites connected with the lake and the territory of Aricia, — rites which, though ancient in origin, continued as late as the historic period. Likewise, the rite of the stuffed figures thrown into the Tiber on the 15th of May, gave occasion to the Roman scholars for discovering therein traces of ancient customs. (See FESTUS, p. 334, M.) I have endeavored to prove in my *Storia di Roma* (I. 1, pp. 183.191; II. p. 202) that the legend of Turnus Herdonius is to be connected with the worship of a fountain.

⁶⁹ MOMMSEN, *Röm. Forschungen*, II. pp. 199 sqq.; *Röm. Strafrecht*, p. 551; PERNICE, *Parerga*, VI. in *Zeitschrift der Savigny-Stiftung*, XVII. (1896) p. 186; FERRINI, *Diritto penale romano*, pp. 170 sqq. I propose to examine this question minutely hereafter.

⁷⁰ LYCURG., *in Leocr.*, 125 = TELFY, *Corpus Iuris Attici*, 1032; ANDOC., *De myster.*, 96; cf. PERNICE, *l. c.*, p. 188, n. 3.

⁷¹ XENOPH., *Hier.*, 4.

⁷² See the texts edited by MICHEL, *Recueil d'inscriptions grecques*, for the rule in Ilium (n. 524), Chios (n. 364), and Eresus (n. 358). Compare the commentary to these laws in DARESTE, HAUSOULLIER, RHEINACH, *Recueil des inscript. jurid. grecques*, II. série, fasc. I. pp. 25 sqq.; 160 sqq.

⁷³ PHAN., fr. 14, in M., *F.G.H.*, II. p. 298. From fragment 16 it results that also in the Italiot Heraclea there were laws which rewarded the tyrannicide.

⁷⁴ DION. HAL., VIII 80 ἐπιβαλλομένων δέ τινων καὶ τοὺς παῖδας ἀποκτεῖναι τοῦ Κασσίου, δεινὸν τὸ ἔθος ἔδοξεν εἶναι τῇ βουλῇ καὶ ἀσύμφορον.

⁷⁵ Regarding the transmission of the penalty to the heirs as a fundamental maxim of the penal law of the Roman Republic, and for the exceptions

thereto, consult the material gathered by MOMMSEN, *Röm. Strafrecht*, and by FERRINI, *Diritto penale romano*, p. 33. Compare also SALVIOLI, *Rivista ital. p. l. scienze giuridiche*, II. (1886) pp. 2 sqq.; pp. 173 sqq.

[76] MOMMSEN, *Röm. Strafrecht*, pp. 591. 941.

[77] DIONYSIUS (VIII. 80, cf. n. 65), mentions the *senatus consultum* regarding the sons of Spurius Cassius as differing from the procedure of Sulla against the sons of the proscribed. It appears to me that this story teaches us two things. Firstly, it shows that the sources of Dionysius (as usual) followed the tradition generally accepted in the annals, and endeavored to strengthen with contemporary tendencies the dubious tales of the early history. Secondly, it positively proves that the transmission of the pain of death to the sons existed before 485 B. C. (the year in which Spurius Cassius was killed), and that, according to the annals, it was abolished on that very occasion.

Our lack of certain knowledge regarding the history of Roman law for the period extending from the end of the fifth century B. C. to the Punic Wars, prevents our determining with precision when such abolition was actually made. It will be remembered that the tribunes of the people intervened when the Carthaginian hostages who had been entrusted to the widow of Attillius Regulus were tortured. (DIOD., XXIV. 12.) This event, it is true, is to be referred to international law, and to a class of events of an entirely different legal character. Nevertheless, it offers conclusive proof that Roman customs, even as early as the fourth century, had already become less harsh.

Rome must have traversed a period which is found in the law of all primitive races, or races somewhat backward in the course of civilization. (POST, *Grundriss der ethnologischen Jurisprudenz*, II. p. 325, Oldenburg, 1895; SACHAU, *Muhamedanisches Recht*, p. 844, Berlin, 1897.) The traces of such a period, though feeble and scanty, nevertheless are yet visible in the Athenian law of the fourth century. (See THONISSEN, *Le droit pénal d. l. répubi. Athénienne*, p. 108, Paris, 1875.)

DIONYSIUS, VIII. 80 affirms the superiority of Roman laws to those Greek ones that punished with death even the sons of persons guilty of a state crime. Such statement, however, is parallel to one made by the same author, in which he considers the laws of the Twelve Tables superior to the Hellenic (XI. 44). And this too, notwithstanding the fact that but shortly previous he had declared them an imitation of those of Solon and of other cities of Magna Graecia (X. 57).

Even MOMMSEN (*Röm. Strafrecht*, p. 593), in reproducing the thought of Dionysius, does not duly consider that the Roman superiority represents a very late historic phase and also the fruit of Greek investigation and philosophy. I doubt, too, whether (as Mommsen seems to consider) that passage in CICERO (*de nat.*, III. 38; *de invent.*, II. 144), is an exclusively Roman thought. For Cicero, in criticising the theory that the sins of the father are to be visited upon the sons, the grandsons, and posterity, merely represents a discussion of the various schools of Greek philosophy. Even the extension of the penalty to the confiscation of property, which seemed to Caesar quite unjust, was approved of by Cicero, even granted that he was actuated by political reasons. SENECA (*De ira*, II. 34) complains of such extension; others seem to commend it. The crimes perpetrated during the civil wars, and the excesses of the imperial period prove that, in the Roman conscience, this conception of the transmission of penalties had not been altogether extinguished. Indeed, the events at Rome during the period of the proscriptions vividly recall what had already occurred at Locris and at Syracuse in the time of the second Dionysius and of Hieronymus.

[78] On this question I but partly accept the views of Mommsen. See my *Storia di Roma*, I. 1, Chap. IV.

[79] We learn from FESTUS, p. 290, M, that the *Lacus Servilius* was situated *in principio vici Iugarii, continens basilicae Iuliae*. And we deduce from CICERO (*pro Roscio Am.*, 32.89) and from SENECA (*De prov.*, III. 7) that the heads of the proscribed were there exposed in the age of Sulla. This *lacus*, which was near the site later occupied by the Basilica Julia, is to be connected with the sacrifice *diis manibus Servilibus*. This, as we learn from VARRO, *L.L.*, VI. 24, was one of the most ancient cults of Rome, — a cult in the same class with the one observed at the neighboring sepulchre of Acca Larentia, — that is, near the *porta Romanula*.

[80] Another characteristic example is that sentence passed upon the thieves which was placed in relation with the eponyms of the public market-place. For this question see the chapter on Minucius and on Spurius Maelius.

NOTES TO CHAPTER VII

SERVIUS TULLIUS

[1] For a discussion of these paintings see KORTE, *Jahrbuch d. arch. Instituts*, XII. (1897) pp. 57 sqq.; MUENZER, in *Rhein. Mus.*, 53 (1898), p. 596; *De Sanctis*, in *Beiträge z. alt. Geschichte*, II. (1902) pp. 96 sqq.; cf. my *Storia di Roma*, I. 1, pp. 338 sqq.

[2] VARRO, *L.L.*, V. 46.

[3] *Caelius* (according to the etymology of the annalists) is in the same relation to *Celes*, as the *Aequimaelium* to the *eques Maelius*. This proves what great caution is necessary on the part of modern critics in deriving conclusions etymological in character.

[4] FESTUS, p. 355, M.

[5] The speech of Claudius (as is well known) is preserved on the bronze tablet of Lyons, *CIL.*, XIII. 1668.

[6] TAC., *Ann.*, IV. 65: *sedem eam acceperat* (i. e., Vibenna) *a Tarquinio Prisco, seu quis alius regum dedit: nam scriptores in eo dissentiunt*.

[7] The tradition of *Lucumo vir inpiger ac divitiis potens*, who comes from Tarquinii to Rome, and who there becomes King Lucius Tarquinius, is well known. See LIVY, I. 34. Also that tradition which makes him a contemporary of Romulus was received among the official versions. See DION. HAL., II. 37.

[8] *Etrusk. Spiegel*, V. pl. 127.

[9] GELL., in SOLIN., I. 7, M.

[10] TAC., *Ann.*, IV. 65: *cetera non ambigua sunt, magnas eas copias per plana etiam ac foro propinqua habitavisse, unde Tuscum vicum e vocabulo advenarum dictum*.

[11] FESTUS, p. 355, M.

[12] LIVY, II. 14; DION. HAL., V. 36.

[13] Compare TACITUS, *Ann.*, IV. 65, with the speech of Claudius. The former says that Caelius occupied the hill; Emperor Claudius (in the Lyons speech) asserts that Mastarna settled upon the Caelian.

[14] LIVY, I. 30.33; DION. HAL., III. 1.

[15] CIC., *de rep.*, II. 18.33. STRABO, V. 234, C.

[16] Speech of Emperor Claudius, *CIL.*, XIII. 1668, lines 22, 23: *mutatoque nomine (nam Tusce Mastarna ei nomen erat) ita appellatus est ut dixi*.

[17] VERGIL, *Aen.*, X. 150 sqq.; XI. 184 sqq.

[18] Upon this subject consult my *Storia di Roma*, I. 1, pp. 462 sqq.; 2, pp. 321 sqq.

[19] *Ibid.*, I. 1, pp. 147 sqq., 624.

[20] The legend of Mezentius is well known. Concerning the death of his son see DION. HAL., I. 65. For the death of Aruns, son of Porsenna, *ib.*, V. 36; cf. LIVY, II. 14.

[21] TAC., *Hist.*, III. 72: *dedita urbe*; PLINY, *N.H.*, XXXIV. 139.

[22] DION. HAL., VII. 1.

[23] LIVY, IV. 29.8.

[24] DION. HAL., IV. 7. In regard to the duplicating of one Tarquin into the two Kings Tarquinii, see my *Storia di Roma*, I. 1, p. 347.

SERVIUS TULLIUS

[25] See above, in the chapter on the Maid Tarpeia.

[26] In fact, it must be noted that, according to tradition itself, Tarquinius Priscus did not dwell on the Capitoline, but on the Velia, where the temple of the Lares was and where later rose the house of Publicola. (CIC., *de rep.*, II. 31.53; SOL., I. 24.) On the other hand, Tarquinius Superbus was said to have dwelled in the Clivus Pullius. (SOL., *l. c.*) That the *Capitolium Vetus* on the Quirinal (VARRO, *L.L.*, V. 158) preserved its political and its religious importance as late as the last century of the Republic, is proved by the gifts which were offered there as well as in the Capitolium on the Capitoline at the time of the Mithridatic Wars. *CIL.*, VI. 373.374; *Notizie degli Scavi*, 1887, p. 321.

[27] Compare LIVY, I. 35.8, with what the same author says in XXXIV. 54. See also VAL. MAX., II. 4.3.

[28] I made this assertion concerning the recent character of the Cloaca Maxima in my *Storia di Roma*, I. 1, p. 349. My statements have now been proved true by the latest excavations of Giacomo Boni.

[29] See the proofs gathered by me in my *Storia di Roma*, I. 2, pp. 228 sqq.

[30] LIVY, I. 42; DION. HAL., IV. 8; CIC., *de rep.*, II. 21.38; *Chron.*, a. 354.

[31] DION. HAL., II. 27, noted, in regard to the laws of the kings, the great divergence between the various annalists, and wondered, therefore, whether the laws had been written or had been handed down by memory.

[32] For the contents and the date of the *lex Poetelia*, consult my *Storia di Roma*, I. 2, pp. 282 sq.

[33] DION. HAL., IV. 25-32.

[34] LIVY, IV. 8.2, *ad a.* 443 B. C. Compare this passage with IV. 22.7, *ad a.* 435 B. C.

[35] SCHWEGLER, *Röm. Geschichte*, I. (ed. 2) pp. 783 sqq.; MOMMSEN, *Röm. Staatsrecht*, I. (ed. 2) pp. 783 sqq.

[36] See my *Storia di Roma*, I. 1, p. 320.

[37] FESTUS, s. v. *praetor*, p. 241, M.

[38] LIVY, VIII. 14.3.

[39] LIVY, III. 71 sq.; IV. 1 sqq. See the chapter on the legend of Virginia. For the origin of the tribe Scaptia, see LIVY, VIII. 17.11.

[40] DION. HAL., IV. 15; LIVY, V. 19.6; cf. X. 46.14.

[41] This has been recognized by such numismatists as SAMWER and BABELON. Moreover, this is a question that can be easily solved by a comparative study of ancient numismatics.

[42] RICHTER, *Beiträge z. röm. Topographie*, Berlin, 1903; cf. in this volume the chapter on the Horatii and the Valerii.

[43] LIVY, I. 60.4; ACCIUS, in CIC., *pro Sestio*, 58.123: *Tullius, qui libertatem civibus stabiliverat*.

[44] I have gathered all the passages referring to this question in my *Storia di Roma*, I. 1, p. 330.

[45] VIB. SEQ., s. v.

[46] SERV., *ad Aen.*, VII. 776: *nam et Virbius inter deos colitur. Virbium autem quidam Solem putant esse;* cf. VII. 761: *numen coniunctum Dianae*.

[47] HELBIG, in L. MORPURGO, *Nemus Aricinum*, in *Monumenti antichi dei Lincei*, XIII. (1903) p. 58.

[48] STRABO, V. 239 C; PAUS., II. 27.4; cf. OVID, *Fasti*, III. 271; *Ars Amat.*, I. 259 sq.; SUET., *Cal.*, 35; VAL. FLACC., *Argon.*, II. 305; STAT., *Silv.*, III. 1.55 sq.

[49] See the chapter on Acca Larentia, notes.

[50] Regarding Servius Tullius and the *vicus Orbius* or *Urbius* and the Dianium, see LIVY, I. 48.6; FEST., p. 182; DION. HAL., IV. 39; SOL., I. p. 25. For the *clivius Virbius* at Aricia, see PERS., VI. 56.

[51] STAT., *Silv.*, III. 1.60; cf. the inscription from Lanuvium, *CIL.*, XIV. 2112.

[52] PLUT., *Quaest. Rom.*, 110; MACROB., I. 13.18; Calendar in *CIL.*, I. (ed. 2), p. 325.
[53] OVID, *Fasti*, VI. 569 sqq. Upon Servius and Fortuna see the passages collected by me in my *Storia di Roma*, I. 1, pp. 327 sqq.
[54] *CIL.*, XIV. 2213: *Dianae Nemorensi Vestae.*
[55] OVID, *Fasti*, VI. 615 sqq.
[56] HYG., *Fab.* 261; SERV., *ad Aen.*, II. 116.
[57] Some critics have wrongly attributed a strictly Italic character to the cult of Diana Aricina. They have deduced this from the fact that oxen were sacrificed to her, and not deer or stags. (PLUT., *Quaest. Rom.*, 4.) But the name *cervi* given to the slaves who were under the protection of this goddess (FESTUS, s. v. *servorum dies*, p. 343, M) proves the opposite view true. Moreover, STRABO (IV. 179, C), in speaking of the statue of Diana Aventinensis, says that it was quite similar to that worshipped by the Phocaeenses of Massilia. This proves that the cult of Diana Aricina and Aventinensis was transformed in very early times by contact with the Greeks. The statement of Strabo must be connected with the fact that the cult of Diana Aricina was said to be derived from the cult of Diana and of Orestes at Rhegium and at Messana. We know that the Phocaeenses, the founders of the Greek Massilia, were kindly received by the inhabitants of Rhegium. (HERODOT., I. 167.) This rapid Hellenizing of the Italic cult of Diana Aricina must be connected with a famous relief found at Aricia, representing the myth of Hippolytus. (See HARRISON, *Prolegomena to the Study of Greek Religion*, Cambridge, 1903, p. 354.)

Another point of contact serves to show how rapidly the Roman cults were Hellenized. The proof is offered by the statue of Semo Sanctus, now in the Vatican (Galleria dei Candelabri), the character of which is that of an Apollo of archaic type.

We have still another proof of the great antiquity of this transformation of Italic cults, — the fact that, notwithstanding Greek influence, the Latin divinity retained her name of Diana. The same happened in the case of Ceres, though the cult of this goddess was purely Hellenic, and though Greek priestesses from Naples or from Sicily were brought to Rome to perform her rites. On the other hand, those divinities that were transported to Rome in a later age retained their Hellenic names, — such as Apollo and Aesculapius.
[58] TAC., *Ann.*, XII. 8.
[59] CATO in PRISC., IV. p. 129, H; FEST., p. 145.
[60] STRABO, V. 234 C, beginning. The original connection between the Egeria of Aricia and that of Rome explains why OVID (*Met.*, XV. 487 sqq.) says that on the death of Numa, Egeria went to the Arician grove to bewail his loss. WISSOWA (in his article on *Egeria* in ROSCHER's dictionary) has not clearly understood this connection, and he consequently supposes the statement a creation of Ovid's fancy.
[61] DION. HAL., IV. 26.
[62] See the chapter on the archaic stele of the Forum, n. 16.
[63] DION. HAL., II. 56.
[64] For the *Poplifugium* see my *Storia di Roma*, I. 2, pp. 84 sqq.
[65] Both versions were in the mind of PLUTARCH, *Quaest. Rom.*, 36.
[66] For the *lacus fagutalis* and for the abode of Servius Tullius, see SOLIN., I. 25, M; cf. VARRO, *L.L.*, V. 49.

NOTES TO CHAPTER VIII

HORATII AND VALERII

[1] I shall make such chronological problems the subject of a special examination, in a volume upon the *Fasti* and the *Annales* of Rome.

[2] For a discussion of all these problems see my *Storia di Roma*, I. 1, pp. 370 sqq., 470 sqq.

[3] I have nothing to add to the observations already made by me in this regard. (See my *Storia di Roma*, I. 1, p. 352; 2, pp. 176 sqq., 339 sqq.) In the foundations of the Capitoline temple the older foot of 278 mm. was employed, and not the later Attic-Roman foot of 296 mm. This fact has induced RICHTER (*Beiträge zur röm. Topographie*, Berlin, 1903, p. 24) to assign the Capitolium to the regal period, in contradistinction to the Servian Wall, which reveals the later Attic-Roman foot of 296 mm.

There are strong arguments against this hypothesis of Richter. In the first place, we have proofs that at Athens and at Tarentum the old system of weights and measures continued side by side with the new system. It cannot, therefore, be argued from the mere presence of the new system that the old one must have been immediately discarded. Even to-day two different systems are to be seen contemporaneously in several countries.

Secondly, even admitting that the presence of the two systems (the old one for the Capitolium and the new one for the Servian Wall) is a proof of different periods, we are not obliged to believe in a difference of three centuries any more than in one of 30 years. For we do not know the precise time limits within which the new foot of 296 mm. displaced the older one of 278 mm.

Thirdly, tradition speaks of substructions built on the Capitoline in 388 B. C., in other words, in the year following the departure of the Gauls. (LIVY, VI. 4.12: *Capitolium quoque saxo quadrato substructum est.*) Ten years later (378 B. C.) it is said that *murum a censoribus locatum saxo quadrato faciundum* (LIVY, VI. 32.1), and finally there is mention of the rebuilding of walls and towers in 353 B. C. (LIVY, VII. 20.9). Therefore tradition itself admits that the walls of Rome were not the creation of one single epoch, but, instead, the product of a decade or so.

Indeed, if due consideration be paid to the extent of Servian *agger*, we shall more easily reach the conclusion that the walls were built rather towards the end of the fourth century than in its first decades. Tradition is right in affirming that the substructures of the Capitoline Hill were the earliest defensive works, and that they were built after the departure of the Gauls. Therefore I do not see that anything prevents our assigning to this same period also the substructures of the Capitoline Temple, even though built according to the ancient foot. I see no reason for assigning the use of the foot of 278 mm. to the sixth century rather than to 388 B. C.

Again, it must be noted that the question of the founding of the Capitolium in the regal period depends entirely on a mass of information and of cults which I have proved as belonging, not to the era of the kings, but, indeed, to the fourth century. The problem, therefore, is to be examined from a broader and a more comprehensive standpoint. If Prof. Richter will undertake such examination, he will recognize that, just as it is false that the walls of Rome were the work of the Tarquins or of Servius, it is likewise false that the Tarquins laid the foundations of the temple of Jupiter Optimus Maximus. For this, to repeat, is a work of the fourth century.

In opposition it may, perhaps, be argued that GNAEUS FLAVIUS (in PLINY, *N.H.*, XXXIII. 19) affirmed (in a tablet placed on the Temple of Concord) that this temple was built by him 203 or 204 years after the dedication of the Capitoline temple. This would lead us back to 507 or 508 B. C. as the date of the latter. I shall omit discussing the many objections that can be adduced regarding the exactness of both this text and of all the passages referring to this dedication and temple. (See my *Storia di Roma*, I. 2, pp. 139, 270, 458, 569.) The fact remains that the synchronism between the expulsion of the Tarquins and that of the Pisistratidae, and between the foundation of the Parthenon and that of the Roman temple, arose in the years in which Timaeus had already invented the contemporaneity between the founding of Rome and that of Carthage. This theory was adopted by Vergil in his national poem. I do not at all doubt but that Timaeus, who visited Rome and wrote a book on the war with Pyrrhus, exercised a great influence upon the Roman scholars of his time. If Appius Claudius, a contemporary of Timaeus and the reformer of the Latin alphabet, was represented as imbued with Pythagorean learning (CIC., *Tusc.*, IV. 2.4), we are inclined to consider as a learned man also his friend and collaborator, Gnaeus Flavius, who published the Fasti and the Calendar. This knowledge of Greek culture, and the kind reception at Rome, not only of commerce, but of everything Hellenic, explain why philosophers like Heraclides Ponticus (who lived at about the time of Appius Claudius and Gnaeus Flavius) called Rome πόλις Ἑλληνίς. (PLUT., *Cam.*, 22.)

[4] Compare my *Storia di Roma*, I. 1, p. 472.

[5] LIVY, II. 10.11; FLOR., I. 4.3, Halm. There are some who still admit the credibility of the traditional history of Rome during the kingly period and the early years of the Republic. Several such are to be found in Italy itself. For these it will be sufficient to recall that Horatius Cocles, who, according to the generally accepted version, saved himself by swimming across the river, according to POLYBIUS, VI. 55.3 (the earliest writer to make any mention of the story), died instead beneath the waters of the Tiber. MOMMSEN, moreover, in his *History of Rome*, I. (ed. 6) p. 246; cf. 463, barely pauses to note the historical worthlessness of the legend. Likewise IHNE, in *Röm. Geschichte*, I. p. 78.

[6] POLYB., VI. 55.3.

[7] PLUT., *Publ.*, 16.7: Κύκλωπα βουλόμενοι καλεῖν αὐτὸν οἱ πολλοί τῆς γλώττης ὀλισθαινούσης ἐκράτησεν ὑπὸ πλήθους Κόκλιον καλεῖσθαι.

[8] ENN., in VARRO, *L.L.*, VII. 71; PLINY, *N.H.*, XI. 150; SERV., *ad Aen.*, VIII. 649; PLAUT., *Curc.*, 393 sq.: *de coc<u>litum prosapia te esse arbitror — nam i sunt unoculi.* Compare VARRO, *l. c.*

[9] PLUT., *l. c.*, 16.10: Πρὸς δὲ τούτοις εἰκόνα χαλκῆν ἔστησαν [αὐτῷ] ἐν τῷ ἱερῷ τοῦ Ἡφαίστου, τὴν γενομένην ἐκ τοῦ τραύματος τῷ ἀνδρὶ χωλότητα μετὰ τιμῆς παρηγοροῦντες.

[10] DION. HAL., V. 25; cf. SER., *ad Aen.*, VIII. 646.

[11] *Ann. Max.*, in GELL., *N.A.*, IV. 5. Mention of the statue of Horatius Cocles, *quae durat hodieque*, is made by PLINY, *N.H.*, XXXIV. 22.

[12] PLINY, *N.H.*, XVI. 236; DION. HAL., II. 50, 54; PLUT., *Rom.*, 24.8.

[13] FESTUS, s. v. *piscatorii ludi*, pp. 210, 238, M; PRELLER-JORDAN, *op. cit.*, pp. 151 sqq.

[14] *CIL.*, XIV. p. 5.

[15] SERV., *ad Aen.*, VII. 678: *virgines aquatum euntes iuxta ignem inventum sustulerunt qui (i. e., Caeculus) haud longe a fonte erat: unde Vulcani dictus est filius.*

[16] SERV., *l. c.*: *Caeculus autem, ideo quia oculis minoribus fuit; quam rem*

frequenter efficit fumus; ad Aen., VIII. 649 : *nam luscos "coclites" dixerunt antiqui: unde et Cyclopas coclitas legimus dictos;* cf. PLINY, *N.H.*, XI. 150.

[17] RAPP, s. v. *Hephaistos*, in ROSCHER'S *Lex.*, and the authorities there cited in regard to the Indian Agnis, who is similarly connected with water and with the divinities of the water.

[18] VAL. ANT., in ARNOB., V. 1.

[19] PLUT., *Publ.*, 19.11 : εἰστήκει . . . ἀνδριὰς . . . ἁπλοῦς καὶ ἀρχαϊκὸς τῇ ἐργασίᾳ.

[20] According to JUSTINUS, his father was not Poseidon, but Aratus (JUST., III. 4.8) ; and his mistress, Agathiadas (DIOD., VIII. 21).

[21] See the just remarks of DOEHLE, *Geschichte Tarents* (Strassburg, 1877), pp. 13 sqq., and of STUDNICZKA, *Kyrene* (Leipzig, 1890), pp. 175 sqq.

[22] HERODOT., I. 23 sq. ; cf. PAUS., X. 13.10.

[23] HERODOT., IV. 15.

[24] HERODOT., I. 66 : Λυκούργῳ τελευτήσαντι ἱρὸν εἰσάμενοι σέβονται μεγάλως.

[25] See in this volume, the chapter on the archaic stele in the Forum.

[26] For the gesture and the statues, see the articles *adoratio* and *ara* in DAREMBERG and SAGLIO. A characteristic example is furnished by the coin of Eryx, edited by POOLE, *Sicily*, p. 62, n. 7 ; cf. a coin from Metapontum in GARRUCCI, *Le monete dell'Italia antica*, tav. CV. n. 5.

[27] DION. HAL., II. 54 ; PLUT., *Rom.*, 24.8.

[28] For the good use which HERODOTUS makes of the inscriptions of statues and monuments see, for example, I. 51–55, regarding the gifts of Croesus and Delphi; IV. 87 sqq., regarding the bas-relief of Mandrocles of Sannus; IX. 85, regarding the tombs of the dead of Plataeae ; and, for the *quadriga* with the inscription referring to the victory of the Chalcidians, V. 77 ; cf. *C.I.A.*, IV. 334 a. For legends originating in monuments, we may think of the tomb of Alyattes, I. 93 ; of that of Queen Nitocris, I. 185, 187. See, too, what THUCYDIDES says of the tombs of the Carians, I. 8 ; of the monuments of Sparta and of Athens, *ib.*, 10 ; of the walls of Themistocles, *ib.*, 93 ; and of the temple of the Pisistratidae, V. 53 ; cf. *C.I.A.*, IV. 373 e.

[29] HERODOT., VI. 137 ; V. 64 ; cf. ED. MEYER, *Forschungen*, p. 10.

[30] See NIESE, *De Sardanapalli epitaphio* (Breslau, 1880) ; ED. MEYER, *Forschungen*, I. pp. 203 sqq.

[31] HERODOT., II. 131.

[32] See the material collected by A. GRAF, *Roma nella memoria e nelle immaginazioni del Medio Evo*, I. pp. 141 sqq.

[33] DANTE, *Purg.*, X. 73 sq.; GRAF, *op. cit.*, II. pp. 37 sqq.

[34] GRAF, *op. cit.*, II. pp. 211 sqq. It is hardly necessary to recall the legends which connect Roman and Neapolitan monuments with the name of Vergil. See COMPARETTI, *Virgilio nel Medio Evo*, II. pp. 72 sqq.

[35] The statue attributed to Cinzica and described by GHIRARDINI, in *Rendiconti dei Lincei*, belongs to the Roman period.

[36] DEM. PHAL., and PANAET., in PLUT., *Arist.*, I. 2. The Attic inscription published by KOEHLER, *C.I.A.*, II. 1257, shows that Panaetius was right.

[37] PLINY, *N.H.*, VII. 69 ; OVID, *Fasti*, IV. 763. Compare VARRO, in LYD., *De mens.*, fragm. Hase (M., *F.H.G.*, IV. p. 325), with PSEUDO-PLUTARCH, *parall. min.*, 35. See, also, in the text the coins of the Valerii, which represent a girl upon a bull. BABELON, *Monn. d. l. rép. rom.*, II. p. 519.

It is not necessary to insist on a perfect resemblance between the snakelike divinity (perhaps a god of the Valerii) represented on the relief in the Magazzino Comunale di Roma and that on the coins of the Valerii. See BABELON, *op. cit.*, II. p. 520, n. 21.

[38] I have brought together the passages proving this in my *Storia di Roma*, I. 1, pp. 432, 480, 489 sqq.

[39] LIVY, X. 9.3; cf. I. 26.6; II. 8.2; III. 55.4.
[40] LIVY, X. 5.13.
[41] See my *Storia di Roma*, I. 1, p. 490.
[42] PLUT., *Publ.*, 23; *Quaest. Rom.*, 79.
[43] Valerius Publicola had his house on the Velia, where the temple of the Penates was, and where the Palace of Tullus Hostilius had been. (SOL., I. 22; CIC. *de rep.*, II. 31, 53.) From there he was supposed to have transported his house *ubi nunc Vicae Potae est*. (LIVY, II. 7.12; cf. CIC., *de leg.*, II. 11.28; ASCON., *in Pison.*, 52.)
[44] DION. HAL., V. 14: ἱερὸν ἥρωος Ὁρατίου. See my *Storia di Roma*, I. 1, pp. 301 sq.
[45] CALP. PISO, and HYLL., in MACROB., III. 2.14.
[46] SUET., *Vitell.*, 1.
[47] Concerning Vacuna, see VARRO, in ACR., *ad Horat., Ep.*, I. 10.49; cf. DION. HAL., I. 15.
[48] DION. HAL., I. 32.
[49] BABELON, *Monn. d. l. rép. rom.*, II. p. 519.
[50] With this sacrifice of bulls are to be connected the *ludi saeculares*, which the Valerii affirmed to have been established by them. VAL. MAX., II. 4.5; ZOSIM., II. 1 sq.

NOTES TO CHAPTER IX

THE FABII

[1] DION. HAL., I. 6.
[2] See my *Storia di Roma*, I. 2, p. 670, and chapter on the *Horatii*, n. 3.
[3] PLUT., *Fab. Max.*, I.; OVID, *Fasti*, II. 237; *ex Ponto*, III. 3.99; SIL. ITAL., II. 3; VI. 628 sq.; JUV., VIII. 14; PAUL., *ep. Fest.*, p. 87, M., s. v. *Fovii*.
[4] The Fabian Luperci are well known. There is a reference to the special cults of the Fabii upon the Quirinal and the Palatine, in the story of the Fabii who left the Capitolium during the Gallic Siege. (LIVY, V. 46.2.)
[5] See, for example, the characteristic comment of CATO, in GELL., *N.A.*, III. 7, following the comparison between Leonidas and the tribune Q. Caedicius. The former, he says, was honored with statues, eulogies, tales, — *at tribuno militum parva laus*.
[6] LIVY, II. 49.4.
[7] FESTUS, *ep. Paul.*, s. v. *scelerata*, p. 335, M.
[8] LIVY, II. 50.11: *dubiisque rebus populi Romani saepe domi belliqueve vel maximum futurum auxilium*.
[9] DION. HAL., IX. 22: μύθοις γὰρ δὴ ταυτά γε καὶ πλάσμασιν ἔοικε θεατρικοῖς.
[10] NIEBUHR, *Röm. Geschichte*, II. pp. 219 sqq.; SCHWEGLER, II. (ed. 2) pp. 519 sqq.; MOMMSEN, *Röm. Forschungen*, II. p. 247; RICHTER, *Die Fabier am Cremera*, in *Hermes*, XVII. (1882) pp. 425 sqq. The work of ORESTE BARATTIERI, *La leggenda dei Fabi, saggio di critica militare* (Roma, 1886), is without historic and topographic value.
[11] DIOD., XI. 53; cf. MOMMSEN, *op. cit.*, pp. 246 sqq.
[12] IHNE, *Röm. Geschichte*, I. (ed. 2) pp. 159 sqq.
[13] I do not believe with MOMMSEN, *op. cit.*, p. 257, that the τινες τῶν συγγραφέων mentioned in this connection by Diodorus are the records of the Fabii. Diodorus, while drawing mainly upon the *Annales Maximi*, is wont to cite, occasionally, his minor sources also. It is from one of these that he must have taken the number of 300 Fabii instead of 306, — a modification which was made for reasons shortly to be related.
[14] Concerning the value of Diodorus as a source for Roman History, I have given a full discussion in my *Storia di Roma*. The opinion of B. NIESE must here be refuted. For this period he considers good and authentic only that which is given by Diodorus, and condemns at once important information, only because it is not found in the source which to him appears trustworthy.
[15] LIVY, VII. 15.10: *nec in acie tantum ibi cladis acceptum, quam quod trecentos septem milites Romanos captos Tarquinienses immolarunt*.
[16] LIVY, V. 36.11; PLUT., *Cam.*, 18 seq.; OVID. *Fasti*, II. 195 sqq.; *CIL.*, I. (ed. 2) p. 322, and my *Storia di Roma*, I. 2, pp. 94 sqq.
[17] LIVY, V. 47.2: *animadverso ad Carmentis saxo*.
[18] PLUT., *Cam.*, 30; SILV., *ad. id. Februar, CIL.*, I², p. 310; SUID., s. v. Φεβρουάριος. Concerning this last, see my *Storia di Roma*, I. 2, p. 94, n. 2.
[19] PSEUDO-PLUTARCH, *parall. min.*, 4.

[20] Four years later, 354 B. C., the Romans had their revenge. LIVY, VII. 19.2 sq.: *In Tarquinienses acerbe saevitum: multis mortalibus in acie caesis ex ingenti captivorum numero trecenti quinquaginta octo delecti, nobillissimus quisque, qui Romam mitterentur; volgus aliud trucidatum. nec populus in eos, qui missi Romam erant, mitior fuit: medio in foro omnes virgis caesi ac securi percussi. id pro immolatis in foro Tarquiniensium Romanis poenae hostibus redditum.* All this, unless I am greatly mistaken, bears the stamp of plain truth and recalls some well-known and terrible Etruscan wall-paintings. LIVY, VII. 15.10: *Qua foeditate supplicii aliquanto ignominia populi Romani insignitior fuit.*

[21] FESTUS, p. 170, s. v. *Numerius;* cf. AUCT., *de praen.*, 6. The praenomen Numerius appears in the years $333 = 421$ B. C., $339 = 415$ B. C., and $347 = 407$ B. C. See LIVY, IV. 49.

[22] Likewise, we have not sufficient data for understanding the connection between the Fabii and the temple of Janus outside the Porta Carmentalis, in which it was not allowed to assemble the senate. See FESTUS, s. v. *Religioni*, p. 285, M.

[23] PLUT. (VARRO), *Quaest. Rom.*, 27; *de curiosit.*, 6.

[24] According to HERODOTUS, VII. 202, there were with Leonidas at Thermopylae, besides his 300 Spartans, also 1,000 men from Tegea and Mantinea, 120 men from Orchomenus in Arcadia, 1,000 from the rest of Arcadia, 400 Corinthians, 200 from Phlius, 80 from Mycenae, 700 from Thespiae, and 400 Thebans,—in all, 3,900 men in addition to the Spartans. According to DIODORUS, XI. 4, Leonidas had with him, 300 Spartans, 1,000 Lacedaemonians, and 3,000 men from the rest of the Peloponnese,—in all, 4,000 men besides his Spartans.

[25] The number of 300 Fabii is given, not only by the poets, such as SILIUS ITALICUS, II. 4; VI. 637, but also by some historians, as DIODORUS, XI. 53, and PLUTARCH, *Cam.*, 19.1; cf. SEN., *de benef.*, V. 3.2.

[26] HERODOT., VII. 221.

[27] GELL., *N.A.*, XVII. 21.13 sq.

[28] LIVY, II. 46 sqq.

[29] For imitations from the Iliad, see E. ZARNCKE, *Der Einfluss der griechischen Litteratur auf die Entwicklung der römischen Prosa*, in *Comment. philol.*, published in honor of RIBBECK (Lipsiae, 1888), pp. 267 sqq.

[30] Precisely because the Fabii considered themselves Heraclides did Fabius Maximus transport to Rome the statue of Hercules which he had captured in the Heraclean-Spartan Tarentum. See PLUT., *Fab. Max.*, 22.8. Concerning the Sabine origin of the Fabii, see DION. HAL., II. 48.

[31] LIVY, XXII. 60.11: *priore Punico bello Calpurnius Flamma trecentis voluntariis . . . dixit;* OROS., IV. 8.2.

[32] PLUT., *Cato Maior*, 13.1: τὴν δὲ Περσικὴν ἐκείνην περιήλυσιν καὶ κύκλωσιν ὁ Κάτων εἰς νοῦν βαλόμενος; cf. 14.2 sq.

[33] Regarding the Sabines and the Spartans, see the sources known to DION. HAL., II. 49. Concerning the Spartan origin of the 300 Roman *celeres* and of the *curiae, ib.*, II. 13,23. For the Spartan Ephors and the Roman tribunes, CIC., *de leg.*, III. 7.16; VAL. MAX., IV. 1 Ext. 8; for the five tribunes, see LIVY, II. 33.2; DION. HAL., VI. 89. The historian Posidonius, *apud* ATHEN., VI. p. 273 f., assigned a Spartan origin to all the Roman institutions; on the other hand, the sources known to LYDUS, *de mag.*, I., assigned them all to Athens.

[34] FESTUS, s. v. *obsidionalis*, p. 190, M.

NOTES TO CHAPTER X

LUCRETIA AND VIRGINIA

¹ The embassy to Athens, for the purpose of studying the customs which were to fashion the laws of the Twelve Tables, is well known. Side by side with this generally diffused tradition, there was another mentioning an embassy to Greece in the time of Tarquinius Superbus. (LYD., *de mag.* I. 31.) Later, however, this embassy is represented as having gone to Greece, not to study laws, but to propitiate the Delphic oracle in favor of the tyrant. With the more ancient version is to be connected the passage in CICERO, *de rep.*, II. 19.34. In this passage Cicero, in speaking of the laws of Tarquinius Priscus (a Corinthian in origin), refers to the relations of the Roman laws to those of Corinth.

² These are well-known tales. It will be sufficient to refer to LIVY, I. 57 sq., and DION. HAL., IV. 64 sqq. Compare, also LIVY, III. 44 sqq., and DION. HAL., XI. 28 sqq.

³ Concerning Gaia Caecilia or Tanaquil, the chaste spouse of Tarquinius, and concerning Servius and his relations with other female characters, see my *Storia di Roma*, I. 1, p. 360. For the wife of Servius, who commits suicide, DION. HAL., IV. 40. For the legend of the Decemvirate and the late tradition of the laws of the Twelve Tables, my *Storia di Roma*, I. 1, p. 572; I. 2, pp. 618 sqq.

⁴ ARISTOT., *Pol.*, V. 3, p. 1303, Bkk.

⁵ These examples could easily be multiplied. Besides the story of Xenocrite of Cuma (related by PLUTARCH, *de mulier. virt.*, 26), recall also that one of the tyrant of Heracleia, lover of Hipparinos (in PHANIAS ERES., M., *F.H.G.*, II. p. 298, fr. 16), of the ravished Phocian women (DURIS, fr. 2, *ib.* p. 469), of the Argive Bryas (PAUS., II. 20.2), of the maid who, violated by Aristomelidas, tyrant of Tegea, saved her honor by death. (PAUS., VIII. 47.6.)

⁶ LIVY, IV. 9.

⁷ LIVY, II. 32.4: *sine ullo duce vallo fossaque communitis castris quieti rem nullam nisi necessariam ad victum sumendo.* Compare, instead, II. 34.10: *rapiant frumenta ex agris, quem ad modum tertio anno rapuere.*

⁸ LIVY, I. 23; II. 39.

⁹ LIVY, III. 66.5.

¹⁰ For the duplicating of the deeds of Cincinnatus, see my *Storia di Roma*, I. 1, pp. 524 sqq.

¹¹ The year 304 A. U. C. (according to Varro, 450 B. C.), corresponds to Olympiad 84.2, the 443 B. C. of Diodorus Siculus.

¹² LIVY, IV. 6. Concerning the *lex Canuleia*, consult what I have said in my *Storia di Roma*, I. 1, pp. 589 sqq.

¹³ In the official legend, Lucretia was surprised by Tarquinius in the city of Collatia, where she was supposed to be living. See LIVY, I. 58; DION. HAL., IV. 64.

¹⁴ Concerning the magistrates and the deeds of 444 B. C., LIVY (IV. 7.2-10) repeatedly expresses his doubts. DIONYSIUS, XI. 62., affirms his belief in the documents referring to this year: πιστεύοντες δὲ ταῖς ἐκ τῶν ἱερῶν τε καὶ τῶν ἀποθέτων βίβλων μαρτυρίαις.

This fact suggests that the doubts had already been expressed by some more ancient source, — a source common to both.

[15] Compare LIVY, III. 71, with IV. 9, and particularly with IV. 7.2, where he explicitly refers to different and contradictory accounts concerning the course of events.

[16] LIVY, III. 25.
[17] LIVY, III. 28; IV. 10.
[18] DION. HAL., XI. 61; LIVY, IV. 7.
[19] LIVY, IV. 11.10; DIOD., XII. 34.1. Aebutius Helva was consul, according to Diodorus; according to Livy, a triumvir.
[20] I have given the proofs of this *passim* in my *Storia di Roma*. I shall present still more detailed proofs in my volume on the *Fasti*. It will be sufficient here to recall Spurius Cassius, Aternius, and Tarpeius, who were, according to the different sources, made either consuls or tribunes.
[21] LIC. MACER, in LIVY, IV. 7.10; IV. 8.7. Compare, instead, DION. HAL., XI. 62.
[22] LIVY, IV. 8.7; cf. IV. 22.7.
[23] I have given the detailed proofs in my two papers, one on the Siceliot elements in the early history of Rome, the other on the Italiot elements (Pisa, 1893, and Naples, 1900).
[24] VARRO, *R.R.*, II. 11.10.
[25] PLINY, *N.H.*, XXXV. 154.
[26] PLINY, *N.H.*, XXXV. 115.
[27] SERV., *ad Aen.*, I. 48.
[28] For the cult of Helen in the Peloponnese, see WIDE, *Lakonische Kulte*, pp. 322 sqq.; 342 sqq.; for the same in Agrigentum, PINDAR, *Ol.*, 3.1 sqq.; in Rome, see FAB. PICTOR, in DION. HAL., VII. 72.
[29] STRABO, V. p. 232, C.
[30] LIVY, VIII. 14.2 sq.
[31] See my *Storia di Roma*, I. 2, pp. 327 sqq.
[32] LIVY, VIII. 11.15; cf. VIII. 14.2.
[33] Compare my *Storia di Roma*, I. 1, pp. 183
[34] XENAG., in DION. HAL., I. 72.
[35] FESTUS, *Ep.*, p. 119, s. v. *Lucereses*.
[36] GELL., in DION. HAL., II. 72.
[37] CIC., *de nat. deor.*, III. 18.47.
[38] LIVY, III. 71 sq.; IV. 10.6; IV. 11.3; DION. HAL., XI. 52 sqq.
[39] LIVY, I. 38; XXVI. 33; POLYB., XXXVI. 2; cf. SERV., *ad Aen.*, VII. 188. The last enumerates the *pignora quae imperium Romanum tenent*, among which were the *quadriga fictilis* of Veii, and the ashes of Orestes which had been transported from Aricia. Compare SERV., *ad Aen.*, II. 116; HYG., *Fab.*, 261. Regarding the sacrifices performed at Ardea by the Decemvirs in 217 B. C., see LIVY, XXII. 1.19.
[40] For Lavinium and Laurentum, see LIVY, VIII. 11.15; MACROB., III. 4.11; for Ardea, LIVY, XXII. 1.19. See my *Storia di Roma*, I. 1, pp. 183 sq.
[41] LIVY, III. 48.5: *data venia seducit filiam ac nutricem prope Cloacinae ad tabernas, quibus nunc novis est nomen, atque ibi ab lanio cultro abrepto.* For the knife taken from the wound of Lucretia and brandished by Brutus, see LIVY, I. 59.
[42] Regarding Amata, see my *Storia di Roma*, I. 1, p. 184.
[43] For the temple of Juno Moneta, LIVY VII. 28.4.
[44] The fragment was published by KRUEGER and MOMMSEN in *Hermes*, IV. (1870) p. 371.
[45] LIVY, X. 23; cf. PROP., II. 6.25; JUV., VI. 308.
[46] FESTUS, p. 242, s. v. *Pudicitiae signum*, informs us that the temple of Fortuna Virgo in the Forum Boarium, erected by Servius Tullius, was sacred to Pudicitia, or at least, that it contained a statue of that goddess.

This divinity was, moreover, placed in connection with maidens who married. VARRO, in PLINY, *N.H.*, VIII. 194, and in NON., p. 189, M.; OVID, *Fasti*, VI. 579; ARNOB., II. 67.

[47] Concerning the character of the cult of Venus Cloacina, see PLINY, *N.H.*, XV. 119 sqq.; PLUT., *Quaest. Rom.*, 20; cf. AUG., *de civ. dei*, IV. 23; VI. 10; LACT., I. 20.11; FESTUS, p. 290, M, s. v. *Sacram Viam*. For the Temple and the myth of Fortuna Seia, which was connected with Servius Tullius and perhaps with the temple of Mala Fortuna, see CIC., *de nat. deor.*, III. 25.63; PLINY, II. 16; VIII. 197; XXXVI. 163.

[48] For the Iunii, Bruti, and the plebeian *tabernae*, FESTUS, p. 230, s. v. *Plebeias tabernas*.

[49] I refer to facts on which there can be no discussion. LIVY, I. 2.6, says in regard to Aeneas who fell into the Numicius: *Iovem Indigetem appellant*; cf. DION. HAL., I. 64. See the parallel stories given in my *Storia di Roma*, I. 1, pp. 183 sqq.

[50] DION. HAL., I. 55.

[51] Turnus, King of the Rutuli, is by VERGIL called the brother of the fountain Juturna (XII. 139 sqq.). Near Aricia, too, there was a *Turni lacus* (COLUM., X. 138), whence the inhabitants of that region were called *Lacuturnenses*. (cf. PLINY, *N.H.*, XIX. 141.) Critics, consequently, are wrong in changing *Turni lacus* to *Turris lacus*. We lack a thorough topographical study regarding the homes of all these myths. It is very probable that with these myths is related the ancient emissary joining the lake of Aricia with the valley of Aricia.

[52] Concerning the river deity Numa, — the author, therefore, of the *pons sublicius* and lover of the fountain Egeria, — I refer the reader to the demonstrations given in my *Storia di Roma*, I. 1, pp. 288 sqq.

[53] The Egerius Laevius who, according to CATO (in PRISC., IV. 129, H), was *dictator Tusculanus* and the founder of the temple of Diana in the *nemus Aricinum* (*Manius Egerius* in FESTUS, p. 145) is merely Αἴγεστος, the leader of the priests, — that is, the ἡγεμών who brought back to Lavinium the cults which Ascanius had transported to Alba. (DION. HAL., I. 67.) Compare the forms *Aegesta, Segesta, Egesta, Aequimaelium, eques Maelius*. This Aigestos is but a localized duplicate of the famous Αἴγεστος, companion of Aeneas (DION. HAL., I. 47,52), who was originally connected with the Elymean-Sicilian Segesta, and who reappears as Αἴγεστος, the son of Numitor, King of Alba. In other words, he reappears as that brother of Rhea Silvia, who was killed by Amulius while hunting. (DION. HAL., I. 76.) He is also found as Egerius, a kinsman of Tarquinius Priscus (DION. HAL., III. 50,57), and from Egerius, FABIUS PICTOR (in DION. HAL., IV. 64; cf. LIVY, I. 57), traced the descent of Tarquinius of Collatia, the husband of the chaste Lucretia.

[54] LIVY, I. 50; DION. HAL., IV. 45.
[55] DION. HAL., I. 57.
[56] PLUT., *Phoc.*, 19.
[57] CIC., *de off.*, III. 22.87.

NOTES TO CHAPTER XI

MINUCIUS AND MAELIUS

¹ LIVY, IV. 12 sqq.; DION. HAL., XII. 1 sqq.; cf. CIC., *de rep.*, II. 27.49; DIOD., XII. 37; ZONAR., VII. 20.

² DION. HAL., XII. 4. Above all, we must call attention to the following words: οἵ φασι (Cincius and Calpurnius) οὔτε δικτάτορα ὑπὸ τῆς βουλῆς ἀποδειχθῆναι τὸν Κοίντιον οὔτε ἱππάρχην ὑπὸ τοῦ Κοιντίου τὸν Σερουίλιον.

³ LIVY, IV. 12.7: *seu adversus annus frugibus fuit, seu dulcedine contionum et urbis deserto agrorum cultu, nam utrumque traditur.*

⁴ T. Quinctius Capitolinus was consul in 439 B. C.

⁵ LIVY, IV. 16.2: *L. Minucius bove aurato extra portam Trigeminam est donatus ne plebe quidem invita.* DION. HAL., XII. 4, extr: τῷ δὲ τὴν κατὰ τοῦ Μαιλίου μήνυσιν ἀποδόντι Μηνυκίῳ στάσιν ἀνδριάντος ἐψηφίσατο ἡ βουλή. PLINY, *N.H.*, XVIII. 15: *qua de causa statua ei extra portam Trigeminam a populo stipe collata statuta est.*

⁶ LIVY, IV. 16.3 sq.: *hunc Minucium apud quosdam auctores transisse a patribus ad plebem, undecimumque tribunum plebis cooptatum seditionem motam ex Maeliana caede sedasse invenio. ceterum vix credibile est numerum tribunorum patres augeri passos, idque potissimum exemplum a patricio homine introductum; nec deinde id plebem concessum semel obtinuisse aut certe temptasse. sed ante omnia refellit falsum imaginis titulum paucis ante annis lege cautum, ne tribunis collegam cooptare liceret.*

⁷ MOMMSEN, *Röm. Forschungen*, II. pp. 214 sqq.

⁸ LIVY, IV. 13.7: *nihil enim constat nisi in libros linteos utroque anno relatum inter magistratus praefecti nomen.*

⁹ DION. HAL., XII. 1, init.

¹⁰ LIVY, IV. 21.3.

¹¹ Regarding the Menenii and their participation in the legends of the agrarian agitations, I have given a full discussion in my paper on the *Elementi Sicelioti nella più antica civiltà romana.*

¹² BABELON, *Monn. d. l. rép. rom.*, II. pp. 229 sqq.

¹³ According to LIVY XL. 34, the first occurrence of a gilt statue at Rome is in the year 181, B. C.; cf. VAL. MAX., II. 5.1. See, also, LIVY, XXXVII. 3.7, *ad a.* 190 B. C.

¹⁴ CIC., *de div.*, II. 17.39.

¹⁵ VELLEIUS, II. 8.3, says that Minucius, *porticus, quae hodie celebres sunt, molitus est;* and from the *Not. Reg.* we learn that in the ninth region there were the *porticus Minucia vetus* and the *porticus Minucia frumentaria.* Both served similar purposes. And since one of the *porticus* built by Minucius was called *vetus*, it may be supposed that, when he erected a new *porticus*, he, at the same time, enlarged and repaired one already in existence. The latter, indeed, may have been erected by an ancestor of our Minucius. We find a Minucius among the defenders of the plebs in 216 B. C. (LIVY, XXIII. 21.6), and among the enemies of the aristocratic Scipio family (GELL., *N.A.*, VI. 19.2).

¹⁶ FESTUS, p. 290, M : *Servilius lacus appellabatur † eo, qui eum faciendum curaverat in principio vici Iugari, continens basilicae Iuliae, in quo loco fuit*

MINUCIUS AND MAELIUS 325

effigies hydrae posita a M. Agrippa ; CIC., *pro Rosc. Am.,* 32.89: *multos caesos non ad Trasumennum lacum, sed ad Servilium vidimus ;* SEN., *Dial.,* I. 3.7: *videant. . . . supra Servilianum lacum* (*id enim proscriptionis Sullanae spoliarum est*) *senatorum capita.*
[17] VARRO, *L.L.,* V. 146 sq.; PAUL., *ep. Fest.,* 48.125, M, s. v. *Cuppes* and *Macellum ;* PLUT., *Quaest. Rom.,* 54.
[18] ATHEN., II. 39, c; IV. 173 a, sq.; EUST., *ad Od.,* pp. 1413.20 sqq.
[19] FEST., *ep. Paul.,* p. 122, s. v. *Minutia ; ib.,* p. 147, s. v. *Minucia porta.*
[20] LIVY, I. 7.7, and DIONYSIUS, I. 39, refer to the lowing of the cows. On the other hand, Vergil (as is customary with him) preserves the more ancient version in VIII. 217 sq.:

> *Reddidit una boum vocem vastoque sub antro*
> *Mugiit et Caci spem custodita fefellit.*

This version is given also in the *Origo Gentis Romanae,* where it is stated that the story was derived from the *Annales Maximi.*
[21] The *ara maxima* of Hercules and the bull in the Forum Boarium are well known. See PLINY, *N.H.,* XXXIV. 10; TAC., *Ann.,* XII. 24. For the altar and the temple of Hercules at the Porta Trigemina, see LIVY, XXXV. 10.12; XL. 51; XLI. 27.8; VARRO, in MACROB., III. 6.10: *Romae autem Victoris Herculis aedes duae sunt, una ad portam Trigeminam, altera in foro Boario ;* DION. HAL., I. 39; SERV., *ad Aen.,* VIII. 363; SOL., I. 7; *Fast. All., ad d.* 13 Aug. in *CIL.,* I. (ed. 2) p. 325, where the Hercules *ad portam Trigeminam* is called *Invictus.*
[22] *CIL.,* I. (ed. 2) p. 319, *ad d.* 4 June.
[23] FESTUS, *ep. Paul.,* p. 122, s. v.: *Minutia porta Romae est dicta ab ara Minuti, quem deum putabant ; ib.,* p. 147, s. v.: *Minucia porta appellata est eo, quod proxima esset sacello Minutii.*
[24] It is not necessary to insist on the fact that the name *Italia* is derived from *Vitellia.* Regarding *Vitellia, quae multis locis pro numine coleretur,* see SUET., *Vit.,* 1. This author refers also to the *via Vitellia* near Rome. We must place in close connection with *Vitellia* the Sabine goddess *Vacuna,* who, according to VARRO (in ACR., *ad Horat., ep.,* I. 10.49) was the same as the goddess *Victoria.* Likewise, it is probable that the goddess *Victoria,* who was worshiped on the Palatine, was merely the goddess of the *Vitulatio.* For the goddess *Victoria* worshiped under the form of a bull, see the notes to the chapter on the Horatii.
[25] VARRO, *L.L.,* V. 164; DION. HAL., II. 50; FEST., *ep. Paul.,* 144, M, s. v. *Mugionia porta Romae dicta a Mugio quodam qui eidem tuendae praefuit ;* SOL., I. 24, M; NON., p. 531, M.
[26] ACIL., in STRABO, V. p. 130, C : καὶ ὅ γε Κοίλιος, ὁ τῶν Ῥωμαίων συγγραφεύς, τοῦτο τίθεται σημεῖον τοῦ Ἑλληνικὸν εἶναι κτίσμα τὴν Ῥώμην, τὸ παρ' αὐτῇ τὴν πάτριον θυσίαν Ἑλληνικὴν εἶναι τῷ Ἡρακλεῖ. In my studies on Strabo, I have already brought to notice that Strabo, even in Roman things, never made use of Latin authors who wrote in their native tongue. It is therefore evident that the historian here cited is Acilius, the well-known annalist of the second century, rather than the later Coelius Antipater.
[27] LIVY, IV. 13.8, expressly says of Minucius: *rem conpertam ad senatum refert.* DIONYSIUS, in giving in Greek the story that had already been written in Greek by Cincius Alimentus, says, XII. 4: τῷ . . . μήνυσιν ἀποδόντι Μηνυκίῳ, and shortly before, XII. 2, calls the denunciation by Minucius μήνυσις, and says of Minucius, τῷ δὲ Μηνυκίῳ τόν τε μηνυτὴν ἄγοντι.
[28] According to STEPHANUS BYZANTINUS, the city of Μοτύη in Western Sicily was named ἀπὸ Μοτύης γυναικὸς μηνυσάσης Ἡρακλεῖ τοὺς ἐλάσαντας τοὺς αὐτοῦ βοῦς. LACT., *div. inst.,* I. 20.36: *Colitur et Caca, quae Herculi fecit indicium de furto boum, divinitatem consecuta quia prodidit fratrem.*

[29] FESTUS, p. 343, s. v. *Servorum dies*; cf. p. 169, col. 2, *Naeviam silvam*.
[30] PLINY, XI. 123, gives the story as one well known in *Latia historia*. Also VALERIUS MAXIMUS, V. 6.3, presents it as authentic history. The myth of Cipus Gaenucius is perhaps to be compared with the cult of the Gallic god *Cernunnos*.
[31] CIC., *de off.*, II. 17.58; PLINY, *N.H.*, XV. 2.
[32] CIC., *Brut.*, 16.62: *quamquam his laudationibus historia rerum nostrarum est facta mendosior. multa enim scripta sunt in eis quae facta non sunt: falsi triumphi, plures consulatus, genera etiam falsa et ad plebem transitiones*; LIVY, VIII. 40.4, sq. *ad a.* 322 B. C.: *vitiatam memoriam funebribus laudibus reor falsisque imaginum titulis, dum familiae ad se quaeque famam rerum gestarum honorumque fallenti mendacio trahunt. inde certe et singulorum gesta et publica monumenta rerum confusa. nec quisquam aequalis temporibus illis scriptor extat, quo satis certo auctore stetur*.
The authors could not be more explicit. It is the modern scholars that know not how to draw therefrom the logical conclusions.
[33] LIVY, VI. 1 sq. explicitly states that all that he had narrated up to the time of the burning of Rome was material *cum vetustate nimia obscuras, velut quae magno ex intervallo loci vix cernuntur, tum quod parvae et rarae per eadem tempora litterae fuere, una custodia fidelis memoriae rerum gestarum, et quod, etiam si quae in commentariis pontificum aliisque publicis privatisque erant monumentis, incensa urbe pleraeque interiere*.
[34] DIONYSIUS, VIII. 62, who drew upon ancient Latin sources, declares that even in his own times the memory of Coriolanus was celebrated, ᾄδεται καὶ ὑμνεῖται πρὸς πάντων ὡς εὐσεβὴς καὶ δίκαιος ἀνήρ. From this, however, is not to be derived the historic authenticity of Coriolanus, but only (as I have shown in my *Storia di Roma*) the sacred character of the myth. Even Romulus and Remus were the subjects of national songs, as DIONYSIUS himself states (I. 79): ἐν τοῖς πατρίοις ὕμνοις ὑπὸ Ῥωμαίων ἔτι καὶ νῦν ᾄδεται. Surely no one would venture to derive thence the historic character of the wolf-nurtured twins.
On the other hand, we have traces of true historical ballads of the Gauls fighting at Sentinum (295 B. C.). In fact, the Gauls themselves were supposed to have celebrated the deeds they performed in the first skirmishes of that battle, — *ovantesque moris sui carmine*, LIVY, X. 26.11. Therefore, we are to put faith in Cato, who speaks of the historic and the convivial songs of the Romans, — songs that had already perished in the age of Cicero. For the importance of these songs, consult what I have already set forth in my *Storia di Roma*, I. 1, pp. 8 sqq.

NOTES TO CHAPTER XII

ON THE TOPOGRAPHY OF ROME

¹ In this map I have purposely omitted to draw the entire line of the limits of the ancient Septimontium, because (in the present state of our knowledge) such precise indication seems to me to be premature.
² MOMMSEN, *Röm. Forschungen*, II. p. 39.
³ ENN., in FESTUS, s. v. *Quadrata Roma*, p. 258, M.
⁴ DION. HAL., I. 88: περιγράφει (i. e. Romulus) τετράγωνον σχῆμα τῷ λόφῳ. Cf. II. 65; PLUT., *Rom.*, 9: 'Ρωμύλος μὲν οὖν τὴν καλουμένην 'Ρώμην κουαδράτην, ὅπερ ἐστὶ τετράγωνον, ἔκτισε, κ.τ.λ.
⁵ SOL., I. 17.
⁶ GELL., *N.A.*, XIII. 14: *Palatini montis radicibus terminabatur.*
⁷ TAC., *Ann.*, XII. 24: *Sed initium condendi, et quod pomerium Romulus posuerit, noscere haud absurdum reor. igitur a foro Boario, ubi aereum tauri simulacrum aspicimus, quia id genus animalium aratro subditur, sulcus designandi oppidi coeptus, ut magnam Herculis aram amplecteretur; inde certis spatiis interiecti lapides per ima montis Palatini ad aram Consi, mox curias veteres, tum ad sacellum Larum inde forum Romanum; forum et Capitolium non a Romulo sed a Tito Tatio additum urbi credidere.* The Medicean copy, after the words *ad sacellum Larum* has *deforüque Romanum*. This is not the place for discussing the reading of this passage, as was done by Richter and others, because it has no bearing on our question. I do not agree with RICHTER, *Top. d. Stadt Rom* (1902), pp. 31 sqq.
⁸ LIVY, I. 7.2: *vulgatior fama est ludibrio fratris Remum novos transiluisse muros; inde ab irato Romulo cum verbis quoque increpans adiecisset, " sic deinde quicumque alius transiliet moenia mea" interfectum.* DION. HAL., I. 88: βοὸς ἄρρενος ἄμα θηλείᾳ ξευχθέντος ὑπ' ἄροτρον ἑλκύσας αὔλακα διηνεκῆ τὴν μέλλουσαν ὑποδέξεσθαι τὸ τεῖχος.
⁹ FESTUS, p. 213, M, s. v.: *Pectuscum Palatii dicta est ea regio Urbis, quam Romulus obversam posuit, ea parte, in qua plurimum erat agri Romani ad mare versus, et quia † mollissime adibatur Urbs, cum Etruscorum agrum a Romano Tiberis discluderet, ceterae vicinae civitates colles aliquos haberent oppositos.*
¹⁰ LIVY, I. 44, in speaking of the enlargement of the *pomerium* by Servius Tullius, says that it included not only land on the inside of the walls, but also *extrinsecus puri aliquid ab humano cultu pateret soli. hoc spatium, quod neque habitari neque arari fas erat, non magis quod post murum esset, quam quod murus post id, pomerium Romani appellarunt, et in urbis incremento semper, quantum moenia processura erant, tantum termini hi consecrati proferebantur.* To this definition of the *pomerium* MOMMSEN (*Röm. Forsch.*, II. pp. 233 sqq.) opposes the more ancient one given by VARRO, *L.L.*, V. 143: *terram unde exculpserant, Fossam vocabant et introrsum iactam Murum. Post ea qui fiebat orbis, Urbis principium.* He opposes to it also the definition of the Roman augurs cited by GELLIUS, *N.A.*, XIII. 14, according to whom the *pomerium* was the *locus intra agrum effatum per totius urbis circuitum pone muros regionibus certeis determinatus, qui facit finem urbani auspicii.* As is well known, the opinion of Mommsen has been combated by NISSEN, in *Pomp. Studien*, pp. 466 sqq., and by DETLEFSEN, in *Hermes*, XXI, pp. 497 sqq.

[11] SOL., I. 24.
[12] PLINY, *N.H.*, XXXIV. 10.
[13] PLINY, *N.H.*, XXXIV. 33.
[14] SILEN., in SOLIN., I. 15.
[15] ACIL., in STRABO, V. p. 230, C. For the relation of Hercules to the origins of Rome, see my *Storia di Roma*, I. pp. 152 sqq.
[16] CATO in SERV., *ad Aen.*, V. 575, et apud ISID., *Orig.*, XV. 2.3 = fr. 18* P. VARRO, *L.L.*, V. 143, et apud FRONT., *de limit.*, p. 27, L, considered the rite an Etruscan one, as did also LIVY, I. 44.
[17] See above, n. 7.
[18] SOL., I. 17: *dictaque est primum Roma quadrata, quod ad aequilibrium foret posita. ea incipit a silva, quae est in area Apollinis, et ad supercilium scalarum Caci habet terminum, ubi tugurium fuit Faustuli.*
[19] PLINY, *N.H.*, III. 66: *urbem tres portas habentem Romulus reliquit, aut (ut pluribus tradentibus credamus) quattuor;* cf. VARRO, *L.L.*, V. 165.
[20] OVID, *Fasti*, I. 260 sqq.; MACROB., I. 9.17.
[21] DION. HAL., II. 50.
[22] For the *casa Romuli* upon the Capitolium, see VITRUVIUS, II. 1.5; SEN., *Contr.*, II. 1.4; CON., *Narr.*, 48.
[23] VARRO, *L.L.*, V. 143: *Oppida condebant in Latio Etrusco ritu multi, id est iunctis bobus, tauro et vacca. . . . Terram unde exculpserant, Fossam vocabant et introrsum iactam Murum. Post ea qui fiebat orbis, Urbis principium . . . oppida quae prius erant circumducta aratro ab orbe et urvo Urbes; ideo coloniae nostrae omnes in litteris antiquis scribuntur urbis, quod item conditae ut Roma.*
[24] Consult the drawings illustrating the text of the *Gromatici Veteres*, in the edition of LACHMANN, tab. 15 sqq. The historical importance of these drawings has recently been recognized also by SCHULTEN, in *Hermes*, XXXIII. (1898), pp. 534 sqq. I think it worthy of note that also in the ancient drawing at the head of the text of the *Gromatici Veteres* there is a sculptural detail to the seat which (as far as I know) is met with only in one marble from Pompeii, found by me in the cellars of the National Museum of Naples.
[25] VITRUVIUS, *de arch.*, I. 5.2: *conlocanda autem oppida sunt non quadrata nec procurrentibus angulis sed circumitionibus, uti hostis ex pluribus locis conspiciatur.*
[26] FRONT., *de limit.*, p. 27, L; HYG., *de limit. const.*, p. 166, L.
[27] PLUT., *Rom.*, 11.
[28] HYG., *de limit. const.*, p. 166, L : *constituti enim limites non sine mundi ratione, quoniam decumani secundum solis decursum diriguntur, kardines a poli axe. unde primum haec ratio mensure constituta ad Etruscorum aruspicum . . . disciplina; quod illi orbem terrarum in duas partes secundum solis cursum diviserunt, dextram appellaverunt quae septentrioni subiacebat, sinistram quae ad meridianum terrae esset, ab oriente ad occasum, quod eo sol et luna spectaret; alteram lineam duxerunt a meridiano in septentrionem, et a media ultra antica, citra postica nominaverunt ex quo haec constitutio liminibus templorum adscribitur.* The Roman surveyors naturally recommended not to adhere to abstract theory, but to the nature of the ground whenever boundary lines of private property were to be established on the edges of hills. See FRONT., *de cont. agr.*, II. p. 42, L.
[29] ANT. LAB., in FESTUS, p. 348, M, s. v. *Septimontio;* cf. *ep. Paul.*, p. 341, M; *Act. Arg.*, in VARRO, *L.L.*, V. 50 sqq.
[30] Romulus determined to establish his city in the place where he had had his home and had been exposed, — namely, on that angle of the Palatine facing the valley of the Circus Maximus. See DION. HAL., I. 85; PLUT., *Rom.*, 9, 20; SOL., I. 17.
[31] FESTUS, p. 258, M, s. v.: *Quadrata Roma in Palatio ante templum Apol-*

ON THE TOPOGRAPHY OF ROME 329

linis dicitur, ubi reposita sunt, quae solent boni ominis gratia in urbe condenda adhiberi, quia saxo munitus est initio in speciem quadratam. eius loci Ennius m. cum ait " et quis est erat † Romae regnare quadratae." For the *mundus*, see CATO, in FESTUS, p. 154, M; cf. OVID, *Fasti*, IV. 821 sqq.; PLUT., *Rom.*, 11. For the area called *Roma Quadrata*, see *Act. Lud. Saec.*, II. 12, in *Eph. Ep.*, VIII. p. 283; JOSEPH., *Ant. Jud.*, XIX. 3.2.

[32] FESTUS, p. 262, M, s. v.: *Romanam portam . . . porta Romana instituta est ab Romulo infimo clivo Victoriae, qui locus gradibus in quadram formatus est;* cf. VARRO, *L.L.*, V. 164; VI. 24.

[33] DION. HAL., I. 79. Compare also Chapter III of this volume.

[34] OVID, *Fasti*, V. 150; CIC., *de domo*, 53.136.

[35] For all that has been said see Chapters II-IV of this volume.

[36] According to PLUTARCH, *Rom.*, 11, the βόθρος was κυκλοτερής.

[37] See my *Storia di Roma*, I. 2, pp. 737 sqq.

[38] It is natural that also OVID (*Fasti*, IV. 802), on occasion of the feast of the Parilia (or Palatuar) which is particularly a feast of the Palatine, should have recorded that *Transferri iussos in nova tecta Lares*.

[39] See above, n. 30.

[40] The Palatine had already lost its original outlines in the time of Dionysius, on account of the numerous edifices erected thereon. This clearly results from the words of DIONYSIUS, I. 32.

[41] The legend of Aius Loquens (CIC., *de divin.*, I. 45.101; II. 32.69; LIVY, V. 32.6, and my *Storia di Roma*, I. 2, p. 204), should be connected with the verses *olim Fauni vatesque canebant* (ENN., fr. 155, B), and with the legend of the voice of Silvanus heard at the battle of the Arsia. A similar part was (as we have seen) attributed to Pan in the Hellenic myths.

[42] TAC., *Ann.*, XIII. 58: *Eodem anno Ruminalem arborem in Comitio, quae octingentos et quadraginta ante annos Remi Romulique infantiam texerat, mortuis ramalibus et arescente trunco deminutam prodigi loco habitum est, donec in novos fetus revivesceret.*

[43] ANT. LAB., in FESTUS, p. 348, M, s. v. *Septimontio;* cf. 341, M.

[44] VARRO, *L.L.*, V. 48: *Succusanus nunc scribitur tertia littera C non B. Pagus Succusanus quod succurrit Carinis.* Compare WISSOWA, in *Satura Viadrina*, Breslau (1896), pp. 1 sqq.

[45] PAUL., *ep. Fest.*, p. 131, M.

[46] VARRO, *L.L.*, V. 48: *Subura Iunius scribit ab eo, quod fuerit sub antiqua urbe; cui testimonium potest esse, quod subest ei loco qui terreus murus vocatur.*

[47] See Excursus VI.

[48] LIVY, I. 26.14: *Horatiae sepulcrum, quo loco corruerat icta, constructum est saxo quadrato.*

[49] OVID, *Fasti*, I. 259 sqq.; MACR., I. 9.17 sq.; cf. VARRO, *L.L.*, V. 156. This passage of Varro is so very clear that I cannot understand how Huelsen can possibly have left undetermined the site of the *Velabrum Minus* in his *Formae Urbis Romae Antiquae*.

[50] MACR., *ib.*

[51] VARRO, *L.L.*, V. 51, 52.

[52] VARRO, *L.L.*, V. 47: *Cum Caelio coniunctum Carinae et inter eas quem locum Ceroniensem appellatum apparet, quod primae regionis quartum sacrarium scriptum sic est: Ceroliensis quarticeps circa Minervium qua in Caelio monte itur in Tabernola est. Ceroliensis a carinarum iunctu dictus;* *Carinae postea Cerionia, quod hinc oritur caput sacrae viae ab Streniae sacello. . .*

[53] OVID, *Fasti*, I. 257:

> *Cum tot sint Iani, cur stas sacratus in uno,*
> *Hic ubi iuncta foris templa duobus habes?*

[54] See my *Storia di Roma*, I. 2, p. 341, and in this volume, Chapter II, n. 51.

[55] VITRUVIUS, II. 1.6; cf. VERG., VIII. 654; OVID, *Fasti*, I. 199; III. 179 sqq.
[56] CORN. NEPOS, in PLINY, *N.H.*, XVI. 36.
[57] IUL. OBSEQ., 8. (62).
[58] PLUT., *Publ.*, 10.
[59] LIVY, XXIV. 47; XXVI. 27; XXXV. 40.
[60] PLINY, *N.H.*, XXIX. 72; cf. SUET., *Aug.*, 28; SEN., *ep.*, XIV. 3.13.
[61] VITRUVIUS, II. 1.6; STRABO, IV. p. 197, C.
[62] THUC., I. 10.

NOTES TO EXCURSUS I

THE STIPS VOTIVA

[1] *Nuova Antologia*, Nov. 1899–Jan. 1900.
[2] *Notizie degli Scavi*, April, 1900, pp. 143 sqq.
For the formation of this accumulation called the *stips votiva*, see the just remarks of G. DE SANCTIS (*Riv. di Fil.*, XXVIII. pp. 16 sqq.). Arguments based on the *stips votiva* are still employed by E. PETERSEN (*Comitium, Rostra und Grab des Romulus*, Rom, 1904, pp. 28 sq.). Without any valid reasons (as appears to me) this eminent scholar attributes a great antiquity to the so-called tomb of Romulus.
[3] In this regard, I set scholars aright in my paper, *Le scoperte archeologiche e la buona fede scientifica*, in the *Rivista di Storia Antica*, Vol. V. fasc. 2, Messina, 1900.
[4] See also the strange and contradictory declarations of GAMURRINI, in *Rendiconti dei Lincei* (1900), pp. 185 and 193. He blames the method pursued by Boni in his excavations, and at the same time declares having seen the *stips votiva*, which "undoubtedly dates back as early as the middle of the sixth century B. C."
[5] In *Neue Heidelberger Jahrbücher*, 1899, p. 111.
[6] In *Jahrbuch d. d. arch. Inst.*, 1900, p. 2, n. 4, extr.
[7] *Inchiesta sul Museo di Villa Giulia*, in the *Bullettino del Ministero della Pubblica Instruzione*, Supplement of June 10, 1899 (Rome 1899). See, in particular, pp. 2, 14, 32, 34.

NOTES TO EXCURSUS II

THE ETRUSCAN TEGULA

[1] The text of the Etruscan tegula from Capua was published by FR. BÜCHELER, in *Rheinisches Museum*, LV. (1900), pp. 1 sqq.

[2] LATTES, in *Rendiconti dell'Instituto Lombardo* (1900), pp. 345 sqq., 541 sqq.

[3] I have discussed the data of the texts concerning Etruscan domination in Campania in my *Storia di Roma*, I. 2, p. 360, n. 1; cf. p. 209, n. 1.

[4] For the relations between Capua and Casilinum see my *Storia di Roma*, I. 2, pp. 209 sq. In addition to what I have there set forth, I shall observe that the topographical relations of the temple of Diana Tifatina (S. Angelo in Formis) prove that this famous and very early religious centre of the Campanian nation was co-ordinated in earliest times with Casilinum, — that is, with Volturnum; rather than with S. Maria di Capua Vetere, — the Roman Capua.

[5] G. DE PETRA, *Intorno al Museo Nazionale di Napoli* (Napoli, 1901).

[6] *Bullettino Ufficiale della Pubblica Instruzione*, Roma, Feb. 8, 1901, pp. 410 sq. Compare my remarks in same work, p. 1267.

NOTES TO EXCURSUS III

THE AEMILIAN PALISADES

[1] PIGORINI has given an exposition of his theories in *Rendiconti dei Lincei*, 1903, pp. 61–69. To the confutation of PROF. S. SERGI (*Arii e Italici*, Torino, 1898) may be added that of PROF. ED. BRIZIO, in *Storia Politica d'Italia del Vallardi* (Milano, — no date). Though the latter is not successful in reconstructing the earliest period of Italian history, he nevertheless is very exhaustive in the negative portion of his work, which destroys the theories of Pigorini. On the excavations on the Sarno I refrain from commenting, and shall continue so to do until the excavations will have been further continued and the material published.

[2] See the work of L. FOGLIA, *Osservazioni intorno alla pretesa terramara di Taranto*, in *Atti d. Accademia di Archeologia*, Napoli, 1903.

NOTES TO EXCURSUS IV

CAELIUS VIBENNA

[1] LIVY, IV. 13; VARRO, *L.L.*, V. 147, in DONAT., *ad* TER. *Eun.*, II. 2.25; PAUL., *ep. Fest.*, 48, 125, s. v. *Cuppes* and *Macellum*.
[2] VARRO, *L.L.*, V. 46.
[3] DION. HAL., II. 13 sq.
[4] LIVY, I. 59.7.
[5] DION. HAL., I. 87.
[6] LIVY, I. 7.2.
[7] DION. HAL., I. 87; cf. also PLUT., *Rom.*, 10.
[8] FEST., *ep. Paul.*, p. 55, s. v. *Celeres*.
[9] OVID, *Fasti*, IV. 837 sqq.; V. 469 sqq.
[10] DION. HAL., I. 87.
[11] See my *Storia di Roma*, I. 2. p. 708; 2, pp. 737 sqq.
[12] DION. HAL., III. 1.

NOTES TO EXCURSUS V

THE LEX AELIA-SENTIA

[1] DION. HAL., IV. 24.
[2] GAIUS, I. 13, 18, 27, 29, 31, 37 sq., 47, 66–71, 80, 139; III. 5.73 sq.
[3] GELL., *N.A.*, X. 28.
[4] DION. HAL., IV. 11; cf. MOMMSEN, *Röm. Chronol.*, 2d ed. p. 168.
[5] See my *Storia di Roma*, I. 2, p. 687.

NOTES TO EXCURSUS VI

VIA NOVA

[1] VARRO, *L.L.*, VI. 59; *vocabulum ei pervetustum ut Novae Viae, quae via iam diu vetus.* On the whole RICHTER has judged correctly, *Top. d. Stadt Rom*, 1902, p. 33.

[2] VARRO, *L.L.*, V. 43, 164 sq. That the *novalia* of the manuscript is to be changed to *nova via* results clearly from VARRO, *ib.*, VI. 23, as was seen by Scaliger.

[3] CIC., *de div.*, I. 45.101; II. 32.69; LIVY, V. 32.6; OVID, *Fasti*, VI. 395 sq.; GELL., *N.A.*, XVI. 17. See, too, PLUT., *de fort. Rom.*, 5.

[4] LIVY, I. 41.4; SOL., I. 24.

[5] OVID, *Fasti*, VI. 395 sq.; cf. passages cited in n. 3.

[6] Consult my *Storia di Roma*, I. 1. p. 336.

[7] LIVY, I. 48.6.

[8] DION. HAL., IV. 39; LIVY, I. 48.

[9] SOL., I. 22–25.

[10] VARRO, *L.L.*, V. 159.

[11] DION. HAL., III. 22: ἐν τῷ στενωπῷ τῷ φέροντι ἀπὸ Καρίνης κάτω τοῖς ἐπὶ τὸν Κύπριον ἐρχομένοις στενωπὸν, κ.τ.λ.

[12] SOL., I. 23 sq.; cf. POLYB., VI. 2.14; LIVY, I. 44.

[13] CIC., *de nat. deor.*, III. 25.63; PLINY, *N.H.*, II. 16.

[14] PLINY, *N.H.*, VIII. 197.

[15] PLINY, *N.H.*, XXXVI. 163.

[16] VARRO, *L.L.*, V. 159.

Augsburg College
George Sverdrup Library
Minneapolis, Minnesota 55454